Lecture Notes of the Institute
for Computer Sciences, Social Informatics
and Telecommunications Engineering 144

T0214375

More information about this series at http://www.springer.com/series/8197

Phan Cong Vinh · Emil Vassev
Mike Hinchey (Eds.)

Nature of Computation and Communication

International Conference, ICTCC 2014
Ho Chi Minh City, Vietnam
November 24–25, 2014
Revised Selected Papers

 Springer

Editors
Phan Cong Vinh
Nguyen Tat Thanh University
Ho Chi Minh City
Vietnam

Emil Vassev
Lero at University of Limerick
Limerick
Ireland

Mike Hinchey
Irish Software Engineering Research Centre
Lero at University of Limerick
Limerick
Ireland

ISSN 1867-8211   ISSN 1867-822X   (electronic)
Lecture Notes of the Institute for Computer Sciences, Social Informatics
and Telecommunications Engineering
ISBN 978-3-319-15391-9   ISBN 978-3-319-15392-6   (eBook)
DOI 10.1007/978-3-319-15392-6

Library of Congress Control Number: 2015930815

Springer Cham Heidelberg New York Dordrecht London

Printed on acid-free paper

Springer International Publishing AG Switzerland is part of Springer Science+Business Media
(www.springer.com)

Preface

ICTCC 2014 was an international scientific conference for research in the field of nature of computation and communication held during November 24–25, 2014 in Ho Chi Minh City, Vietnam. The aim of the conference was to provide an internationally respected forum for scientific research related to the natural aspects of computation and communication. This conference provided an excellent opportunity for researchers to discuss natural approaches and techniques for computation and communication. The proceedings of ICTCC 2014 were published by Springer in series Lecture Notes of the Institute for Computer Sciences, Social Informatics and Telecommunications Engineering (LNICST) (indexed by DBLP, EI, Google Scholar, Scopus, Thomson ISI).

For this edition, the Program Committee received over 100 submissions from 20 countries and each paper was reviewed by at least three expert reviewers. We chose 34 papers after intensive discussions held among the Program Committee members. We really appreciate the excellent reviews and lively discussions of the Program Committee members and external reviewers in the review process. This year we chose three prominent invited speakers, Prof. Mike Hinchey, Director of Lero (the Irish Software Engineering Research Centre) at University of Limerick in Ireland; Prof. Giacomo Cabri from University of Modena and Reggio Emilia in Italy and Dr. Phan Cong Vinh from Nguyen Tat Thanh University in Vietnam. The abstracts of their talks were included in these proceedings.

ICTCC 2014 was jointly organized by The European Alliance for Innovation (EAI) and Nguyen Tat Thanh University (NTTU). This conference could not have been organized without the strong support from the staff members of both organizations. We would especially like to thank Prof. Imrich Chlamtac (University of Trento and Create-NET), Sinziana Vieriu (EAI), and Elisa Mendini (EAI) for their great help in organizing the conference. We also appreciate the gentle guidance and help from Dr. Nguyen Manh Hung, Chairman and Rector of NTTU.

November 2014

Phan Cong Vinh
Emil Vassev
Mike Hinchey

Organization

Steering Committee

Imrich Chlamtac   CREATE-NET and University of Trento, Italy
Phan Cong Vinh   Nguyen Tat Thanh University, Vietnam

Organizing Committee

General Chair

Phan Cong Vinh   Nguyen Tat Thanh University, Vietnam

Technical Program Committee Chairs

Dang Quang A   Vietnam Academy of Science and Technology, Vietnam
Nguyen Thanh Tung   Ha Noi Vietnam National University, Vietnam

Technical Program Committee Session or Track Leader

Nguyen Van Phuc   Nguyen Tat Thanh University, Vietnam

Workshops Committee Chair

Nguyen Van Luong   Nguyen Tat Thanh University, Vietnam

Publications Committee Chair

Nguyen Kim Quoc   Nguyen Tat Thanh University, Vietnam

Marketing and Publicity Committee Chair

Le Tuan Anh   Posts and Telecommunications Institute of Technology, Vietnam

Patron Sponsorship and Exhibits Committee Chair

Bach Long Giang   Nguyen Tat Thanh University, Vietnam

Panels and Keynotes Committee Chairs

Vangalur Alagar	Concordia University, Canada
Emil Vassev	University of Limerick, Ireland

Demos and Tutorials Committee Chairs

Ashish Khare	University of Allahabad, India
Nguyen Thanh Binh	Ho Chi Minh City University of Technology, Vietnam

Posters Committee Chair

Do Nguyen Anh Thu	Nguyen Tat Thanh University, Vietnam

Industry Forum Committee Chair

Le Huy Ba	Nguyen Tat Thanh University, Vietnam

Special Sessions Committee Chair

Jason Jung	Yeungnam University, South Korea

Local Arrangements Committee Chair

Nguyen Tuan Anh	Nguyen Tat Thanh University, Vietnam

Web Site Committee Chair

Thai Thi Thanh Thao	Nguyen Tat Thanh University, Vietnam

Technical Program Committee

Abdur Rakib	The University of Nottingham, UK
Aniruddha Bhattacharjya	Amrita University, India
Asad Masood Khattak	Kyung Hee University, South Korea
Ashad Kabir	Swinburne University of Technology, Australia
Ashish Khare	University of Allahabad, India
Charu Gandhi	Jaypee Institute of Information Technology, India
Chien-Chih Yu	National ChengChi University, Taiwan
David Sundaram	The University of Auckland, New Zealand

Dinh Duc Anh Vu	University of Information Tecnology – HCMVNU, Vietnam
Do Thanh Nghi	Can Tho University, Vietnam
Emil Vassev	University of Limerick, Ireland
Gabrielle Peko	The University of Auckland, New Zealand
Giacomo Cabri	University of Modena and Reggio Emilia, Italy
Govardhan Aliseri	Jawaharlal Nehru Technological University, Hyderabad, India
Hoang Huu Hanh	Hue University, Vietnam
Huynh Quyet Thang	Hanoi University of Science and Technology, Vietnam
Huynh Trung Hieu	Ho Chi Minh City University of Industry, Vietnam
Huynh Xuan Hiep	Can Tho University, Vietnam
Issam Damaj	American University of Kuwait, Kuwait
Jason Jung	Yeungnam University, South Korea
Jonathan Bowen	Birmingham City University, UK
Krishna Asawa	Jaypee Institute of Information Technology, India
Kurt Geihs	University of Kassel, Germany
Le Tuan Anh	Posts and Telecommunications Institute of Technology, Vietnam
Ly Quoc Ngoc	Ho Chi Minh City University of Science-HCMVNU, Vietnam
Mubarak Mohammad	Concordia University, Canada
Ngo Quoc Viet	Ho Chi Minh City Pedagogical University, Vietnam
Nguyen Dinh Thuc	Ho Chi Minh City University of Science – HCMVNU, Vietnam
Nguyen Thanh Thuy	University of Engineering and Technology – HNVNU, Vietnam
Nong Thi Hoa	Thai Nguyen University of Information Technology and Communication, Vietnam
Ondrej Krejcar	University of Hradec Králové, Czech Republic
Pham Ngoc Hung	University of Engineering and Technology – HNVNU, Vietnam
Pham The Bao	Ho Chi Minh City University of Science – HCMVNU, Vietnam
Tran Dinh Que	Posts and Telecommunications Institute of Technology, Vietnam
Tran Van Lang	Institute of Applied Mechanics and Informatics, Vietnam
Vangalur Alagar	Concordia University, Canada
Vikas Saxena	Jaypee Institute of Information Technology, India
Vo Thanh Tu	Hue University, Vietnam
Vo Viet Minh Nhat	Hue University, Vietnam
Waralak V. Siricharoen	UTCC, Thailand
Yaser Jararweh	Jordan University of Science and Technology, Jordan

List of Reviewers

Anuranjan Misra	Bhagwant Institute of Technology, India
Apostolos Syropoulos	Freelance Researcher, Greece
Chandresh Chhatlani	Janardan Rai Nagar Rajasthan Vidyapeeth University, India
Christer Karlsson	South Dakota School of Mines and Technology, USA
Do Anh Tuan	Hung Yen University of Technology and Education, Vietnam
Hatem Zakaria	Benha University, Egypt
Ibrahim Kucukkoc	University of Exeter, UK
Ingyu Lee	Advanced Institutes of Convergence Technology, South Korea
José Santos Reyes	University of A Coruña, Spain
Maha Abdelhaq	National University of Malaysia, Malaysia
Masoud Rahiminezhad Galankashi	University of Technology, Malaysia
Nguyen Dang	University of Information Technology – HCMVNU, Vietnam
Nguyen Le Thu	People Security Academy, Vietnam
Nguyen Thanh Phuong	Polytechnic University of Bari, Italy
Rajiv Singh	University of Allahabad, India
Ramu Balu	Bharathiar University, India
Shervan Fekri Ershad	Amin University, Iran
Suleman Khan	University of Malaya, Malaysia
The Anh Han	Vrije Universiteit Brussel, Belgium
Vishal Gupta	Utttarakhand Technical University, India
Walter Delashmit	Independent Consultant, USA
Yilun Shang	Hebrew University of Jerusalem, Israel

Contents

Formal Methods
for Self-Adaptive Systems

Modular Design and Verification of Distributed Adaptive Real-Time Systems

Thomas Göthel[(✉)] and Björn Bartels

Technische Universität Berlin, Berlin, Germany
{thomas.goethel,bjoern.bartels}@tu-berlin.de

Abstract. We present and apply a design pattern for distributed adaptive real-time systems using the process calculus Timed CSP. It provides a structured modelling approach that is able to cope with the complexity of distributed adaptive real-time systems caused by the interplay of external stimuli, internal communication and timing dependencies. The pattern allows to differentiate between functional data and adaptive control data. Furthermore, we enable the modular verification of functional and adaptation behaviour using the notion of process refinement in Timed CSP. The verification of refinements and crucial properties is automated using industrial-strength proof tools.

Keywords: Adaptive Systems · Modelling · Verification · Timed CSP

1 Introduction

Modern adaptive systems are distributed among different network nodes. One of the advantages of (distributed) adaptive systems is their robustness, which must not be corrupted by single points of failures as provoked by centralized components. Thus, adaptation of the entire network's behaviour should be distributed as well. This means that adaptive components should be able to adapt both, their local behaviour and the behaviour of the overall network. This, however, makes these systems very complex to design and analyse.

In this paper, we present a generic design pattern for distributed adaptive real-time systems. Its aim is threefold. First, it describes an architecture, which helps formally designing adaptive systems. Second, it enables a strict separation of functional and adaptation behaviour. Third, due to this separation, it allows for modular refinement of adaptive systems and thereby facilitates formal verification of possibly crucial properties.

As in our previous work [3], we enable the refinement-based verification of adaptation and functional behaviour. However, in this work we focus on a strict distinction between functional data and control data following [4]. This enables the separate verification of functional and adaptive properties. A functional component manipulates its functional data but may be controlled by possibly dynamic control data that can only be changed by some corresponding adaptation component. The adaptation component gathers information of the

© Institute for Computer Sciences, Social Informatics and Telecommunications Engineering 2015
P.C. Vinh et al. (Eds.): ICTCC 2014, LNICST 144, pp. 3–12, 2015.
DOI: 10.1007/978-3-319-15392-6_1

functional component, which it uses for an analysis concerning whether or not adaptation is necessary. Then, a plan is created that results in new control data, which is finally set in the functional component or sent to another distributed adaptive component. The separation of functional and control data allows for the clear separation of functional and adaptation components, which allows for modular verification. We show how this idea can be modelled and verified with Timed CSP in a modular and stepwise manner using automatic tool support.

The rest of this paper is structured as follows. In Section 2, we briefly introduce the process calculus Timed CSP and then discuss related work in Section 3. In Section 4, we introduce our timed adaptive specification pattern and discuss its refinement and verification capabilities. We illustrate the benefits of our approach using an example in Section 5. Finally, we conclude the paper in Section 6 and give pointers to future work.

2   Timed CSP

Timed CSP is a timed extension of the CSP (Communicating Sequential Processes) process calculus [9]. It enables the description and the compositional refinement-based verification of possibly infinite-state real-time systems. To this end, process operators like *Prefix* (a -> P), *Sequential Composition* (P ; Q), *External Choice* (P [] Q), *Internal Choice* (P |~| Q), *Parallel Composition* (P [|A|] Q), *Hiding* (P \ A), and special timed operators like WAIT(t) are used. A discretely-timed dialect of Timed CSP that is amenable to automatic model checking techniques is tock-CSP. Here, the passage of time is explicitly modelled using a distinguished event *tock*. In FDR3 [5], which is the standard tool for CSP, tock-CSP is supported via timed operators and the prioritise operator with the internal τ event and other events can be given priority over tock. This is necessary to inherit the notion of refinement and its compositional features from Timed CSP. Refinement is usually considered in the semantical traces or failures model. This means, for example, that the refinement $P \sqsubseteq_T Q$ expresses that $traces(Q) \subseteq traces(P)$ where $traces(\_)$ denotes all finite traces of a process.

3   Related Work

Dynamic reconfiguration of systems is supported by the architecture description language (ADL) Dynamic Wright presented in [2]. Reconfiguration of interacting components is modelled separately from steady-state behaviour in a central specification. Our work aims to support the stepwise construction of distributed adaptive systems in which adaptation is realised in a decentralised way.

The work in [1] provides a development approach for adaptive embedded systems starting with model-based designs in which adaptation behaviour is strictly separated from functional behaviour. Verification is based on transition systems which are connected by input and output channels. Our approach aims to support development processes for adaptive systems with the powerful notion of CSP refinement and the mature proof tools for automatic refinement checking.

In [7], CSP is used to model self-adaptive applications where nodes in a network learn from the behaviour of other nodes. Behavioural rules of nodes are described by CSP processes, which are communicated between the nodes and used to adapt the individual behaviour. Our work focusses on modelling entire adaptive systems and verifying properties of the modelled systems.

Timed automata are used in [6] for modelling and verifying a decentralised adaptive system. Verification of crucial properties is done using the Uppaal model checker. In contrast, we focus on the stepwise development of and modular verification of distributed timed adaptive systems.

In [8], a UML-based modelling language for untimed adaptive systems is presented. Based on its formal semantics, deadlock freedom and stability can be verified. Our work enables the stepwise development and furthermore the verification of general functional and adaptation properties in a timed setting.

In [3], we have presented an approach for the specification and verification of untimed distributed adaptive systems in CSP. A main goal of this work was the separation of functional behaviour from adaptation behaviour. The application of this framework in [10] has shown that the high level of abstraction becomes problematic when supplementing the adaptive system model with functional behaviours. While functional and adaptation events and also their respective parts of the system variables are separated, it remains rather unclear how the interface between them can be modelled in a systematic manner. This drawback is addressed in this paper. Furthermore, we introduce mechanisms to specify and verify timed adaptive behaviour.

4   Timed Adaptive System Pattern

In this section, we introduce an abstract pattern for timed adaptive systems. It describes a general structure of timed adaptive systems, which is amenable to modular refinement-based verification. In Figure 1, the overall architecture is illustrated. We consider adaptive systems that consist of a network of adaptive components (AC(i)) that communicate using channels. Communication channels are categorised, depending on their origin, as either functional channels (FE) or adaptation channels (EA). A single component can perform some computation (also depicted by FE) or adapt its internal behaviour (IA) due to the violation of some (local) invariant. Internal adaptation can also be triggered by an internal timeout (TO). Timeouts can, for example, be used to indicate that during a certain amount of time, functional events of a certain class have not been communicated. When some internal adaptation takes place, other components can be triggered to adapt their behaviour accordingly using EA events as introduced above. The environment interacts with the adaptive system using functional events only. As it might be necessary to restrict the behaviour of the environment, it can be constrained using the process ENV.

In a model-driven development process, an abstract design is continuously refined until an implementation model is reached. To start with more abstract models offers the advantage that properties can be verified, whose verification would be too complex on more concrete levels. Below, we sketch how the

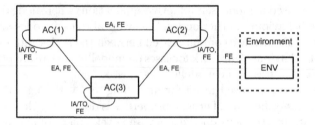

Fig. 1. Architecture of our Adaptive Pattern

described pattern can be formally defined on an abstract level in Timed CSP and how it can be refined in a stepwise way so that the verification of properties can be performed in a modular manner. The primary focus of the models lies on the separation of functional behaviour and adaptation behaviour. The refinement calculus of Timed CSP allows us to verify both of these aspects separately while leaving out concrete details of the respective other part. In addition to functional and adaptive behaviour, also timing behaviour can be specified and verified. To this end, we use the real-time capabilities of Timed CSP and FDR3.

4.1 Abstract Model

The overall adaptive system consists of a set of (distributed) adaptive components. Each such component consists of an adaptation component, a functional component, and, if necessary, a timer.

AdaptiveComponent(i) = (AC(i) [| {timeout} |] TIMER(i))
          [| union (FE(i) , {| getData , setControlData |}) |] FC(i)

The adaptation component checks whether adaptation of the functional component is necessary every `t(i)` time units. As the adaptation component has no direct access on the functional or control data, it has to explicitly fetch the data from the functional component using the `getData` event, analyse it, plan adaptation and execute the plan by setting the control data and possibly notifying other adaptive components, thereby implementing IBM's MAPE (monitor, analyse, plan, execute) approach. This is captured in the `CHECKADAPT` and `ADAPT` processes described below. The adaptation component can also be triggered by some external adaptation event or be notified that the timeout has elapsed. The timeout can for example be used to denote that during the last `timer(i)` time units no functional event took place (see `TIMER` below).

AC(i) = [] WAIT(t (i)) ; CHECKADAPT(i)
           [] ([] x :EA(i) @ x —> getData?d?cd —> ADAPT(i , x))
           [] timeout   —> getData?d?cd —> ADAPT(i , timeout)

To check whether adaptation is necessary, the current (necessary) functional data and control data is fetched from the functional component. According to local violations of the invariant, actual adaptation of control data takes place. On this level of abstraction, the invariant is not explicitly captured but possible violations are modelled via internal choices.

CHECKADAPT(i) = getData?d?cd ->
                (|~| x:IA(i) @ x -> ADAPT(i ,x)
                |~| AC(i))

Adaptation takes some time `ta(i,x)`, depending on the component in which adaptation takes i place and depending on the cause of adaptation x. After the plan is created, the corresponding control data is set in the functional component and further adaptive components are notified using external adaptation EA events. Notification is realised in `NotifyACs` process.

ADAPT(i ,x) = WAIT(ta(i ,x)) ;
            |~| cd : CD @ setControlData.cd ->
                   (NotifyACs(i ,x) ; AC(i))

The timer keeps track of whether some functional event took place within the last timer(i) time units.

TIMER(i) = [] x:FE(i) -> TIMER(i)
           [] WAIT(timer (i)) ; timeout -> TIMER(i)

The functional component provides information about the internal data to the adaptation component and the control data can be set by the adaptation component. On this abstract level, we abstract away state information using constructions based on internal choices. The functional component can also communicate with other functional components or manipulate its functional data.

FC(i) = |~| (d ,cd):{(d ,cd) | d <- D , cd <- CD}
                    @ getData.d.cd -> FC(i)
      [] setControlData?cd' -> FC(i)
      [] |~| x:FE(i) @ x -> FC(i)

The abstract components have a far smaller state space than the refined components that we introduce in the following subsection. Only by this, the verification on the abstract level is possible in reasonable time. The relatively complicated construction for coping with state information based on internal choices (e.g. `getData` in the functional component) is necessary to allow for later refinements in the failures model of CSP. It is certainly a radical way to leave out all of the state information here. However, it would be possible to keep at least a part of the state information.

4.2 Refined Model

In the abstract model, state information of the components is not present. A refined model needs to make clear when the actions actually take place. To do this in the context of CSP, non-determinism is usually reduced by replacing internal choices ($|^{\sim}|$) with guarded deterministic choices ($\square$). For the adaptation component, the adaptation logic is refined by reducing non-determinism in CHECKADAPT and ADAPT. In the CHECKADAPT' subcomponent, the invariant is now explicitly modelled by the g(i,d,cd,ia) predicate. Note that CHECKADAPT' and ADAPT' now depend on the functional (d) and control data (cd).

```
AC'( i ) = WAIT( t )  ;  CHECKADAPT'( i )
           [] ( [] x:EA @ x -> getData?d?cd -> ADAPT'( i ,d,cd ,x))
           [] timeout  -> getData?d?cd -> ADAPT'( i ,d,cd ,timeout )

CHECKADAPT'( i ) = getData?d?cd ->
                   ( [] ia:IA( i ) @ g(i,d,cd,ia) & ia -> ADAPT'( i ,d,cd ,ia )
                     [] else & none -> AC'( i ))

ADAPT'( i ,d,cd ,x) = WAIT( ta( i ,x))  ;
                      setControlData. f( i ,d,cd ,x) ->
                      NotifyACs '( i ,d,cd ,x)  ; AC'( i )
```

The functional component no longer abstracts from the data, but makes use of it to implement the actual functional logic using, e.g., guards (gf(...)).

```
FC'( i ,d,cd) = getData.d.cd -> FC'( i ,d,cd)
           [] setControlData?cd ' -> FC'( i ,d,cd '))
           [] ( [] fe:FE( i ) @ gf( i ,d,cd , fe) & fe -> FC'( i ,h(d,x) ,cd ))
```

In the next section, we explain the refinement and verification process in the context of the presented adaptive system pattern. This makes it also clearer why it is beneficial for a designer to provide models on different abstraction levels.

4.3 Proving Refinement

The aim of the described pattern is to facilitate the modular refinement and verification of adaptive real-time systems. By separating functional from adaptive behaviour, we are able to verify the respective properties separately.

The most abstract system model leaves out most of the details concerning adaptation and functional behaviour. When adaptation takes place, it has no direct influence on the functional behaviour of the components. Thus, the most abstract model is suited to verify properties, which focus neither on the adaptation behaviour nor the functional behaviour. By introducing detailed adaptation or functional behaviour, we refine the abstract model to a refined model that fulfils more required properties w.r.t. adaptation behaviour or w.r.t. functional behaviour due to the preservation of properties. The key point is that for many properties only the functional behaviour or the adaptation behaviour needs to be refined, not necessarily both at the same time.

A refinement-based verification approach has two major advantages. First, we can verify functional correctness and adaptation correctness separately. On the most abstract level, we have a system that is composed of a functional component FC and an adaptation component AC. Both of these abstract components leave out most of the details. By refining the functional component to FC' and the adaptive component to AC', we can verify functional properties and adaptation properties while leaving out details of the respective component, which is not of interest for the respective property. Formally, we have $FC \otimes AC \sqsubseteq_{FD} FC' \otimes AC$ and $FC \otimes AC \sqsubseteq_{FD} FC \otimes AC'$. Furthermore, we have that $FC' \otimes AC \sqsubseteq_{FD} FC' \otimes AC'$ and $FC \otimes AC' \sqsubseteq_{FD} FC' \otimes AC'$. This means that all properties that are valid on the partly refined models $FC' \otimes AC$ and $FC \otimes AC'$ remain valid in the refined model $FC' \otimes AC'$. The second advantage is related to the environment model. In CSP, a model is more abstract than another when it contains fewer constraints. This means that a refined system has fewer behaviours than an abstract one. Ideally, we would like to verify an adaptive system with a most abstract or most unconstrained environment. However, this is almost never possible especially in the context of adaptive systems. Refinement allows us to include necessary constraints to the environment to prove the overall system correct.

5   Example

In this section, we present a simple adaptive system with which we illustrate the main ideas of the adaptive system pattern from the previous section. It consists of two adaptive components: a light dimmer and a daylight sensor. When the daylight sensor recognises a change in light intensity that stays stable for a certain amount of time, the dimmer is notified that it possibly should adapt to the new situation by changing the dim intensity. Furthermore, the dimmer can be adjusted manually, which represents the actual functional behaviour of the dimmer. On the abstract level, we omit details concerning the state information in the components. This means that all choices, which should depend on the state information are realised by internal choices.

The dimmer is adjusted manually using the **higher** and **lower** events. Furthermore, the dim intensity can be set using the **setGoal** event leading to an automatic adjustment phase thereafter. Finally, the current dim value can be queried. The **obs** event is used as an observation event for later verification only.

```
DimmerFC_0(y)  =   higher -> obs?x -> DimmerFC_0(y)
              []  lower -> obs?x -> DimmerFC_0(y)
              []  setGoal?ny -> DimmerFC_0(9)
              []  (y>0 & (adjust -> DimmerFC_0(y-1)
                          |~| DimmerFC_0(0)))
              []  y==0 & obs?x -> DimmerFC_0(-1)
              []  getCurrent?x -> DimmerFC_0(y)
```

The corresponding adaptation component can be notified that the intensity of the surrounding light has changed such that it subsequently adapts the behaviour of the functional component.

```
DimmerAC_0 = newIntensity?y ->
          getCurrent?x -> (DimmerAC_0
                          |~| setGoal?x -> DimmerAC_0)
```

```
AdaptiveComponent1_00 =
        DimmerAC_0 [| {| getCurrent , setGoal |} |] DimmerFC_0(-1)
```

The light sensor recognises the daylight intensity. If it remains stable for 5 time units, the dimmer is possibly notified using the **newIntensity** event. On this abstraction level, details of the check are hidden through an internal choice.

```
LightSensorTimer =   WAIT(5) ; timeout -> LightSensorTimer
                  [] light?y -> LightSensorTimer

LightSensorAC_0 = timeout ->
          getIntensity?y -> (newIntensity?x -> LightSensorAC_0
                            |~| LightSensorAC_0)

LightSensorFC_0 =   light?x -> LightSensorFC_0
                  [] getIntensity?x -> LightSensorFC_0

AdaptiveComponent2_00 =
((LightSensorAC_0 [| {timeout} |] LightSensorTimer) \{timeout})
     [| {| getIntensity |} |] LightSensorFC_0
```

The environment model formalises the restriction that at most once a second the system is interacted with. This is a severe restriction but eases presentation. Finally, the system model assembles the adaptive components and the environment model according to the architecture given by our adaptive pattern.

```
ENV =   WAIT(1) ; (light?y->ENV [] higher->ENV [] lower->ENV)

System_abs = ((AdaptiveComponent1_00 [|{|newIntensity|}|]
                AdaptiveComponent2_00)
                   [|{|light , higher , lower|}|]
     ENV) \{| newIntensity , getCurrent , getIntensity |}
```

We have modelled three safety properties as CSP processes. Thus, trace refinement is sufficient to express that a system fulfils them. Due to the lack of space, we omit their CSP definitions here. The first property states that two consecutive **setGoal** events always occur with different values. The second one states that there is a delay of at least 4 time units between consecutive **setGoal** events. Finally, the third property states that there are only small jumps in the dimmer. The dim value before and after setting it can differ by two at most.

These properties are not valid in the abstract model presented above. We first need to refine the model to be able to show them. All three properties are concerned with the adaptation behaviour of the two components. So we need to refine the adaptation mechanisms accordingly.

```
DimmerAC_1 =
  newIntensity?y ->
    getCurrent?x -> if (x-y < 0) or (x-y > 9) then DimmerAC_1
                    else setGoal.(x-y) -> DimmerAC_1
```

```
LightSensorAC_1(x) =
   timeout -> getIntensity?y ->
   if (y!=x) then newIntensity.lDiff(x,y) -> LightSensorAC_1(y)
            else                            LightSensorAC_1(x)
```

The adaptation components above are updated with these refined parts accordingly (taking 0 as the initial value for x). The corresponding new system description System_abs2 is sufficiently refined to show the second property using FDR3. Note that we need to prioritise internal events over tock and have to specify that the setGoal and obs events are urgent but visible.

```
assert P2 [T= prio(System_abs2,<{|setGoal,obs|},{tock}>)
```

The first and the third property do not hold on this model, because they depend on the functional behaviour of the dimmer. So, we also refine DimmerFC.

```
DimmerFC_1(x,y) =
    x<9 & higher -> obs.(x+1) -> DimmerFC_1(x+1,-1)
[] x>0 & lower -> obs.(x-1) -> DimmerFC_1(x-1,-1)
[] setGoal?ny -> DimmerFC_1(x,ny)
[] y>=0 and y>x & adjust -> DimmerFC_1(x+1,y)
[] y>=0 and x>y & adjust -> DimmerFC_1(x-1,y)
[] y>=0 and x==y & obs.x -> DimmerFC_1(x,-1)
[] getCurrent.x -> DimmerFC_1(x,y)
```

With this refined version, we can finally show the first and the third property.

```
assert P1/P3 [T= prio(System_abs3,<{|setGoal,obs|},{tock}>)
```

Note that the last property is not as obvious as it appears at first glance. If we did not have the environmental assumptions that there is a delay of at least one time unit between external events, a setGoal event could be arbitrarily delayed while higher and lower events have an effect on the dimmer.

For completeness, we also give the refined version of the functional component of the light sensor. Here, the last intensity value that has been recognised is memorised and can be given to the adaptation component accordingly.

```
LightSensorFC_1(x) =    light?y -> LightSensorFC_1(y)
                  [] getIntensity.x -> LightSensorFC_1(x)
```

In summary, we have shown that it is possible to verify the example above in a modular way by focussing especially on adaptation behaviour while abstracting from functional behaviour as much as possible. Although being a relatively simple example, we are confident that we benefit from applying our approach to more complex systems as described in the next section.

6   Conclusion and Future Work

In this paper, we have presented a design pattern that supports the modular design and verification of distributed adaptive real-time systems. It clarifies how functional and control data is processed and communicated within the individual components of a distributed adaptive system. Adaptation is achieved in a decentralised fashion. Moreover, we have demonstrated how timing dependencies of adaptation behaviours can be modelled and analysed. Using an example, we have shown how the approach facilitates the stepwise development of distributed adaptive real-time systems and helps to cope with the complexity of such systems by using automated verification methods.

In future work, we plan to apply our approach to an adaptive multicore system, which was previously only incompletely verified [10], because of limited scalability due to not separating functional from adaptation behaviour. As another piece of work, we want to analyse whether we can exploit the compositional structure of systems in our approach to enable runtime verification. This would especially enable the integration of more flexible adaptation strategies at design time such that the system could apply the correct strategies at runtime while preserving functional and adaptation correctness.

References

1. Adler, R., Schaefer, I., Schuele, T., Vecchié, E.: From model-based design to formal verification of adaptive embedded systems. In: Butler, M., Hinchey, M.G., Larrondo-Petrie, M.M. (eds.) ICFEM 2007. LNCS, vol. 4789, pp. 76–95. Springer, Heidelberg (2007)
2. Allen, R.B., Douence, R., Garlan, D.: Specifying and analyzing dynamic software architectures. In: Astesiano, E. (ed.) ETAPS 1998 and FASE 1998. LNCS, vol. 1382, pp. 21–37. Springer, Heidelberg (1998)
3. Bartels, B., Kleine, M.: A CSP-based framework for the specification, verification and implemenation of adaptive systems. In: 6th Int. Symp. on Software Engineering for Adaptive and Self-Managing Systems (SEAMS 2011). ACM (2011)
4. Bruni, R., Corradini, A., Gadducci, F., Lluch Lafuente, A., Vandin, A.: A conceptual framework for adaptation. In: de Lara, J., Zisman, A. (eds.) Fundamental Approaches to Software Engineering. LNCS, vol. 7212, pp. 240–254. Springer, Heidelberg (2012)
5. Gibson-Robinson, T., Armstrong, P., Boulgakov, A., Roscoe, A.W.: FDR3 — A modern refinement checker for CSP. In: Ábrahám, E., Havelund, K. (eds.) TACAS 2014 (ETAPS). LNCS, vol. 8413, pp. 187–201. Springer, Heidelberg (2014)
6. Iftikhar, M.U., Weyns, D.: A case study on formal verification of self-adaptive behaviors in a decentralized system. In: Kokash, N., Ravara, A. (eds.) FOCLASA. EPTCS, vol. 91, pp. 45–62 (2012)
7. Jaskó, S., Simon, G., Tarnay, K., Dulai, T., Muhi, D.: CSP-based modelling for self-adaptive applications. Infocommunications Journal LVIV (2009)
8. Luckey, M., Engels, G.: High-quality specification of self-adaptive software systems. In: 8th Int. Symp. on Software Engineering for Adaptive and Self-Managing Systems (SEAMS 2013). ACM (2013)
9. Schneider, S.: Concurrent and Real Time Systems: The CSP Approach. John Wiley & Sons Inc., New York (1999)
10. Schwarze, M.: Modeling and verification of adaptive systems using Timed CSP. Master thesis, Technische Universität Berlin (2013)

Modeling Swarm Robotics with KnowLang

Emil Vassev and Mike Hinchey

Lero–the Irish Software Engineering Research Centre,
University of Limerick, Limerick, Ireland
{emil.vassev,mike.hinchey}@lero.ie

Abstract. Swarm robotics has emerged as a paradigm whereby intelligent agents are considered to be autonomous entities that interact either cooperatively or non-cooperatively. The concept is biologically-inspired and offers many advantages compared with single-agent systems, such as: greater redundancy, reduced costs and risks, and the ability to distribute the overall work among swarm members, which may result in greater efficiency and performance. The distributed and local nature of these systems is the main factor in the high degree of parallelism displayed by their dynamics that often results in adaptation to changing environmental conditions and robustness to failure. This paper presents a formal approach to modeling self-adaptive behavior for swarm robotics. The approach relies on the KnowLang language, a formal language dedicated to knowledge representation for self-adaptive systems.

1 Introduction

Aside from complex mechanics and electronics, building robots is about the challenge of interacting with a dynamic and unpredictable world, which requires the presence of intelligence. In swarm robotics systems, in addition to this challenge, we also need to deal with the dynamic local interactions among robots, often resulting in emergent behavior at the level of the entire swarm. Real swarm intelligence systems such as social insects, bird flocks and fish schools, leverage such parallelism to achieve remarkable efficiency and robustness to hazards. The prospect of replicating the performance of natural systems and their incredible ability of self-adaptation is the main motivation in the study of swarm robotics systems.

Swarm robotics brings most of the challenges that the theories and methodologies developed for self-adaptive systems are attempting to solve. Hence, self-adaptation has emerged as an important paradigm making a swarm robotics system capable of modifying the system behavior and/or structure in response to increasing workload demands and changes in the operational environment. Note that robotic artificial intelligence (AI) mainly excels at formal logic, which allows it, for example, to find the appropriate action from hundreds of possible actions.

In this paper, we present a formal approach to modeling self-adaptive behavior of swarm robotics. We use KnowLang, a formal framework under development

© Institute for Computer Sciences, Social Informatics and Telecommunications Engineering 2015
P.C. Vinh et al. (Eds.): ICTCC 2014, LNICST 144, pp. 13–22, 2015.
DOI: 10.1007/978-3-319-15392-6_2

under the mandate of the FP7 project, ASCENS [1]. KnowLang's notation is a formal language dedicated to knowledge representation for self-adaptive systems, so the framework provides both a notation and reasoning to deal with self-adaptation.

The rest of this paper is organized as follows. Section 2 presents the ARE approach that helps us capture the requirements for self-adaptive behavior. Section 3 describes our swarm robotics case study. Section 4 presents our approach to specifying the self-adaptive behavior of swarm robots with KnowLang. Finally, Section 5 provides brief concluding remarks and a summary of our future goals.

2   Requirements for Self-adaptive Behavior

We aim to capture self-adaptive behavior so that it can be properly designed and subsequently implemented. To do so, we consider that self-adaptive behavior extends the regular objectives of a system upstream with special self-managing objectives, also called self-* objectives [6]. Basically, the self-* objectives provide autonomy features in the form of a system's ability to automatically discover, diagnose, and cope with various problems. This ability depends on the system's degree of autonomicity, quality and quantity of knowledge, awareness and monitoring capabilities, and quality characteristics such as adaptability, dynamicity, robustness, resilience, and mobility. The approach for capturing all of these requirements is called Autonomy Requirements Engineering (ARE) [4–6]. This approach aims to provide a complete and comprehensive solution to the problem of autonomy requirements elicitation and specification. Note that the approach exclusively targets the self-* objectives as the only means to explicitly determine and define autonomy requirements. Thus, it is not meant to handle the regular functional and non-functional requirements of the systems, presuming that those might by tackled by the traditional requirements engineering approaches, e.g., use case modeling, domain modeling, constraints modeling, etc. Hence, functional and non-functional requirements may be captured by the ARE approach only as part of the self-* objectives elicitation.

The ARE approach starts with the creation of a goals model that represents system objectives and their interrelationships for the system in question. For this, we use GORE (Goal-Oriented Requirements Engineering) where ARE goals are generally modeled with intrinsic features such as type, actor, and target, with links to other goals and constraints in the requirements model. Goals models may be organized in different ways copying with the system's specifics and the engineers' understanding of the system's goals. Thus we may have hierarchical structures where goals reside at different level of granularity and concurrent structures where goals are considered as being concurrent to each other.

The next step in the ARE approach is to work on each one of the system goals along with the elicited environmental constraints to come up with the self-* objectives providing the autonomy requirements for this particular system's behavior. In this phase, we apply a special Generic Autonomy Requirements model to a system goal to derive autonomy requirements in the form of the goal's supportive and alternative self-* objectives along with the necessary capabilities and quality characteristics.

Finally, the last step after defining the autonomy requirements per the system's objectives is the formalization of these requirements, which can be considered as a form of formal specification or requirements recording. The formal notation used to specify the autonomy requirements is KnowLang [7]. The process of requirements specification with KnowLang extends over a few phases:

1. Initial knowledge requirements gathering – involves domain experts to determine the basic notions, relations and functions (operations) of the domain of interest.
2. Behavior definition – identifies situations and behavior policies as "control data", helping to identify important self-adaptive scenarios.
3. Knowledge structuring – encapsulates domain entities, situations and behavior policies into KnowLang structures such as concepts, properties, functionalities, objects, relations, facts and rules.

To specify self-* objectives with KnowLang, we use special policies associated with goals, special situations, actions (eventually identified as system capabilities), metrics, etc.[7]. Hence, self-* objectives are represented as policies describing at an abstract level what the system will do when particular situations arise. The situations are meant to represent the conditions needed to be met in order for the system to switch to a self-* objective while pursuing a system goal. Note that policies rely on actions that are *a priori* defined as functions of the system. In the case that such functions have not been defined yet, the needed functions should be considered as autonomous functions and their implementation will be justified by the ARE's selected self-* objectives.

According to the KnowLang semantics, in order to achieve specified goals (objectives), we need to specify policy-triggering *actions* that will eventually change the system states, so the desired ones, required by the goals, will become effective [7]. Note that KnowLang policies allow the specification of autonomic behavior (autonomic behavior can be associated with self-* objectives), and therefore, we need to specify at least one policy per single goal; i.e., a policy that will provide the necessary behavior to achieve that goal. Of course, we may specify multiple policies handling same goal (objective), which is often the case with the self-* objectives and let the system decide which policy to apply taking into consideration the current situation and conditions. The following is a formal presentation of a KnowLang policy specification [7].

Policies (Π) are at the core of autonomic behavior (autonomic behavior can be associated with autonomy requirements). A policy π has a goal (g), policy situations (Si_π), policy-situation relations (R_π), and policy conditions (N_π) mapped to policy actions (A_π) where the evaluation of N_π may eventually (with some degree of probability) imply the evaluation of actions (denoted with $N_\pi \xrightarrow{[Z]} A_\pi$ (see Definition 2). A condition is a Boolean function over ontology (see Definition 4), e.g., the occurrence of a certain event.

Definition 1. $\Pi := \{\pi_1, \pi_2, ..., \pi_n\}, n \geq 0$ (Policies)

Definition 2. $\pi :=< g, Si_\pi, [R_\pi], N_\pi, A_\pi, map(N_\pi, A_\pi, [Z]) >$
$\quad A_\pi \subset A, N_\pi \overset{[Z]}{\rightarrow} A_\pi$ (A_π - *Policy Actions*)
$\quad Si_\pi \subset Si, Si_\pi := \{si_{\pi_1}, si_{\pi_2}, ..., si_{\pi_n}\}, n \geq 0$
$\quad R_\pi \subset R, R_\pi := \{r_{\pi_1}, r_{\pi_2}, ..., r_{\pi_n}\}, n \geq 0$
$\quad \forall r_\pi \in R_\pi \bullet (r_\pi :=< si_\pi, [rn], [Z], \pi >), si_\pi \in Si_\pi$
$\quad Si_\pi \overset{[R_\pi]}{\rightarrow} \pi \rightarrow N_\pi$

Definition 3. $N_\pi := \{n_1, n_2, ..., n_k\}, k \geq 0$ (Conditions)

Definition 4. $n := be(O)$ (Condition - Boolean Expression)

Definition 5. $g := \langle \Rightarrow s' \rangle | \langle s \Rightarrow s' \rangle$ (Goal)

Definition 6. $s := be(O)$ (State)

Definition 7. $Si := \{si_1, si_2, ..., si_n\}, n \geq 0$ (Situations)

Definition 8. $si :=< s, A \overset{\leftarrow}{si}, [E \overset{\leftarrow}{si}], A_{si} >$ (Situation)
$\quad A \overset{\leftarrow}{si} \subset A$ ($A \overset{\leftarrow}{si}$ - Executed Actions)
$\quad A_{si} \subset A$ (A_{si} - Possible Actions)
$\quad E \overset{\leftarrow}{si} \subset E$ ($E \overset{\leftarrow}{si}$ - Situation Events)

Policy situations (Si_π) are situations that may trigger (or imply) a policy π, in compliance with the policy-situations relations R_π (denoted with $Si_\pi \overset{[R_\pi]}{\rightarrow} \pi$), thus implying the evaluation of the policy conditions N_π (denoted with $\pi \rightarrow N_\pi$)(see Definition 2). Therefore, the optional policy-situation relations (R_π) justify the relationships between a policy and the associated situations (see Definition 2). In addition, the self-adaptive behavior requires relations to be specified to connect policies with situations over an optional probability distribution (Z) where a policy might be related to multiple situations and vice versa. Probability distribution is provided to support *probabilistic reasoning* and to help the KnowLang Reasoner choose the most probable situation-policy "pair". Thus, we may specify a few relations connecting a specific situation to different policies to be undertaken when the system is in that particular situation and the probability distribution over these relations (involving the same situation) should help the KnowLang Reasoner decide which policy to choose (denoted with $Si_\pi \overset{[R_\pi]}{\rightarrow} \pi$ - see Definition 2).

A goal g is a desirable transition to a state or from a specific state to another state (denoted with $s \Rightarrow s'$) (see Definition 5). A state s is a Boolean expression over ontology ($be(O)$)(see Definition 6), e.g., "a specific property of an object must hold a specific value". A situation is expressed with a state (s), a history of actions ($A \overset{\leftarrow}{si}$) (actions executed to get to state s), actions A_{si} that can be performed from state s and an optional history of events $E \overset{\leftarrow}{si}$ that eventually occurred to get to state s (see Definition 8).

Ideally, policies are specified to handle specific situations, which may trigger the application of policies. A policy exhibits a behavior via actions generated in the environment or in the system itself. Specific conditions determine which specific actions (among the actions associated with that policy - see Definition 2) shall be executed. These conditions are often generic and may differ from the situations triggering the policy. Thus, the behavior not only depends on the specific situations a policy is specified to handle, but also depends on additional conditions. Such conditions might be organized in a way allowing for synchronization of different situations on the same policy. When a policy is applied, it checks what particular conditions are met and performs the mapped actions (see $map(N_\pi, A_\pi, [Z])$) - see Definition 2). An optional probability distribution can additionally restrict the action execution. Although initially specified, the probability distribution at both mapping and relation levels is recomputed after the execution of any involved action. The re-computation is based on the consequences of the action execution, which allows for reinforcement learning.

3   The Ensemble of Robots Case Study

The ensemble of robots case study targets swarms of intelligent robots with self-awareness capabilities that help the entire swarm acquire the capacity to reason, plan, and autonomously act. The case study relies on the marXbot robotics platform [2], which is a modular research robot equipped with a set of devices that help the robot interact with other robots of the swarm or the robotic environment. The environment is defined as an arena where special cuboid-shaped obstacles are present in arbitrary positions and orientations. Moreover, the environment may contain a number of light sources, usually placed behind the goal area, which act as environmental cues used as shared reference frames among all robots.

Each marXbot robot is equipped with a set of devices to interact with the environment and with other robots of the swarm:

- a light sensor, that is able to perceive a noisy light gradient around the robot in the 2D plane;
- a distance scanner that is used to obtain noisy distances and angular values from the robot to other objects in the environment;
- a range and bearing communication system, with which a robot can communicate with other robots that are in line-of-sight;
- a gripper, that is used to physically connect to the transported object;
- two wheels independently controlled to set the speed of the robot.

Currently, the marXbots robots are able to work in teams where they coordinate based on simple interactions in group tasks. For example, a group of marXbots robots may collectively move a relatively heavy object from point A to point B by using their grippers.

For the purpose of the Ensemble of Robots case study, we developed a simple scenario that requires self-adaptive behavior of the individual marXbot robots

[3]. In this scenario, a team of marXbot robots, called *rescuers*, is deployed in a special area, called a *deployment area*. We imagine that some kind of disaster has happened, and the environment is occasionally obstructed by *debris* that the robots can move around. In addition, a portion of the environment is dangerous for robot navigation due to the presence of *radiation*. We assume that prolonged exposition to radiation damages the robots. For example, short-term exposition increases a robot's sensory noise. Long-term damage, eventually, disables the robot completely. To avoid damage, the robots can use debris to build a *protective wall*.

Further, we imagine that a number of *victims* are trapped in the environment and must be rescued by the robots. Each victim is suffering a different injury. The robots must calculate a suitable *rescuing behavior* that maximizes the number of victims rescued. A victim is considered rescued when it is deposited in the deployment area alive. To perform its activities, a robot must take into account that it has limited energy.

4   Formalizing Swarm Robotics with KnowLang

Following the scenario described in Section 3, we applied the ARE approach (see Section 2) and derived the goals along with the *self-* objectives* assisting these goals when self-adaptation is required. Note that the required analysis and process of building the goals model along with the process of deriving the adaptation-supporting self-* objectives is beyond the scope of this paper. These will be addressed in a future paper.

Based on the rationale above, we applied the ARE approach (see Section 2) and derived the system's goals along with the self-* objectives assisting these goals when self-adaptation is required. Note that the required analysis and process of building the goals model for swarm robotics along with the process of deriving the adaptation-supporting self-* objectives is beyond the scope of this paper.

Figure 1 depicts the ARE goals model for swarm robotics where goals are organized hierarchically at three different levels. As shown, the goals from the first two levels (e.g., "Rescue Victims", "Protect against Radiation", and "Move Victims away") are *main system goals* captured at different levels of abstraction. The 3rd level is resided by *self-* objectives* (e.g., "Clean Debris", "Optimize Rescue Operation", and "Avoid Radiation Zones") and *supportive goals* (e.g., "Exploration and Mapping" and "Find Victim") associated with and assisting the 2nd-level goals. Basically, all self-* objectives inherit the system goals they assist by providing behavior alternatives with respect to these system goals. The system switches to one of the assisting self-* objectives when alternative autonomous behavior is required (e.g., a robot needs to avoid a radiation zone). In addition, Figure 1 depicts some of the environmental constraints (e.g., "Radiation" and "Debris"), which may cause self-adaptation.

In order to specify the autonomy requirements for swarm robotics, the first step is to specify a knowledge base (KB) representing the swarm robotics system in question, i.e., robots, victims, radiation, debris, etc. To do so, we need

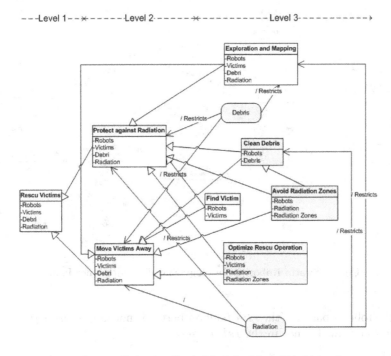

Fig. 1. Swarm Robotics Goals Model with Self-* Objectives

to specify ontology structuring the knowledge domain of the case study. Note that this domain is described via domain-relevant concepts and objects (concept instances) related through relations. To handle explicit concepts like situations, goals, and policies, we grant some of the domain concepts with explicit state expressions where a state expression is a Boolean expression over the ontology (see Definition 6 in Section 2). Note that being part of the autonomy requirements, knowledge plays a very important role in the expression of all the autonomy requirements (see Section 2).

Figure 2, depicts a graphical representation of the swarm robotics ontology relating most of the domain concepts within a swarm robotics system. Note that the relationships within a concept tree are "is-a" (inheritance), e.g., the *Radiation_Zone* concept is an *EnvironmentEntity* and the *Action* concept is a *Knowledge* and consecutively *Phenomenon*, etc. Most of the concepts presented in Figure 2 were derived from the Swarm Robotics Goals Model (see Figure 1). Other concepts are considered *explicit* and were derived from the KnowLang specification model [8].

The following is a sample of the KnowLang specification representing the *Robot* concept. As specified, the concept has properties of other concepts, functionalities (actions associated with that concept), states (Boolean expressions validating a specific state), etc. For example, the *IsOperational* state holds

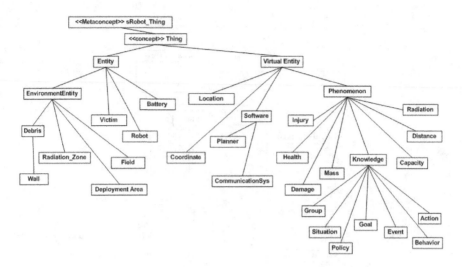

Fig. 2. Swarm Robotics Ontology Specified with KnowLang

when the robot's battery (the *rBattery* property) is not in the *batteryLow* state and the robot itself is not in the *IsDamaged* state.

```
CONCEPT Robot { ....
 PROPS {
  PROP rBattery {TYPE{swarmRobots.robots.CONCEPT_TREES.Battery} CARDINALITY{1}}
  PROP rPlanner {TYPE{swarmRobots.robots.CONCEPT_TREES.Planner} CARDINALITY{1}}
  PROP rCommunicationSys {TYPE{swarmRobots.robots.CONCEPT_TREES.CommunicationSys} CARDINALITY{1}}
  PROP liftCapacity {TYPE{NUMBER} CARDINALITY{1}}
  PROP dragCapacity {TYPE{swarmRobots.robots.CONCEPT_TREES.Capacity} CARDINALITY{1}}
  PROP rDamages {TYPE{swarmRobots.robots.CONCEPT_TREES.Damage} CARDINALITY{*}}
  PROP distDebries {TYPE{swarmRobots.robots.CONCEPT_TREES.Distance_to_Debries} CARDINALITY{1}}
  PROP victimToCareOf {TYPE{swarmRobots.robots.CONCEPT_TREES.Victim} CARDINALITY{1}}}
 FUNCS {
  FUNC plan {TYPE {swarmRobots.robots.CONCEPT_TREES.Plan}}
  FUNC explore {TYPE {swarmRobots.robots.CONCEPT_TREES.Explore}}
  FUNC selfCheck {TYPE {swarmRobots.robots.CONCEPT_TREES.CheckForDamages}}
  FUNC dragVictimAway {TYPE {swarmRobots.robots.CONCEPT_TREES.DragVictim}}
  FUNC carryVictim {TYPE {swarmRobots.robots.CONCEPT_TREES.CarryVictim}}
  FUNC buildWall {TYPE {swarmRobots.robots.CONCEPT_TREES.BuildWall}}}
 STATES {
  STATE IsOperational{ NOT swarmRobots.robots.CONCEPT_TREES.Robot.PROPS.rBattery.STATES.batteryLow AND
   NOT NOT swarmRobots.robots.CONCEPT_TREES.Robot.STATES.IsDamaged }
  STATE IsDamaged { swarmRobots.robots.CONCEPT_TREES.Robot.FUNCS.selfCheck > 0 }
  STATE IsPlaning { IS_PERFORMING{swarmRobots.robots.CONCEPT_TREES.Robot.FUNCS.plan} }
  STATE IsExploring { IS_PERFORMING{swarmRobots.robots.CONCEPT_TREES.Robot.FUNCS.explore} }
  STATE HasDebrisNearby { swarmRobots.robots.CONCEPT_TREES.Victim.PROPS.distDeplArea < 3 } //less than 3 m
}}
```

Note that *states* are extremely important to the specification of *goals*, *situations*, and *policies*. For example, states help the KnowLang Reasoner determine at runtime whether the system is in a particular situation or a particular goal has been achieved. The following code sample presents a partial specification of a simple goal.

```
CONCEPT_GOAL Protect_Victim_against_Radiation { ....
 SPEC {
  DEPART { swarmRobots.robots.CONCEPT_TREES.Victim.STATES.underRadiation  }
  ARRIVE { swarmRobots.robots.CONCEPT_TREES.Victim.STATES.radiationSafe }}}
```

The following is the specification of a policy called *ProtectVictimAgainst Radiation*. As shown, the policy is specified to handle the *Protect_Victim_against_Radiation* goal and is triggered by the situation *VictimNeedsHelp*.

Further, the policy triggers via its $MAPPING$ sections conditionally the execution of a sequence of actions. When the conditions are the same, we specify a probability distribution among the $MAPPING$ sections involving same conditions (e.g., $PROBABILITY\{0.6\}$), which represents our initial belief in action choice.

```
CONCEPT_POLICY ProtectVictimAgainstRadiation { ....
  SPEC {
  POLICY_GOAL { swarmRobots.robots.CONCEPT_TREES.Protect_Victim_against_Radiation }
  POLICY_SITUATIONS { swarmRobots.robots.CONCEPT_TREES.VictimNeedsHelp }
  POLICY_RELATIONS { swarmRobots.robots.RELATIONS.Policy_Situation_1 }
  POLICY_ACTIONS { swarmRobots.robots.CONCEPT_TREES.DragVictim,
    swarmRobots.robots.CONCEPT_TREES.CarryVictim,swarmRobots.robots.CONCEPT_TREES.BuildWall}
  POLICY_MAPPINGS {
    MAPPING {
      CONDITIONS { swarmRobots.robots.CONCEPT_TREES.Robot.STATES.IsOperational AND
      swarmRobots.robots.CONCEPT_TREES.Robot.PROPS.victimToCareOf.PROPS.victimMass >
      swarmRobots.robots.CONCEPT_TREES.Robot.PROPS.liftCapacity AND
      swarmRobots.robots.CONCEPT_TREES.Robot.STATES.HasDebrisNearby}
      DO_ACTIONS {swarmRobots.robots.CONCEPT_TREES.Robot.FUNCS.dragVictimAway} PROBABILITY {0.6}}
    MAPPING {
      CONDITIONS { swarmRobots.robots.CONCEPT_TREES.Robot.STATES.IsOperational AND
      swarmRobots.robots.CONCEPT_TREES.Robot.PROPS.victimToCareOf.PROPS.victimMass >
      swarmRobots.robots.CONCEPT_TREES.Robot.PROPS.liftCapacity AND
      swarmRobots.robots.CONCEPT_TREES.Robot.STATES.HasDebrisNearby}
      DO_ACTIONS {swarmRobots.robots.CONCEPT_TREES.Robot.FUNCS.buildWall} PROBABILITY {0.4}}
    MAPPING {
      CONDITIONS { swarmRobots.robots.CONCEPT_TREES.Robot.STATES.IsOperational AND
      swarmRobots.robots.CONCEPT_TREES.Robot.PROPS.victimToCareOf.PROPS.victimMass <=
      swarmRobots.robots.CONCEPT_TREES.Robot.PROPS.liftCapacity}
      DO_ACTIONS {swarmRobots.robots.CONCEPT_TREES.Robot.FUNCS.carryVictim} PROBABILITY {0.6}}
    MAPPING {
      CONDITIONS { swarmRobots.robots.CONCEPT_TREES.Robot.STATES.IsOperational AND
      swarmRobots.robots.CONCEPT_TREES.Robot.PROPS.victimToCareOf.PROPS.victimMass <=
      swarmRobots.robots.CONCEPT_TREES.Robot.PROPS.liftCapacity}
      DO_ACTIONS { swarmRobots.robots.CONCEPT_TREES.Robot.FUNCS.dragVictimAway} PROBABILITY {0.4}
}}}}
```

As specified, the probability distribution gives the designer's initial preference about what actions should be executed if the system ended up running that policy. Note that at runtime, the KnowLang Reasoner maintains a record of all the action executions and re-computes the probability rates every time when a policy has been applied and subsequently, actions have been executed. Thus, although initially the system will execute the function $dragVictimAway$ (it has the higher probability rate of 0.6), if that policy cannot achieve its goal with this action, then the probability distribution will be shifted in favor of the function $buildWall$, which may be executed the next time when the system will try to apply the same policy. Therefore, probabilities are recomputed after every action execution, and thus the behavior changes accordingly.

5   Conclusion and Future Work

Swarm robotics systems generally exhibit a number of autonomic features resulting in complex behavior and complex interactions with the operational environment, often leading to a need for self-adaptation. The need of self-adaptation arises when a system needs to cope with changes in order to ensure realization of its objectives. To properly develop such systems, it is very important to appropriately handle their self-adaptive behavior. In this paper, we have presented an approach to capturing the requirements for, and modeling self-adaptive behavior, of swarm robotics. We consider that self-adaptive behavior extends the regular goals of a system upstream with special self-* objectives in the form of system's ability to automatically discover, diagnose, and cope with various problems. To formalize self-* objectives, the approach relies on the KnowLang language, a formal language dedicated to knowledge representation for self-adaptive systems.

Future work is mainly concerned with further development of the Autonomy Requirements Engineering approach along with full implementation of KnowLang, involving tools and a test bed for autonomy requirements verification and validation.

Acknowledgments. This work was supported by the European Union FP7 Integrated Project Autonomic Service-Component Ensembles (ASCENS) and by Science Foundation Ireland grant 03/CE2/I303_1 to Lero–the Irish Software Engineering Research Centre.

References

1. ASCENS: ASCENS - Autonomic Service-Component Ensembles. ascens-ist.eu (2014). http://www.ascens-ist.eu/
2. Bonani, M., Baaboura, T., Retornaz, P., Vaussard, F., Magnenat, S., Burnier, D., Longchamp, V., Mondada, F.: marXbot, Laborotoire de Systemes Robotiques (LSRO), Ecole Polytechnique Federale de Lausanne. mobots.epfl.ch (2011). http://mobots.epfl.ch/marxbot.html
3. Serbedzija, N., Hoch, N., Pinciroli, C., Kit, M., Bures, T., Monreale, G., Montanari, U., Mayer, P., Velasco, J.: D7.3: Third Report on WP7 Integration and Simulation Report for the ASCENS Case Studies. ASCENS Deliverable (2013)
4. Vassev, E., Hinchey, M.: Autonomy requirements engineering. In: Proceedings of the 14th IEEE International Conference on Information Reuse and Integration (IRI 2013), pp. 175–184. IEEE Computer Society (2013)
5. Vassev, E., Hinchey, M.: Autonomy requirements engineering: A case study on the bepicolombo mission. In: Proceedings of C* Conference on Computer Science & Software Engineering (C3S2E 2013), pp. 31–41. ACM (2013)
6. Vassev, E., Hinchey, M.: On the autonomy requirements for space missions. In: Proceedings of the 16th IEEE International Symposium on Object/Component/Service-oriented Real-time Distributed Computing Workshops (ISCORCW 2013). IEEE Computer Society (2013)
7. Vassev, E., Hinchey, M., Gaudin, B.: Knowledge representation for self-adaptive behavior. In: Proceedings of C* Conference on Computer Science & Software Engineering (C3S2E 2012), pp. 113–117. ACM (2012)
8. Vassev, E., Hinchey, M., Montanari, U., Bicocchi, N., Zambonelli, F., Wirsing, M.: D3.2: Second Report on WP3: The KnowLang Framework for Knowledge Modeling for SCE Systems. ASCENS Deliverable (2012)

Reasoning on Data Streams: An Approach to Adaptation in Pervasive Systems

Nicola Bicocchi[1], Emil Vassev[2], Franco Zambonelli[1], and Mike Hinchey[2(✉)]

[1] Universita di Modena e Reggio Emilia, Modena, Italia
{nicola.bicocchi,franco.zambonelli}@unimore.it
[2] Lero–the Irish Software Engineering Research Centre, University of Limerick,
Limerick, Ireland
{emil.vassev,mike.hinchey}@lero.ie

Abstract. Urban environments are increasingly invaded by devices that acquire sensor information and pave the way for innovative forms of context awareness. Collecting knowledge from loosely-structured data streams and reasoning about changes are two key elements of the process. This paper illustrates a possible way to combine these two elements in a coordinated way. We make use of a recently-developed framework for classifying data streams with service-oriented, reconfigurable components. Furthermore, we embed the KnowLang Reasoner, allowing logical and statistical reasoning on the acquired knowledge aiming to achieve self-adaptation.

1 Introduction

The widespread adoption of sensor networks, actuators and computational resources capable of interacting with people is transforming urban environments as well as domestic spaces [1,3,6]. However, the design of such systems presents challenges for current approaches. Designing with a top-down approach means that all the requirements of a software architecture have to be taken into account *a priori*. Systems engineered in this way have a predictable and measurable behaviour but are not well suited to cope with dynamic execution contexts. On the other hand, bottom-up design delivers robust systems that can eventually be used in pervasive environments. However, modelling system behaviour of such pervasive systems is not a trivial task and potential urban scenarios call for a balanced trade-off between the two approaches.

Situational awareness appears to be one of the key drivers that guide this trade-off. In fact, it can be used to provide systems with adaptation capabilities — essential in dynamic, interconnected, and yet, heterogeneous environments — without compromising predictable behaviours. For example, it would be possible to envision a system capable of continuously inferring its operating context and executing actions accordingly. Increasing both the number of inferred contexts and possible actions leads to seemingly-adaptive systems [2].

This paper illustrates how situational awareness and reasoning can be put to work together in order to implement adaptive behaviours. For awareness collection, we have made use of a recently-developed framework [4], centered around

© Institute for Computer Sciences, Social Informatics and Telecommunications Engineering 2015
P.C. Vinh et al. (Eds.): ICTCC 2014, LNICST 144, pp. 23–32, 2015.
DOI: 10.1007/978-3-319-15392-6_3

the concept of dynamic service reconfiguration, which is able to gather data from a number of different sources, and classify them using general-purpose algorithms. For reasoning, instead, we used the KnowLang framework [10]. The combination of these tools allows systems to collect data on situational aware-ness, reason about it, and select the most proper chain of actions accordingly in a closed loop fashion (see Figure 1). As an example, we discuss a case study describing the implementation of a self-driving, self-adapting drone. Situational awareness data is collected via various sensors, classified and provided to the KnowLang Reasoner to select the appropriate actions.

The rest of this paper is organised as follows. Section 2 presents our approach to data collection and classification. Section 3 provides a brief introduction to KnowLang along with a short discussion on how it can cope with the collected data. Then, in Section 4 we present a small proof-of-concept case study. Finally, Section 5 provides concluding remarks and a summary of our future goals.

2   Knowledge Collection and Understanding

In this section the framework for knowledge collection is described. It is based on reconfigurable components and its goal is to provide a starting point for many diverse applications. Developers are only required to select the required modules, and define their topology and reconfiguration strategies as depicted in Figure 1. It has been conceived around the following requirements [12] [7].

- *Adaptation.* The framework should be the key source of the applications' adaptive capabilities. It has to provide the mechanisms and tools neces-sary for knowledge processing. Applications relying on the framework must receive compact and structured information about the environment and use this as triggers for adaptation.
- *Self-Adaptation.* Given a specific classification task and a situation, the framework should select the most appropriate components. For example, it is possible to roughly recognise the vehicle used by a user with either GPS or an accelerometer or microphone. An energy constrained system could constantly monitor its residual energy and select the most appropriate trade-off between consumption and classification accuracy. Service-oriented and dynamically reconfigurable components have been recently proposed. They allow us to select among different components (i.e., sensors, classifiers) depending on the situation. Furthermore, reconfigurable components can transparently modify their internal parameters. For example, classifiers can analyse temporal win-dows of different sizes considering the availability of computational resources or energy boundaries.
- *Extensibility.* The framework should be extensible in several ways, without the need to restart it. First, it should be possible to deploy, modify, and remove context services. Second, the infrastructure should support the evo-lution of supported types of contexts by dynamic load context definitions, functionality, and acquisition mechanisms.

- *Modelling abstractions.* The type of situational information that is relevant for modelling and handling varies across application settings. For example, in a hospital, items like beds, pill-containers, and medicines are important information for the work of clinicians, but this is specific to hospitals. Hence the application programmer should be able to model and handle context data specific to various settings.
- *Software Engineering.* Organising the framework around the idea of reconfigurable components (i.e., sensors, classifiers) leads to modularity and composability of the software ecosystem. Developers are allowed to deploy components that are either: *(i)* already included in the framework or *(ii)* developed by third parties.
- *Event-based.* The core quality of situation-aware applications is their ability to react to changes in their environment. Hence, applications should be able to subscribe to relevant events and be notified when such events occur.

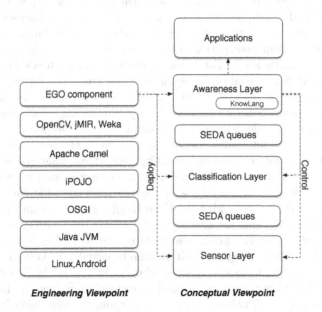

Fig. 1. The framework architecture is structured around three layers, namely *sensor*, *classifier* and *awareness* layers

The architecture is structured around three layers, namely the *sensor*, *classifier* and *awareness* layers. Each layer can host multiple modules connected to each other via application-definable topologies. The data flow from sensors through the whole architecture is by means of in-memory queues enabling modules decoupling and many-to-many asynchronous communications. Each layer can host multiple modules.

The sensor layer hosts modules that are responsible for retrieving raw data from physical sensors and pre-processing them. An example could be a module acquiring images from a camera and cropping and resizing them. At the time of writing, we have already implemented modules for reading data from Android devices.

The classification layer hosts modules that consume data coming from the sensor layer and classify them (i.e., generate semantically richer information). An example could be a module able to classify the activity performed by a user by processing accelerometer data. At the time of writing, we have implemented modules for classifying user activity, location, speed, and vehicle used on the basis of common smartphone sensors. It is worth noting that our goal is to build a general-purpose awareness framework that can be used as a common basis for both research and application development, not to solve every possible classification problem. Specific applications will need their own modules to be developed.

The awareness layer hosts modules consuming labels produced in the classification layer and feeding external applications with situational information. These modules might have different goals depending on the application. However, they can be divided into two main classes. The former comprises modules delegated to sensor fusion processes. These modules receive labels, eventually conflicting, coming from multiple classification modules and apply algorithms to achieve higher semantic levels. For example, common-sense knowledge has been recently proposed [5] and could be integrated at this level. The latter, instead, is related with the capability of the framework of monitoring and controlling itself. In a sense, the awareness layer could be the key to building a *self-aware* awareness module. For example, it would be possible within this level to integrate modules observing the internal status of the framework and activating different classifiers and sensors depending on operating conditions. This capability could be used to achieve both improved classification accuracies and reduced power consumption levels by continuously selecting the most suitable classifiers and sensors. In this work, we embedded the KnowLang reasoner within this layer. It receives labels from the classification layer and selects the arriving actions.

From an engineering viewpoint, the architecture is implemented on top of industrial-level Java technologies. Each module is actually an OSGi component able to meet the requirements mentioned above. On top of OSGi, we have an iPOJO layer. iPOJO is a container-based framework handling the lifecycle of *Plain Old Java Objects (POJOs)* and supporting management facilities such as dynamic dependency handling, component reconfiguration, component factory, and introspection. Moreover, the iPOJO container is easily extensible and allows pluggable handlers, typically for the management of non-functional aspects. On top of the iPOJO framework we build the support for the staged and layered architecture by making use of Apache Camel. This framework provides components with the capability of asynchronously processing data streams and communicating through in-memory queues. These queues allow modules belonging to different layers to continuously communicate with each other with minimum hardware requirements. Considering that pattern recognition has a central role in situation awareness, we wrapped well-known data manipulation libraries within the framework such as Weka, OpenCV, and jMIR.

3   KnowLang

KnowLang [10] is a formal language dedicated to knowledge representation for self-adaptive systems. The language implies a multi-tier specification model allowing for integration of ontologies together with rules and Bayesian networks [8]. The language aims at efficient and comprehensive knowledge structuring and awareness based on logical and statistical reasoning coping with the non-deterministic behaviour of self-adaptive systems by handling uncertain knowledge via additive probabilities used to represent degrees of belief. With KnowLang, we build a knowledge base (KB) with a variety of knowledge structures such as *ontologies, facts, rules* and *constraints*. The KnowLang ontologies are composed of hierarchically organised *concepts* and *objects*. Moreover, concepts and objects may be additionally related via *relations*. Relations are binary, i.e., connect two concepts, two objects, or an object with a concept, and may have probability-distribution attributes (e.g., over time, over situations, etc.). The relations can be expressed graphically as *concept maps* (see Figure 2). Probability distribution is provided to support probabilistic reasoning and by specifying relations with probability distributions, we actually specify Bayesian networks connecting the concepts and objects of an ontology.

Figure 2 shows a KnowLang specification sample demonstrating both the language syntax [9] and its visual counterpart — a concept map based on interrelations with no probability distributions.

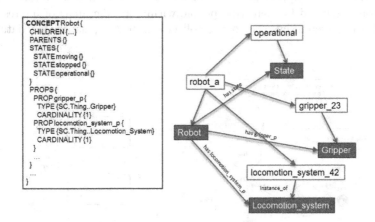

Fig. 2. KnowLang Specification Sample

For reasoning purposes, every concept specified with KnowLang, has an intrinsic *STATES* attribute (see Figure 2) that may be associated with a set of possible states that a concept's instances may be in. In general, a concept may occupy a new state when *concept properties* have been changed or some events or actions have occurred in the system or environment. KnowLang employs special knowledge structures and a reasoning mechanism for modelling self-adaptive behaviour [11]. Such a behaviour can be expressed via special *policies, events, actions*, *situations*, and *relations* between policies and situations. Policies (Π) are at the core of self-adaptive behavior. A policy π has a *goal* (g), *policy situations* (Si_π), *policy-situation relations* (R_π), and *policy conditions* (N_π) mapped to *policy actions* (A_π) where the evaluation of N_π may eventually (with some degree of probability) imply the evaluation of actions (formally denoted with $N_\pi \xrightarrow{[Z]} A_\pi$). A condition is a Boolean expression over the ontology, e.g., the occurrence of a certain event. A goal g is a desirable transition to a state, or from a specific state, to another state (formally denoted with $s \Rightarrow s'$). A state s is a Boolean expression over ontology ($be(O)$). Ideally, KnowLang policies are specified to handle specific situations, which may trigger the application of policies. A policy exhibits a behaviour via actions generated in the environment or in the system itself. Specific conditions determine which specific actions (among the actions associated with that policy) will be executed. When a policy is applied, it checks what particular conditions are met and performs the mapped actions. An optional probability distribution may additionally restrict the action execution. Although initially specified, the probability distribution is recomputed after the execution of any involved action. The re-computation is based on the consequences of the action execution, which allows for *reinforcement learning*.

4   Case Study

To demonstrate our approach, we describe an example of a self-aware surveillance drone designed for detecting people within specific areas of interest (see Figure 3). The system has the goal to collect sensor data, classify the data, and

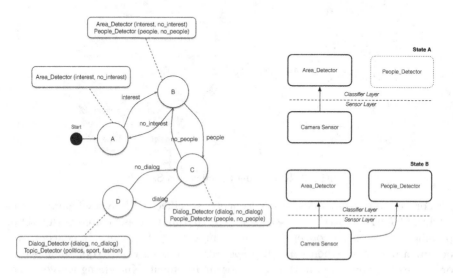

Fig. 3. A self-aware surveillance drone designed for detecting people within specific areas of interest

define the situation the data are immersed in. However, instead of using a single complex classifier, we provide developers a means of using a number of simpler and more specific classifiers. These modules can be enabled, disabled, wired and rewired in a dynamic way by making use of their output to navigate the state automata. Each status has a name and is associated with a set of classifiers — and associated sensors — that have to be active and a set of possible transitions. Each time the output of an active classifier changes, a reconfiguration is applied. Needed modules are deployed and inactive ones are automatically removed to reach the new status. In this way, the overall problem of situation recognition is modularised in a way similar to the way we believe our brain works. Each node embeds the knowledge acquired by the former and activates more specific classifiers to collect further details.

Figure 3, drives the reconfiguration of a surveillance drone. State A is activated as soon as the drone takes off and tries to detect areas of interests. As soon as an area of interest is spotted, state B is activated and eventual people are detected. State C, activated only when people are detected in an area of interest analyses audio signals to detect dialogs. Finally, state D, refines state C by inferring the general topic of the conversation using common sense knowledge and speech recognition techniques.

It is worth noting that this example shows the internal logic of the awareness module of two different applications. However, despite the fact that the logic used to collect situational awareness has to be linked with the application logic, these automata are agnostic about *how* the situational knowledge is actually collected. In fact one could completely change sensors and classifiers used in each and every state without altering the application logic. We think this feature could both: *(i)* sensibly speed up the prototyping of pervasive applications and *(ii)* help in the development of pattern recognition modules. If fact, one could quickly assess different algorithms, libraries, and approaches without altering anything within the actual application. For the purpose of this case study, we used KnowLang to support the behaviour outlined above. The first step was to specify a simple knowledge base (KB) representing the domain outlined in the case study, e.g., the drone itself and the drone's operational environment with entities such as areas of interest, people, drone base, etc. Recall that this domain is described via a domain ontology expressed through domain-relevant concepts and objects (concept instances) related through relations (see Section 3). To handle explicit concepts such as situations, goals, and policies, we gave some of the domain concepts explicit state expressions. The following is a partial specification of the Drone concept. As shown, the Drone has properties, functionalities, and states (Boolean expressions validating states).

```
CONCEPT Drone {
  PARENTS {srvllnceDrone.drones.CONCEPT_TREES.System}
  CHILDREN { }
  PROPS {
    PROP dFlyCapacity {TYPE{srvllnceDrone.drones.CONCEPT_TREES.FlyingCapacity} CARDINALITY{1}}
    PROP dPlanner {TYPE{srvllnceDrone.drones.CONCEPT_TREES.Planner} CARDINALITY{1}}
    PROP dCommunicationSys {TYPE{srvllnceDrone.drones.CONCEPT_TREES.CommunicationSys} CARDINALITY{1}}
  }
  FUNCS {
    FUNC plan {TYPE {srvllnceDrone.drones.CONCEPT_TREES.Plan}}
    FUNC lineExplore {TYPE {srvllnceDrone.drones.CONCEPT_TREES.LineExplore}}
    FUNC spiralExplore {TYPE {srvllnceDrone.drones.CONCEPT_TREES.SpiralExplore}}
    FUNC takeoff {TYPE {srvllnceDrone.drones.CONCEPT_TREES.TakeOff}}
    FUNC flyTowardsBase {TYPE {srvllnceDrone.drones.CONCEPT_TREES.FlyTowardsBase}}
    FUNC lookForPeople {TYPE {srvllnceDrone.drones.CONCEPT_TREES.LookForPeople}}
  }
  STATES {
    STATE IsUp { PERFORMED{srvllnceDrone.drones.CONCEPT_TREES.Drone.FUNCS.takeoff} }
    STATE IsPlaning { IS_PERFORMING{srvllnceDrone.drones.CONCEPT_TREES.Drone.FUNCS.plan} }
    STATE IsExploring { IS_PERFORMING{srvllnceDrone.drones.CONCEPT_TREES.Drone.FUNCS.lineExplore} OR
        IS_PERFORMING{srvllnceDrone.drones.CONCEPT_TREES.Drone.FUNCS.spiralExplore} }
    STATE InLowFlayCapacity {
        srvllnceDrone.drones.CONCEPT_TREES.Drone.PROPS.dFlyCapacity.STATES.smallFlyingTime}
    STATE FoundAreaOfInterest { srvllnceDrone.drones.CONCEPT_TREES.Drone.STATES.IsExploring AND
        srvllnceDrone.drones.CONCEPT_TREES.SpottedAreasOfInterest >= 1 }
    STATE FlayingOverAreaOfInterest { }
    STATE IsExploringAreaOfInterest { srvllnceDrone.drones.CONCEPT_TREES.Drone.STATES.IsExploring AND
        srvllnceDrone.drones.CONCEPT_TREES.Drone.STATES.FlayingOverAreaOfInterest }
    STATE FoundPeopleOfInterest {
        srvllnceDrone.drones.CONCEPT_TREES.Drone.STATES.IsExploringAreaOfInterest AND
        srvllnceDrone.drones.CONCEPT_TREES.SpottedPeople >= 1 }
} }
```

To specify the drone's behaviour with KnowLang, we used goals, policies, and situations (see Section 3). The following is a specification sample showing a drone's policy called *GoFindAreaOfInterest*. As shown, the policy is specified to handle the goal *FindAreaOfInterest* and is triggered by the situation *DroneIsOnAndAreaNotFound*. Further, the policy triggers via its *MAPPING* sections conditionally (e.g., there is a *CONDITONS* directive that requires the drone's flying capacity be higher than the estimated time needed to get back to the base) the execution of a sequence of actions. When the conditions were the same, we specified a probability distribution among the *MAPPING* sections involving same conditions (e.g., *PROBABILITY* 0.6), which represents our initial belief in action choice.

```
CONCEPT_POLICY GoFindAreaOfInterest {
  CHILDREN {}
  PARENTS { srvllnceDrone.drones.CONCEPT_TREES.Policy}
  SPEC {
    POLICY_GOAL { srvllnceDrone.drones.CONCEPT_TREES.FindAreaOfInterest }
    POLICY_SITUATIONS { srvllnceDrone.drones.CONCEPT_TREES.DroneIsOnAndAreaNotFound }
    ....
    POLICY_MAPPINGS {
      MAPPING {
        CONDITIONS { srvllnceDrone.drones.CONCEPT_TREES.TimeToDroneBase <
          srvllnceDrone.drones.CONCEPT_TREES.drone.PROPS.dFlyCapacity }
        DO_ACTIONS { srvllnceDrone.drones.CONCEPT_TREES.drone.FUNCS.lineExplore }
        PROBABILITY {0.6}
      }
      MAPPING {
        CONDITIONS { srvllnceDrone.drones.CONCEPT_TREES.TimeToDroneBase <
          srvllnceDrone.drones.CONCEPT_TREES.drone.PROPS.dFlyCapacity }
        DO_ACTIONS { srvllnceDrone.drones.CONCEPT_TREES.drone.FUNCS.spiralExplore }
        PROBABILITY {0.4}
      }
      ....
} } }
```

As specified, the probability distribution gives the designer's initial preference about what actions should be executed if the system ends up running the *GoFindAreaOf Interest* policy. Note that at runtime, the KnowLang Reasoner maintains a record of all the action executions and re-computes the probability rates every time when a policy has been applied, and subsequently when actions have been executed. Thus, although initially the system will execute the function *lineExplore* (it has the higher probability rate of 0.6), if that policy cannot achieve its goal with this action, then the probability distribution will be shifted in favour of the function *spiralExplore*, which might be executed next time when the system will try to apply the same policy. Therefore, probabilities are recomputed after every action execution, and thus, the behaviour changes accordingly.

As mentioned above, policies are triggered by situations. Therefore, while specifying policies handling the drone's objectives (e.g., *FindAreaOfInterest*), we need to think of important situations that may trigger those policies. Note that these situations will eventually be outlined by scenarios providing alternative behaviours or execution paths out of that situation. The following code represents the specification of the situation *DroneIsOnAndAreaNotFound*, used for the specification of the *GoFindAreaOfInterest* policy.

```
CONCEPT_SITUATION DroneIsOnAndAreaNotFound {
....
   SPEC {
      SITUATION_STATES {srvllnceDrone.drones.CONCEPT_TREES.drone.STATES.IsUp,
         srvllnceDrone.drones.CONCEPT_TREES.drone.STATES.IsExploring}
      SITUATION_ACTIONS {srvllnceDrone.drones.CONCEPT_TREES.LineExplore,
         srvllnceDrone.drones.CONCEPT_TREES.FlyTowardsBase}
}}
```

As shown, the situation is specified with $SITATION\_STATES$ (e.g., the drone's states *IsUp* and *IsExploring*) and $SITUATION\_ACTIONS$ (e.g., *LineExplore*, *SpiralExplore*, and *FlyTowardsBase*). To consider a situation effective (i.e., the system is currently in that situation), the situation states must be respectively effective (evaluated as true). For example, the *DroneIsOnAndAreaNotFound* situation is effective if the Drone's state *IsExploring* is effective (is on hold). The possible actions define what actions can be undertaken once the system fails in a particular situation.

Note that the specification presented is a part of the KB that is operated by the KnowLang Reasoner. The reasoner encapsulates that KB and acts as a module in the awareness layer of the *framework for knowledge collection* (see Figure 1). The reasoner is "fed" with classified sensory data (labels), produced by the classification layer, and returns situational information and proposed behaviour upon request. The consumed labels help the reasoner update the KB, which results in re-evaluation of the specified concept states (recall that states are specified as a Boolean expression over the ontology, i.e., a state expression may include any element in the KB). Subsequently, the evaluation of the specified states helps the reasoner determine at runtime whether the system is in a particular situation or if a particular goal has been achieved. Moreover, it can deduce an appropriate policy that may help the drone "go out" of a particular situation.

5   Conclusion and Future Work

In this paper we proposed a combination of two innovative frameworks for context-awareness and reasoning aimed at self-aware systems. The former has been designed around the concept of reconfiguration and built using well-established Java technologies. It is able to collect data from a number of different sources and classify them using general-purpose algorithms. The latter has been designed for reasoning and action selection using both logical and statistical techniques. To test their mutual synergies, a case study describing a self-aware surveillance drone has been described in greater detail.

We are planning to challenge this approach in more complex scenarios to better understand how the framework self-* structure could simplify the engineering of pervasive applications, particularly on mobile platforms.

Acknowledgments. This work was supported by the European Union FP7 Integrated Project Autonomic Service-Component Ensembles (ASCENS) and by Science Foundation Ireland grant 03/CE2/I303_1 to Lero—the Irish Software Engineering Research Centre.

References

1. Smart cities Ranking of European medium-sized cities, Vienna, Austria (2007). http://tinyurl.com/bqh83np
2. Abeywickrama, D.B., Bicocchi, N., Zambonelli, F.: Sota: towards a general model for self-adaptive systems. In: Reddy, S., Drira, K. (eds.) WETICE, pp. 48–53. IEEE Computer Society (2012)
3. Bicocchi, N., Cecaj, A., Fontana, D., Mamei, M., Sassi, A., Zambonelli, F.: Collective awareness for human-ict collaboration in smart cities. In: WETICE, pp. 3–8 (2013)
4. Bicocchi, N., Fontana, D., Zambonelli, F.: A self-aware, reconfigurable architecture for context awareness. In: IEEE Symposium on Computers and Communications, Madeira, Portugal (2014)
5. Bicocchi, N., Lasagni, M., Zambonelli, F.: Bridging vision and commonsense for multimodal situation recognition in pervasive systems. In: International Conference on Pervasive Computing and Communications, Lugano, Switzerland (2012)
6. Kehoe, M., et al.: Understanding ibm smart cities. Redbook Series (2011)
7. Khan, W.Z., Xiang, Y., Aalsalem, M.Y., Arshad, Q.: Mobile phone sensing systems: A survey. IEEE Communication Survey and Tutorials **15**, 402–427 (2013)
8. Neapolitan, R.: Learning Bayesian Networks. Prentice Hall (2003)
9. Vassev, E.: KnowLang Grammar in BNF. Tech. Rep. Lero-TR-2012-04, Lero, University of Limerick, Ireland (2012)
10. Vassev, E., Hinchey, M.: Knowledge representation for cognitive robotic systems. In: Proceedings of the 15th IEEE International Symposium on Object/Component/Service-Oriented Real-Time Distributed Computing Workshops (ISCORCW 2012), pp. 156–163. IEEE Computer Society (2012)
11. Vassev, E., Hinchey, M., Gaudin, B.: Knowledge representation for self-adaptive behavior. In: Proceedings of C* Conference on Computer Science and Software Engineering (C3S2E 2012), pp. 113–117. ACM (2012)
12. Ye, J., Dobson, S., McKeever, S.: Situation identification techniques in pervasive computing: A review. Pervasive and Mobile Computing **8**, 33–66 (2012)

Autonomic Computing Software
for Autonomous Space Vehicles

Carlos C. Insaurralde[1] and Emil Vassev[2(⊠)]

[1] Institute of Sensors, Signals and Systems, Heriot-Watt University, Edinburgh
EH14 4AS, UK
`c.c.insaurralde@hw.ac.uk`
[2] Lero–the Irish Software Engineering Research Centre, University of Limerick,
Limerick, Ireland
`emil.vassev@lero.ie`

Abstract. Current space missions increasingly demand more autonomy in control architectures for Unmanned Space Vehicles (USVs), so unmanned long-term missions can be afforded. Continuous assurance of effective adaptation to unpredictable internal and external changes, along with efficient management of resources is essential for such requirements. One of the attractive solutions is that inspired by the physiology of living systems, where self-regulation helps to achieve continuous adaptation to the environment by changing internal conditions. The physiological functions are performed by nervous system reflexes that are the foundations for self-regulatory mechanisms such as homeostasis. Building artificial self-regulation similar to biological ones into USVs makes them highly-viable and ultra-stable in order to support very long missions. This paper presents aspects of how to endow USVs with Artificial Nervous Reflexes (ANRs) by means of applying physiological principles of self-regulation to the USV's control architecture, so resilience and persistence can be supported. A case study of a composite orbiter is presented. The studied ANRs are needed to guarantee the self-regulation of response time (latency), operation temperature (thermoregulation), and power consumption (energy balance). Results from a cross-checked analysis of the above self-regulation mechanisms are also presented.

1   Introduction

The technological evolution of Unmanned Space Vehicles (USVs) is making them progressively more sophisticated by increasing the complexity of their structural control architecture (e.g., integration of multiple capabilities for robotic exploration of very large and hostile areas in planet surveys), and the degree of behavioral autonomy (e.g., non-stop operation supporting in-service adaptation to expected and unexpected situations). The main challenge in dealing with the above systems involves the continuous assurance of effective adaptation to unpredictable internal and external changes, and efficient management of resources. One of the attractive inspirations for tackling these issues is that provided by the physiology of living systems, in particular, auto-configuration, auto-reproduction, and auto-regulation abilities. These self-

© Institute for Computer Sciences, Social Informatics and Telecommunications Engineering 2015
P.C. Vinh et al. (Eds.): ICTCC 2014, LNICST 144, pp. 33–41, 2015.
DOI: 10.1007/978-3-319-15392-6_4

adapting capabilities endow organisms with resilience having the vital goal of surviving. The self-adaptation is inspired by the physiological functions performed by single/multi-operational combination of nervous system reflexes. It is able to support autonomic management and persistent sustainment (including self-maintenance and self-suitability) in order to make systems more viable and stable. Resilient operation is a qualitative aspect supported by highly-viable and ultra-stable control engineering systems. Applying this system quality to USVs means that they can know how to regulate themselves internally to cope with different external operational conditions. The implementation of this self-management in USVs is rather a very complex development task that requires concurrent control architecture.

The motivation of this research work is to propose a physiologically-inspired control approach for USVs by endowing them with well-defined self-regulatory capabilities to persist (even in adverse conditions), i.e., reflex-driven homeostasis properties as in living systems. By means of homeostasis, a system regulates its internal environment and tends to maintain a stable and constant condition regarding the external environment.

This paper presents aspects of how to endow USVs with Artificial Nervous Reflexes (ANRs) by means of applying physiological principles of self-regulation to the USV Control Architecture, so resilience and persistence can be supported. The architectural approach is realized on the basis that autonomy requirements for USVs are satisfied. A case study based on orbiters for the BepiColombo Mission to Mercury [1] is presented. The ANRs, studied in this paper for those orbiters, are needed to guarantee the self-regulation of response time (latency), operation temperature (thermoregulation), and power consumption (energy balance).

The rest of the paper is structured as follows. Section 2 presents a review of fundamental biology concepts and related work. Section 3 presents the Autonomic System Specification Language (ASSL) used in this project to specify the ANRs. Section 4 presents a case study based on the BepiColombo Mission where an algorithm of ANRs for the mission's orbiters is proposed. Section 5 presents our experiments and results. Finally, the last section presents concluding remarks and directions for future work.

2   Related Work

The nervous system has neural pathways named reflex arcs that control reflex actions in order to implement regulatory functions. Reflex arcs are divided into two types: somatic reflex arcs and autonomic reflex arcs. The former are reflexes from SNS classified as withdrawal, stretch, and extra-pyramidal reflexes. The latter are from the ANS classified as autonomic reflexes. Same examples of reflexes are [2]:

- Withdrawal Reflexes, e.g., pain impulses initiated by touching a very hot surface with the finger.
- Stretch Reflexes, e.g., the knee jerk; the sensory nerve endings in the tendon and the thigh muscles are stretched by tapping the tendon just below the knee when it is bent.

- Extra-pyramidal (Upper-Motor) Reflexes, e.g., maintenance of upright neck and head where many muscles are contracting in a coordinated manner.
- Autonomic Reflexes, e.g., the self-regulation of the cardiovascular functions such an increase of the heart rate to increasing blood pressure.

Homeostasis is the property of a system to maintain stable its condition regarding the external environment by regulating its internal environment.

Major pioneering research is focused on mobile robots as an excellent test-bed for research on Autonomic Computing (AC) [3] and Organic Computing (OC) [5]. It recognizes self-management power by exploring the use of AC techniques in the domain of ground-based mobile robots [4]. The main focus is on robustness and fault-tolerance. This research work only presents the ideas to apply AC to mobile robots but not any implementation.

Active adaptation of systems requires non-stop monitoring and control. Thus, the two main OC components are an observer and a controller dealing with the system under observation and regulation. Since its emergence, OC has brought the attention of researchers from different domains. Once the methodology has been proposed, the question is how to design and implement OC systems. Some approaches coin the combination of model-driven engineering with OC [6].

The viability provided by the Viable System Model (VSM) [7] is based on the ultra-stability concept. A system is said to be ultra-stable when it can survive arbitrary and un-forecast interference. This high stability is also applied to systems that are able to deal with various principles for states. If a system can cope with its environment by successfully absorbing the variety from it (attenuating the incoming variety, and amplifying its own variety when needed), it achieves an ultra-stabile state. If a system is capable of working in such a manner, then it can maintain homeostasis. This means it can maintain itself in a state of equilibrium. Maintaining a balance of variety is essential for self-organizing systems. An approach based on VSM principles was used to build resilience into enterprise systems [8]. It demonstrated how a combination of systems thinking and a physiology inspiration based on homeostatic mechanisms of the human body can provide a blueprint for resilience.

The idea of building a self-adaptable man-made system capable of taking into account environment changes was proposed by mid-20th century. The "homeostat", as its inventor W. Ross Ashby called it, was developed to support habituation, reinforcement and learning through its ability to maintain homeostasis in a changing environment [9]. The homeostat caught the attention of the control community that saw it as an interesting implementation for adaptive control based on cybernetics and general systems theory [10].

3   Autonomic System Specification Language

The Autonomic System Specification Language (ASSL) [11, 12] is defined through formalization tiers. Over these tiers, ASSL provides a multi-tier specification model that is designed to be scalable and exposes a judicious selection and configuration of infrastructure elements and mechanisms needed by an AS. ASSL defines the latter with interaction protocols and autonomic elements (AEs), where the ASSL tiers and their sub-tiers describe different aspects of the AS under consideration, such as policies, communication interfaces, execution semantics, actions, etc. There are three main tiers in the ASSL specification model:

- The AS Tier specifies an AS in terms of service level objectives (AS SLO), self-management policies, architecture topology, actions, events, and metrics. The AS SLO is a high-level form of behavioral specification that establishes system objectives such as performance. The self-management policies could be the four self-management policies (also called self- CHOP) of an AS: self-configuring, self-healing, self-optimizing, and self-protecting, or they could be others. The metrics constitute a set of parameters and observables controllable by the AEs.
- At the AS Interaction Protocol tier, the ASSL framework specifies an AS-level interaction protocol (ASIP). ASIP is a public communication interface, expressed with channels, communication functions and messages.
- At the AE Tier, the ASSL formal model considers AEs to be analogous to software agents able to manage their own behavior and their relationships with other AEs. In this tier, ASSL describes the individual AEs of the AS.

We used ASSL in this project to specify the orbiters' ANRs.

4   Autonomic ANRs for BepiColombo Mission

The BepiColombo Mission is to be performed by two orbiters: a Mercury Planetary Orbiter (MPO) and a Mercury Magnetospheric Orbiter (MMO) [1]. The physiologically-inspired adaptation for the orbiters is defined through three self-regulatory functions based on autonomic ANRs by parameterizing the autonomicity and quality attributes of BepiColombo [13].

There are three parameters in the studied USVs (MPO and MMO) that are under self-regulation: (1) the end-to-end latency regulation; (2) the system-context temperature regulation; and (3) the power consumption regulation. These self-regulated parameters have the following requirements as to operation ranges.

The states generated by the USV latency (L):

$$S_L(L) \equiv \{s(L)\} \quad \forall L \in 50\ \mu s < L < 200\ \mu s$$

The states generated by the USV temperature (T):

$$S_T(T) \equiv \{s(T)\} \quad \forall T \in -65\ °C < T < 175\ °C$$

The states generated by the USV power (P):

$$S_P(P) \equiv \{s(P)\} \quad \forall P \in 10\ W < P < 30\ W$$

The states of homeostatic balance in the AES (S_{hb}) are derived as the intersection of the above states:

$$S_{hb} = S(L) \cap S(T) \cap S(P)$$

The states of homeostatic imbalance in the AES (SHI) are the exclusion of states given by:

$$S_{hi} = S(L) / S(T) / S(P)$$

The self-regulation of the above three operational parameters (L, T, and P) is working as follows:

End-to-end Latency Regulation (L). This requirement is basically to optimize by guaranteeing the USV performance in terms of time response, including processing and communication times. The USV under study is required to work within a certain end-to-end latency range (50 μs < L < 200 μs), no matter the processes and tasks it has to execute, and in order to get its right time response. Thus, any system state generated by L between 50 μs and 200 μs makes the USV to be in homeostatic end-to-end latency balance. Otherwise, the USV is in homeostatic end-to-end latency imbalance.

System-Context Temperature Regulation (T). This requirement is basically to optimize by guaranteeing the USV performance in terms of temperature of operation. The USV temperature can be affected by the heat generated by the electronic devices and other heat sources inside the system as well as outside it (environment). The USV under study is required to work within a certain temperature range (-65 °C < T < 175 °C), no matter the environmental temperature the USV has to deal with, and in order to maintain operational performance. Thus, any USV state generated by T between -65 °C and 175 °C makes the USV to be in homeostatic temperature balance. Otherwise, the system is in homeostatic temperature imbalance.

Power Consumption Regulation (P). This requirement is basically to optimize by guaranteeing the USV performance in terms of power consumption. The USV under study is required to work within a certain power range (10 W < P < 30 W), no matter the USV operation, and in order to make a good use of the energy. Thus, any USV state generated by p between 10 W and 30 W makes the USV to be in homeostatic power consumption balance. Otherwise, the USV is in homeostatic power consumption imbalance.

The artificial homeostatic balance state (collective; three-parameters) can be formally specified as follows.

$$S_{hb} = S_L \cap S_T \cap S_P, \forall 50 \text{ μs} \leq L \leq 200 \text{ μs} \wedge \forall \text{-65 °C} \leq T \leq 175 \text{ °C} \wedge \forall 10 \text{ W} \leq P \leq 30 \text{ W}$$

Any other state outside S_{hb} makes the system to be in homeostatic imbalance. The homeostatic balance states can be formally defined as follows:

$$S_{hi} = S_L / S_T / S_P \; \forall 50 \text{ μs} \leq L \leq 200 \text{ μs} \wedge \forall \text{-65 °C} \leq T \leq 175 \text{ °C} \wedge \forall 10 \text{ W} \leq P \leq 30 \text{ W}$$

5   Experiments

The self-regulation behavior based on the three operational parameters (**L**, **T**, and **P**) was specified with the ASSL framework and consecutively, Java code was generated. For more information on the self-regulation specification model, please, refer to [13]. Note that all Java applications generated with ASSL can generate run-time log records that show important state-transition operations ongoing in the system at runtime and the behavior of the generated system can be easily followed by the generated log records. Hence, the log records produced by the generated Java application for the ASSL self-regulation specification model for USVs allowed us to trace the simulated USV behavior and so, to perform a variety of experiments outlined in this section.

The USV deals with the following two drivers that impact on the self-regulatory functions (applied to the parameters under auto-regulation, i.e. end-to-end latency, system-context temperature, and power consumption) based on autonomic ANRs:

- **Data Processing Rate (DPR).** The USV under study is able to process data and dispatch tasks with a sampling time, an execution time, a deadline, a delivery time, and within a range defined by them from 825 Mips to 3300 Mips. The USV data processing is defined by delays generated by software/hardware controllers. A typical application case is that a USV is a real-time system. Thus, data processing time constraints must be guaranteed all the time.
- **Data Transfer Rate (DTR).** The USV under study is able to transfer data up to 2000 Mbits/sec. However, it is required to work at least at 500 Mbits/sec in order to keep a desired operational performance. The USV optimizes its performance by increasing the transfer rate when the data volume is bigger, and decrease it when the data volume is smaller. USV DTR can also be changed when a priority list for messages is applied; transmission rules for different communication channels are set or network availability policies are required.

Increments in the DPR increase the temperature and power consumption of the USV but decrease its end-to-end latency. On the contrary, decrements in the DPR decrease the temperature and power consumption of the USV but increase its end-to-end latency. It is the same situation for the DTR. In addition, a higher USV clock speed means an increase of the DPR and DTR, and a lower one means a decrease of them. There are other drivers that influence on the USV parameters under regulation such as the environment temperature, and cooling mechanics of the USV. A higher environment temperature increases the USV temperature, and lower one decreases the USV temperature. An activated cooling mechanism lowers the USV temperature but increases the power consumption and the environment temperature.

The cross-checked tests of the self-regulatory functions and their drivers is carried out by running a software application which code was automatically generated by the ASSL framework.

Different tests were carried out. They go from reduced-load system operations with slight load changes up to full-load system operations with strong load changes. Reduction in loads entails the USV in a state defined as follows: power-up and communication and computation load (randomly variable but up to 20 % of the maximum).

Full loads entail the USV in an operational state where transferring and processing loads were simulated in order to evaluate the USV self-regulatory capabilities under load (randomly variable, and up to 100 % of the maximum).

The following figures show results from the tests of the self-regulatory mechanisms studied on a USV. They show the cross-regulation impact during 140 minutes, and with a randomly-variable load on the data processing and transferring rates. Figure 1 shows the evolution of the self-regulation for the system-context temperature (one of the three parameters under self-regulation) when the loads can vary from 0% to 100 % of the maximum value (with slight load changes from 0 min to ~65 min, and strong ones from ~65 min to 140 min).

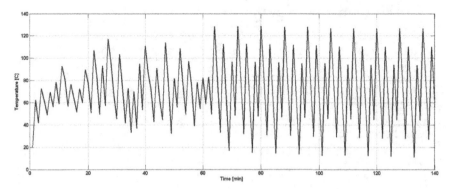

Fig. 1. Thermoregulation performance (variable load) for a USV

Just after the USV is started up, its temperature quickly reaches 60 °C, and from there it starts increasing and decreasing based on the system demands. The power consumption evolution is according to the system process, and somehow it is proportional to the variation of the temperature which makes sense. The end-to-end latency got an increase at the beginning (no transferring or processing demands).

Figure 2 shows a snapshot of the trace when the application is executed. When the system temperature (ST) reaches 60 °C, the cooling mechanism is activated. This makes ST to drop for a while and then ST varies according to the workload of the USV (transfer and processing loads) as shown in Figure 1. Figures 1 and 2 show results of the performance of the self-regulation mechanism implemented in the USV when transferring and processing loads are applied by means of slight and strong load changes. The USV starts in idle state, and then some variable loads are applied at ~4 min and ends at ~65 min. Then, some stronger variable loads are applied again at ~65 min and end at ~135 min. Then, an abruptly-decreased load is applied. In any case, the USV jumps accordingly from one state to the other, and comes back to the previous state adequately.

There is a slight increment in the power consumption when the cooling mechanism is activated but no changes are seen on the end-to-end latency due to this increment since the power consumption remains below the limit configured (30 W). This energy rise does not make any change in the system clock that can indirectly modify the end-to-end latency (through data processing and transfer rates). The cooling mechanism prevents the system temperature going beyond 140 °C (upper temperature threshold for performance optimization), and helps dissipate more temperature in the system even though the USV could support temperatures up to 175 °C. The above figures do not show the evolution of the drivers, i.e., environment temperature, DPR, and DTR.

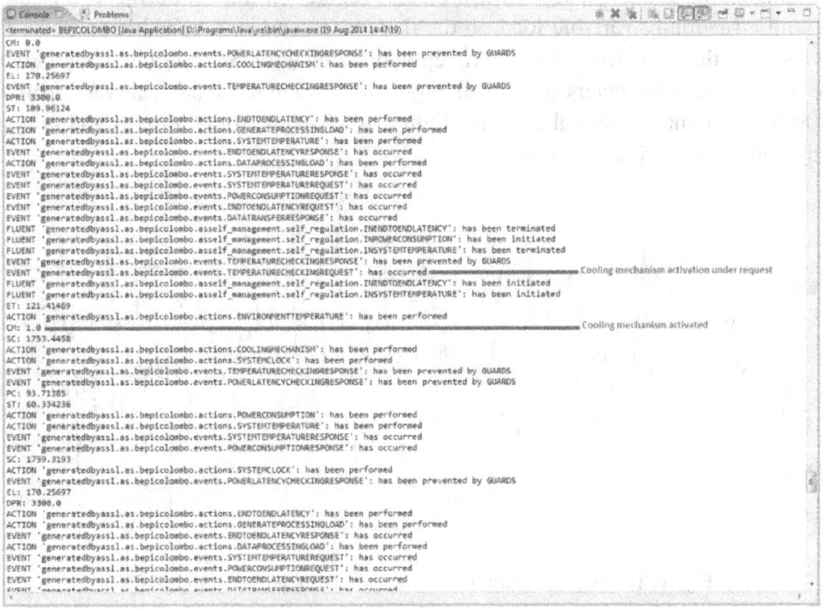

Fig. 2. Generated Java Packages for USVs

All three parameters are simultaneously and successfully regulated along the USV operation with and without workload. No one of them goes beyond the boundaries set by the artificial homeostasis principles to optimize the USV performance.

6   Conclusions

An approach to implementing operational resilience and persistence based on ANRs for USVs has been presented in this paper. Three reference technologies inspired by human physiology as well as biological foundations have been reviewed. A case study on orbiters (USVs) for the BepiColombo Mission to Mercury and outcomes of experimental tests have been presented. Initial results show the feasibility of the approach proposed. Three self-regulatory functions based on autonomic ANRs for Mercury orbiters (USVs) have been identified to show how physiological principles of self-regulation can be applied to the USV control architecture. This approach is able to comply with the USV autonomy requirements and extends the USV autonomicity through other self-managing capabilities that are suitable for either manned or unmanned spacecraft.

Future work will be mainly concerned with further development of the approach presented in this paper, including adding more self-regulated parameters and an improvement of the current code generation. It will also integrate KnowLang [14] – a formal framework that can be particularly used for formal specification of ANRs.

Acknowledgments. This work was supported by ESTEC ESA (contract No. 4000106016), by the European Union FP7 Integrated Project Autonomic Service-Component Ensembles (ASCENS), and by Science Foundation Ireland grant 03/CE2/I303_1 to Lero–the Irish Software Engineering Research Centre.

References

1. Benkhoff, J.: BepiColombo: Overview and Latest Updates, European Planetary Science Congress, p. 7. EPSC Abstracts (2012)
2. Waugh, A., Grant, A.: Anatomy and Physiology in Health and Illness. Ross and Wilson (2004)
3. Horn, P.: Autonomic Computing: IBM's perspective on the state of information technology. IBM Research Report (2001)
4. Melchior, N.A., Smart, W.D.: Autonomic systems for mobile robots. In: Proceedings of the 2004 International Conference on AC, New York, USA (2004)
5. Schmeck, H.: Organic computing – a new vision for distributed embedded systems. In: Proceedings of the 8th IEEE International Symposium on Object-Oriented Real-Time Distributed Computing. IEEE Computer Society (2005)
6. Kishi, T.: Model driven design and organic computing: from the viewpoint of application production. In: Proceedings of the IEEE International Symposium on ISORC 2009, pp. 97–98. IEEE Computer Society (2009)
7. Beer, S.: Brain of the Firm. 2nd ed. Wiley (1994)
8. Hilton, J., Wirght, C., Kiparoglou, V.: Building resilience into systems. In: Proceedings of the International Systems Conference, Vancouver, Canada (2012)
9. Ashby, W.R.: The William Ross Ashby Digital Archive (2014). http://www.rossashby.info/index.html
10. Cariani, P.A.: The Homeostat as Embodiment of Adaptive Control. International Journal of General Systems **38**(2) (2008)
11. Vassev, E.: ASSL: Autonomic System Specification Language - A Framework for Specification and Code Generation of Autonomic Systems. LAP Lambert Academic Publishing, Germany (2009)
12. Vassev, E.: Towards a Framework for Specification and Code Generation of Autonomic Systems. Ph.D. Thesis, Department of Computer Science and Software Engineering, Concordia University, Montreal, Canada (2008)
13. Insaurralde, C.C., Vassev, E.: Software specification and automatic code generation to realize homeostatic adaptation in unmanned spacecraft. In: Proceedings of the International C* Conference on Computer Science and Software Engineering (C3S2E 2014), pp. 35–44. ACM (2014)
14. Vassev, E., Hinchey, M., Montanari, U., Bicocchi, N., Zambonelli, F., Wirsing, M.: D3.2: Second Report on WP3: The KnowLang Framework for Knowledge Modeling for SCE Systems. ASCENS Project Deliverable (2012)

Logic-Based Modeling of Information Transfer in Cyber-Physical Multi-Agent Systems

Christian Kroiß[1]([⊠]) and Tomáš Bureš[2]

[1] Ludwig Maximilian University of Munich,
Institute for Informatics, Munich, Germany
kroiss@pst.ifi.lmu.de
[2] Charles University in Prague,
Faculty of Mathematics and Physics, Prague, Czech Republic
bures@d3s.mff.cuni.cz

Abstract. In modeling multi-agent systems, the structure of their communication is typically one of the most important aspects, especially for systems that strive toward self-organization or collaborative adaptation. Traditionally, such structures have often been described using logic-based approaches as they provide a formal foundation for many verification methods. However, these formalisms are typically not well suited to reflect the stochastic nature of communication in a cyber-physical setting. In particular, their level of abstraction is either too high to provide sufficient accuracy or too low to be practicable in more complex models. Therefore, we propose an extension of the logic-based modeling language SALMA, which we have introduced recently, that provides adequate high-level constructs for communication and data propagation, explicitly taking into account stochastic delays and errors. In combination with SALMA's tool support for simulation and statistical model checking, this creates a pragmatic approach for verification and validation of cyber-physical multi-agent systems.

Keywords: Statistical model checking · Cyber-physical systems · Situation calculus · Discrete event simulation

1 Introduction

With SALMA (Simulation and Analysis of Logic-Based Multi-Agent Systems) [2], we have recently introduced an approach for modeling and analysis of multi-agent systems that is aimed to provide a lightweight solution for approximated verification through *statistical model checking* [4] with the system model still being grounded on a rigorous formal foundation. SALMA's modeling language is based on the well-established *situation calculus* [7], a first-order logic language for describing dynamical systems.

In this paper, we provide an extension of SALMA (and the situation calculus in general) to explicitly address one aspect that is particularly important for *cyber-physical* multi-agent systems, namely the distributed gathering and

© Institute for Computer Sciences, Social Informatics and Telecommunications Engineering 2015
P.C. Vinh et al. (Eds.): ICTCC 2014, LNICST 144, pp. 42–52, 2015.
DOI: 10.1007/978-3-319-15392-6_5

transfer of information. Agents not only have to continuously sense their environment, but also share these readings with other agents, acquire information of others, and participate in coordination activities. In the cyber-physical context, these information transfer processes are subject to stochastic effects, e.g. due to sensor errors or unreliable communication channels. Furthermore, accuracy and timing of information transfer processes can strongly influence the behavior of the whole system. In particular, the efficacy of mechanisms for self-adaptation or optimization typically degrades when certain time-constraints are violated or the accuracy of sensors is insufficient.

Using pure logical formalisms like the basic situation calculus for describing such scenarios results in rather verbose and low-level representations that are not practicable in more complex cases. What is needed instead are high-level constructs that establish a bridge between the underlying logical semantics and the typical requirements for modeling information transfer in multi-agent CPS. Although higher-level extensions on top of the situation calculus have been designed for related aspects like sensing and knowledge (e.g. [9]), there has, to our knowledge, not been a detailed reflection of information propagation in CPS in the context of the situation calculus.

We have therefore developed a generic model of information transfer that is based on a stochastic timed version of the situation calculus and allows capturing a wide range of effects that may be imposed on information transfer processes. Additionally, we have defined a set of macro-like abstractions for common information transfer scenarios within CPS, such as message passing or sensor data propagation. This creates a concise interface for the modeler that hides the stochastic details of information propagation but makes them fully accessible in simulation and verification. The following sections introduce both the generic model and the high-level language and demonstrate their use by means of an example.

2 Example: Optimized Parking Lot Assignment

As a running example to illustrate our approach, we employ the e-mobility case-study of the ASCENS EU project[1] that has been described before, e.g., in [1]. The case study focuses on a scenario in which electric vehicles compete for parking lots with integrated charging stations (PLCS) in an urban area. The goal is to find an optimal assignment of PLCS to vehicles. Technically, the assignment is performed by an agent called super-autonomic manager (SAM) that coordinates a number of PLCS. The basic idea is that vehicles send *assignment requests* to the SAM, including a start time, a duration, and a list of preferred PLCS that is compiled by the vehicle's on-board computer. The SAM tries to find optimal suggestions for parking lot assignments, based on the knowledge about driver's intentions, and on occupancy information that is sent repeatedly by the PLCS.

---

[1] www.ascens-ist.eu

True to the distributed CPS principle, all the agents (vehicles, PLCS, SAM) are autonomous and communicate via some wireless data transmission infrastructure like a VANET or 3G/4G network. This implies that neither transmission delays nor the possibility of errors can be neglected. However, timing clearly plays an important role in the scenario described above. First of all, the reservation service would simply not be accepted if the delay between reservation requests and reservation responses was too high. Also, the communication timing affects the convergence of the optimization, thus directly it influences the functionality of the distributed CPS.

3   Background: Situation Calculus

The situation calculus [7] is a first-order logic language for modeling dynamic systems. Its foundation is based on the notion of *situations*, which can be seen as histories of the world resulting from performing *action sequences*. The state of the world in a given situation is defined by the set of all *fluents*, which are situation-dependent predicates or functions. Since the models discussed here are meant to be used in *discrete event simulation*, time itself is simply modeled as an integer fluent named *time* that is increased with each simulation step. How other fluents are affected by *actions* and *events* is defined by *successor state axioms (SSAs)*. Additionally, a situation calculus model also contains *precondition axioms* that define whether or not an action or event is possible in a given situation. Actions can either be deliberately executed by agents or *exogenous*, i.e. external events caused by the environment. In general, both the effects of actions and events, and also the occurrence of exogenous actions, are of stochastic nature. Consequently, simulation involves sampling from a set of probability distributions that the modeler can define as part of the simulation's configuration (cf. section 6).

One of the most prominent applications of the situation calculus is GOLOG [5], a language that combines elements from procedural with logic programming. It has been used for modeling and implementation in various domains, ranging from robotics to the semantic web. In particular, GOLOG's core principles have strongly inspired the SALMA approach, which is introduced in the next section.

4   The SALMA Approach

In [2], we introduced SALMA (Simulation and Analysis of Logic-Based Multi-Agent Systems), an approach that adapts the concepts of the situation calculus and GOLOG for discrete event simulation and *statistical model checking*. The approach is outlined in Figure 1. The *domain* model, i.e. the general mechanisms of the simulated world, is described by means of situation calculus axioms that are encoded in Prolog. Based on this axiomatization, the modeler defines the behavior of the agents in the system with a Python-based procedural language that provides access to the situation calculus model. Finally, a concrete simulation model instance is created by defining initial values and *probability distributions* for stochastic actions and events.

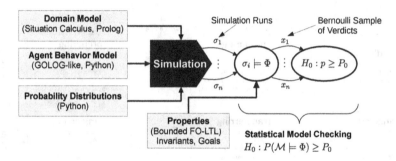

Fig. 1. Overview of the SALMA Approach

In addition to the system model, a set of invariants and goals can be specified with a language that is mainly a first-order version of linear temporal logics (LTL) with time-bounds for the temporal modalities. Since the simulated system model is also described by means of first-order logics, the property specification language is able to provide a very detailed and direct access to the system's state (i.e. fluents), actions, and events.

Given the system model together with invariants and goals, the SALMA interpreter performs *discrete event simulations*. For each simulation run, the engine eventually decides whether it satisfies the given properties or not. The set of resulting verdicts yields a *Bernoulli sample* that is used to test the statistical hypothesis $H_0 : p \geq P_0$ which asserts that the probability of a success (a run fulfills the property) is at least as high as a given lower bound. By using the sequential probability ratio test (SPRT) by A. Wald [10], the number of required simulation runs for given statistical error bounds can be determined dynamically. This way of approximative assertion of properties defined by temporal logics is generally called *statistical model checking* [4] and provides a pragmatic alternative to exact model checking techniques that does not suffer from the same scalability problems since only individual simulation runs are inspected instead of the complete state space.

5   A Generic Model for Information Transfer

In order to use SALMA for analyzing scenarios like the one described in Section 2, concepts like sensing and communication have to be mapped to SALMA's modeling language framework. As a first step, we propose a generic model for information transfer in the situation calculus. This model is able to describe both sensing and inter-agent communication in a unified way and allows capturing stochastic effects with a variable level of detail.

In general, our approach is based on the notion that information is transferred from a *source fluent* to a *destination fluent* that is directly accessible by the receiving agent. The source fluent can either represent a *feature of the physical world* or data created by some artificial process, e.g. a message queue. A *connector* defines modalities of an information transfer process, including the

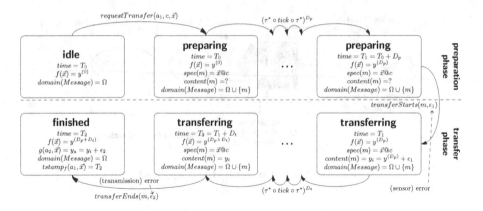

Fig. 2. General Information Transfer Model

fluent endpoints and the types and roles of participating agents. The *messages* that are transmitted over connectors are treated as first-level model citizens by representing them as entities of the dedicated sort *Message*. Both the content and the state of each message are stored separately by a set of fluents and evolve independently as result to several types of events. This representation provides great flexibility for the realization of arbitrary propagation structures. However, it requires that message entities can be created and removed dynamically as effect to actions and events. Unlike traditional realizations of the situation calculus, SALMA supports this by using a special (meta-)fluent *domain(sort)* to store the sets of entities that manifest the current *domains* of all sorts in the model. Creation and destruction of entities can therefore be controlled through regular successor state axioms.

Based on the foundational concepts described above, we distinguish two phases of information transfer that are sketched in Figure 2:

a) The **preparation phase** starts when an agent (a_1 in Figure 2) executes a *transfer request action*, specifying a *connector* (c) and a parameter vector ($\vec{x}$) that fully qualifies the information source and, in case of a point-to-point transmission, contains the identity of the receiving agent. In response to this action, a new message (m) is created and initialized with the transfer metadata but without content yet. Depending on the concrete scenario, there can be various reasons for the actual transfer being delayed, e.g. initialization of sensors or communication devices. This means that there may be an arbitrary sequence of time steps (*tick* events) interleaved with actions and events (denoted as τ in Figure 2) that may change the information source (f) but are not recognized by the agent. After that sequence, the actual value that is eventually used as message content can deviate from the information source value present at the time when the transfer was initiated.

b) The **transfer phase** follows the preparation phase and begins when a *transferStarts* event occurs. At that point, the current value of the source fluent f is fixated as the content of the message that is now actually transferred to its destination over the connector c whose stochastic characteristics are specified within the simulation model. Like above, this phase may take an arbitrary amount of time during which unrecognized or unrelated actions and events occur. Eventually, a *transferEnds* event finishes the transfer process. Thereupon, the destination fluent instance $g(a_2, \vec{x})$ is updated and the message entity is removed. This moment, as well as the starting points of both phases, are memorized in timestamp fluents that can, for instance, be used to reason about the age of a measurement.

The diagram in Figure 2 omits the fact that, due to malfunctions and disturbances in the environment, the transfer could *fail* at any time, which would be represented by an additional event *transferFails*. Additionally, the transfer process may be affected by stochastic errors that eventually cause the received value to deviate from the original input, which is reflected by the error terms ϵ_1 and ϵ_2 in the events *transferStarts* and *transferEnds*.

In general, both stochastic errors and delays are governed by a set of probability distributions that are used during simulation to decide when the events mentioned above occur and which errors they introduce. By adjusting these parameters, a wide variety of different scenarios can be modeled, ranging from nearly perfect local sensing to wireless low-energy communication with interferences. The simulation engine supports probabilistic sampling both in an *anticipatory* and in a *momentary* way. In the first case, a random value is sampled in advance to set the time for which the corresponding event will be scheduled. By contrast, in momentary sampling mode, the effective delay is generated by stochastically choosing in each time step, whether the event should occur or not. While the second approach obviously increases computational effort, it is typically better suited for capturing highly dynamic effects, e.g. when the position of a moving agent has significant impact on communication quality.

6   A High-Level Modeling Language for Information Transfer Processes

To turn the generic information transfer model to a practical solution for modeling real-size systems, we provide high-level constructs that reflect the way a modeler normally thinks about information transfer processes in a CPS. These constructs can be seen as macros that are internally mapped to situation calculus axioms, agent process fragments, and probability distributions. How the variation points of the generic model are resolved depends largely on the type of information transfer that is modeled. In particular, we distinguish the following two core concepts:

Channel-Based Communication: an agent actively sends data to one or several other agents. The well-known channel paradigm fits well to the asynchronous communication style predominant in CPS and to the relational way of identifying information in the situation calculus.

Gerneralized Sensing: an agent acquires information about a feature of the world that can be assessed through sensing. In the case of **direct (local)** sensing, the querying agent can produce the desired result on its own, although the sensing process may take a considerable amount of time and can be disturbed by internal or external factors. **Remote sensing**, on the other hand, makes it possible to observe features that are not directly reachable by local sensors but have to be gathered from one or several other agents. The remote sensing abstraction reflects the delays and disturbances of the involved communication processes but abstracts away their technical details.

6.1   Usage of High-Level Constructs

SALMA's high-level language support for communication and generalized sensing spans across several sections of the model. First, all *connector types* for sensors and channels are declared in the domain model. As an example, the parking lot assignment model contains the following lines:

```
channel(assignments, v:vehicle, sam:sam).
sensor(freeSlotsL, plcs, freeSlots).
remoteSensor(freeSlotsR, sam, freeSlotsL, plcs).
```

Here, `assignments` is defined to be a type of channel over which agents of the sort `vehicle` can communicate directly with agents of the sort `sam` in order to request and receive a PLCS assignment. Each channel declaration actually specifies two *roles*, whose names are given on the left of the colons, that agents can play within the communication. The sensors of type `freeSlotsL` allow PLCS agents to count the current number of free slots at their station, i.e. access the fluent `freeSlots`. This information is propagated to the SAM via *remote sensors* of type `freeSlotsR` that effectively install unidirectional channels and periodic background processes at each SAM and PLCS agent which transmit and receive the content of `freeSlotsL`, respectively.

With the necessary declarations in place, the communication and sensing infrastructure can be used in agent processes by means of several special statements of the SALMA process definition language. As an example, the following lines appear in the definition of the main SAM process that handles incoming requests from vehicles, calculates optimal assignments, and sends them back to the vehicles:

```
Receive("assignments", "sam", SELF, vehicle,
req), Assign(resp, optimizeAssignments, [req]),
Iterate(resp, (v, p), Send("assignments", "sam",
v, "v", ("aresp", p)))
```

First, all available assignment requests are retrieved from the agent's incoming message queue with a call to `Receive` which stores a message list in the variable `req`. The actual assignment optimization logic is integrated by means of an external Python function `optimizeAssignments` that is not shown here due to space limitations. Through the `Assign` statement, the function is called with the received request list as a parameter and the function's result is stored in the variable `resp`. One of the most important inputs for this optimization is certainly the number of free slots at each PLCS. This information is made available by the remote sensor `freeSlotsR` from above that transparently gathers occupancy information from all PLCS. The result of `optimizeAssignments`, stored in `resp`, is a list of tuples that assign each requesting vehicle to a PLCS. The agent process iterates over this list and sends the PLCS id to each corresponding vehicle.

6.2 Predicate-Based Addressing

An important concern that arises in modeling multi-agent information propagation is how the set of receiving agents is determined. In many cases, it is either impossible or impracticable to do this statically. A particularly elegant alternative, supported by SALMA, is *predicate-based addressing* [3]. In this approach, the set of recipients for each information transfer is determined by a *characteristic ensemble predicate* that is evaluated for each (properly typed) agent pair. An *ensemble predicate* may describe *intentional selection criteria* as well as *intrinsic constraints* imposed by agent attributes or the environment. For instance, the channel declaration from Section 6.1 could be accompanied by the following predicate that declares that assignment requests issued by vehicles are only received by SAM agents within a given maximal communication range:

ensemble(assignment, Vehicle, SAM, S) :-
  distance(Vehicle, SAM, D, S), D <max_comm_dist.

7 Statistical Model Checking for Information Transfer

Once a system model has been created and configured in the way described above, SALMA's statistical model checker can be used to approximately assert system properties based on simulation results (cf. Section 4). SALMA's property specification language provides deep access to all elements of the communication and sensing processes. This allows direct reasoning about various aspects that are particularly important in CPS. For instance, the following invariant requires that when any vehicle agent sends an assignment request to the SAM, it will not take longer than 55 time units until a target PLCS has been set:

forall(v:vehicle,
implies(**messageSent**(assignments, v, ?, ?, ?, ?),
  eventually(55, currentTargetPLCS(v) \= **none**)))

Here, `messageSent` is a predicate that is true when the message has been sent in the current time step and `eventually` is the time bounded version of the well-known temporal operator. The question marks serve as wildcard arguments for pattern matching, applied here to the recipient and arguments of the message.

As another example, the next invariants define for all entries of the remote sensor `freeSlotsR` a maximum value age of 10 time units and a maximum deviation of 1 from the original sensor `freeSlotsL`:

forall([s:sam, p:plcs], age(freeSlotsR, [s, p]) =<10)
forall([s:sam, p:plcs], abs(freeSlotsR(s, p) - freeSlotsL(p)) =<1)

8   Experiments and Preliminary Evaluation

In order to test the presented approach and its integration in the SALMA toolkit, we implemented a reduced version of the scenario introduced in Section 2. It contains only a simple mock-up version of the optimization mechanism but realizes the full communication structure according to the approach presented in this paper. Both the SALMA toolkit and the model are available at the SALMA website[2]. By varying parameters and replacing the Python optimization function, different optimization schemes can be tested and the impact of factors like delays or transmission errors can be analyzed. A detailed evaluation of the model is still ongoing and beyond the scope of this paper. However, first experiences show that our information transfer model is well applicable also for complex communication scenarios. In particular, our proposed declarative high-level language has proven to be able to significantly improve clarity and conciseness of the model. For instance, the declarative part related to communication and sensing in the model mentioned above requires only about 30 lines in the style of the examples in Section 6.1. In contrast, the corresponding part of a functionally equivalent model that employs a direct axiomatization instead of the high-level abstractions, contains 15 fluents and 21 actions and events together with their associated axioms, which requires more than 200 lines of Prolog code.

9   Related Work

Information in the situation calculus has traditionally been viewed from an epistemic perspective, i.e. as knowledge that agents gain through (communication) actions. In [6], the epistemic model has been extended to model inter-agent communication by means of channels in a similar way as in our model described above. However, neither time nor stochastic effects are covered. In contrast to that, the approach presented in [8] combines the epistemic model with time and concurrency and allows reasoning about time-related aspects like the age of measurements. Unlike the approaches mentioned above, our model does not consider knowledge in the epistemic sense but leaves the interpretation of transferred information to the agent processes. While we think that this perspective is better suited in the particular context of cyber-physical systems, it would be possible to combine both views in a straight-forward way.

In [3], the authors introduce a stochastically timed process calculus that is centered around predicate-based communication. Like our model, the most

---

[2] www.salmatoolkit.org

detailed semantical variant they describe distinguishes between a preparation and a transmission phase and allows assigning separate probability distributions for delays and errors to each of them. However, since the semantics is based on continuous time markov chains (CMTC), only exponential distributions can be used and delays or errors are effectively determined at the start of each phase. This can be too coarse-grained in very dynamic situations, e.g. when the movement of agents has significant effect.

10   Conclusion

We have presented a new logic-based approach for modeling channel-based communication, sensing, and other kinds of information transfer within cyber-physical multi-agent systems. The proposed high-level language provides means to embrace the stochastic nature of these systems, like transmission delays and errors. At the same time it has a precise formal semantics based on the first-order logic situation calculus. Therefore, it can be integrated in existing logic-based approaches for verification and validation, in particular SALMA, a framework for simulation and statistical model checking we have introduced earlier in [2]. A major advantage of this combination is that SALMA's property specification language, based on a first-order temporal logic, allows fine-grained reasoning about the inner details of information transfer processes.

First experiences show that our approach offers great flexibility with respect to the level of detail and accuracy with which both the system model and corresponding requirements are formulated. Altogether, we hope that, in the long run, SALMA will contribute to making verification and validation practicable for self-adaptive cyber-physical multi-agent systems.

Acknowledgments. This work has been partially sponsored by the EU project ASCENS, FP7 257414.

References

1. Bureš, T., et al.: A Life Cycle for the Development of Autonomic Systems: The e-Mobility Showcase. In: 3rd Workshop on Challenges for Achieving Self-Awareness in Automatic Systems, pp. 71–76. IEEE (2013)
2. Kroiß, C.: Simulation and Statistical Model Checking of Logic-Based Multi-Agent System Models. In: Jezic, G., Kusek, M., Lovrek, I., J. Howlett, R., C. Jain, L. (eds.) Agent and Multi-Agent Systems: Technologies and Applications. AISC, vol. 296, pp. 151–160. Springer, Heidelberg (2014)
3. Latella, D., et al.: Stochastically timed predicate-based communication primitives for autonomic computing. Technical report, QUANTICOL Project (2014)
4. Legay, A., Delahaye, B., Bensalem, S.: Statistical Model Checking: An Overview. In: Barringer, H., Falcone, Y., Finkbeiner, B., Havelund, K., Lee, I., Pace, G., Roşu, G., Sokolsky, O., Tillmann, N. (eds.) RV 2010. LNCS, vol. 6418, pp. 122–135. Springer, Heidelberg (2010)

5. Levesque, H.J., et al.: Golog: A logic programming language for dynamic domains. The Journal of Logic Programming **31**(1), 59–83 (1997)
6. Marcu, D., et al.: Distributed software agents and communication in the situation calculus. In: International Workshop on Intelligent Computer, Communication, pp. 69–78 (1995)
7. Reiter, R.: Knowledge in action: logical foundations for specifying and implementing dynamical systems. MIT Press (2001)
8. Scherl, R.B.: Reasoning about the interaction of knowledge, time and concurrent actions in the situation calculus. In: 18th International Joint Conference on Artificial Intelligence (IJCAI 2003), pp. 1091–1098 (2003)
9. Scherl, R.B., Levesque, H.J.: Knowledge, action, and the frame problem. Artificial Intelligence **144**(1), 1–39 (2003)
10. Wald, A., et al.: Sequential tests of statistical hypotheses. Annals of Mathematical Statistics **16**(2), 117–186 (1945)

Nature of Computation
and Communication

Categorical Structures of Self-adaptation in Collective Adaptive Systems

Phan Cong Vinh[✉]

Faculty of Information Technology, Nguyen Tat Thanh University (NTTU),
300A Nguyen Tat Thanh Street, Ward 13, District 4, HCM City, Vietnam
pcvinh@ntt.edu.vn

Abstract. An adaptive system is currently on spot: collective adaptive system (CAS), which is inspired by the socio-technical systems. CASs are characterized by a high degree of adaptation, giving them resilience in the face of perturbations. In CASs, highest degree of adaptation is *self-adaptation*. The overarching goal of CAS is to realize systems that are tightly entangled with humans and social structures. Meeting this grand challenge of CASs requires a fundamental approach to the notion of self-adaptation. To this end, taking advantage of the categorical approach we construct, in this paper, algebraic structures of self-adaptation in CASs.

Keywords: Adaptedness · Categorical approach · Collective adaptive system · Self-adaptation · Self-adaptive trait

1 Introduction

The socio-technical structure of our community increasingly depends on systems, which are built as a collection of varied agents and are tightly coupled with humans and social interrelations. Their agents more and more need to be able to develop, cooperate and work all by themselves as a part of an artificial community. Hence, for such collective adaptive systems (CASs), one of major challenges is how to support self-adaptation in the face of changing interactions [8,9]. In other words, how does a CAS understand relevant interrelations and then self-adapt to become better able to live in its interactions?

Dealing with this grand challenge of CASs requires a well-founded modeling and in-depth analysis on the notion of self-adaptation. With this aim, we construct, in this paper, categorical structures of self-adaptation in CASs where a collective of entities is able to self-adapt its configuration and self-optimize its performance in the face of changing interactions [10].

2 Outline

The paper is a reference material for readers who already have a basic understanding of CAS and are now ready to know the novel approach for formalizing self-adaptation in CAS using categorical language [1–5].

© Institute for Computer Sciences, Social Informatics and Telecommunications Engineering 2015
P.C. Vinh et al. (Eds.): ICTCC 2014, LNICST 144, pp. 55–62, 2015.
DOI: 10.1007/978-3-319-15392-6_6

Formalization is presented in a straightforward fashion by discussing in detail the necessary components and briefly touching on the more advanced components. Several notes explaining how to use the formal aspects, including justifications needed in order to achieve the particular results, are presented.

We attempt to make the presentation as self-contained as possible, although familiarity with the notion of self-adaptation in CAS is assumed. Acquaintance with the algebra and the associated notion of categorical language is useful for recognizing the results, but is almost everywhere not strictly necessary.

The rest of this paper is organized as follows: Sections 3 and 4 present the notions of collective adaptive systems (CASs) and self-adaptation, respectively. In section 5, categorical structures of self-adaptation in CASs are developed in detail. Finally, a short summary is given in section 6.

3   Collective Adaptive Systems (CASs)

We define collective adaptive systems (CASs) as the following among various definitions that have been offered by different researchers:

Definition 1. CASs *are systems that consist of a collective of heterogeneous components, often called agents, that interact and adapt or learn.*

Hence, CASs are characterized by a high degree of adaptation, giving them resilience in the face of perturbations. We see that, in CASs, highest degree of adaptation is *self-adaptation* and we are interested in approaches to this characteristic of CASs.

This definition is concerned with three major factors of CAS:

- *A collective of heterogeneous agents* is large enough to build up systems that are tightly entangled with humans and social structures. Their agents increasingly need to be able to evolve, collaborate and function as a part of an artificial society. More importantly, the agents interact dynamically, and their interactions are either physical or involving the exchange of information.
- *Interactions* are rich, non-linear and primarily, but not exclusively, with immediate neighbors. They can be recurrent, i.e. any interaction can feed back onto itself directly or after a number of intervening stages. CASs are dynamic networks of interactions
- *Self-adaptation* is the self-evolutionary process whereby a CAS becomes better able to live in its interactions.

4   Self-adaptation

An interesting aspect of CASs is that it makes distinction between self-adaptation (i.e. system-driven personalization and modifications) and self-adaptability (i.e. user-driven personalization and modifications). *Self-adaptedness* is the state of being self-adapted, i.e. the degree to which a CAS is able to live and reproduce in a given set of interactions. *Self-adaptive trait* is an aspect of the developmental pattern of the CAS which enables or enhances the probability of that CAS surviving and reproducing.

Formally, let self-* be the set of self-_'s. Each self-_ to be an element in self-* is called a *self-* facet* [6]. That is,

$$\text{self-*} = \{\text{self-}\_ \mid \text{self-}\_ \text{ is a self-* facet}\} \tag{1}$$

Thus, self-adaptation is a facet of self-*, that is, self-adaptation is a member of self-*. In other words, using categorical language, this is written as $1 \xrightarrow{\text{self-adaptation}} \text{self-*}$. CASs are self-adaptive in that the individual and collective behavior mutate and self-organize corresponding to interactions. Self-adaptation indicates that CAS is a mimicry of socio-technical systems.

5   Categorical Structures of Self-adaptation

In this section, we construct self-adaptation monoid and then a category of self-adaptation monoids in order to consider the significant properties of the self-adaptation.

5.1   Self-adaptation Monoid

In [7], self-adaptation is specified by the morphism $Self\text{-}A : (CAS \times Inter^{n \in T}) \longrightarrow (CAS \times Inter^{n \in T})$, which defines the set $\{Self\text{-}A_{i \in \mathbb{N}}(CAS \times Inter^{n \in T}, CAS \times Inter^{n \in T})\}$ of self-adaptive traits. Let $\textbf{Self-A}^{n \in T}$ be the set of such self-adaptive traits, then

$$\textbf{Self-A}^{n \in T} = \{Self\text{-}A_{i \in \mathbb{N}}(CAS \times Inter^{n \in T}, CAS \times Inter^{n \in T})\} \tag{2}$$

Note that, in the case, we write $Self\text{-}A_{i \in \mathbb{N}}^{n \in T}$ to stand for $Self\text{-}A_{i \in \mathbb{N}}(CAS \times Inter^{n \in T}, CAS \times Inter^{n \in T})$. Thus, we have

$$\textbf{Self-A}^{n \in T} = \{Self\text{-}A_{i \in \mathbb{N}}^{n \in T}\} \tag{3}$$

This set with the composition operation ";" satisfies two following properties:

Composition of self-adaptive traits. Let f and g be members of $\textbf{Self-A}^{n \in T}$, then the composition of self-adaptive traits $f; g : (CAS \times Inter^{n \in T}) \longrightarrow (CAS \times Inter^{n \in T})$ is as $g : (f : (CAS \times Inter^{n \in T}) \longrightarrow (CAS \times Inter^{n \in T})) \longrightarrow (CAS \times Inter^{n \in T})$. In other words, let $f = Self\text{-}A_{i \in \mathbb{N}}^{n \in T}$ and $g = Self\text{-}A_{j \in \mathbb{N}}^{n \in T}$ then

$$(Self\text{-}A_{i \in \mathbb{N}}^{n \in T} \ ; \ Self\text{-}A_{j \in \mathbb{N}}^{n \in T}) = Self\text{-}A_{j \in \mathbb{N}}(Self\text{-}A_{i \in \mathbb{N}}^{n \in T}, CAS \times Inter^{n \in T}) \tag{4}$$

Identity of self-adaptive traits. There exist identities $1_{n \in T} : (CAS \times Inter^{n \in T}) \longrightarrow (CAS \times Inter^{n \in T})$ of self-adaptive traits in **Self-A**$^{n \in T}$ such that, for every f in **Self-A**$^{n \in T}$, $1_{n \in T}; f = f; 1_{n \in T} = f$ to be held. In other words, this can be specified by

$$Self\text{-}A_{i \in \mathbb{N}}^{n \in T} = Self\text{-}A_{i \in \mathbb{N}}(1_{n \in T}, CAS \times Inter^{n \in T}) \tag{5}$$
$$= Self\text{-}A_{i \in \mathbb{N}}(CAS \times Inter^{n \in T}, 1_{n \in T})$$
$$= Self\text{-}A_{i \in \mathbb{N}}(CAS \times Inter^{n \in T}, CAS \times Inter^{n \in T})$$

Thus, **Self-A**$^{n \in T}$ with the composition operation "$;$" is called *self-adaptation monoid*. Moreover, the monoid **Self-A**$^{n \in T}$ is also a monoid category including only one object to be the set $\{Self\text{-}A_{i \in \mathbb{N}}^{n \in T}\}$, each of whose members is a self-adaptive trait, and by the composition operation as a morphism, then the associativity and identity on the morphisms are completely satisfied.

5.2 A Category of Self-adaptation Monoids

By the self-adaptation monoids **Self-A**$^{i \in T}$, we can construct **Cat(Self-A)** to be a category of self-adaptation monoids. In fact, **Cat(Self-A)** is constructed as follows:

• *Objects*: $Obj(\textbf{Cat(Self-A)})$ is the set of self-adaptation monoids **Self-A**$^{i \in T}$. That is,

$$Obj(\textbf{Cat(Self-A)}) = \{\textbf{Self-A}^{i \in T}\} \tag{6}$$

• *Morphisms*: Associated with each object **Self-A**$^{i \in T}$ in $Obj(\textbf{Cat(Self-A)})$, we define a morphism **Self-A**$^{i \in T} \xrightarrow{\;1_{\textbf{Self-A}^{i \in T}}\;}$ **Self-A**$^{i \in T}$, the identity morphism on **Self-A**$^{i \in T}$ such that

$$\textbf{Self-A}^{i \in T} \xrightarrow{\;1_{\textbf{Self-A}^{i \in T}} \overset{def}{=} 1_{i \in T}\;} \textbf{Self-A}^{i \in T} \tag{7}$$

or

$$\{Self\text{-}A_{k \in \mathbb{N}}^{i \in T}\} \xrightarrow{\;1_{\textbf{Self-A}^{i \in T}} \overset{def}{=} 1_{i \in T}\;} \{Self\text{-}A_{k \in \mathbb{N}}^{i \in T}\} \tag{8}$$

and to each pair of morphisms **Self-A**$^{i \in T} \xrightarrow{\;f\;}$ **Self-A**$^{j \in T}$ and **Self-A**$^{j \in T} \xrightarrow{\;g\;}$ **Self-A**$^{j \in T}$ such that

$$\textbf{Self-A}^{i \in T} \xrightarrow{\;f \overset{def}{=} 1_{i \in T} \times Inter^{j-i}\;} \textbf{Self-A}^{j \in T} \tag{9}$$

and

$$\textbf{Self-A}^{j \in T} \xrightarrow{\;g \overset{def}{=} 1_{j \in T} \times Inter^{k-j}\;} \textbf{Self-A}^{k \in T} \tag{10}$$

there is an associated morphism **Self-A**$^{i \in T} \xrightarrow{\;f;g\;}$ **Self-A**$^{k \in T}$, the composition of f with g, such that

$$\textbf{Self-A}^{i \in T} \xrightarrow{\;f;g = 1_{i \in T} \times Inter^{k-i}\;} \textbf{Self-A}^{k \in T} \tag{11}$$

For every object in $Obj(\mathbf{Cat}(\mathbf{Self\text{-}A}))$ and the morphisms

$$\mathbf{Self\text{-}A}^{i\in T} \xrightarrow{\;f \overset{def}{=} 1_{i\in T} \times Inter^{j-i}\;} \mathbf{Self\text{-}A}^{j\in T} \tag{12}$$

$$\mathbf{Self\text{-}A}^{j\in T} \xrightarrow{\;g \overset{def}{=} 1_{j\in T} \times Inter^{k-j}\;} \mathbf{Self\text{-}A}^{k\in T} \tag{13}$$

and

$$\mathbf{Self\text{-}A}^{k\in T} \xrightarrow{\;h \overset{def}{=} 1_{k\in T} \times Inter^{m-k}\;} \mathbf{Self\text{-}A}^{m\in T} \tag{14}$$

in $Arc(\mathbf{Cat}(\mathbf{Self\text{-}A}))$, the following equations hold:

Associativity: $(f; g); h = f; (g; h) = 1_{i\in T} \times Inter^{m-i}$
Identity: $1_{\mathbf{Self\text{-}A}^{i\in T}}; f = f = f; 1_{\mathbf{Self\text{-}A}^{j\in T}}$

(i.e., $1_{i\in T}; 1_{i\in T} \times Inter^{j-i} = 1_{i\in T} \times Inter^{j-i} = 1_{i\in T} \times Inter^{j-i}; 1_{j\in T}$)

As a result, the above-mentioned monoid morphisms can be diagrammatically drawn such as

$$\mathbf{Self\text{-}A}^{i\in T} \xrightarrow{\;1_{i\in T} \times Inter^{\pm k}\;} \mathbf{Self\text{-}A}_{i \pm k \in T} \tag{15}$$

or

$$\{Self\text{-}A^{i\in T}_{l\in\mathbb{N}}\} \xrightarrow{\;1_{i\in T} \times Inter^{\pm k}\;} \{Self\text{-}A^{i\pm k\in T}_{l\in\mathbb{N}}\} \tag{16}$$

These are all the basic ingredients we need to have the category $\mathbf{Cat}(\mathbf{Self\text{-}A})$. Let us see a general definition of category in [7] for reference.

5.3 Some Properties of Category *Cat(Self-A)*

By the construction of category $\mathbf{Cat}(\mathbf{Self\text{-}A}))$, some emerging significant properties are presented in this subsection.

Property 1.   *All monoid morphisms of* $\mathbf{Cat}(\mathbf{Self\text{-}A})$ *is monoid isomorphisms*

Proof: This result immediately stems from diagram (15). In fact, for every pair of monoid morphisms in $Arc(\mathbf{Cat}(\mathbf{Self\text{-}A}))$ between $\mathbf{Self\text{-}A}^{i\in T}$ and $\mathbf{Self\text{-}A}^{j\in T}$, we always have the following diagram:

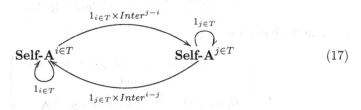

$$\tag{17}$$

These monoid morphisms satisfy an isomorphic relationship.   Q.E.D.

Property 2.   *Isomorphisms between any pair of monoids in* **Cat(Self-A)** *are ever isomorphisms between the pair of* CASs.

Proof: This comes from the fact that each object of category **Cat(Self-A)** is just a CAS.   Q.E.D.

From the above-mentioned justification of **Cat(Self-A)**, we are able to derive **Self-A**$^{i \in T}$. Derivation of every **Self-A**$^{i \in T}$ is simplified by the following facts:

Property 3.   *There exists always a self-adaptation monoid* **Self-A**, *as simply as it can, in* **Cat(Self-A)** *constructed. Hence, it is available to start with.*

Proof: It emerges that

$$\textbf{Self-A} = \{Self\text{-}A_{i \in \mathbb{N}}(CAS \times Inter^0, CAS \times Inter^0)\} \tag{18}$$
$$= \{Self\text{-}A_{i \in \mathbb{N}}(CAS, CAS)\}$$

thus

$$1 \xrightarrow{\quad \textbf{Self-A} \quad} Obj(\textbf{Cat}(\textbf{Self-A})) \tag{19}$$

Q.E.D.

Property 4.   *Given* **Self-A**, *we can compute* **Self-A**$^{i \in T}$.

Proof: We evaluate self-adaptation monoid **Self-A**$^{i \in T}$ such that

$$1 \xrightarrow{\quad \textbf{Self-A}^{i \in T} \quad} Obj(\textbf{Cat}(\textbf{Self-A})) \tag{20}$$

based on the facts that

$$\left(\begin{array}{c} 1 \xrightarrow{\quad \textbf{Self-A} \quad} Obj(\textbf{Cat}(\textbf{Self-A})) \\ \text{and} \\ \textbf{Self-A} \xrightarrow{\quad 1_0 \times Inter^i \quad} \textbf{Self-A}^{i \in T} \end{array} \right) \tag{21}$$

Note that $\textbf{Self-A} \xrightarrow{\quad 1_0 \quad} \textbf{Self-A}$ Q.E.D.

Property 5.   *Given* **Self-A**$^{i \in T}$, *we can compute* **Self-A**$^{j \in T}$ *for every* $j \neq i$.

Proof: Self-adaptation monoid **Self-A**$^{j \in T}$ is evaluated such that

$$1 \xrightarrow{\quad \textbf{Self-A}^{j \in T} \quad} Obj(\textbf{Cat}(\textbf{Self-A})) \tag{22}$$

based on the facts that

$$\left(\begin{array}{c} 1 \xrightarrow{\quad \textbf{Self-A}^{i \in T} \quad} Obj(\textbf{Cat}(\textbf{Self-A})) \\ \text{and} \\ \textbf{Self-A}^{i \in T} \xrightarrow{\quad 1_{i \in T} \times Inter^{j-i} \quad} \textbf{Self-A}^{j \in T} \end{array} \right) \tag{23}$$

Q.E.D.

From the construction of $\mathbf{Cat(Self\text{-}A)}$, we see that every $\mathbf{Self\text{-}A}^{i \in T}$ can be formed in the unifying way based on properties 3, 4 and 5. As a result, we gain a substantial procedure of construction at a high abstract level without any excessive inclination towards a specific implementation detail. This is quite helpful when we want to justify whether or not some certain properties of the construction are true. In fact, we can prove

Property 6. *Every monoid* $\mathbf{Self\text{-}A}^{i \in T}$ *can be constructed by any other monoid in* $\mathbf{Cat(Self\text{-}A)}$

Proof: Applying properties 3, 4 and 5 to construct every monoid $\mathbf{Self\text{-}A}^{i \in T}$ from another monoid in $\mathbf{Cat(Self\text{-}A)}$ Q.E.D.
This is certainly a property we expect of any construction procedure.

Property 7. $\mathbf{Cat(Self\text{-}A)}$ *is a complete graph*

Proof: In fact, this is a consequence stemming from property 6   Q.E.D.
This is indeed a property of our abstract construction mechanism.

6   Conclusions

In this paper, we have investigated algebraic structures of self-adaptation in CASs based on categorical approach.

We have started with investigating self-adaptation in CASs. Then, $\mathbf{Self\text{-}A}^{i \in T}$ has been constructed as a self-adaptation monoid. By the self-adaptation monoids, we have formed $\mathbf{Cat(Self\text{-}A)}$ as a category of the self-adaptation monoids for discovering the significant properties of the self-adaptation.

Acknowledgments. Thank you to NTTU[1] for the constant support of our work which culminated in the publication of this paper. As always, we are deeply indebted to the anonymous reviewers for their helpful comments and valuable suggestions which have contributed to the final preparation of the paper.

References

1. Adamek, J., Herrlich, H., Strecker, G.: Abstract and Concrete Categories. John Wiley and Sons (1990)
2. Asperti, A., Longo, G.: Categories, Types and Structures. M.I.T Press (1991)
3. Bergman, G.M.: An Invitation to General Algebra and Universal Constructions. Henry Helson, 15 the Crescent, Berkeley CA 94708, US (1998)
4. Lawvere, F.W., Schanuel, S.H.: Conceptual Mathematics: A First Introduction to Categories, 1st edn. Cambridge University Press (1997)
5. Levine, M.: Categorical algebra. In: Benkart, G., Ratiu, T.S., Masur, H.A., Renardy, M. (eds.) Mixed Motives. Mathematical Surveys and Monographs, chapter I, II, II of Part II, vol. 57, pp. 373–499. American Mathematical Society, USA (1998)

---

[1] Nguyen Tat Thanh University, Vietnam

6. Vinh, P.C.: Autonomic computing and networking. In: Chapter Formal Aspects of Self-* in Autonomic Networked Computing Systems, pp. 381–410. Springer (2009)
7. Vinh, P.C.: Self-Adaptation in Collective Adaptive Systems. Mobile Networks and Applications (2014, to appear)
8. Vinh, P.C., Alagar, V., Vassev, E., Khare, A. (eds.): ICCASA 2013. LNICST, vol. 128. Springer, Heidelberg (2014)
9. Vinh, P.C., Hung, N.M., Tung, N.T., Suzuki, J. (eds.): ICCASA 2012. LNICST, vol. 109. Springer, Heidelberg (2013)
10. Vinh, P.C., Tung, N.T.: Coalgebraic Aspects of Context-Awareness. Mobile Networks and Applications, August 2012. doi:10.1007/s11036-012-0404-0

Self-adaptive Traits in Collective Adaptive Systems

Phan Cong Vinh[1]([⊠]) and Nguyen Thanh Tung [2]

[1] Faculty of Information Technology, Nguyen Tat Thanh University (NTTU),
300A Nguyen Tat Thanh Street, Ward 13, District 4, HCM City, Vietnam
pcvinh@ntt.edu.vn
[2] International School, Vietnam National University (VNU), 144 xuan Thuy Street,
Cau Giay District, Ha Noi, Vietnam
tungnt@isvnu.vn

Abstract. An adaptive system is currently on spot: collective adaptive system (CAS), which is inspired by the socio-technical systems. In CASs, highest degree of adaptation is self-adaptation consisting of *self-adaptive traits*. The overarching goal of CAS is to realize systems that are tightly entangled with humans and social structures. Meeting this grand challenge of CASs requires a fundamental approach to the notion of self-adaptive trait. To this end, taking advantage of the coinductive approach we construct self-adaptation monoid to shape series of self-adaptive traits in CASs and some significant relations.

Keywords: Adaptedness · Bisimulation · Coinduction · Collective adaptive system · Equivalence · Self-adaptation · Self-adaptive trait · Series

1 Introduction

The socio-technical structure of our community increasingly depends on systems, which are built as a collection of varied agents and are tightly coupled with humans and social interrelations. Their agents more and more need to be able to develop, cooperate and work all by themselves as a part of an artificial community. Hence, for such collective adaptive systems (CASs), one of major challenges is how to support self-adaptation in the face of changing interactions [5,6]. In other words, how does a CAS understand relevant interrelations and then self-adapt to become better able to live in its interactions?

Dealing with this grand challenge of CASs requires a well-founded modeling and in-depth analysis on the notion of *self-adaptive trait*. With this aim, we construct self-adaptation monoid to shape series of self-adaptive traits in CASs, then we justify the equivalence between two series of self-adaptive traits based on a powerful method so-called *proof principle of coinduction*.

© Institute for Computer Sciences, Social Informatics and Telecommunications Engineering 2015
P.C. Vinh et al. (Eds.): ICTCC 2014, LNICST 144, pp. 63–72, 2015.
DOI: 10.1007/978-3-319-15392-6_7

2   Outline

The paper is a reference material for readers who already have a basic under-standing of CAS and are now ready to know the novel approach for constructing self-adaptive traits in CAS using coinduction [3].

Construction is presented in a straightforward fashion by discussing in detail the necessary components and briefly touching on the more advanced compo-nents. Several notes explaining how to use the notions, including justifications needed in order to achieve the particular results, are presented.

We attempt to make the presentation as self-contained as possible, although familiarity with the notion of self-adaptive trait in CAS is assumed. Acquain-tance with the algebra and the associated notion of coinduction is useful for recognizing the results, but is almost everywhere not strictly necessary.

The rest of this paper is organized as follows: Sections 3 and 4 present the notions of collective adaptive systems (CASs) and self-adaptive trait, respec-tively. In section 5, self-adaptation monoid is constructed. In section 6, series of self-adaptive traits in CASs is developed in detail. Finally, a short summary is given in section 7.

3   Collective Adaptive Systems (CASs)

We define collective adaptive systems (CASs) as the following among various definitions that have been offered by different researchers:

Definition 1. CASs *are systems that consist of a collective of heterogeneous components, often called agents, that interact and adapt or learn.*

Hence, CASs are characterized by a high degree of adaptation, giving them resilience in the face of perturbations. We see that, in CASs, highest degree of adaptation is *self-adaptation* and we are interested in approaches to this char-acteristic of CASs.

This definition is concerned with three major factors of CAS:

- *A collective of heterogeneous agents* is large enough to build up systems that are tightly entangled with humans and social structures. Their agents increasingly need to be able to evolve, collaborate and function as a part of an artificial society. More importantly, the agents interact dynamically, and their interactions are either physical or involving the exchange of informa-tion.
- *Interactions* are rich, non-linear and primarily, but not exclusively, with immediate neighbors. They can be recurrent, i.e. any interaction can feed back onto itself directly or after a number of intervening stages. CASs are dynamic networks of interactions
- *Self-adaptation* is the self-evolutionary process whereby a CAS becomes bet-ter able to live in its interactions.

4 Self-adaptive Trait

An interesting aspect of CASs is that it makes distinction between self-adaptation (i.e. system-driven personalization and modifications) and self-adaptability (i.e. user-driven personalization and modifications). *Self-adaptedness* is the state of being self-adapted, i.e. the degree to which a CAS is able to live and reproduce in a given set of interactions. *Self-adaptive trait* is an aspect of the developmental pattern of the CAS which enables or enhances the probability of that CAS surviving and reproducing.

Hence, self-adaptation is a set of self-adaptive traits [4]. That is,

$$\text{self-adaptation} = \{y \mid y \text{ is a self-adaptive trait}\} \tag{1}$$

Thus, each self-adaptive trait is an element in self-adaptation. In other words, using categorical language, this is written as $1 \xrightarrow{\text{self-adaptive trait}} \text{self-adaptation}$. CASs are self-adaptive in that the individual and collective behavior mutate and self-organize corresponding to interactions. Self-adaptation indicates that CAS is a mimicry of socio-technical systems.

5 Self-adaptation Monoid

In [4], self-adaptation is specified by the morphism $Self\text{-}A : (CAS \times Inter^{n \in T}) \longrightarrow (CAS \times Inter^{n \in T})$, which defines the set $\{Self\text{-}A_{i \in \mathbb{N}}(CAS \times Inter^{n \in T}, CAS \times Inter^{n \in T})\}$ of self-adaptive traits. Let $\textbf{Self-A}^{n \in T}$ be the set of such self-adaptive traits, then

$$\textbf{Self-A}^{n \in T} = \{Self\text{-}A_{i \in \mathbb{N}}(CAS \times Inter^{n \in T}, CAS \times Inter^{n \in T})\} \tag{2}$$

Note that, in the case, we write $Self\text{-}A_{i \in \mathbb{N}}^{n \in T}$ to stand for $Self\text{-}A_{i \in \mathbb{N}}(CAS \times Inter^{n \in T}, CAS \times Inter^{n \in T})$. Thus, we have

$$\textbf{Self-A}^{n \in T} = \{Self\text{-}A_{i \in \mathbb{N}}^{n \in T}\} \tag{3}$$

This set with the composition operation ";" satisfies two following properties:

Composition of Self-adaptive Traits

Let f and g be members of $\textbf{Self-A}^{n \in T}$, then the composition of self-adaptive traits $f ; g : (CAS \times Inter^{n \in T}) \longrightarrow (CAS \times Inter^{n \in T})$ is as $g : (f : (CAS \times Inter^{n \in T}) \longrightarrow (CAS \times Inter^{n \in T})) \longrightarrow (CAS \times Inter^{n \in T})$. In other words, let $f = Self\text{-}A_{i \in \mathbb{N}}^{n \in T}$ and $g = Self\text{-}A_{j \in \mathbb{N}}^{n \in T}$ then

$$(Self\text{-}A_{i \in \mathbb{N}}^{n \in T} \; ; \; Self\text{-}A_{j \in \mathbb{N}}^{n \in T}) = Self\text{-}A_{j \in \mathbb{N}}(Self\text{-}A_{i \in \mathbb{N}}^{n \in T}, CAS \times Inter^{n \in T}) \tag{4}$$

Identity of Self-adaptive Traits

There exist identities $1_{n \in T} : (CAS \times Inter^{n \in T}) \longrightarrow (CAS \times Inter^{n \in T})$ of self-adaptive traits in **Self-A**$^{n \in T}$ such that, for every f in **Self-A**$^{n \in T}$, $1_{n \in T}; f = f; 1_{n \in T} = f$ to be held. In other words, this can be specified by

$$Self\text{-}A_{i \in \mathbb{N}}^{n \in T} = Self\text{-}A_{i \in \mathbb{N}}(1_{n \in T}, CAS \times Inter^{n \in T}) \tag{5}$$
$$= Self\text{-}A_{i \in \mathbb{N}}(CAS \times Inter^{n \in T}, 1_{n \in T})$$
$$= Self\text{-}A_{i \in \mathbb{N}}(CAS \times Inter^{n \in T}, CAS \times Inter^{n \in T})$$

Thus, **Self-A**$^{n \in T}$ with the composition operation ";" is called *self-adaptation monoid*. Moreover, the monoid **Self-A**$^{n \in T}$ is also a monoid category including only one object to be the set $\{Self\text{-}A_{i \in \mathbb{N}}^{n \in T}\}$, each of whose members is a self-adaptive trait, and by the composition operation as a morphism, then the associativity and identity on the morphisms are completely satisfied.

6 Series of Self-adaptive Traits

A number of different notations are in use for denoting series of self-adaptive traits.

$$sf = (f_0, f_1, f_2, \ldots) \tag{6}$$

is a common notation which specifies a series of self-adaptive traits sf which is indexed by the natural numbers in $T (= \mathbb{N} \cup \{0\})$. We are also accustomed to

$$sf = (f_{t \in T}) \tag{7}$$

Informally, series of self-adaptive traits can be understood as a rope on which we hang up a sequence of self-adaptive traits for display. Hence it follows that

Definition 2 (Series of self-adaptive traits). *For morphisms* $1 \overset{t}{\longrightarrow} T$ *and* $1 \overset{f_t}{\longrightarrow}$ **Self-A**$^{n \in T}$*, there exists a unique morphism* $T \overset{sf}{\longrightarrow}$ **Self-A**$^{n \in T}$ *such that the equation* $t; sf = f_t$ *holds. This is described by the following commutative diagram*

$$\tag{8}$$

Morphism $T \overset{sf}{\longrightarrow}$ **Self-A**$^{n \in T}$ *defines a series of self-adaptive traits.*

Note that morphism $T \overset{sf}{\longrightarrow}$ **Self-A**$^{n \in T}$ is read as

$$\forall t[t \in T \implies \exists! \, f_t[f_t \in \textbf{Self-A}^{n \in T} \, \& \, sf(t) = f_t]]$$

In other words, $T \xrightarrow{sf} \textbf{Self-A}^{n \in T}$ generates series of self-adaptive traits as an infinite sequence of $sf(0) = f_0$, $sf(1) = f_1$, ..., $sf(t) = f_t$, ... which is written as $(sf(0), sf(1), \ldots, sf(t), \ldots)$ or $(f_0, f_1, \ldots, f_t, \ldots)$

Definition 3 (Set of series of self-adaptive traits). *Given* $T \xrightarrow{sf} \textbf{Self-A}^{n \in T}$ *then the set of series of self-adaptive traits, denoted by* $\textbf{Self-A}_{\omega}^{n \in T}$, *is defined by*

$$\textbf{Self-A}_{\omega}^{n \in T} = \{ sf \mid T \xrightarrow{sf} \textbf{Self-A}^{n \in T} \} \tag{9}$$

We obtain

Corollary 1. *If* $T \xrightarrow{sf} \textbf{Self-A}^{n \in T}$ *then* $1 \xrightarrow{sf} \textbf{Self-A}_{\omega}^{n \in T}$

Proof: This result stems immediately from definitions 2 and 3   Q.E.D.

This corollary means that for each morphism $T \xrightarrow{sf} \textbf{Self-A}^{n \in T}$, there is a morphism $1 \xrightarrow{sf} \textbf{Self-A}_{\omega}^{n \in T}$ generating member in $\textbf{Self-A}_{\omega}^{n \in T}$. That is, morphism $T \xrightarrow{sf} \textbf{Self-A}^{n \in T}$ generates series of self-adaptive traits and $1 \xrightarrow{sf} \textbf{Self-A}_{\omega}^{n \in T}$ constructs the set of series of self-adaptive traits.

For series of self-adaptive traits, we can define a mechanism to generate them. This mechanism consists of an object T equipping with structural morphisms $1 \xrightarrow{0} T \xrightarrow{succ} T$ with the property that for $\textbf{Self-A}^{n \in T}$, any $1 \xrightarrow{f_0} \textbf{Self-A}^{n \in T}$ and $\textbf{Self-A}^{n \in T} \xrightarrow{next} \textbf{Self-A}^{n \in T}$ then there exists a unique morphism $T \xrightarrow{sf} \textbf{Self-A}^{n \in T}$ such that the following diagram commutes

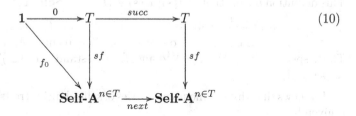

$$\tag{10}$$

Definition 4 (Construction of series of self-adaptive traits). *We define a construction morphism of series of self-adaptive traits, denoted by* $\ddagger$, *such that*

$$\textbf{Self-A}^{n \in T} \times [T \xrightarrow{sf} \textbf{Self-A}^{n \in T}] \xrightarrow{\ddagger} [T \xrightarrow{sf} \textbf{Self-A}^{n \in T}] \tag{11}$$

This definition means that $\ddagger(A \times B \xrightarrow{f \times g} C \times D) = A \ddagger B \xrightarrow{f \ddagger g} C \ddagger D$. It follows that any series of self-adaptive traits $T \xrightarrow{sf} \textbf{Self-A}^{n \in T}$ can be represented in a format including two parts of *head* and *tail* to be connected by "‡" such that

$$
T \xrightarrow{sf} \text{Self-A}^{n \in T} \stackrel{equiv}{\equiv} \overbrace{1 \xrightarrow{0} T \xrightarrow{sf} \text{Self-A}^{n \in T}}^{f_0} \ddagger \overbrace{1 \xrightarrow{t>0} T \xrightarrow{sf} \text{Self-A}^{n \in T}}^{f_{t>0}}
$$

(12)

where $\overbrace{1 \xrightarrow{0} T \xrightarrow{sf} \text{Self-A}^{n \in T}}^{f_0} = sf(0)$ and $\overbrace{1 \xrightarrow{t>0} T \xrightarrow{sf} \text{Self-A}^{n \in T}}^{f_{t>0}} = (sf(1), sf(2), \ldots)$ to be called head and tail, respectively.

Definition 5 (Head of series of self-adaptive traits). *We define a head construction morphism, denoted by* $1 \xRightarrow{0} (\_)$, *such that*

$$
1 \xRightarrow{0} (\_) : [T \xrightarrow{sf} \text{Self-A}^{n \in T}] \longrightarrow \text{Self-A}^{n \in T}
$$

(13)

This definition states that $\forall (a \ddagger s)[(a \ddagger s) \in [T \xrightarrow{sf} \text{Self-A}^{n \in T}] \implies \exists! f_0[f_0 \in \text{Self-A}^{n \in T} \ \& \ 1 \xRightarrow{0} (a \ddagger s) = a = f_0]]$

It follows that $1 \xRightarrow{0} (T \xrightarrow{sf} \text{Self-A}^{n \in T}) \stackrel{equiv}{\equiv} 1 \xrightarrow{0} T \xrightarrow{sf} \text{Self-A}^{n \in T}$.

Definition 6 (Tail of series of self-adaptive traits). *We define a tail construction morphism, denoted by* $(\_)'$, *such that*

$$
(\_)' : [T \xrightarrow{sf} \text{Self-A}^{n \in T}] \longrightarrow [T \xrightarrow{sf} \text{Self-A}^{n \in T}]
$$

(14)

This definition means that $\forall (a \ddagger s)[(a \ddagger s) \in [T \xrightarrow{sf} \text{Self-A}^{n \in T}] \implies \exists! (f_1, f_2, \ldots)$
$[(f_1, f_2, \ldots) \in [T \xrightarrow{sf} \text{Self-A}^{n \in T}] \ \& \ (a \ddagger s)' = s = (f_1, f_2, \ldots)]]$

As a convention, $(\_)^{\langle n \rangle}$ denotes applying recursively the $(\_)'$ n times. Thus, specifically, $(\_)^{\langle 2 \rangle}, (\_)^{\langle 1 \rangle}$ and $(\_)^{\langle 0 \rangle}$ stand for $((\_)')', (\_)'$ and $(\_)$, respectively.

It follows that the first member of series of self-adaptive traits $T \xrightarrow{sf} \text{Self-A}^{n \in T}$ is given by

$$
1 \xRightarrow{0} ((T \xrightarrow{sf} \text{Self-A}^{n \in T})') \stackrel{equiv}{\equiv} 1 \xrightarrow{1} T \xrightarrow{sf} \text{Self-A}^{n \in T}
$$

(15)

and, in general, for every $k \in T$ the k-th member of series of self-adaptive traits $T \xrightarrow{sf} \text{Self-A}^{n \in T}$ is provided by

$$
1 \xRightarrow{0} ((T \xrightarrow{sf} \text{Self-A}^{n \in T})^{\langle k \rangle}) \stackrel{equiv}{\equiv} 1 \xrightarrow{k} T \xrightarrow{sf} \text{Self-A}^{n \in T}
$$

(16)

Series of self-adaptive traits to be an infinite sequence of all $f_{t \in T}$ is viewed and treated as single mathematical entity, so the derivative of series of self-adaptive traits $T \xrightarrow{sf} \text{Self-A}^{n \in T}$ is given by $(T \xrightarrow{sf} \text{Self-A}^{n \in T})'$

Now using this notation for derivative of series of self-adaptive traits, we can specify series of self-adaptive traits $T \xrightarrow{sf} \textbf{Self-A}^{n \in T}$ as in

Definition 7. *A series of self-adaptive traits $T \xrightarrow{sf} \textbf{Self-A}^{n \in T}$ can be specified by*

- *Initial value:* $1 \xrightarrow{0} T \xrightarrow{sf} \textbf{Self-A}^{n \in T}$ *and*
- *Differential equation:* $((T \xrightarrow{sf} \textbf{Self-A}^{n \in T})^{\langle n \rangle})' = (T \xrightarrow{sf} \textbf{Self-A}^{n \in T})^{\langle n+1 \rangle}$

The initial value of $T \xrightarrow{sf} \textbf{Self-A}^{n \in T}$ is defined as its first element $1 \xrightarrow{0} T \xrightarrow{sf} \textbf{Self-A}^{n \in T}$, and the derivative of series of self-adaptive traits, denoted by $(T \xrightarrow{sf} \textbf{Self-A}^{n \in T})'$, is defined by $((T \xrightarrow{sf} \textbf{Self-A}^{n \in T})^{\langle n \rangle})' = (T \xrightarrow{sf} \textbf{Self-A}^{n \in T})^{\langle n+1 \rangle}$, for any integer n in T. In other words, the initial value and derivative equal the head and tail of $T \xrightarrow{sf} \textbf{Self-A}^{n \in T}$, respectively. The behavior of a series of self-adaptive traits $T \xrightarrow{sf} \textbf{Self-A}^{n \in T}$ consists of two aspects: it allows for the observation of its initial value $1 \xrightarrow{0} T \xrightarrow{sf} \textbf{Self-A}^{n \in T}$; and it can make an evolution to the new series of self-adaptive traits $(T \xrightarrow{sf} \textbf{Self-A}^{n \in T})'$, consisting of the original series of self-adaptive traits from which the first element has been removed. The initial value of $(T \xrightarrow{sf} \textbf{Self-A}^{n \in T})'$, which is $1 \xRightarrow{0} ((T \xrightarrow{sf} \textbf{Self-A}^{n \in T})') = 1 \xrightarrow{1} T \xrightarrow{sf} \textbf{Self-A}^{n \in T}$ can in its turn be observed, but note that we have to move from $T \xrightarrow{sf} \textbf{Self-A}^{n \in T}$ to $(T \xrightarrow{sf} \textbf{Self-A}^{n \in T})'$ first in order to do so. Now a behavioral differential equation defines a series of self-adaptive traits by specifying its initial value together with a description of its derivative, which tells us how to continue.

Note that every member $f_{t \in T}$ in $\textbf{Self-A}^{n \in T}$ can be considered as a series of self-adaptive traits in the following manner. For every $f_{t \in T}$ in $\textbf{Self-A}^{n \in T}$, a unique series of self-adaptive traits is defined by morphism f:

$$\overbrace{1 \xrightarrow{f_t} \textbf{Self-A}^{n \in T} \xrightarrow{f} \textbf{Self-A}_{\omega}^{n \in T}}^{(f_t, \circ, \circ, \dots)} \tag{17}$$

such that the equation $f_t; f = (f_i, \circ, \circ, \dots)$ holds, where $\circ$ denotes empty member (or null member) in $\textbf{Self-A}^{n \in T}$. Thus $(f_t, \circ, \circ, \dots)$ is in $\textbf{Self-A}_{\omega}^{n \in T}$.

Definition 8 (Equivalence). *For any $T \xrightarrow{sf1} \textbf{Self-A}^{n \in T}$ and $T \xrightarrow{sf2} \textbf{Self-A}^{n \in T}$, $sf1 = sf2$ iff $1 \xrightarrow{t} T \xrightarrow{sf1} \textbf{Self-A}^{n \in T} = 1 \xrightarrow{t} T \xrightarrow{sf2} \textbf{Self-A}^{n \in T}$ with every t in T.*

Definition 9 (Bisimulation). *Bisimulation on $\textbf{Self-A}_{\omega}^{n \in T}$ is a relation, denoted by $\sim$, between series of self-adaptive traits $T \xrightarrow{sf1} \textbf{Self-A}^{n \in T}$ and*

$T \xrightarrow{sf2} \textbf{Self-A}^{n \in T}$ *such that if* $sf1 \sim sf2$ *then* $1 \xRightarrow{0} (sf1) = 1 \xRightarrow{0} (sf2)$ *and* $(sf1)' \sim (sf2)'$.

Two series of self-adaptive traits are bisimular if, regarding their behaviors, each of the series "simulates" the other and vice-versa. In other words, each of the series cannot be distinguished from the other by the observation. Let us consider the following corollaries related to the bisimulation between series of self-adaptive traits.

Corollary 2. *Let* sf, $sf1$ *and* $sf2$ *be in* $\textbf{Self-A}_\omega^{n \in T}$. *If* $sf \sim sf1$ *and* $sf1 \sim sf2$ *then* $(sf \sim sf1) \circ (sf1 \sim sf2) = sf \sim sf2$, *where the symbol* $\circ$ *denotes a relational composition. For more descriptive notation, we can write this in the form*

$$\frac{sf \sim sf1, sf1 \sim sf2}{(sf \sim sf1) \circ (sf1 \sim sf2) = sf \sim sf2} \tag{18}$$

and conversely, if $sf \sim sf2$ *then there exists* $sf1$ *such that* $sf \sim sf1$ *and* $sf1 \sim sf2$. *This can be written as*

$$\frac{sf \sim sf2}{\exists sf1 : sf \sim sf1 \quad and \quad sf1 \sim sf2} \tag{19}$$

Proof: Proving (18) originates as the result of the truth that the relational composition between two bisimulations $L_1 \subseteq sf \times sf1$ and $L_2 \subseteq sf1 \times sf2$ is a bisimulation obtained by $L_1 \circ L_2 = \{\langle A, y \rangle \mid A \ L_1 \ z \text{ and } z \ L_2 \ y \text{ for some } z \in sf1\}$, where $A \in sf$, $z \in sf1$ and $y \in sf2$.

Proving (19) comes from the fact that there are always $sf1 = sf$ or $sf1 = sf2$ as simply as they can. Hence, (19) is always true in general.   Q.E.D.

Corollary 3. *Let* $sf_i, \forall i \in \mathbb{N}$, *be in* $\textbf{Self-A}_\omega^{n \in T}$ *and* $\bigcup_{i \in \mathbb{N}}$ *be union of a family of sets. We have*

$$\frac{sf \sim sf_i \quad with \ i \in \mathbb{N}}{\bigcup_{i \in \mathbb{N}} (sf \sim sf_i) = sf \sim \bigcup_{i \in \mathbb{N}} sf_i} \tag{20}$$

and conversely,

$$\frac{sf \sim \bigcup_{i \in \mathbb{N}} sf_i}{\exists i \in \mathbb{N} : sf \sim sf_i} \tag{21}$$

Proof: Proving (20) stems straightforwardly from the fact that sf bisimulates sf_i (i.e., $sf \sim sf_i$) then, sf bisimulates each series in $\bigcup_{i \in \mathbb{N}} sf_i$.

Conversely, proving (21) develops as the result of the fact that for each $\langle A, y \rangle \in \bigcup_{i \in \mathbb{N}} (sf \times sf_i)$, there exists $i \in \mathbb{N}$ such that $\langle A, y \rangle \in sf \times sf_i$. In other words, it is formally denoted by $\bigcup_{i \in \mathbb{N}} (sf \times sf_i) = \{\langle A, y \rangle \mid \exists i \in \mathbb{N} : A \in sf$ and $y \in sf_i\}$, where $A \in sf$ and $y \in sf_i$.   Q.E.D.

The union of all bisimulations between sf and sf_i (i.e., $\bigcup_{i\in N}(sf \sim sf_i)$) is the greatest bisimulation. The greatest bisimulation is called the *bisimulation equivalence* or *bisimilarity* [1,2] (again denoted by the notation $\sim$).

Corollary 4. *Bisimilarity $\sim$ on $\bigcup_{i\in N}(sf \sim sf_i)$ is an equivalence relation.*

Proof: In fact, a bisimilarity $\sim$ on $\bigcup_{i\in N}(sf \sim sf_i)$ is a binary relation $\sim$ on $\bigcup_{i\in N}(sf \sim sf_i)$, which is reflexive, symmetric and transitive. In other words, the following properties hold for $\sim$

– Reflexivity:

$$\frac{\forall(a \sim b) \in \bigcup_{i\in N}(sf \sim sf_i)}{(a \sim b) \sim (a \sim b)} \quad (22)$$

– Symmetry:

$$\frac{\forall(a \sim b), (c \sim d) \in \bigcup_{i\in N}(sf \sim sf_i), \quad (a \sim b) \sim (c \sim d)}{(c \sim d) \sim (a \sim b)} \quad (23)$$

– Transitivity:

$$\frac{\forall(a \sim b), (c \sim d), (e \sim f) \in \bigcup_{i\in N}(sf \sim sf_i), \quad ((a \sim b) \sim (c \sim d)) \wedge ((c \sim d) \sim (e \sim f))}{(a \sim b) \sim (e \sim f)} \quad (24)$$

to be an equivalence relation on $\bigcup_{i\in N}(sf \sim sf_i)$.   Q.E.D.

For some constraint α, if $sf1 \sim sf2$ then two series $sf1$ and $sf2$ have the following relation.

$$\frac{sf1 \models \alpha}{sf2 \models \alpha} \quad (25)$$

That is, if series $sf1$ satisfies constraint α then this constraint is still preserved on series $sf2$. Thus it is read as $sf1 \sim sf2$ in the constraint of α (and denoted by $sf1 \sim_\alpha sf2$).

For validating whether $sf1 = sf2$, a powerful method is so-called *proof principle of coinduction* [3] that states as follows:

Theorem 1 (Coinduction). *For any $T \xrightarrow{sf1} \textbf{Self-A}^{n\in T}$ and $T \xrightarrow{sf2} \textbf{Self-A}^{n\in T}$, if $sf1 \sim sf2$ then $sf1 = sf2$.*

Proof: In fact, for two series of self-adaptive traits $sf1$ and $sf2$ and a bisimulation $sf1 \sim sf2$. We see that by inductive bisimulation for $k \in T$, then $sf1^{\langle k \rangle} \sim sf2^{\langle k \rangle}$. Therefore, by definition 9, $1 \xrightarrow{0} (sf1^{\langle k \rangle}) = 1 \xrightarrow{0} (sf2^{\langle k \rangle})$.

By the equivalence in (16), then $1 \xrightarrow{k} sf1 = 1 \xrightarrow{k} sf2$ with every $k \in T$. It follows that, by definition 8, we obtain $sf1 = sf2$ Q.E.D.
Hence in order to prove the equivalence between two series of self-adaptive traits $sf1$ and $sf2$, it is sufficient to establish the existence of a bisimulation relation $sf1 \sim sf2$. In other words, using coinduction we can justify the equivalence between two series of self-adaptive traits $sf1$ and $sf2$ in $\textbf{Self-A}_\omega^{n\in T}$.

Corollary 5 (Generating series of self-adaptive traits). *For every sf in* **Self-A**$_\omega^{n \in T}$, *we have*

$$sf = 1 \overset{0}{\Longrightarrow} (sf) \ddagger (sf)' \tag{26}$$

Proof: This stems from the coinductive proof principle in theorem 1. In fact, it is easy to check the following bisimulation $sf \sim 1 \overset{0}{\Longrightarrow} (sf) \ddagger (sf)'$. It follows that $sf = 1 \overset{0}{\Longrightarrow} (sf) \ddagger (sf)'$ Q.E.D.

In (26), operation $\ddagger$ as a kind of series integration, the corollary states that series derivation and series integration are inverse operations. It gives a way to obtain sf from $(sf)'$ and the initial value $1 \overset{0}{\Longrightarrow} (sf)$. As a result, the corollary allows us to reach solution of differential equations in an algebraic manner.

7   Conclusions

In this paper, we have constructed self-adaptation monoid to establish series of self-adaptive traits in CASs based on coinductive approach.

We have started with defining CASs and self-adaptive traits in CASs. Then, **Self-A**$^{i \in T}$ has been constructed as a self-adaptation monoid to shape series $T \overset{sf}{\longrightarrow}$ **Self-A**$^{i \in T}$ of self-adaptive traits. In order to prove the equivalence between two series of self-adaptive traits, using coinduction, it is sufficient to establish the existence of their bisimulation relation. In other words, we can justify the equivalence between two series of self-adaptive traits in **Self-A**$_\omega^{n \in T}$ based on a powerful method so-called *proof principle of coinduction*.

Acknowledgments. Thank you to NTTU[1] for the constant support of our work which culminated in the publication of this paper. As always, we are deeply indebted to the anonymous reviewers for their helpful comments and valuable suggestions which have contributed to the final preparation of the paper.

References

1. Jacobs, B., Rutten, J.: A Tutorial on (Co)Algebras and (Co)Induction. Bulletin of EATCS **62**, 222–259 (1997)
2. Rutten, J.J.M.M.: Universal Coalgebra: A Theory of Systems. Theoretical Computer Science **249**(1), 3–80 (2000)
3. Rutten, J.J.M.M.: Elements of Stream Calculus (An Extensive Exercise in Coinduction). Electronic Notes in Theoretical Computer Science **45** (2001)
4. Vinh, P.C.: Self-Adaptation in Collective Adaptive Systems. Mobile Networks and Applications (2014, to appear)
5. Vinh, P.C., Alagar, V., Vassev, E., Khare, A. (eds.): ICCASA 2013. LNICST, vol. 128. Springer, Heidelberg (2014)
6. Vinh, P.C., Hung, N.M., Tung, N.T., Suzuki, J. (eds.): ICCASA 2012. LNICST, vol. 109. Springer, Heidelberg (2013)

---

[1] Nguyen Tat Thanh University, Vietnam.

A Context-Aware Traffic Engineering Model for Software-Defined Networks

Phuong T. Nguyen[1]([✉]), Hong Anh Le[2], and Thomas Zinner[3]

[1] Research and Development Center, Duy Tan University, Da Nang, Vietnam
phuong.nguyen@duytan.edu.vn
[2] Hanoi University of Mining and Geology, Hanoi, Vietnam
lehonganh@humg.edu.vn
[3] Lehrstuhl für Informatik III, Universität Würzburg, Würzburg, Germany
zinner@informatik.uni-wuerzburg.de

Abstract. Software-Defined Networking is a novel paradigm, based on the separation of the data plane from the control plane. It facilitates direct access to the forwarding plane of a network switch or router over the network. Though it has a lot advantages, the SDN technology leaves considerable room for improvement. Research problems like efficient techniques for customization and optimization for SDN networks are under investigation. This paper aims at proposing a model for traffic engineering in SDN-based networks.

Keywords: Software-Defined Networking · Traffic Engineering · Context-Aware Systems

1 Introduction

Performing experiments in production networks with legacy switches had been a costly and arduous task for a long time, until the Software-Defined Networking approach (SDN) appeared. SDN is a novel paradigm, based on the separation of the data plane from the control plane. While the former remains in switches, the latter is ported to a programmable controller which can either be a physical computer or a virtual machine. By this way, SDN gives researchers the flexibility in working with networks, it allows to perform their own experiments on network devices. The emergence of SDN provides users with a convenient way to customize network applications, without intervening the internal design of commodity switches [5],[6]. Though its technical aspects are still under development, SDN has found its way going into other formulation, SDN is widely adapted by network, content, and datacenter providers.

OpenFlow is a protocol for the communication between controllers and OpenFlow switches. It provides direct access to the forwarding plane of a switch or router. OpenFlow is widely accepted and considered to be the most notable deployment of SDN [5]. The protocol has recently received a growing attention both from academe and industry. As of June 2014, there are more than 150

© Institute for Computer Sciences, Social Informatics and Telecommunications Engineering 2015
P.C. Vinh et al. (Eds.): ICTCC 2014, LNICST 144, pp. 73–82, 2015.
DOI: 10.1007/978-3-319-15392-6_8

members registered to the Open Networking Foundation - the consortium for the development and standardization of SDN.

Despite a myriad of advantages, the SDN technology leaves considerable room for improvement. Research problems like efficient techniques for customization and optimization for SDN networks are under investigation. Our paper aims at introducing state of the art of SDN. Afterward, it is going to present a proposal for a traffic engineering model in SDN-based networks. The paper is organized as follows. In Section 2 we present the reader an overview of SDN functionalities. Recent developments on SDN performance are reviewed in Section 3. A running example is introduced in Section 4. Section 5 highlights the motivations, research objectives as well as our proposed solution. Finally, Section 6 concludes the paper.

2   SDN Functionalities

An SDN switch may hold a number of flow tables, each of them stores forwarding rules. A flow entry consists of three components: headers, actions, and statistics. The flow tables of a switch are used as the base for manipulating packets. Figure 1 illustrates how the first packet of a new flow is processed at an SDN switch.

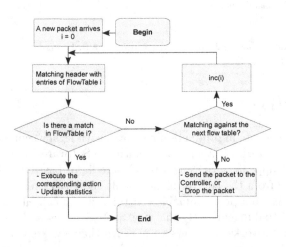

Fig. 1. Processing for the first packet of a flow

Upon the arrival of the packet, the packet's header is compared with the rules in the first flow table. If there is a match, the corresponding actions are executed and statistics are updated. The packet can also be discarded depending on the rules defined at the switch. In contrast, if there is no match, the header is compared against rules in the next tables or the packet is encapsulated and forwarded towards the controller. This is left at programmer's discretion. When receiving the packet, the controller may create a new rule and sends back to the switch which in turn updates the new rule to the flow table.

Figure 2 shows the fields for matching defined by the OpenFlow standard.

Fig. 2. Fields for matching [17],[18]

The following components are essential for an SDN implementation:

- The data plane is a set of flow tables and the actions corresponding to the table entries.
- The control plane is the controller that manages the flow tables through a pre-defined protocol.
- A flow is normally a group of consecutive packets sharing same features.

Using SDN's centralized intelligence, an administrator can exploit some advantages. SDN is used to route flow at Layer 2, Layer 3, and Layer 4 separately or concurrently according to packet's header information. In conventional networks, to configure network flows, an administrator needs to manipulate network devices separately using CLI (Command Line Interface). This poses a great difficulty, especially for networks with heterogeneous hardware units. In addition, it is almost impossible to program the network so that it can self configure during operation; any re-configuration needs to be manually done by the administrator. SDN helps the administrator do his work in a smoother way. It is not necessary for the administrator to know the specification of each hardware. He can configure a wide range of hardwares from different vendors using a single language.

3 Technical Issues

One might argue that SDN is no more useful if the time for processing incoming packets is longer that that of a legacy switch. It is, therefore, necessary to investigate the performance of SDN-based switches. The performance of data plane and control plane has received much interest from the research community. This section gives an overview of some notable studies on the problem.

It is worth noting that controller and switch - representing the control plane and the data plane - are the integral parts of the SDN approach. Correspondingly, performance evaluations have been done pertaining to these aspects. Parameters regarding response time, throughput of controller implementation as well as OpenFlow switches have been thoughtfully investigated. In [6] a performance evaluation for the data plane is presented. In this paper, the performance the of OpenFlow data plane is compared to that of IP routing and switching. It has been shown that, the performance of the data plane is comparable with that of the two technologies. Similarly, in [8] the authors introduce a performance comparison for an OpenFlow switch implementation and a native router. The two studies, [6] and [8], show that the efficiency of the forwarding plane of OpenFlow switches is similar to that of commodity switches.

Investigating performance of control plane helps promote an understanding of the feasibility, scalability, and robustness of the SDN concept. This helps network administrators know the number of controllers launched to handle the network. In addition, this helps further provision suitable resources. There are lots of studies conducted to investigate performance of control plane for SDN implementations. A performance comparison for different OpenFlow controllers is presented in [7]. Alongside some existing controllers, the authors propose NOX-MT, an enhancement of NOX with multi-threads. The performance tests are then conducted on the four OpenFlow implementations: NOX, NOX-MT, Maestro, and Beacon. The measurement metrics are controller's throughput and response time. The experimental results demonstrate that NOX-MT outperforms the other implementations.

In [5] the authors conduct performance tests to evaluate the performance of the control plane and the data plane of three OpenFlow switches: Open vSwitch, Pronto 3290 and NetFPGA OpenFlow switch. The experiments aim to measure the delay time at each OpenFlow switch for different packet sizes. The experimental results show that the NetFPGA OpenFlow switch has the lowest delay time compared to those of Open vSwitch and Pronto 3290. The Open vSwitch needs much more time to process a packet since it frequently accesses memory. In addition to the performance measurement, the authors also propose a simple model of an OpenFlow architecture based on queueing theory. In their approach, the performance of a controller is measured with the following parameters: the delay time at controllers and switches, the probability a packet is dropped given that the controller is out of service. The model has the advantage of swiftly delivering results but it has also some limitations. Despite the fact that an OpenFlow controller can host a number of switches, the model allows only one switch for a controller. In addition, only TCP traffic is considered and UDP traffic is missing.

A model for flexible benchmarking OpenFlow controllers has been proposed in [2]. Along with the model a software tool was implemented. The benchmark allows the emulation of scenarios and topologies, it helps build performance evaluation scenarios using several virtual switches. The performance of the benchmark is compared with that of Cbench. The experimental results show that the tool produces comparable results to those of Cbench. In addition, the benchmark is able to provide more performance statistics, i.e. round trip time, number of sent/received packets per second, and the number of outstanding packets per switch. It is also possible to examine whether the controller treats switches equally or not. This helps study further the performance characteristics of different OpenFlow controller implementations.

A model for the optimization of flow scheduling for datacenter networks is presented in [9]. The system, named Hedera can schedule in an adaptive fashion, in order to utilize network resources more efficiently. From a global view, the system can monitor flow and based on the information collected calculates a more efficient path to redirect flows. Similarly, with the model proposed in [11], [12], an OpenFlow system can detect traffic congestion of a virtual link and migrate flows away from the congested links.

In summary, different technical issues of OpenFlow have been thoroughly examined in many studies. Important parameters relating to the performance of the OpenFlow concept have been identified. A number of different performance benchmarks are already implemented to measure performance of OpenFlow network

components. The performance of data plane of an OpenFlow switch is close to that of a legacy switch while the performance of control plane depends on controller implementation. Some studies have taken the first steps towards network traffic tailoring based on network's conditions. However, the issue of using up-to-date performance information to control network is yet at an early stage and remains an open research problem.

4   Running Example: Datacenter

Network technologies prior to SDN supported a certain level of virtualization. Nevertheless, customizing traffics to meet user's demands was not only a costly but also daunting task, since technologies did not offer a convenient way to do. SDN has been applied in datacenters and helps eliminate the limitations. The SDN architecture facilitates flexible control of the whole network. Through the separation of control plane and data plane, it is possible to route network traffic with regard to the content of flows.

SDN provides a better way to utilize resources while hiding the underlying physical networks. It allows for decoupling the logical layer and physical layer to create virtual networks working on a shared physical network infrastructure. Switches are responsible for basic data forwarding while the control functionalities are handled at a virtual machine/programmable server. As a result, administrators are able to add new resources without needing to re-configure the existing devices. In network virtualization, a slice is defined as a set of flows and formed based on pooling of different network resources. The SDN scheme helps manage network slices and automate network management. This facilitates the development of a multi-tenant network environment. Each slice is handled by a single, logical controller and runs through multiple switches. Slicing enables flexible connection of servers, storage equipments and switches. Users are able to independently customize their own load and policies [19].

In datacenters, a common task is to move a large amount of data from a location to another location. Using SDN, one can configure network based on packet header at execution time to efficiently exploit existing bandwidth. To see how SDN helps optimize network resources and bandwidth, we consider a datacenter as depicted in Figure 3 and Figure 4 where a caching scheme is applied.

In this scenario, file server FS is used to provide data for the whole network and CS works as a cache server. Big volume data is frequently transferred from FS to CS. Another data stream with lower bandwidth requirement flows continuously from $SW1 \rightarrow SW3$. Figure 3 shows how a datacenter in legacy network operates. All traffics including that from FS to CS are routed through the high bandwidth channel. The low bandwidth channel is inadvertently left free.

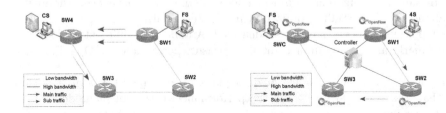

Fig. 3. Data transmission in legacy networks

Fig. 4. Data transmission in SDN networks

The SDN paradigm provides a productive way to manage the transmission. In such a network the cache station CS is about to serve a number of nodes and therefore should be deemed of importance. Flows from the file server to the cache server are given a certain level of priority. In Figure 4 the same network topology is deployed with SDN switches superseding legacy switches. A controller is added to handle all the switches. Flows are distinguished by their features, e.g. the MAC addresses of CS and FS. Since the controller has a global view of the network and knows the network topology, it is able to customize flows to maximize network utilization. The controller assigns the highest bandwidth channel to flows from FS to CS, i.e. $SW1 \rightarrow SW4$, whilst moving out subordinate traffics to the low bandwidth channel, i.e. $SW1 \rightarrow SW2 \rightarrow SW3$. Once the data has been completely transmitted, the controller allocates the released traffic to other flows. By doing this, flows are manipulated to tailor network traffic. As a result, network bandwidth is more efficiently utilized.

Implementing the SDN concept in a datacenter brings benefits. However, from our perspective, there are still issues that need to be addressed. Considering the above mentioned scenario, some questions might arise. For example, what would happen if the channel from $SW1 \rightarrow SW2 \rightarrow SW3 \rightarrow SW4$ has been beefed up and got a higher bandwidth than that between $SW1 \rightarrow SW4$? The controller program is upgraded, does its processing ability affect the overall performance? Can the controller be aware of changes if an SDN switch with greater processing capability has been added? There is a need to adaptively react to changes happening in the surrounding environment. We consider these issues as our research problems.

5 A Proposed Model for the Adaptive Control of an SDN-Based Datacenter

5.1 Motivations

SDN ushers in a new era of the network technology. Nevertheless, the concept is still in its infancy. There is a potential of souping up network applications using SDN/OpenFlow. A main question is how to further exploit the centralized intelligence of SDN to increase network utilization. It is also necessary to further facilitate the cooperation between controllers and switches.

The survey in Section 3 implies that the performance of an SDN network is substantially dependent on the controller's performance and switch's status. An SDN/OpenFlow controller might be suitable for a specific type of applications than for an other. In a network where there is the presence of several SDN switches and corresponding controllers, a change in controller's implementation may produce adverse or beneficial effects on to the network. Applications themselves also have influence on the system, their behaviours can possibly place a burden on the performance over the course of time. **Given the circumstances, the regular monitoring of controllers, switches, flows, and application behaviours is intrinsic to a good performance of the whole system**.

So far, several researches have been conducted to study different aspects of the SDN approach. **However, comparatively little of them has addressed the issue of utilizing the performance metrics for controlling SDN networks**.

5.2 Goals

From our perspective, a control model for SDN networks which has the ability to deal with changes or perturbations occuring at execution time is meaningful. Based on investigations, our work aims at developing a management model for OpenFlow networks which performs operations according to the performance information of the underlying network. The proposed model is expected to facilitate traffic engineering techniques for OpenFlow networks. It will, therefore, pave the way for further developments in the SDN domain. The specific aims of our work are as follows.

Aim #1: To propose techniques for employing flow statistics, information about switches, application, and controllers to control OpenFlow networks.

- Hypothesis #1: Information about flows, switches and controllers as well as bandwidth demand from applications is beneficial to the autonomous reaction to changes or disruptions happening in the network.
- Expected Result #1: To develop a traffic engineering model that exploits information about the conditions of the surrounding environment as the input.

Aim #2: To validate the efficiency of the proposed model in an SDN-based system - a datacenter.

- Hypothesis #2: The prototype helps the datacenter efficiently utilize network resources and deal with environmental stimuli.
- Expected Result #2: To realize the model by building a software prototype based on the OpenFlow standard and to deploy test scenarios in a datacenter, either a real system or simulation.

Our work aims at proposing and evaluating a traffic engineering model for SDN-based datacenters. The traffic engineering model is realized using the Open-Flow standard. Figure 5 displays an abstract view of the prospective model. The succeeding sections will give a brief introduction to the model.

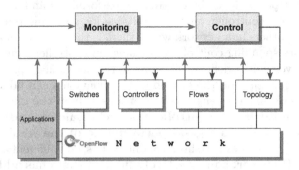

Fig. 5. An abstract view of the proposed model

5.3 Performance Monitoring

The proposed architecture consists of two main modules: Monitoring and Control as shown in Figure 5. The monitoring of controllers, switches, and flows contributes towards the optimization of the overall performance. In the first place, it is necessary to identify the factors that best represent the performance of an OpenFlow network. The existing studies on the performance of OpenFlow implementations provide a comprehensive analysis that can be used to derive a performance model suited to the requirements. The model will either exploit existing techniques or propose novel methods for the extraction of OpenFlow network's features.

The aim of performance monitoring is to provide the metrics reflecting network conditions. This module frequently communicates with switches, controllers, and flows to get up-to-date information about the network situation.

5.4 Topology Discovery

Information about network topology helps the control module calculate feasible paths for flows. The monitoring module needs to collect topology information to maintain a view of the network topology.

Each OpenFlow switch is programmed with some predefined configuration. The controller programs a rule in the new switch when it connects to the network.

The switch periodically sends data packets to all ports and waits for responses. This aims at testing the availability of neighbour switches as well as measuring sojourn time. The information is collected by the monitoring modul which then supplies the controller with status of links and transfer time. Once the controller collects enough information about network topology from all switches, it is able to construct network topology.

5.5 Network Control

Information collected by the monitoring module serves as the input for the control module (cf Figure 5). This includes information from flows, switches, controllers and applications. Switches report collision or disruption occurring in the constituent network segments. The statistics collected from the flow tables provide a view of the flows. Each application sends up-to-date information about bandwidth demand. The capacity of the existing communication channels will also be frequently reported from the switches.

The control module receives the information and conducts adequate countermeasures. It orders the controller to move or re-distribute flows to avoid collision and disruption. New routes are then calculated and programmed into related switches. The changes enable efficient bandwidth distribution and result in tailoring bandwidth demand and channel capacity. This contributes towards the efficient utilization of network resources and optimization of overall performance.

6   Conclusions and Future Work

In this paper we have introduced our proposal for a traffic engineering model for Software-Defined Networks. To turn the proposals into realization, we are working towards a software prototype for the management of OpenFlow networks based on an existing OpenFlow controller implementation, e.g. NOX, Maestro, Floodlight, etc. The software prototype operates as an overlay between the OpenFlow architecture and its applications. Afterwards, to validate the efficiency of the proposed model, its features are going to be investigated. This is done by deploying the software prototype in the selected use case datacenter. A testbed will be built and the test infrastructure should emulate the activities of a datacenter. Simulation might be necessary given that the available resources are not sufficient to perform tests for a large scale. Experiments will be conducted to measure network throughput, transfer time under different system configurations. The evaluations aim at examining the performance, feasibility, and scalability of the proposed approach in the datacenter. It is expected that the deployment of the software prototype will help the datacenter utilize network resources efficiently.

References

1. Curtis, A.R., Mogul, J.C., Tourrilhes, T., Yalag, P., Sharma, P., Banerjee, S.: Devoflow: Scaling flow management for high-performance networks. ACM SIGCOMM (2011)

2. Jarschel, M., Lehrieder, F., Magyari, Z., Pries, R.: A Flexible OpenFlow-Controller Benchmark. In: European Workshop on Software Defined Networks (2012)
3. Rotsos, C., Sarrar, N., Uhlig, S., Sherwood, R., Moore, A.W.: OFLOPS: An open framework for openflow switch evaluation. In: Taft, N., Ricciato, F. (eds.) PAM 2012. LNCS, vol. 7192, pp. 85–95. Springer, Heidelberg (2012)
4. Heller, B., Sherwood, R., McKeown, N.: The controller placement problem. In: Proceedings of the First Workshop on Hot Topics in Software Defined Networks (HotSDN 2012) (2012)
5. Jarschel, M., Oechsner, S., Schlosser, D., Pries, R., Goll, S., Tran-Gia, P.: Modeling and performance evaluation of an OpenFlow architecture. In: Proceedings of the 23rd International Teletraffic Congress (2011)
6. Bianco, A., Birke, R., Giraudo, L., Palacin, M.: OpenFlow switching: data plane performance. In: Proceedings of IEEE International Conference on Communications (2010)
7. Tootoonchian, A., Gorbunov, S., Ganjali, Y., Casado, M., Sherwood, R.: On controller performance in software-defined networks. In: Proceedings of the 2nd USENIX Conference on Hot Topics in Management of Internet, Cloud, and Enterprise Networks and Services, Hot-ICE 2012 (2012)
8. Moreira, et al.: Packet forwarding using openflow. In: First Workshop on Network Virtualizaton and Intelligence for Future Internet, WNetVirt 2010 (2010)
9. Al-Fares, M., Radhakrishnan, S., Raghavan, B., Huang, N., Vahdat, A.: Hedera: dynamic flow scheduling for data center networks. In: Proceedings of the 7th USENIX Conference on Networked Systems Design and Implementation, NSDI 2010 (2010)
10. Open Networking Foundation. https://www.opennetworking.org/membership/members (accessed June 20, 2014)
11. Mattos, et al.: OMNI: OpenFlow management infrastructure. In: Proceedings of the 2nd IFIP International Conference Network of the Future, NoF 2011 (2011)
12. Fernandes, et al.: Multinetwork control using openflow. In: First Workshop on Network Virtualizaton and Intelligence for Future Internet (2010)
13. Yu, M.: Scalable Management of Enterprise and Data-Center Networks. PhD Dissertation (2011)
14. Sherwood, et al.: FlowVisor: A Network Virtualization Layer. OpenFlow Switch (2009)
15. Pisa, P.S., Fernandes, N.C., Carvalho, H.E.T., Moreira, M.D.D., Campista, M.E.M., Costa, L.H.M.K., Duarte, O.C.M.B.: OpenFlow and xen-based virtual network migration. In: Pont, A., Pujolle, G., Raghavan, S.V. (eds.) WCITD 2010. IFIP AICT, vol. 327, pp. 170–181. Springer, Heidelberg (2010)
16. Rotsos, et al.: Cost, performance & flexibility in openflow: pick three. In: Proceedings of IEEE International Conference on Communications (2012)
17. Simeonidou, D., Nejabati, R., Azodolmolky, S.: Enabling the Future Optical Internet with OpenFlow: A Paradigm Shift in Providing Intelligent Optical Network Services
18. McKeown, et al.: OpenFlow: Enabling Innovation in Campus Networks. SIGCOMM Comput. Commun, Rev. (2008)
19. Google Inc.: Inter-Datacenter WAN with centralized TE using SDN and OpenFlow

Efficient *k*-Nearest Neighbor Search for Static Queries over High Speed Time-Series Streams

Bui Cong Giao$^{(\boxtimes)}$ and Duong Tuan Anh

Faculty of Computer Science and Engineering,
Ho Chi Minh City University of Technology, Ho Chi Minh City, Vietnam
giao.bc@cb.sgu.edu.vn, dtanh@cse.hcmut.edu.vn

Abstract. In this paper, we propose a solution to the multi-step *k*-nearest neighbor (*k*-NN) search. The method is the reduced tolerance-based *k*-NN search for static queries in streaming time-series. A multi-scale filtering technique combined with a multi-resolution index structure is used in the method. We compare the proposed method to the traditional multi-step *k*-NN search in terms of the CPU search time and the number of distance function calls in the post-processing step. The results reveal that the reduced tolerance-based *k*-NN search outperforms the traditional *k*-NN search. Besides, applying multi-threading to the proposed method enables the system to have a fast response to high speed time-series streams for the *k*-NN search of static queries.

Keywords: *k*-NN search · Streaming time-series · Multi-scale filtering · Multi-resolution index structure · Static query

1 Introduction

At present, a significant number of real-world applications deal with time-series streams: performance measurements in network monitoring and traffic management, online stock analysis, earthquake prediction, etc. The major common characteristic of these applications is that they are all time-critical. In such applications, similarity search is often a core subroutine, yet the time taken for similarity search is almost an obstacle since time-series streams might transfer huge amount of data at steady high-speed rates. As a result, time-series streams are potentially unbounded in size within a short period and the system runs out of memory soon. Due to this, if an element of time-series stream has been processed, it is quickly discarded and cannot be retrieved so that it yields to a new-coming one. To achieve real-time response, one-pass scan and low time complexity are usually required for handling streaming time-series. However, available methods used to manage static time-series are hardly to satisfy the above requirements because they commonly need to scan time-series database many times for processing time-series data and often have high time complexity. Therefore, according to Yang and Wu [1], high-speed data streams and high dimensional data are the second ranking challenge among ten top challenging problems in nowadays' data mining. In addition, Fu [2] has recently conducted a review on time-series data mining and reckoned that mining on streaming time-series is an attractive research

© Institute for Computer Sciences, Social Informatics and Telecommunications Engineering 2015
P.C. Vinh et al. (Eds.): ICTCC 2014, LNICST 144, pp. 83–97, 2015.
DOI: 10.1007/978-3-319-15392-6_9

direction. In the scope of this paper, we only focus on pattern discovery by similarity search in streaming context. That is similarity-based streaming time-series retrieval, which is to find those streaming time-series similar to a time-series query.

Kontaki et al. [3] summarized that there are three similarity search types extensively experimented in the literature: range search, k-NN search and join search. Liu and Ferhatosmanoglu [4] reckoned that applications of streaming time-series might involve two query kinds: static queries that are predefined patterns as well as ad hoc and streaming queries that are continuously changed. In our previous work [5], we proposed a solution to range search for static queries in streaming time-series. In the paper, we will address a problem of improving the performance of the multi-step k-NN search for static queries in streaming time-series. Specifically, we deal with an important scenario in streaming applications where incoming data are from concurrent time-series streams at high speed rates, and queries are a fixed set of time-series patterns.

The existing multi-step k-NN search method [6] is to achieve a fixed tolerance and use the tolerance in the whole range query process. As a result, a large number of candidate sequences are retrieved by a range query with a large tolerance. Too many candidates incur CPU overheads in the post-processing step and eventually degrade the overall k-NN search performance. To reduce the number of candidates, we apply a tolerance reduction-based approach, which improves the search performance by tightening the tolerance of a query when its k-NN set is modified. The approach is similar in spirit to one suggested by Lee et al. [7]. Our method also uses a multi-resolution index structure is built on an array of R^*-trees [8] that supports the multi-scale filtering in similarity search. The index structure stores features of time-series subsequences of queries, extracted by any transform that satisfies the lower bounding condition and has multi-resolution property.

The main contributions of the paper are

- Using a tolerance reduction-based approach in k-NN search for static queries over high speed time-series streams;
- Adjusting range search in an R^*-tree for many queries at a time.

The rest of paper is organized as follows. Section 2 presents supporting techniques for our approach. Section 3 describes the proposed method. Section 4 discusses experimental evaluation, and Section 5 gives conclusions and future work.

2   Supporting Techniques

The section briefly describes supporting techniques for the proposed method. Some of the techniques were presented in detail in [5].

2.1   Multi-resolution Dimensionality Reduction Methods

A time-series X of length l might be considered as a point in l-dimensional space. It would be costly if we perform similarity search directly on the time-series X. Therefore, X is often transformed into a new space with lower dimensionality.

We use three common dimensionality reduction transforms: Discrete Fourier Transforms (DFT) [9], Harr Wavelet Transform (Haar DWT) [10], and PAA [11]. They all satisfy the lower bounding condition and have multi-resolution property.

2.2   Storing Coefficients at Resolutions

Each predefined query is segmented into non-overlapped segments. This makes sure that segments of queries are filtered continuously and this is suitable for streaming environment. These segments are normalized and transformed into coefficients by Haar DWT, PAA, or DFT.

Let denote *maxlevel* as the maximum level of the multi-resolution structure and *l* as the length of a query. We assume that the minimum length of queries is *min*. A query is separated into segments: *min*, 2*min*, 4*min*... from backward direction, such that $\exists n$, *n* is largest and *min* $\times$ (2*n* - 1) $\leq$ MIN (*l*, *maxlevel* $\times$ *min*). Therefore, *n* is the maximum level to which the query might be filtered. Fig. 1 depicts the segmentation from the backward direction of a query.

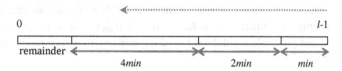

Fig. 1. The query segmentation [5]

The number of coefficients must be an integer power of two (2^i) since we want to compare the results of three transform methods: Haar DWT, PAA, and DFT. There is a maximum value of the number of coefficients; in [5] we recommend the maximum is 16. The number of coefficients at levels might be different. Assume that *min* = 8 and *maxlevel* = 5, we have the number of coefficients as shown in Table 1.

Table 1. Coefficient table

Level	Length	Number of Coefficients
1	8	2
2	16	4
3	32	8
4	64	16
5	128	16

2.3   Multi-resolution Index Structure

An array of R*-trees is used to store coefficients extracted from query segments. The index of the array corresponds to the resolution level that filters out the data. For example, the coefficients of the first segment (its length is *min*) of the query are stored in the first R*-tree of the array (i.e. level 1). The coefficients of the second segment (its length is 2*min*) of the query are stored in the second R*-tree (i.e. level 2), etc. Notice that all static queries share the same array of R*-trees as their index.

2.4   Improved Range Search in R*-tree

R*-tree is an index structure organized as B-tree. It contains hierarchical nodes and parent (upper) nodes link to their child (lower) nodes. Only leaf nodes refer to spatial data object. Each node has its own minimum bounding rectangle (MBR). Because we use R*-tree for point (coefficients of query segments) query, we can have the information about whichever points lie in a MBR. The minimum distance h_{min} from a query point in a MBR to the margin of the MBR can be calculated after the R*-tree is constructed.

During the stage of k-NN search, a time-series point is checked to determine whether the time-series subsequence is a k-NN candidate of a query within its own tolerance tl. The procedure is done as follows: Firstly, the distance dt from a time-series point to the MBR is calculated. Next, we consider the query points in the MBR; if $dt < tl$, the time-series subsequence might be a k-NN candidate of that query. To reduce false alarms we additionally note that if $dt + h_{min} < tl$ then the time-series subsequence is a more probable candidate. Fig. 2 depicts the improved range search in 2-dimensional space.

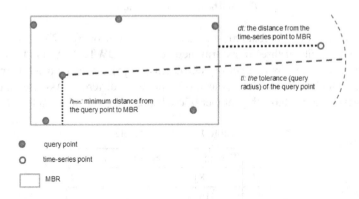

Fig. 2. The improved range search for a query point to a time-series point in the 2-dimensional space

2.5   Data Structures

To simulate data streams, we use a round-robin buffer to contain data points from a time-series stream. When the round-robin buffer is full, the new-coming element is put into the position of the oldest one; whereas in case of a common buffer, all elements of the buffer are forcibly shifted forward to have an available position for the new-coming one.

Each query has its own k-NN candidate set. The k-NN candidates of a query have their distance to the query less than a tolerance. We expect that the tolerance of a query is the maximum distance in the k-NN candidate set. When a time-series subsequence has its distance to the query less than the tolerance, it is added into the k-NN candidate set. Because time-series streams are potentially unbounded in size, so if the tolerance is large, the number of candidates in the k-NN set is too numerous and this incurs memory overflow in the execution of similarity search. For this reason, we cannot use a common in-memory set to store all candidates that have their distances less than the tolerance of a query. We propose using a priority queue organized as a max-heap to keep k candidates of a query. Therefore, the top item in the priority queue is the time-series subsequence that has the maximum distance to the corresponding query. Another advantage of using priority queues as the k-NN sets of queries is that the system can return the sorted k-NN items of a query at any time, while in the traditional k-NN search it takes time to sort the final candidates before the k-NN items are returned. However, using priority queues also costs some time for removing the top item to yield to a new time-series subsequence whose distance is less.

3   Proposed Method

The k-NN search algorithm consists of three main phases as follows:

Phase 1: **Preprocessing**

At the beginning of the program, the k-NN sets of all queries are initialized with k false items whose distances are a maximum value (∞). Let denote *NotFullQueryList* as the global list of queries whose k-NN set has still false items; initially the list contains all queries. Also, let *kNNinfo* be the global list of queries whose entire k-NN sets contain true items; initially the list is empty.

Next, queries are segmented and normalized. Their coefficients are calculated and stored in a multi-resolution index structure which is an array of R*-trees. Notice that segments of predefined queries only need normalizing once in this phase, but segments of time-series stream have to be normalized at every new-coming data point.

Phase 2: **k-NN search**

When there is a new-coming data point of a time-series stream, segments on the streaming time-series are incrementally normalized. Using the incremental data normalization based on z-score [5] enables the method not to compute data normalization from the scratch. After that, the coefficients of the normalized segments are calculated. These coefficients are matched with the coefficients of query segments already stored in the nodes of R*-tree within each tolerance of the queries from the lowest to upper levels. Fig. 3 illustrates the backward matching of each pair of the coefficients. This matching step, which applies multi-step filtering, helps to prune unsatisfying queries. Lastly, the query candidates are checked in the post-processing phase.

Phase 3: **Post-processing**

For each query candidate, the real distance between the query candidate and the corresponding piece of streaming time-series is calculated to find a true k-NN item (time-series subsequence). If a true k-NN item is found, the k-NN set is updated and the tolerance might be reduced.

Table 2 shows some notations we will use in the following.

Table 2. Frequently used notations

Notation	Meaning
q	a query sequence
$q.kNN$	the priority queue of q
$q.normal$	the normalized sequence of q
m	the number of queries
SortedByToleranceList	data structure of lists sorted by descending tolerance
$S = \{\dots T_{n-2}, T_{n-1}, T_n\}$	a streaming time-series
s_i	the ith time-series segment of S, i: $0..maxlevel$-1
T_n	new-coming data at time point n
T_{n-1}	new-coming data at time point n-1

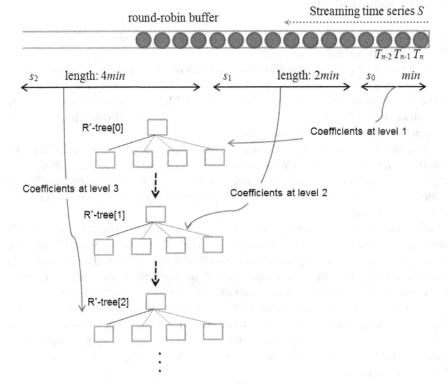

Fig. 3. Query filter through resolution levels [5]

The algorithm has two options. Firstly, when the *k*-NN set of a query is full (that means all items in the set are real), the tolerance is the maximum distance in the set and since then, it is not changed. Secondly, when the *k*-NN set of a query is full, the tolerance is the maximum distance in the set and it might be changed whenever the set is updated. We will evaluate the performance of the two options in section 4. The following pseudo codes illustrate the *k*-NN search for static queries over a time-series stream.

Algorithm *k*-NNSearch(Streaming time-series *S*)

---

variables
- *SCandidates*: a static local list contains candidate queries whose *k*-NN sets are full. Its type is *SortedByToleranceList*.
- *SNotFullQueryList*: a static local list contains candidate queries whose *k*-NN sets are not full.
- *postCheckSet*: a set of queries for post-processing
- *tempList*: a query list whose type is *SortedByToleranceList*
- *res*: a query candidate list
- d_{max}: the maximum distance of *q.kNN*
- *s*: a corresponding piece of *S* with a current query

begin
When there is a new-coming data of *S*: T_n // Phase 2
1. **if** *SCandidates* is different from *kNNinfo* **then**
2.   Copy *kNNinfo* to *SCandidates*
3.   **if** |*SCandidates*| < *m* **then**
4.   Copy *NotFullQueryList* to *SNotFullQueryList*
5. **if** |*SCandidates*| > 0 **then**
6.   *postCheckSet* = ∅
7.   *tempList* = *SCandidates*
8.   **for** *i* = 0 **to** *maxlevel* - 1
9.   *res* = Search*k*-NN(Coef(IncNormalize(s_i)),*tempList*,R*-tree[*i*])
10.   **foreach** (Query *q* **in** *res*)
11.   **if** *i* is the maximum resolution level of *q* **then**
12.   *postCheckSet* = *postCheckSet* ∪ *q*
13.   Remove *q* from *res*
14.   **end foreach**
15.   **if** *res* is empty **then**
16.   **break**
17.   *tempList* = Sort *res* by descending tolerances
18.   **end for**
19.   **foreach** (Query *q* **in** *postCheckSet*)   // Phase 3
20.   *d* = d_o(*q.normal*, Normalize(*s*))
21.   Get d_{max} from *q.kNN*

```
22.       if d < d_max then
23.           q.kNN.Dequeue
24.           q.kNN.Enqueue(s) with d
25.           Get d_max from q.kNN
26.           Update q and its d_max in kNNinfo
27.    end foreach
28. foreach (Query q in SNotFullQueryList) //Phase filling k-NN
sets
29.    d = d_o(q.normal, Normalize(s))
30.    q.kNN.Dequeue
31.    q.kNN.Enqueue(s) with d
32.    Get d_max from q.kNN
33.    if d_max < ∞ then
34.        Add q and its d_max into kNNinfo
35.        Remove q from NotFullQueryList
36. end foreach
end
```

There are some noticeable issues in the phases of *Algorithm k-NNSearch*:

- *Phase 2:* If *SCandidates* does not contain all queries then *NotFullQueryList* is copied to *SNotFullQueryList* (lines 3-4). Copies (lines 2 and 4) ensure that the algorithm manipulates local resources, not shared global ones. Next, the two static local resources are *SCandidates* and *SNotFullQueryList* considered one by one. Line 9 implies that segments s_i is incrementally normalized and a coefficient vector is extracted from the normalized segment; then a k-NN search in the R^*-tree of the ith filter level is performed. *Searchk-NN* calls *Algorithm Searchk-NN* with *node* as the root node of the R^*-tree. The query results are checked (line 11) to create a candidate set for phase 3. Going through filter levels might ends early if the candidate set for the next traverse is empty (lines 15-16). Because the return results of the k-NN search in the R^*-tree is not to follows the type of *SortedByToleranceList*, the results need sorting by descending tolerance for the next filter level (line 17).

- *Phase 3:* Line 20 implies that the real distance between the normalized query sequence, which is calculated beforehand, and the time-series subsequence, which is normalized at the moment, is performed. As mentioned before, the algorithm has two options: the reduced tolerance-based k-NN search and the traditional k-NN search. Lines 25-26 exist for the first option while these codes are omitted for the second option. It is obvious that when we compare the two options, the execution cost of lines 2-4 is less in the second option.

- *Phase filling k-NN sets:* the phase illustrates filling k-NN queues of queries with real items. If a k-NN queue is full, that means the condition of line 33 is true, the query information is added into *kNNinfo* (line 34) and the query is removed out of *NotFullQueryList* (line 35).

To support the k-NN search in an R^*-tree, the nodes in the index structure need to include the information of points that lies in the MBR of the nodes. The information is a list of items whose structure consists of *pointID*, *entryID*, and *hmin*. The list is in order of *pointID*. *pointID* is the *queryID*. *entryID* is *ID* of the entry that refers to the child node containing the point. *hmin* is the minimum distance from the point to the MBR margin of the node. For example, a node has *entrieIDs*: 10, 14, 21 and *pointIDs*: 2, 4, 9, 10, 15, 22, and 35. *entryID* 10 contains 9 and 22; *entryID* 14 contains 2, 15, and 35; and *entryID* 21 contains 4 and 10. Let *node.information* be the information of the points in the node. Fig. 4 illustrates an example of *node.information*.

pointID	2	4	9	10	15	22	35
entryID	14	21	10	21	14	10	14
hmin	0	1.2	2.3	0	1.5	4.6	2.8

Fig. 4. An illustration of *node.information*

We note that *hmin* is 0 if the point lies at the margin of the MBR of the node.

Algorithm Searchk-NN elaborates the function *Searchk-NN* used in line 9 of *Algorithm k-NNSearch*. This important algorithm performs the *k*-NN search of a coefficient point against a query list, whose type is *SortedByToleranceList*, on a node of an R^*-tree.

Algorithm Search*k*-NN(*point, ql, node*)

---

variables
- *cl*: an array of lists of query candidates in *node*, which needs considering in the lower level of the R^*-tree. The indexes of the array are entry IDs of *node*.
- *res*: a query candidate list. Initially, *res* is empty.

begin
1. calculate distance *dt* between *point* and the MBR of *node*
2. **if** *dt* = 0 **then**
3.   **foreach** (*item* **in** *ql*)
4.   Get *entryID* of *item* from *node.information*
5.   Add *item* into *cl*[*entryID*]
6.   **end foreach**
7. **else**
8.   **foreach** (*item* **in** *ql*)
9.   **if** *dt* >= *item.tolerance* **then**
10.   **break**
11.   Get *hmin* of *item* from *node.information*
12.   **if** *dt* + *hmin* < *item.tolerance* **then**
13.   Get *entryID* of *item* from *node.information*
14.   Add *item* into *cl*[*entryID*]
15.   **end foreach**
16.   **if** *cl* is empty **then**
17.   **return** *res*
18. **if** *node* is leaf **then**

```
19.      foreach (item in cl)
20.          calculate distance dt between point and the point of
item
21.          if dt < item.tolerance then
22.              item.tolerance = item.tolerance - dt;
23.              Add item into res
24.      end foreach
25.  else                              // internal node
26.      foreach (SortedByToleranceList el in cl)
27.          child is a child node of node, entryID of el refers to
child
28.          Add results of Searchk-NN(point,el,child) to res
29.      end foreach
30.  return res
end
```

We have some notes about *Algorithm Searchk-NN*:

In the first stage, if the condition in line 2 is true, that means the point lies in the MBR or at the margin of the MBR, an array of lists of query candidates is created from items of *ql* (line 5). Otherwise, if distance *dt* is larger than the tolerance of an item (query), the loop ends early because surely this item and the remaining items are not candidates (lines 9-10). If not, an additional check is performed to make sure that *item* is a candidate (see more in section 2.4). If the condition in line 12 is true, *item* is added to the list that is identified by the *entryID* of *item* (lines 13-14). At the end of the stage, if the array of lists of query candidates does not have any item, the algorithm ends early (line 17).

In the second stage, if *node* is leaf, entries of *node* refer to point objects (coefficient vectors). If the condition in line 21 is true, *item* is a candidate of the *k*-NN set (line 23). The tolerance of *item* is reduced by distance *dt* for the next filter level (line 22). If *node* is not a leaf, each list in array *cl* has an *entryID* as the index of the list and the entry refers to a child node (line 27). The algorithm is called recursively again and the results are added into *res* (line 28).

The process of the *k*-NN search must begin from the root node. So the function *Searchk-NN (Algorithm Searchk-NN)* should be invoked at the first time by the following statement: *Searchk-NN(point, ql, Index-tree.root)*.

To clarify the structure of *ql* and *cl*, we reconsider the example in Fig. 4. Fig. 5 is an example of *ql* and Figure 6 is one of *cl*.

pointID	15	10	2	35	9
tolerance	16.5	12.2	8.7	0.4	0.1

Fig. 5. An illustration of *ql*

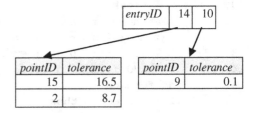

Fig. 6.
entryID	14	10

pointID	tolerance
15	16.5
2	8.7

pointID	tolerance
9	0.1

Fig. 6. An illustration of *cl*

4   Experimental Evaluation

In this section, we present experiments on the proposed method and the traditional *k*-NN search method, and evaluate the performance of the system. All experiments have been conducted on an Intel Dual Core i3 M350 2.27 GHz, 4GB RAM PC.

To take advantage of the strength of today's CPU and due to the characteristic of the search method, we use multi-threaded programming. Each threading process handles one time-series stream to implement *Algorithm k-NNSearch*. For simplicity, all threading processes have the same priority. The programming language used in this work is C# since the language is powerful for multi-threading. Because threading processes can compete to update the same global resources (e.g. *k*-NN sets) at a time, the system must lock the shared resources before updates can be done. However, this technique degrades the performance of the system. To mitigate the problem, locks for update must occur as quickly as possible by optimizing update operations.

We used ten text files containing the time-series datasets that are input for ten time-series streams. The sources of the datasets are given in column 4 of Table 3. One thousand text files created from ten above datasets play a role of static queries. The number of queries created from a dataset is proportional to the number of points in the text file that simulates the dataset. The size of the queries varies from 8 to 256. The number of filter levels is 5 for these queries. Level 1 can filter queries whose lengths are greater than or equal to 8. Level 2 can filter queries whose lengths are greater than or equal to 24, and so on. The total number of data points in the queries is 133,771. Other parameter setting in the experiments is as follows. Buffer length of each time-series stream is 1,024. R^*-tree has the setting: $m = 4$ and $M = 10$.

Table 3. Text files used to simulate time-series streams

No	Datasets	Number of Points	Source
1	carinae.txt	1,189	[12]
2	D1.txt	8,778	[13]
3	D2.txt	50,000	[13]
4	darwin.slp.txt	1,400	[12]
5	eeg7-6.txt	3,600	[12]
6	Hawea-91757.txt	7,487	[14]
7	infraredwave.txt	4,096	[13]
8	lightcurve.txt	27,204	[13]
9	Pukaki-877571.txt	7,487	[14]
10	wirewave.txt	4,096	[13]
	Total points	115,337	

We have implemented experiments to compare the reduced tolerance-based *k*-NN search to the traditional *k*-NN search. The criteria for comparing the two approaches are the CPU search time and the number of distance function calls in post-processing step of Haar DWT, PAA, and DFT. The parameter k is from 1 to 3.

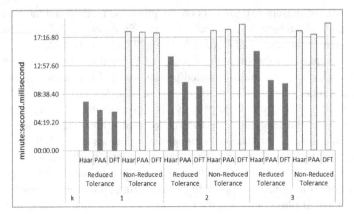

Fig. 7. CPU search times of k-NN search for the two methods

Fig. 7 shows the first approach is better than the second one in the CPU search time. For the first method, the CPU search time has increasing tendency when k increases and the CPU search time of Haar DWT is largest and that of DFT is least. As for the second method, the CPU search times of three dimensionality reduction transforms are nearly the same.

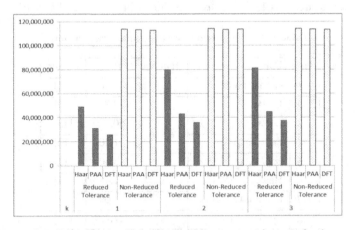

Fig. 8. The number of distance function calls in the post- processing step for the two methods

Fig. 8 shows that in the post-processing step, the first approach has the number of distance function calls less than the second does. For the first approach, the number increases when k increases and DFT has the least number and Haar DWT has the largest one. However, in the second approach, these numbers are almost the same thought k increases.

From Fig. 7 and Fig. 8 we can conclude that although the tradition *k*-NN search does not change tolerances, (that means the locking time for the global resource (*kNNInfo*) is less than our approach), tolerances in this approach are often large and the number of distance function calls in the post-processing step is too much. This degrades the overall performance.

We have already implemented the *k*-NN search method without multi-threading; in the case, the system only has a process to scan time-series streams sequentially for handling new-coming data points, whereas the proposed method has every threading process for a time-series stream. Fig. 9 shows the average CPU times for processing a new-coming data point over the ten time-series streams with *k* varying from 1 to 10 in case of the system handling time-series streams sequentially. We note that when *k* increases, in general, the average CPU times of the dimensionality reduction transforms also increase. With each *k*-NN search, the average CPU time of DFT is least, while that of Haar DWT is largest; the average CPU time of PAA is slightly larger than that of DFT.

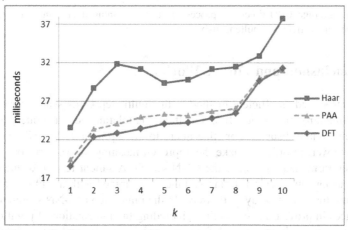

Fig. 9. The average CPU times for processing a new-coming data point when the system handles time-series streams sequentially

Since the proposed method processes time-series streams simultaneously, the performance of the system is improved significantly. The average CPU times for processing a new-coming data point of the system are slightly small in case of the system handling time-series streams simultaneously. For the 1-NN search, the average CPU time of DFT in Fig. 9 is 18 milliseconds, while in Fig. 10 the value is only 3 milliseconds. For the 5-NN search, the average CPU time of PAA in Fig. 9 is 25 milliseconds, while in Fig. 10 the value is about 6 milliseconds. For 10-NN search, the average CPU time of Haar DWT in Fig. 9 is 38 milliseconds, while in Fig. 10 the value is 10 milliseconds. Therefore, multi-threaded programming as a whole offers dramatic improvements in speed (up to roughly 4 times) over traditional programming. The comparison demonstrates the usability of multi-threading to proposed method for real-time applications that need perform *k*-NN search for static queries over time-series streams at high-speed rates.

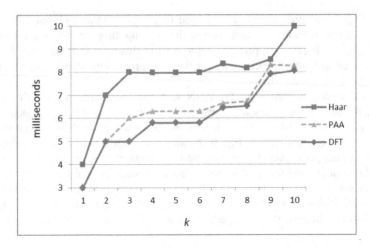

Fig. 10. The average CPU times for processing a new-coming data point when the system handles time-series streams simultaneously

5   Conclusions and Future Work

We have introduced an efficient method to the multi-step k-NN search for static queries over streaming time-series. In the method, the tolerance of each query is reduced when the maximum distance from that query to the top item in its k-NN queue is reduced. Moreover, in order to make the approach meaningful, we carry out the incremental data normalization before the k-NN search. A salient feature of the proposed method is using multi-scale filtering technique combined with a multi-resolution index structure that are an array of R^*-trees. In the range step of k-NN search, the method introduces improved range search by including the information of point objects in nodes of R^*-trees, and range search for many queries can be performed simultaneously. The experimental results show that for static queries in streaming time-series, the reduced tolerance-based k-NN search outperforms the traditional k-NN search. Finally yet importantly, with the proposed method, we have recorded the average CPU times for processing a new-coming data point of in case of the system handling time-series streams sequentially, and in case of the system handling time-series streams simultaneously. The results show multi-threading makes the approach increase approximately 4 times in speed. From the extensive experiments, the proposed method combined with multi-threading presents a fast response to process high-speed time-series streams for k-NN search of static queries.

As for future work, we plan to adjust the proposed method to handle k-NN search for streaming queries in high-speed streaming time-series.

References

1. Yang, Q., Wu, X.: 10 challenging problems in data mining research. International Journal of Information Technology and Decision Making (2006)
2. Fu, T.-C.: A review on time series data mining. Journal of Engineering Applications of Artificial Intelligence (24), 164–181 (2011)
3. Kontaki, M., Papadopoulos, A., Manolopoulos, Y.: Adaptive similarity search in streaming time series with sliding windows. Data and Knowledge Engineering **16**(6), 478–502 (2007)
4. Liu, X., Ferhatosmanoglu, H.: Efficient k-NN search on streaming data series. In: Hadzilacos, T., Manolopoulos, Y., Roddick, J., Theodoridis, Y. (eds.) SSTD 2003. LNCS, vol. 2750, pp. 83–101. Springer, Heidelberg (2003)
5. Giao, B., Anh, D.: Efficient similarity search for static queries in streaming time series. In: Proceedings of the 2014 International Conference on Green and Human Information Technology, HoChiMinh City, pp. 259–265 (2014)
6. Korn, F., Sidirapoulos, N., Faloutsos, C., Siegel, E., Protopapas, Z.: Fast nearest neighbor search in medical databases. In: Proceedings of the 22nd International Conference on Very Large Data Bases, Bombay, India, pp. 215–226 (1996)
7. Lee, S., Kim, B.-S., Choi, M.-J., Moon, Y.-S.: An approximate multi-step k-NN search in time-series databases. Advances in Computer Science and its Applications **279**, 173–178 (2014)
8. Beckmann, N., Kriegel, H.-P., Schneider, R., Seeger, B.: The R*-tree: an efficient and robust access method for points and rectangles. In: ACM SIGMOD International Conference on Management of Data, Atlantic City, New Jersey, USA, pp. 322–331 (1990)
9. Agrawal, R., Faloutsos, C., Swami, A.: Efficient similarity search in sequence databases. In: Lomet, D.B. (ed.) FODO 1993. LNCS, vol. 730, pp. 69–84. Springer, Heidelberg (1993)
10. Chan, K.-P., Fu, A.: Efficient time series matching by wavelets. In: Proceedings of the 15th IEEE International Conference on Data Engineering, pp. 126–133 (1999)
11. Keogh, E., Chakrabarti, K., Mehrotra, S., Pazzani, M.: Locally adaptive dimensionality reduction for indexing large time series databases. In: Proceedings of the 2001 ACM SIGMOD International Conference on Management of Data, pp. 151–163 (2001)
12. West, M.: http://www.isds.duke.edu/~mw/data-sets/ts_data/ (accessed December 2013)
13. Weigend, A.: Time series prediction: Forecasting the future and understanding the past. http://www-psych.stanford.edu/~andreas/Time-Series/SantaFe.html (accessed December 2013)
14. Group, M.: Electricity Authority's market data and reporting portal. ftp://ftp.emi.ea.govt.nz/Datasets/ (accessed December 2013)

Reconstructing Low Degree Triangular Parametric Surfaces Based on Inverse Loop Subdivision

Nga Le-Thi-Thu[1](✉), Khoi Nguyen-Tan[1], and Thuy Nguyen-Thanh[2]

[1] Danang University of Science and Technology, Danang, Vietnam
lenga248@gmail.com, ntkhoi@dut.udn.vn
[2] Vietnam National University, Hanoi, Vietnam
nguyenthanhthuy@vnu.edu.vn

Abstract. In this paper, we present an efficient local geometric approximate method for reconstruction of a low degree triangular parametric surface using inverse Loop subdivision scheme. Our proposed technique consists of two major steps. First, using the inverse Loop subdivision scheme to simplify a given dense triangular mesh and employing the result coarse mesh as a control mesh of the triangular Bézier surface. Second, fitting this surface locally to the data points of the initial triangular mesh. The obtained parametric surface is approximate to all data points of the given triangular mesh after some steps of local surface fitting without solving a linear system. The reconstructed surface has the degree reduced to at least of a half and the size of control mesh is only equal to a quarter of the given mesh. The accuracy of the reconstructed surface depends on the number of fitting steps k, the number of reversing subdivision times i at each step of surface fitting and the given distance tolerance ε. Through some experimental examples, we also demonstrate the efficiency of our method. Results show that this approach is simple, fast, precise and highly flexible.

Keywords: Triangular Bézier · Parametric surface · Loop subdivision · Reconstructing surface · Surface Fitting

1 Introduction

Modeling method using 3D mesh to describe a surface of an object in the real world is widely used in fields. It consists of small polygonal pieces that can be linked together. These small pieces are often triangles or quadrangles. Beside the 3D meshes, the parametric surfaces have also proven to be the most popular representation method for their specific characteristics including continuousness, smoothness and exact processing [18]. Both of them play an important role for versatile design and research tool in many fields [19], such as Computer Graphic (CG), Computer Aided Geometric Design (CAGD), Reverse Engineering (RE) and Virtual Reality (VR), simulating the surfaces of topography, ect...with applications ranging from simulated surgeries to animated films in the movie industry.

The smooth surface reconstruction from the data points of the given polygon mesh, which surface is recreated in the computer and conserved most of its physical charac-

© Institute for Computer Sciences, Social Informatics and Telecommunications Engineering 2015
P.C. Vinh et al. (Eds.): ICTCC 2014, LNICST 144, pp. 98–107, 2015.
DOI: 10.1007/978-3-319-15392-6_10

teristics, is a difficult and challenging problem because of the following reasons: constructing control polygon meshes, complicated procedures of refinement and reparameterization.

The most of methods interpolate or approximate the parametric surfaces or sudivision surfaces from rectangular meshes. The rectangular surfaces as tensor-product surfaces, are reconstructed by solving linear equation systems, solving a least squares problem and it is difficult to control locally [11,12]. Recently, the iterative geometric fitting methods that do not require the solution of a linear system studied and improved. However, those methods recreated the subdivision surfaces [2,7,14,16] or rectangular parametric surfaces [1, 15, 17] as tensor-product Bézier, tensor-product B-splines by using the initial mesh as the control mesh of fitting surface and so they required that the number of control vertices is equal to the number of data points. The most of the input data is large, so the degree of reconstructed parametric surface is very high.

The Bézier surface is a common form of the paramatric surface and a mathematical description of the surface very used in computer graphics as it is much smoother and compact than mesh. We can distinguish a triangular Bézier surface from a rectangular surface by basing on the basic function over the parameter domain, as known Bernstein polynomial, and the number of control points. Comparing with the rectangular paramatric surfaces, the triangular ones allow to join flexibly and suit arbitrary topological type. The other hand, since the triangular Bernstein basic function is more complex than both the rectangular Bernstein and B-spline basic function, the research of multivariata Bernstein basis over a triangular doman is very significant and still an open question.

Besides, the subdivision surfaces have also become very popular in the computer graphics and geometric modeling domain. They have been applied widely for the representation and manipulation of multiresolution surfaces having arbitrary topological type. There are many subdivision schemes that have been studied and applied such as subdivision schemes of Catmull-Clark, Doo-Sabin, Loop, etc [5]. The Loop subdivision scheme is popularly applied to an arbitrary triangular mesh based on the method called approximate vertex insertion [3]. Inverse subdivision aims at constructing a coarse mesh from a given dense mesh. As the inverse subdivision can be stopped after each step, different multiresolution representation can be obtained. Thus, we want to benefit by the inverse subdivision scheme for the simplification of subdivision meshes.

In this paper, we propose an efficient local geometric approximate method for reconstruction of a low degree triangular parametric surface using inverse Loop subdivision scheme. Our proposed technique consists of two major steps. First, using the inverse Loop subdivision scheme to simplify the given dense triangular mesh and employing the result coarse mesh as a control mesh of the triangular Bézier surface. Second, fitting this surface locally to data points of the initial triangular mesh. The obtained parametric surface is approximate to all data points of the given triangular mesh after some steps of local surface fitting. In contrast with traditional reconstruction methods, our method does not solve linear systems. Therefore, this approach completely avoids the parametric dependency problem.

The main contribution of our work is that we proposed an efficient method for re-constructing a triangular Bézier surface from data points of the initial triangular mesh. The reconstructed surface has degree reduced to at least of a half and the size of control mesh is only equal to a quarter of the given mesh. The accuracy of the reconstructed surface depends on the number of fitting steps k, the number of reversing subdivision times i at each step of fitting and the given distance tolerance ε.

The remainder of this article is organized as follows. We describe the inverse Loop subdivision scheme and the triangular Bézier surface in Section 2. In Section 3, an efficient approximate method to recreate the parametric surface from the triangular mesh is proposed. And Section 4 presents some experimental results. Finally, some concluding remarks are drawn in the last Section 5.

2   Inverse Loop Subdivision and Triangular Bézier Surface

In order to simplify the given dense triangular mesh by using an inverse subdivision scheme and employing the result coarse mesh as a control mesh of the triangular Bézier parametric surface, we describe the inverse Loop subdivision scheme and the triangular Bezier surface in this section.

2.1   Inverse Loop Subdivision

Loop subdivision [3] is a process that add new vertices and new faces to a coarse arbitrary triangular mesh to create a finer triangular mesh by breaking triangular faces of this coarse mesh into the smaller triangular faces. In each step of Loop subdivision, to add the new vertices and faces in a triangular mesh, each triangular face is divided into four smaller new triangular faces by splitting each of them and connecting new vertices together (Fig 1).

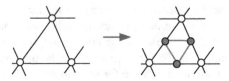

Fig. 1. Each triangular is replaced by the four smaller new triangles

Let us consider an initial coarse triangular mesh $M^0(m)$ with m data points $\{P_j^0 \mid_{j=1...m}\}$. From the initial mesh M^0, by applying the Loop subdivision successively through masks or transformative matrices, a hierarchy of meshes M^1, M^2, M^3, etc is generated then gradually converges to the smooth surface of object. After each step i of Loop subdivision, the vertices of meshes M^i include two types:

- The old vertices of the triangular mesh are modified, which are called vertex-vertices (e.g. vertex p^i of mesh M^i corresponding to vertex p^{i-1} of mesh M^{i-1} in Figure 2).

▪ The new vertices are inserted into the edges of the triangular mesh, which are called edge -vertices (e.g. vertices $p^i_j \mid_{j=1,2,3...l}$ of mesh M^i corresponding to edges of M^{i-1} in Figure 2).

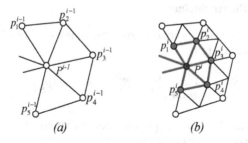

(a)   *(b)*

Fig. 2. A segment of a triangular mesh before (a) and after (b) Loop subdivision

The inverse of Loop subdivision aims at constructing a coarser triangular mesh from the given fine triangular mesh. As the inverse Loop subdivision can be stopped after each step, different multiresolution representation can be obtained.

To reverse Loop subdivision, we have to construct the exact formulas to map the set of vertices of mesh M^i into the set of vertices of mesh M^{i-1}. Assume that the positions of edge-vertices and vertex-vertices in Loop subdivision scheme are correlative with the α and β weights. We have to determine the positions of vertex p^{i-1} from vertices p^i and $p^i_j \mid_{j=1,2,3...l}$. In other words, we must determine the weights η and μ correlative with the α and β weights by using inverse formulas. The expression of the inverse vertex-vertices p^{i-1} based on p^i and the neighbor vertices $p^i_j \mid_{j=1,2,3...l}$ of mesh M^i is determined as follows:

$$p^{i-1} = \mu.p^i + \eta.\sum_{j=1}^{l} p^i_j \qquad (1)$$

With $\alpha = \frac{1}{l}\left(\frac{5}{8} - \left(\frac{3}{8} + \frac{1}{4}\cos\left(\frac{2\pi}{l}\right)\right)^2\right)$; $\beta = 1 - l\alpha$

$$\mu = \frac{5}{8\beta - 3} \text{ and } \eta = \frac{\beta - 1}{n\left(\beta - \frac{3}{8}\right)} \qquad (2)$$

where l is valence of vertex p^i .

For the boundary vertices, by applying the inverse masks for cubic B-spline of Bartels and Samavati [13], we have the inverse formula:

$$P^{i-1} = -\frac{1}{2}P_1^i + 2P^i - \frac{1}{2}P_2^i \qquad (3)$$

2.2   Triangular Bézier Surface

A triangular Bézier parametric surface S over the triangular domain $\Delta(A,B,C)$ defined by the following equation [18]:

$$S(u,v,w) = \sum_{i+j+k=n} B_{i,j,k}^n(u,v,w)p_{ijk} \qquad (4)$$

where n is the degree of surface, p_{ijk} are the control points of the control polyhedron with $(n+1)(n+2)/2$ points, $u+v+w=1$ and

$$B_{i,j,k}^n(u,v,w) = \frac{n!}{i!\,j!\,k!} u^i v^j w^k \qquad (5)$$

is called a Bernstein polynomial over the triangular domain Δ.

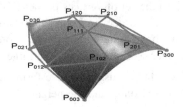

Fig. 3. A triangular Bézier parametric surface for degree 3

A triangular Bézier parametric surface has shape properties as follows: convex hull property, end point interpolation, end point tangency, the boundary curves are Bézier curves formed by the boundary control points and affine invariance. The degree of the triangular Bernstein polynomial function is lower than the rectangular one and the control polyhedron is a triangular mesh, so the triangular Bézier surface allow to perform the surface of 3D objects flexibly.

Let us consider a triangular mesh $M^0(m)$ with m data points, the degree n of the triangular Bezier surface which has $M^0(m)$ as its control mesh is determined as follows:

$$n = \frac{1}{2}(\sqrt{1+8m} - 3) \qquad (6)$$

After steps of reversing Loop subdivision i, the degree of triangular Bézier surface will be equal to $n/2^i$. Then, the number of reversing Loop subdivision i must satisfy the following condition:

$$0 < i \le log_2(\frac{1}{2}(\sqrt{1+8m}-3))$$ (7)

3 Reconstructing the Low Degree Parametric Surface

In this section, we proposed a geometric approximate method to reconstruct the parametric surface S from the given triangular mesh $M^0(m)$ with m data points sampled from the surface of 3D object.

By using the inverse Loop subdivision scheme to simplify the given dense triangular mesh and employing the vertices of this result coarse mesh as the control vertices of a triangular Bézier surface. After that, this parametric surface is locally translated to gradually converge to an ideal smooth surface that pass thought all data points of the initial triangular mesh. After some steps of local surface fitting, the obtained parametric surface is approximate to all data points of the given triangular mesh. The proposed method is presented by diagram in figure 4.

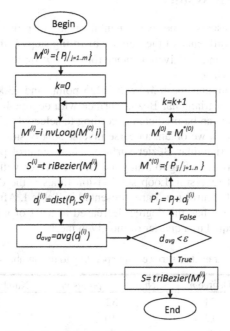

Fig. 4. Approximative surface fitting algorithm

with denoting the expressions as followings:

- $M^{(0)}=\{\ P_j|_{j=1..m}\ \}$ is the initial triangular mesh with P_j are data points sampled from the surface of 3D object.
- $M^{(i)}=invLoop(M^{(0)}, i)$ is the triangular mesh $M^{(0)}$ after i steps of reversing of Loop subdivision.

- $S^{(i)}=triBezier(M^{(i)})$ is the triangular Bézier parametric surface with the control mesh $M^{(i)}$.
- $d_j^{(i)}=dist(P_j,S^{(i)})$ is the distance from point P_j of the given mesh $M^{(0)}$ to the parametric surface $S^{(i)}$.
- $d_{avg}^{(i)}=avg(d_j^{(i)})$ is average of the distances $d_j^{(i)}$.
- P_j^* is point P_j after fitting.
- $M^{*(0)}$ is the triangular mesh that is reconstructed by the new points P_j^*.

The quality and accuracy of the reconstructed surface depends on the number of fitting steps k, the number of reversing subdivision times i at each step of fitting and the given distance tolerance ε.

Considering this computation cost is a constant time, the projections of initial mesh points P_j are executed m times, and suppose that the repeat-until iterates for k times. The value k depends on given tolerance ε. Then the approximative surface fitting algorithm has an asymptotic complexity $\theta(m \times k)$.

4 Experimental Results

In this section, we presents some experimental results to prove the effective of the proposed method, the influence of the number of fitting steps k, the number of reversing subdivision times i and the given distance tolerance ε on the quality and accuracy of the reconstructed surface.

Given an initial triangular mesh M^0 with 1225 points and 2304 faces, corresponding to a control mesh of triangular Bézier surface with degree 48. The size of the inverse subdivision mesh can be predicted according to selected value of i. After $i=4$ of inverse subdivision steps, we obtain a coarse inverse subdivision mesh used as a control polyhedron of a triangular Bézier surface. These control polyhedrons have 10 points and 9 faces, corresponding to triangular Bézier surface with degree 3. The relative of the number of reversing Loop subdivision times i, the degree of parametric surface and the size of control mesh are presented in Table I. After each step of local fitting, the result surface has the degree decreased at least of a half and the size of control mesh is only equal to a quarter of the given mesh.

Table 1. The degree of parametric surface corresponding to the number of inverse subdivision

i	Degree n	Number of points m	Number of faces
1	24	325	576
2	12	91	144
3	6	28	36
4	3	10	9

Figure 5a uses the initial mesh as the control mesh of parametric surface, and figure 5b uses the control mesh of parametric which is the initial mesh simplified by $i=2$ steps of reversing subdivision. Result shows that in case of the obtained parametric surfaces both are equivalent together, but the degree of the second surface reduced to 2^i times.

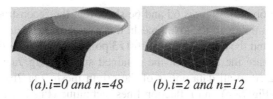

(a).i=0 and n=48   *(b).i=2 and n=12*

Fig. 5. The result surface after i times of inverse subdivision with $k=1$

In order to prove the influence of the number of fitting steps k and the given distance tolerance ε for the convergence of parametric surface to the initial mesh, we analyse the convergence by the maximum distances d_{max} and average distances d_{avg} between the initial mesh points and the reconstructed approximative surface.

Table II shows the distance values d_{max} and d_{avg} depend to the number of fitting steps k. As expected, the higher the number k of surface fitting step, the smaller distance values. This is said that the result surface quickly converge to the parametric surface which is interpolate to the data points after several steps of local geometric fitting.

Table 2. The distance values depend to the number of fitting steps k

k	d_{max}	d_{avg}
1	0.01076160	0.003063370
2	0.00669807	0.001669370
3	0.00490922	0.001163310
4	0.00396409	0.000929139
5	0.00300018	0.000704332

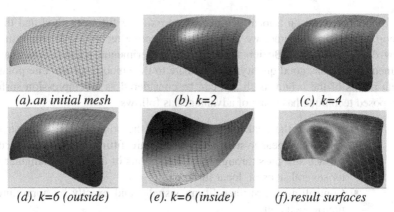

(a).an initial mesh   *(b). k=2*   *(c). k=4*

(d). k=6 (outside)   *(e). k=6 (inside)*   *(f).result surfaces*

Fig. 6. The initial triangular mesh and the obtained approximate parametric surface after k steps of local geometric fitting

Figure 6a illustrates an initial triangular mesh M^0 with 561 points and 1024 faces, corresponding to a control mesh of triangular Bézier surface with degree $n=32$. After $k=2,4,6$ steps of local fitting, the triangular Bézier surface quickly converge to the given mesh (Fig 6b,c,d). Figures 6d and 6e show that the reconstructed surfaces pass through most data points of the given mesh. It is a triangular Bézier surface which has the degree $n=16$ and the control mesh with 153 points và 256 faces (Fig 6f).

Figure 7 compare the quality of the obtained surface (Fig 7a,c) with the smooth surface interpolated to all data points of the origin mesh (Fig 7b,d) by texture mapping technique (Fig 7a,b) and reflection lines technique (Fig 7c,d) after $k=4$ steps of local fitting. The result shows that, the reconstructed surface has good quality, approximate the smooth surface interpolated to all data points of the origin mesh.

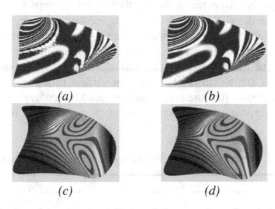

(a)   *(b)*

(c)   *(d)*

Fig. 7. The obtained surface after $k =4$ (a,c) and the smooth surface interpolated to all data points of the origin mesh (b,d).

5   Conclusions

In this paper, base on a local geometric approximate fitting method and the inverse Loop subdivision scheme, we proposed an effective technique for reconstructing of low degree triangular Bézier surfaces. The experimental results show that the obtained surface has good quality, approximate to the smooth surface interpolated to all data points of the origin mesh and can be considered as a compression surface. Our proposed technique has some of advantages as follows:

- Avoiding the peak point problem of the control mesh reconstruction by solving a linear system and least-square fitting method, the recontructed surface still pass through most data points of the initial triangular mesh after several steps of local surface fitting.
- Controlling the surface fitting visually and exactly by approximate geometric technique.
- The obtained parametric surface has the degree reduced to at least of a half and the size of control mesh is only equal to a quarter comparing to methods which use the given mesh as a control mesh of the reconstructed surface.
- The proposed technique apply to triangular meshes, so it take over advantage of triangular meshes and parametric surfaces on triangular doman.

With the inverse Loop subdivision as the control mesh of the parametric surface on triangular doman, our method is promising in areas such as mesh compression, surface editing and manipulation and versatile design, ect.

References

1. Deng, C., Lin, H.: Progressive and iterative approximation for least squares B-spline curve and surface fitting. Computer-Aided Design **47**, 32–44 (2014)
2. Deng, C., Ma, W.: Weighted progressive interpolation of Loop subdivision surfaces. Computer-Aided Design **44**, 424–431 (2012)
3. Loop, C.: Smooth Subdivision Surfaces Based on Triangles. M.S. Mathematics thesis (1987)
4. Zhou, C.Z.: On the convexity of parametric Bézier triangular surfaces. CAGD 7(6) (1990)
5. Zorin, D., Schroder, P., Levin, A., Kobbelt, L., Swelden, W., DeRose, T.: Subdivision for Modeling and Animation. Course Notes, SIGGRAPH (2000)
6. Yoo, D.J.: Three-dimensional surface reconstruction of human bone using a B-spline based interpolation approach. Computer-Aided Design **43**(8), 934–947 (2011)
7. Cheng, F., Fan, F., Lai, S., Huang, C., Wang, J., Yong, J.: Loop subdivision surface based progressive interpolation. Journal of Computer Science and Technology **24**, 39–46 (2009)
8. Farin, G.E., Piper, B., et al.: The octant of a sphere as a non-degenerate triangular Bézier patch. Computer Aided Geometric Design **4**(4), 329–332 (1987)
9. Chen, J., Wang, G.J.: Progressive-iterative approximation for triangular Bézier surfaces. Computer-Aided Design **43**(8), 889–895 (2011)
10. Lu, L.: Weighted progressive iteration approximation and convergence analysis. Computer Aided Geometric Design **27**(2), 129–137 (2010)
11. Eck, M., Hoppe, H.: Automatic reconstruction of B-spline surfaces of arbitrary topological type. In: Proceedings of SIGGRAPH 1996, pp. 325–334. ACM Press (1996)
12. Halstead, M., Kass, M., Derose, T.: Efficient, fair interpolation using Catmull-Clark surfaces. Proceedings of ACM SIGGRAPH **93**, 35–44 (1993)
13. Bartels, R.H., Samavati, F.F.: Reverse Subdivision Rules: Local Linear Conditions and Observations on Inner Products. Journal of Computational and Applied Mathematics (2000)
14. Maekawa, T., Matsumoto, Y., Namiki, K.: Interpolation by geometric algorithm. Computer-Aided Design **39**, 313–323 (2007)
15. Kineri, Y., Wang, M., Lin, H., Maekawa, T.: B-spline surface fitting by iterative geometric interpolation/approximation algorithms. Computer-Aided Design **44**(7), 697–708 (2012)
16. Nishiyama, Y., Morioka, M., Maekawa, T.: Loop subdivision surface fitting by geometric algorithms. In: Poster Proceedings of Pacific Graphics (2008)
17. Xiong, Y., Li, G., Mao, A.: Convergence analysis for B-spline geometric interpolation. Computers & Graphics **36**, 884–891 (2012)
18. Piegl, L., Tiller, W.: The NURBS Book, 2nd edn. Springer, Berlin (1997)
19. Farin, G.: Curves and Surfaces for Computer Aided Geometric Design: A Practical Guide, 5th edn. Morgan Kaufmann, San Mateo (2002)

Maximizing the Lifetime of Wireless Sensor Networks with the Base Station Location

Nguyen Thanh Tung[1(✉)], Dinh Ha Ly[2], and Huynh Thi Thanh Binh[2]

[1] International School, Vietnam National University, Hanoi, Vietnam
tungnt@isvnu.vn
[2] Hanoi University of Science and Technology, Hanoi, Vietnam
greeny255@gmail.com, binhht@soict.hust.edu.vn

Abstract. Nowadays, wireless sensor networks (WSNs) have been increasingly applied in many different areas and fields. However, one major defect of WSNs is limited energy resources, which affects the network lifetime strongly. A wireless sensor network includes a sensor node set and a base station. The initial energy of each sensor node will be depleted gradually during data transmission to the base station either directly or through other sensor nodes, depending on the distance between the sending node and the receiving node. This paper considers specifying a location for the base station such that it can minimize the consumed energy of each sensor node in transmitting data to that base station, in other words, maximizing the network lifetime. We propose a nonlinear programming model for this optimal problem. Four methods, respectively named as the centroid, the smallest total distances, the smallest total squared distances and greedy method, for finding the base station location are also presented, experimented and compared to each other over 30 data sets that are created randomly. The experimental results show that a relevant location for the base station is essential.

Keywords: Base Station Location · Wireless Sensor Network · Routing · Non-Linear Programming

1 Introduction

Nowadays, with the considerable development of integrated circuit engineering, embedded systems and the strong power of network, it is inevitable for the birth of wireless sensor networks.

Wireless Sensor Network (WSN) is a network of sensor nodes in which network nodes are placed in such areas that can collect, exchange then send information to the base station through their sensor function, not links. By this way, it is possible to deploy WSN on almost all types of terrains simply. Hence, people can be aware of dangerous or hard to reach areas easily and frequently. Sensor nodes can collect information related to humidity, temperature, concentration of pesticides, noise, etc; which makes WSN applicable to many fields such as environment, heath, military, industry, agriculture….

Although the benefit of WSNs is extremely great, its one major defect is limited energy resources. When energy source of a sensor node runs out, this node dies,

© Institute for Computer Sciences, Social Informatics and Telecommunications Engineering 2015
P.C. Vinh et al. (Eds.): ICTCC 2014, LNICST 144, pp. 108–116, 2015.
DOI: 10.1007/978-3-319-15392-6_11

which means it can no longer collect, exchange as well as send information to the base station. And the WSN, therefore, will not be able to complete its mission.

In this paper, we are interested in how to use sensor nodes' energy effectively, in other words, to maximize the lifetime of WSNs. We consider the model in which all sensor nodes in the network are responsible for sending data to the base station in every specified period. When a sensor node sends data, its consumed energy depends on the distance between it and the node which receives data. In this research, we suppose that energy for transmitting a data unit is directly proportional to the square of distance between two nodes.

In [1, 2, 3, 6, 7, 12], the base station is placed at a random location. However, the fact shows that the location needs to be optimized. This paper proposes four methods that are the centroid, the smallest total distances, the smallest total squared distances and the greedy method to specify this optimal location. Also, we propose a nonlinear programming model for optimizing the WSN lifetime and use this model to evaluate our proposed methods over 30 randomly created data sets . The experimental results show that a relevant location for the base station is essential, which proves our correct research way.

The rest of this paper is organized as follows: Section 2 describes the related works. Mathematical model for this problem is introduced in section 3. Four methods for specifying the base station location is showed in section 4. Section 5 gives our experiments as well as computational and comparative results. The paper concludes with discussions and future works in section 6.

2   Related Works

Until now, the problem of maximizing the lifetime of WSNs has received a huge interest of the researchers. According to [1], there have two different approaches for maximizing the network lifetime. One is the indirect approach aiming to minimize energy consumption, while the other one directly aims to maximize network lifetime.

With the indirect approach, the authors [2] gave a method to calculate energy consumption in WSNs depending on the number of information packets sent or the number of nodes. Then they proposed the optimal transmission range between nodes to minimize total amount of consumed energy. With this method, the total energy consumption is reduced by 15% to 38%.

Cheng et al. formulated a constrained multivariable nonlinear programming problem to specify both the locations of the sensor nodes and data transmission patterns [3]. The authors proposed a greedy placement scheme in which all nodes run out of energy at the same time. The greed of this scheme is that each node tries to take the best advantage of its energy resource, prolonging the network lifetime. They reason that node i should not directly send data to node j if $j \geq i + 2$ because communication over long links is not desirable. Their greedy scheme offered an optimal placement strategies that is more efficient than a commonly used uniform placement scheme.

In [12] proposed a network model for heterogeneous networks, a set of Ns sensors is deployed in a region in order to monitor some physical phenomenon. The complete set of sensors that has been deployed can be referred as $S=\{s1......sN\}$. Sensor i

generates traffic at a rate of ri bps. All of the data that is generated must eventually reach a single data sink, labeled $s0$. Let $q_{i,j}$ be traffic on the link (i,j) during the time T. The network scenario parameters also include the traffic generation rate ri for each sensor. The power model in [6,7,10,12,13], is used, where the amount of energy to transmit a bit can be represented as:

The total transmission energy of a message of k bits in sensor networks is calculated by:

$$E_t = E_{elec} + \varepsilon_{FS}d^2$$

and the reception energy is calculated by:

$$E_r = E_{elec}$$

where E_{elec} represents the electronics energy, ε_{FS} is determined by the transmitter amplifier's efficiency and the channel conditions, d represents the distance over which data is being communicated.

Maximize: T

Subject to:

$$\sum_{j=1}^{N} q_{j,i} + r_i T = \sum_{j=0}^{N} q_{i,j} : \forall i \in [1...N] \qquad (1)$$

$$\sum_{j=0}^{N} (E_{elec} + \varepsilon_{FS}d^2)q_{i,j} + \sum_{j=1}^{N} E_{elec}q_{j,i} <= E_i : \forall i \in [1...N] \qquad (2)$$

$$q_{i,j} >= 0 : \forall i, j \in [1...n] \qquad (3)$$

3   Problem Formulation of Maximizing the Lifetime of Wireless Sensor Networks with the Base Station Location

A sensor network is modeled as a complete undirected graph $G = (V, L)$ where V is the set of nodes including the base station (denoted as node 0) and L be the set of links between the nodes. The size of V is N. The link between node i and node j shows that node i can send data to node j and vice versa. Each node i has the initial battery energy of E_i. Let Q_i be the amount of traffic generated or sank at node i. Let d_{ij} be the distance between node i and node j. Let T be the time until the first sensor node runs out of energy. Let q_{ij} be the traffic on the link $L_{(ij)}$ during the time T. The problem of maximizing the lifetime of the wireless sensor networks with the base station is formulated as follows:

Maximize: T

Subject to:

$$\sum_{j=1}^{N} q_{ji} + QT = \sum_{j=0}^{N} q_{ij} : \forall i \in [1...N] \tag{4}$$

$$\sum_{j=1}^{N} q_{ij} d_{ij}^2 + q_{i0}[(x_i - x_0)^2 + (y_i - y_0)^2] <= E_i : \forall i \in [1...N] \tag{5}$$

$$\sum_{i=1}^{N} q_{i0} = Q_0 \tag{6}$$

$$q_{ij} >= 0 : \forall i, j \in [0...N] \tag{7}$$

$$x_0, y_0, T : Variable$$

In which, (x_i, y_i) is coordinate of node i in the 2-dimensional space.

4   Four Methods for Specifying the Base Station Location

To maximizing the lifetime of WSNs, the base station location not only is close, but also balances distances with as many sensor nodes as possible. This guarantees that sensor nodes do not consume too much energy in transmitting data to the base station and no sensor node depletes its energy much faster than other nodes. The center of network seems to be in accord with this requirement. However, there are many definitions for the center of network, each definition gives different locations. So this paper proposes four methods corresponding to four different "center" definitions to specify the center of network that is also the base station location.

These four methods are named respectively as the centroid, the smallest total distances, the smallest total squared distances and the greedy methods. After this base station location is determined, the model in section 3 becomes a linear optimal one. By using a tool to find the lifetime of WSN, we can evaluate quality of this base station location as well as that of these methods. Four methods are as follows:

The Centroid Method: defines the base station location as the centroid of all sensor nodes. This location is calculated by (8).

$$x_0 = \frac{\sum_{i=1}^{N} x_i}{N-1}, y_0 = \frac{\sum_{i=1}^{N} y_i}{N-1} \tag{8}$$

The Smallest Total Distances Method: the base station location is a point such that the Euclidean distance summation from it to all sensor nodes is the smallest one. This point satisfies (9). With this definition, easily seen, the base station location should be a point in the convex hull of all sensor nodes. However, for the sake of simplicity, this location is found in the smallest rectangle surrounding all sensor nodes.

$$Min: \sum_{i=1}^{N} \sqrt{(x_i - x_0)^2 + (y_i - y_0)^2} \tag{9}$$

The Smallest Total Squared Distances Method: it is similar to the smallest total distances one, but the base station location has to satisfy that the sum squared distances from it to all sensor nodes is the smallest.

$$Min: \sum_{i=1}^{N} (x_i - x_0)^2 + (y_i - y_0)^2 \tag{10}$$

The Greedy Method: defines a sensor set includes sensor nodes and a delegate center. If the set has only one sensor node, its delegate center is this own sensor node. Also, we define the distance between two sensor sets is the distance between their two delegate centers. The main idea of this method is that starting with one-sensor-node sets (Fig 1(a)), we merge two sets having the smallest distance (sensor node set S1 and S2 in Fig 1(a)). A new delegate center for the merged set (the red node in Fig 1(b)) is specified as follows: this center is on the line segment connecting two old delegate centers and splits this line into two segments with proportional by p. The sensor sets is merged until only one set remains. The delegate center of this last set is the base station location (The green node in Fig 1(c)).

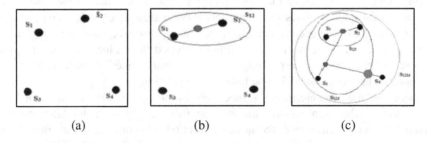

Fig. 1. Illustration of the greedy method

5   Experimental Results

5.1   Problem Instances

In our experiments, we created 30 random instances denoted as *TPk* in which k ($k = 1$, $2,..., 30$) shows ordinal number of a instance. Each instance consists of l lines. Each line has two numbers representing coordinate of a sensor node in the 2-dimensional space.

5.2   System Setting

The parameters in our experiments were set as follows:

Table 1. The experiment parameters

Parameter	Value
The network size	100m x 100m
Number of sensor nodes - l	30
Initial energy of each node - E	1 J
Ratio p in method 4	$\dfrac{\sqrt{cx}}{\sqrt{cy}}$ with cx, cy is the number of sensor nodes in two old sensor sets.
Energy model	$E_{elec} = 50 * 10^{-9}$ J $\varepsilon_{fs} = 10 * 10^{-12}$ J/bit/m^2 $\varepsilon_{mp} = 0.0013 * 10^{-12}$ J/bit/m^4

5.3   Computational Results

Table 2 presents the base station location found by four methods in the section 4 for 30 random instances. The results of the centroid, the smallest total distances, the smallest total squared distances and the greedy method is in BS1, BS2, BS3 and BS4 column respectively. Through this table, we can see that the centroid and the smallest total square distances method gave extremely close locations over all instances. The difference between locations found by these four methods for each instance is inconsiderable.

The lifetime of 30 WSNs corresponding to 30 instances is showed in the table 3. These lifetime were found by using the tool with the found base station locations in the table 2. The maximum lifetime of each instance is traced with green.

The greedy method gave the best lifetime over 20 instances, the best lifetime with the base station location found by the centroid method is over 8 instances, by the smallest total squared distances method is over 7 instances and by the smallest total distances method is over 5 instances.

The lifetime with the base station location of the centroid method and the smallest total squared distances method is about the same over all data sets, which can be explained by the relatively same coordinate of these base station locations.

Despite giving the second best base station location, the centroid is the simplest method which is suitable to real-time or limited computing systems.

The difference among the network lifetimes corresponding to the base station location gave by four methods over all instances shows that the location for the base station should be optimized as mentioned in the section 1.

Table 2. The base station location found by four methods for 30 instances

Ins.	BS1 (x-y)	BS2 (x-y)	BS3 (x-y)	BS4 (x-y)	Ins.	BS1 (x-y)	BS2 (x-y)	BS3 (x-y)	BS4 (x-y)
TP1	55.2-39.9	54-37	55-40	53.1-50.5	TP16	38.3-59.9	36-64	38-60	38.5-54.2
TP2	39.9-55.3	36-60	40-55	40.6-54.8	TP17	59.9-38.5	62-35	60-39	58.1-42.3
TP3	55.3-42.6	55-41	55-43	52.6-53.0	TP18	38.5-61.2	35-66	39-61	38.9-55.0
TP4	42.6-56.2	40-62	43-56	42.1-55.1	TP19	61.2-40.5	64-37	61-41	52.1-40.2
TP5	56.2-42.3	57-39	56-42	52.1-53.4	TP20	40.5-59.6	36-64	41-60	47.0-58.4
TP6	42.3-56.4	39-61	42-56	41.8-55.0	TP21	59.6-40.3	62-37	60-40	57.6-43.4
TP7	56.4-42.9	58-40	56-43	53.3-54.6	TP22	40.3-58.2	36-64	40-58	47.0-57.7
TP8	42.9-56.8	39-63	43-57	44.7-53.6	TP23	58.2-39.0	60-34	58-39	56.8-43.1
TP9	56.8-41.3	59-36	57-41	54.1-53.7	TP24	39.0-55.9	35-63	39-56	45.9-56.3
TP10	41.3-58.4	36-64	41-58	45.9-54.5	TP25	55.9-39.4	58-35	56-39	53.9-44.3
TP11	58.4-42.0	62-38	58-42	54.5-53.5	TP26	39.4-54.6	36-59	39-55	46.2-55.0
TP12	42.0-58.7	36-64	42-59	46.1-54.9	TP27	54.6-41.5	56-38	55-42	53.6-45.5
TP13	58.7-39.9	61-36	59-40	57.4-43.3	TP28	41.5-53.2	39-55	42-53	47.3-54.0
TP14	39.9-59.9	36-65	40-60	46.1-48.9	TP29	53.2-39.4	54-35	53-39	53.9-45.6
TP15	59.9-38.3	62-35	60-38	58.1-41.9	TP30	39.4-50.5	37-51	39-51	45.9-52.6

Table 3. The lifetime of WSNs with the corresponding base station locations in the table 2

Ins.	BS1	BS2	BS3	BS4	Ins.	BS1	BS2	BS3	BS4
TP1	870	811	867	890	TP16	762	739	761	812
TP2	809	652	820	836	TP17	907	907	907	907
TP3	867	845	866	865	TP18	746	726	747	793
TP4	838	885	837	829	TP19	893	870	894	907
TP5	878	839	869	877	TP20	751	695	750	786
TP6	822	832	815	805	TP21	1020	935	1003	1130
TP7	931	926	925	906	TP22	744	682	745	794
TP8	739	706	738	746	TP23	1056	943	1065	1124
TP9	941	910	948	907	TP24	695	587	694	746
TP10	736	700	736	738	TP25	1115	997	1116	1010
TP11	1044	1041	1044	971	TP26	843	741	838	893
TP12	777	722	777	791	TP27	1040	1048	1038	977
TP13	1171	1160	1171	1171	TP28	838	799	845	862
TP14	762	739	762	797	TP29	988	962	988	952
TP15	907	907	907	907	TP30	817	789	810	861

6   Conclusion

In this paper, we proposed a nonlinear programming model for maximizing the lifetime of wireless sensor networks with the base station location. We presented four methods that are the centroid, the smallest total distances, the smallest total squared distances and the greedy method for finding the base station location. These four methods were experimented on 30 random data sets. With the found base station locations, specific lifetime of WSNs were calculated by our model and showed that a relevant location for the base station should be essential.

In the future, we will find a method that provides the best solution in all random topologies tested.

References

1. Dong, Q.: Maximizing System Lifetime in Wireless Sensor Networks. In: Information Processing in Sensor Networks, pp. 13–19 (2005)
2. Shebli, F., CNRS, Dayoub, I., M'foubat, A.O., Rivenq, A., Rouvaen, J.M.: Minimizing Energy Consumption within Wireless Sensors Networks Using Optimal Transmission Range between Nodes. In: Signal Processing and Communications, IEEE International Conference, pp. 105–108 (2007)
3. Cheng, P., Chuah, C.-N., Liu, X.: Energy-aware Node Placement in Wireless Sensor Networks. Global Telecommunications Conference 5, 3210–3214 (2004)
4. Kamyabpour, N., Hoang, D. B.: Modeling Overall Energy Consumption in Wireless Sensor Networks. *arXiv preprint arXiv:1112.5800* (2011)
5. Khan, M. I., Gansterer, W. N., Haring, G.: Static vs. Mobile Sink: The Influence of Basic Parameters on Energy Efficiency in Wireless Sensor Networks. Computer Communications 36(9), 965–978 (2013)
6. Lourthu Hepziba Mercy, M., BalamuruganK., Vijayaraj M.: Maximization of Lifetime and Reducing Power Consumption in Wireless Sensor Network Using Protocol. International Journal of Soft Computing and Engineering 2(6) (2013)
7. Paschalidis, I.C., Wu, R.: Robust Maximum Lifetime Routing and Energy Allocation in Wireless Sensor Networks. International Journal of Distributed Sensor Networks 2012, Article ID 523787, 14 pages (2012)
8. Chang, J.H., Tassiulas, L.: Maximum Lifetime Routing in Wireless Sensor Networks. IEEE/ACM Transactions on Networking 12(4), 609–619 (2004)
9. Giridhar, A., Kumar, P.R.: Maximizing the Functional Lifetime of Sensor Networks. In: Proceedings of the 4th International Symposium on Information Processing in Sensor Networks (IPSN 2005), pp. 5–12 (2005)
10. Nama, H., Mandayam, N.: Sensor Networks over Information Fields: Optimal Energy and Node Distributions. In: Proceedings of the IEEE Wireless Communications and Networking Conference (WCNC 2005), vol. 3, pp. 1842–1847 (2005)

11. Le Thi, H.A., Nguyen, Q.T., Phan, K.T., Pham Dinh, T.: DC Programming and DCA Based Cross-Layer Optimization in Multi-hop TDMA Networks. In: Selamat, A., Nguyen, N.T., Haron, H. (eds.) ACIIDS 2013, Part II. LNCS, vol. 7803, pp. 398–408. Springer, Heidelberg (2013)

12. Cheng, Z., Perillo, M., Heinzelman, W.B.: General Network Lifetime and Cost Models for Evaluating Sensor Network Deployment Strategies. IEEE Transactions on Mobile Computing 7(4), 484–497 (2008)

13. Li, Y., Xiao, G., Singh, G., Gupta, R.: Algorithms for Finding Best Location of Cluster Heads for Minimizing Energy Comsumption in Wireless Sensor Networks. Wireless Network 19(7), 1755–1768 (2013)

Establishing Operational Models for Dynamic Compilation in a Simulation Platform

Nghi Quang Huynh[1($\boxtimes$)], Tram Huynh Vo[2], Hiep Xuan Huynh[1], and Alexis Drogoul[3]

[1] DREAM-CTU/IRD, CICT-CTU, Cantho, Vietnam
{hqnghi,hxhiep}@ctu.edu.vn
[2] Software Engineering Department, CICT-CTU, Cantho, Vietnam
vhtram@ctu.edu.vn
[3] UMI 209 UMMISCO, IRD, Hanoi, Vietnam
alexis.drogoul@ird.fr

Abstract. In this paper we introduce a new approach to dynamic converting conceptual models in a simulation platform as the GAMA platform (represented in form of GAML syntax) into corresponding operational models (represented in form of Java syntax). This approach aims at providing a more flexible solutions to actual simulation models implemented in a simulation platform as the GAMA. This new approach will facilitate the exhibits of a simulation platform to work with different types of simulation models represented in different forms of syntax.

Keywords: Domain-specific language · Operational model · Simulation platform · Dynamic compilation

1 Introduction

GAML [26] is the modeling language of the GAMA platform [22], which was based on XML syntax [3]. This language designed as a simple scripting language for platform of simulation, has grown into a general language dedicated to the modeling (modeling language [24]). From its appearing, the diversity of multi modeling language resulted a difficult challenge to reuse models between platforms, to increase numbers of new features and to have a large developer community. In this context, we propose a generic method of establishing operational model in simulation platforms. Since version 1.4, GAMA has had a developed environment built with the technology XText [4](based on ANTLR [17] grammar) and is considered, ultimately, able to build models directly in Java [5].

The main objective of our work is to convert from a GAML model, represent the Abstract Syntax Tree [11] as one Java class or even one Java project Java which can run alone without the GAMA compiler. From this Java model, we can have another way to combine the models, to attach plugins, and of course to have inheritance of Java. In addition, running the Java models will take less time and memories, gain speed of models processing. With this work, we can

© Institute for Computer Sciences, Social Informatics and Telecommunications Engineering 2015
P.C. Vinh et al. (Eds.): ICTCC 2014, LNICST 144, pp. 117–131, 2015.
DOI: 10.1007/978-3-319-15392-6_12

take a review of what the current grammar can do now, by translation to Java syntax, review the advantages and inconveniences between Java platform and GAMA platform.

This paper will be represented in six parts. The second part introduces related works of three type of model in modeling. In the third part, we talk about our methodology for establishing operational model, due to algorithm of traversing Abstract Syntax Tree and our strategies of creating Java syntax. In the fourth part, this method was implemented into a simulation platform GAMA. Then we'll tell you how our experimental results have been taken in the fifth part, based on converting Bug model with description of model, species, attributes and behaviors. Finally, in sixth part, we give information about our results and ongoing work.

2   Related Work

2.1   From XML to Operational Model

XML [3] has usually been used in modeling domains, which can be considered as an flexible integration approach into modeling and simulation systems [19]. As the effort towards standardization of formalism representations, based on the XML schema definition of a formalism, a binding compiler generates model classes that support the user in constructing models according to the formalism. Although simulators could be built for these declarative model descriptions, they would be hardly efficient. To this end, a separate transformation component is required according to manually pre-defined XML schemas [7].

Other effort of using XML in modeling and simulation is to compose simulations from XML-specified model components [20]. It presents the realization of a component framework that can be added as an additional layer on the top of simulation systems. It builds upon platform independent specifications of components in XML to evaluate dependent relationships and parameters during composition. The process of composition is split up into four stages. Starting from XML documents component instances are created. These can be customized and arranged to form a composition. Finally, the composition is transformed to an executable simulation model.

in the DEVS community , a current notable effort is to provide a worldwide platform for distributed modeling and simulation based on web services and related technologies[24].This infrastructure will allow the sharing and reuse of simulation models and experiments and will permit attacking different aspects of interoperability at the right level of abstraction: the simulation-based interoperability at the level of the data transfer among components in a distributed simulation, the model-based interoperability to share models and experiments. An essential requirement is that a common, unique and complete representation must be adopted to store, retrieve, share and make interoperable simulation models. The author represent all the aspects included in all possible use cases and proposes an XML-based language that can serve as a basis for defining a standard for distributed simulation linking DEVS and non-DEVS simulations.

2.2   From Domain-Specific Language to Operational Model

Domain-specific languages (DSL) [16] are languages tailored to a specific application domain. They offer substantial gains in expressiveness and ease of use compared with general-purpose programming languages in their domain of application. DSL development is hard, and it requires both domain knowledge and language development expertise. Few people have all these two. Not surprisingly, the decision to develop a DSL is often postponed indefinitely, if considered at all, and most DSLs never get beyond the application library stage.

Aspen (Abstract Scalable Performance Engineering Notation) [21] fills an important gap in existing performance modeling techniques and is designed to enable rapidly exploration of new algorithms and architectures. It includes a formal specification of an application's performance behavior and an abstract machine's model. It provides an overview of Aspen's features and demonstrate how it can be used to express a performance model for a three dimensional Fast Fourier Transform [8] . It demonstrates the composability and modularity of Aspen by importing and reusing the FFT model in a molecular dynamics model. It have also created a number of tools that allow scientists to balance application and system factors quickly and accurately.

2.3   Dynamic Compilation

Dynamic compilation [23] is a process used by some programming language implementations to gain performance during program execution. Although the technique is originated in the Self [6] programming language, the best-known language that uses this technique is Java. Since the machine code emitted by a dynamic compiler is constructed and optimized at program runtime, the use of dynamic compilation enables optimizations for efficiency not available to compiled programs except through code duplication or meta-programming. Runtime environments using dynamic compilation typically have programs run slowly for the first few minutes, and after that, most of the compilation and recompilation is done and it runs quickly. Due to this initial performance lag, dynamic compilation is undesirable in certain cases. In most implementations of dynamic compilation, some optimizations that could be done at the initial compile time are delayed until further compilation at run time, causing further unnecessary slowdowns. Just in time compilation is a form of dynamic compilation.

Dynamic compilation bring more and more fast, effective and optimization values [1] [12] due to invariant data computed at run-time. Using the values of these run-time constants, a dynamic compiler can eliminate their memory loads, perform constant propagation and folding, remove branches they determine, and fully unroll loops they bound.

Dynamic compilation increases Java virtual machine (JVM) performance [15] because running compiled codes is faster than interpreting Java byte-codes. However, inappropriate decision on dynamic compilation may degrade performance owing to compilation overhead. A good heuristic algorithm for dynamic compilation should achieve an appropriate balance between compilation overhead and performance gain in each method invocation sequence. A method-size and execution-time heuristic algorithm is proposed in the study.

In brief, dynamic compilation have fully of benefits investing [14]. Dynamic compilation is typically performed in a separate thread, asynchronously with the remaining application threads. It explores a number of issues surrounding asynchronous dynamic compilation in a virtual machine by describing the shortcomings of current approaches and demonstrate their potential to perform poorly under certain conditions. It shown the importance of ensuring a level of utilization for the compilation thread and empirically validate this in a production virtual machine on a large benchmark suite; beside evaluation a range of compilation thread utilizations and quantify the effect on both performance and pause times.

3   From Domain-Specific Language to Operational Model

3.1   What Is a Model?

Model [18], especially scientific model [25], is an abstract construction, that allows to comprehensive functions of the reference system by answering one scientific question. It is an simplify representation of the reference system, relying on generic theory and can be expressed in one specific language which called Modeling language [9].

3.2   Model in a Simulation Platform

Model in simulation platform, especially GAMA, contains 4 main sections:

Global section contains all declaration of variables, parameters at global scope. These declarations can be used anywhere in model. This section also contains starting point when a model is executed, *init* block. This "global" section defines the "world" agent, a special agent of a GAMA model. We can define variables and behaviors for the "world" agent. Variables of "world" agent are global variables thus can be referred by agents of other species or other places in the model source code.

Environment section contains informations about topology which are used by agents. GAMA supports three types of topologies for environments: continuous, grid and graph. By default, the world agent (i.e. the global agent that contains all of the other agents) has a continuous topology. This section could include the definition of one or several environments with grid topology.

Entities section defines of all species which are placed into this section. A model can contain any number of species. Species are used to specify the structure and behaviors of agents. Although the definitions below apply to all the species, some of them require specific declarations: the species of the world and the species of the environmental places.

Experiment section defines experiments to run. Two kinds of experiment are supported: gui (graphic user interface, which displays its input parameters and outputs) and batch (Allows to setup a series of simulations without graphical interface).

3.3   Abstract Syntax Tree

An abstract syntax tree (AST) [11] , is a tree representation of the abstract syntactic structure of source code written in a programming language. Each node of the tree denotes a construct occurring in the source code. The syntax is 'abstract' and doesn't represent every detail appearing in the real syntax. For instance, grouping parentheses are implicit in the tree structure, and a syntactic construction like an if-condition-then expression may be denoted by means of a single node with two branches. This distinguishes abstract syntax trees from concrete syntax trees, traditionally designated parse trees, which are often built by a parser during the source code translation and compiling process. Once built, additional information is added to the AST by means of subsequent processing, e.g., contextual analysis. Abstract syntax trees are also used in program analysis and program transformation systems.

3.4   AST of Operational Model

The current version of GAMA contains five main types of node in AST, with respect to meta-model of Multi-agent systems. There are:

– Model Description: Root node of a model. It contains others children nodes. This "global" section defines the "world" agent, a special agent of a GAMA model. We can define variables and behaviors for the "world" agent. Variables of "world" agent are global variables thus can referred by agents of other species or other places in the model source code.

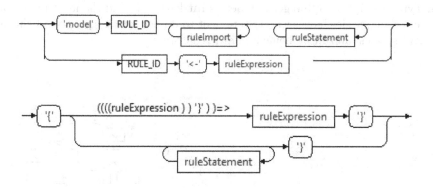

Fig. 1. AST of GAML syntax

– Experiment Description: this type of node describes the inputs, outputs parameters, the way that model would be simulated. Based on concept of MAS, Experiment can be a special species in model.

- Species Description: due to multi-scale hierarchy, a species could be a child of another species, models, or even experiments
- Type Description: more likely in a programming language, we have several base data types, integer, string, double. In fact, modelers can define themself theirs own data types, which is related to complex structures. Especially a species could be a data type, to be declared and assigned as variable later.
- Statement Description: includes simple statement and complex (sequence) statement. It's correspond with the smallest element of programming language. A species can thus contain several statements representing different behaviors that agents of the species can execute. GAMA offers a statement framework that facilitates the extension, i.e., the introduction of new types of agent's behavior. Developer can extend, in case of new needed appear, a new Statement by implement this class.
- Variable Description: In this declaration, information of variables data type refers to the name of a built-in type or a species declared in the model. The value of name can be any combination of letters and digits that does not begin with a digit and that follows certain rules. If the value of the variable is not intended to change over time, it is preferable to declare it as a constant in order to avoid any surprise (and to optimize, a little bit, the compiler's work). This is done with the **const** attribute set to true (if const is not declared, it is considered as false by default):

An example of AST for operational model in GAMA can be found in fig.2. On the right, It's an example in simple model of GAMA. In **entities** section, it's declared 2 species which are type of SpeciesDescription node in AST. In species definition, user can define other children nodes as VariableDescription, TypeDescription, StatementDescription. This example shows the usage of built-in TypeDescription of Integer number as **int** keyword. And the most important description, species have several Statement to do behaviors, e.g. **move** behavior in Ant species, and **hunt** behaviors in Predator.

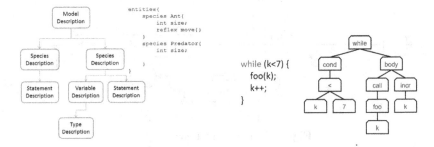

Fig. 2. AST of operational model in GAMA   **Fig. 3.** AST of Java statement

3.5 Converting from GAML Syntax to Operational Model (with Java Syntax)

As both GAMA model and Java program base on a tree (Abstract Syntax Tree), we use the algorithm of traversing to explore AST.

Recursivement, we traverse the AST, from root node. At each node, by considering node's type, compiler will translate into correspond Java syntax. Following pseudo-code describe whole progress.

This function builds a abstract syntax tree which contains each node as Java syntax. It takes input as a GAML_Node, which can be following type: ModelDescription, SpeciesDescription, TypeDescription, VariableDescription, Symbol Description. At first, an empty tree would be created in local scope, with root node that will be created in next steps. This tree has attached the node which was translated in Java syntax. Next, the type of the current node was returned into variable t. Regarding value of this variable, compiler gets pre-defined template as string *tplt*. This template is input parameter of merging method, described in Fig. 5. This method manipulates information of the current node and template *tplt* by combining together at needed XML tag. The output is considered as root node of local tree. The loop of each child node do a recursive calling itself. After calling, root node attachs these results to child node. Finally, method returns thes whole structure tree in Java syntax.

```
1    Function Build Java Tree ( GAML_Node gNode) {
2        Let JavaTree = new tree
3        Let t= type of gNode
4        String tplt=Generate java syntax correspond with type t
5        Node root = Merging description of gNode with template tplt
6        For each child C in gNode
7        {
8            Let tree T = Build JavaTree (C)
9            Add T as child of root
10       }
11       Add tmp as root node of JavaTree
12       Return JavaTree
13   }
```

Fig. 4. Algorithm of traversing on Abstract Syntax Tree, applying to convert from GAML to Java

3.6 Generate Java Syntax

There are 2 types of generating Java syntax. The first way is to use static template, which is pre-defined by programmer. It is used to apply on non-volatile type, like Model, Species's Description, corresponding with a package, a class in Java. The second way is to use more informations inside each node of AST. It's Java annotation, declared for operator, statement and other components.

```
1    Function Build Java Tree ( GAML_Node gNode) {
2        Let JavaTree = new tree
3        Let t= type of gNode
4        String tplt=Generate java syntax correspond with type t
5        Node root = Merging description of gNode with template tplt
6        For each child C in gNode
7        {
8            Let tree T = Build JavaTree (C)
9            Add T as child of root
10       }
11       Add tmp as root node of JavaTree
12       Return JavaTree
13   }
```

Fig. 5. Merging GAML with templates to get Java syntax

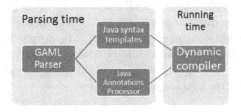

Fig. 6. Modules of G2J plugin

4   G2J Plugin

To facilitate the whole process of establishing, and make it re-usable, we implemented our method as plugin in GAMA platform. This plugin named G2J (fig.6) (GAML to Java) which is implemented in Java language. This plugin contains 4 following modules: GAML Parser, Java syntax template, Java Annotation Processor, Dynamic Compiler, which are separated into 2 phases : parsing and running. In parsing phase, it takes into account 2 process. Firstly, GAML parser is integrated into parsing process of ANTLR as grammar syntax processing. The output of GAML parser is transfered to Java Syntax Templates, and at the same time to Java Annotations Processor. These two module work in collaboration with each other to establish a complete Java Syntax Tree with the most comfortable solutions. After the first phase, Java Syntax Tree uses as input of Dynamic Compiler, which pre-compile to byte code (.class) of Java.

4.1   GAML Parser

This module implements algorithm to traversing AST in fig.4 and builds the Java syntax tree. The input of this module is a Description tree, which is described in part 3. This tree contains several types of nodes. This module is injected into parsing process of GAMA. It provides method parseTree() to call algorithm of traversing tree, return Java syntax tree.

4.2   Java Syntax Template

This module aims at reproduce corresponding Java syntax, due to pre-defined XML templates. It uses an likely-XML parser. With informations of a node from Description Tree, it get XML node in templates.

4.3   Java Annotations Processor

Beside the solution of using pre-defined templates, this module is considered as pre-processer of all Java annotation in all modules, plugins, to build additional information. These information will be used in GAML parser when traversing AST, or be combined with XML templates when calling module 2. This module provides more flexibility, and reusable solutions, in case of pre-defined templates couldn't suitable with large amount of evolving syntax in GAMA.

4.4   Java Dynamic Compiler

In addition to GAMA compiler, we have used a Java Dynamic compiler [2] [10] [13], to compile from Java syntax tree to Java byte-code class. This class is taken into account when we launch the simulation, instead of re-compiling original Abstract Syntax tree each time. In this part we introduce the method to compile the Java model and attach it to the execution tree. When we finished this paper, we had succeeded to translate only the Species entity to Java, by adding a boolean keyword named **compiled**, to tell the compiler if it must use the Java class instead of original species class in the model description tree. After having created the Java class, we use a Java plugin,batch compiler (org.eclipse.jdt.core), to compile the Java class to byte code, and load it to memory, on run time.

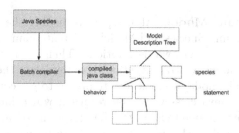

Fig. 7. Compilation process in Java species instead of GAML species

5   Experiments

By applying our manner of establishing operational, we consider below our experimental result in a simple model in simulation platform GAMA. We do some experiences on a simple model which contains **model** and **entities** section. It shows the establishment from GAML to Java on declaration of a **model**, a **species**, which demonstrates the usage of Java Syntax Templates, an **operator** and a **statement**, which are supposed to use Java Annotations Processor.

5.1   Data Described

Let's consider the model below in GAMA platform, it describes a bug which can change its color in a square environment. This species has one attribute, mycolor, representing its body's color. This bug shows itself as a circle of which the radius is 10 units and the color is green as default. At each simulation step, the attribute mycolor will change to a random rgb value, thanks to operator rnd(255). This action is a reaction of species basing on reflex architecture (line 11), which will happen if it reaches the condition following keyword **when**. In this case, it always happens because the condition is always return true.

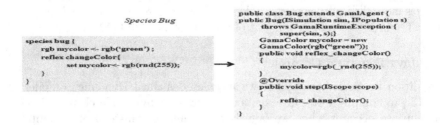

Fig. 8. Definition of Species Bug in GAML and Java

5.2   Convert Domain-Specific Language to Operational Model

By applying algorithm as Fig. 4, there are 3 following cases that we consider as main points.

Convert Species and Model. At first, by regarding the proper syntax of GAML and Java defining Species and Model, we create manually an XML template, content format of these two descriptions. Then when compiler traverses each nodes of constructed Abstract Syntax Tree, we detect the type of the current node. If it's Model node, we look into template to get corresponding XML node. In this case, a Java class would be returned which have class name be name of Model node, extended class ModelDescription to have all default predefined parameters, skills, behaviors. In Fig. 10, we have a normal declaration of model. It contains keyword model, followed by the model's name as a string. This string will be used in place of tag name in its corresponding template. After combination, compiler create an empty Java class. Body of this class will be completed later. When compiler encounters a node with type Species, process flow is much similar with previous type (Model), except some varied in extending class SpeciesDescription. This predefined class contents all must-have attributes of formal Species, ex. location, size, shape...(Fig. 11).

Applying the same manner to some more type of node in AST, we get an advantage of possibility to translate all GAML syntax to Java syntax. But it's a big challenge for modelers to create and develop new operators, skills, behaviors.

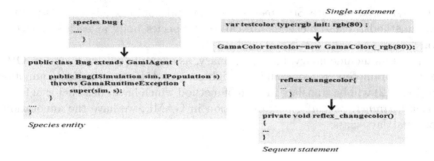

Fig. 9. Converting cases from GAML to Java

Beside of theirs implementations in Java, they must create them-self template for their new things. The job to read and create all correspond templates must take too much time, and actually in future, it will not adapt well and quickly (depend on human-additions templates) when GAML syntax has evolved.

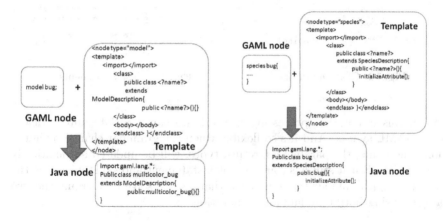

Fig. 10. Case Model   **Fig. 11.** Case Species

Convert Attributes, Behaviors. Almost operators, type, statements, and even skills, are interpreted thanks to annotation, and can execute thanks to GAML additions helpers. The helpers is an Java interface linked to Java class which take care on process the command. The idea is focus to declared annotations, implement a Java class to read all the annotation, and then translate it to Java syntax. When GAML model compiled, by mixing the tree and Java syntax, we have translated whole model into Java class.

Attributes declaration syntax contains two part: type and name, which are converted into declaration of variable in Java. In contructor of species, there is an initialization of these attributes, with default values.

Behaviors, which are Statements (simple and complex), is converted into Java's methods. These methods are called in Species body at each simulation step.

Operators include unary, binary or nnary, as example, binary operator 'OR' take two parameters, left_operand and right_operand. Its description in annotation (Fig. 12) will be translate in form of method which have constructor in form _keyword(param1, param2,...) , expression in GAML, we have the annotation in original Java class.

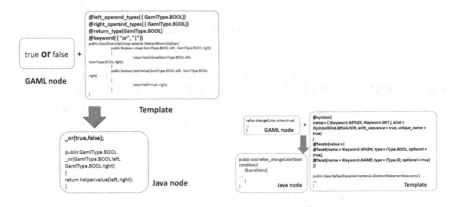

Fig. 12. Case Operators   **Fig. 13.** Case Statements

With this annotation processing method, we can translate automatically almost GAML syntax. And it's so flexible when the grammar change by annotation. The name, the parameters, return types, will be updated automatically by annotation. But it still has some complex statement and skill which face the problem of logical and syntactic in Java, that can be solve by merging the two strategies, using both template and annotation.

5.3   Results of Dynamic Compilation

By using this model, we execute simulation 100 times and get the average statistic about running time, memory using. Regarding the advantages of compiling dynamically species into Java, we can see the following:

- Faster execution (although we can't prove it now, it is fairly obvious that compiled code should be faster than interpreted one, especially because Java code can be compiled on the fly to native code by the JVM).

- Better verification (for the code to compile properly, it needs to be correct in GAML).

- Possibility to further optimize the execution of agents by changing the Java code directly (instead of being restricted by the GAML set of primitives).

Scenario	Number of agents	Compile Time (s)		Running resources (Mb RAM)		Execution time for 400 simulation steps (s)	
		Original	Java	Original	Java	Original	Java
1	100	4	3	225	226	5	8
2	10 000	56	43	310	286	5	9
3	100 000	149	126	531	403	6	10

Fig. 14. Compare between dynamic compilation with original compilation method

6 Conclusion

This paper has established an operational model from conceptual model for a simulation platform, applicant to GAMA platform. With algorithm to traversing AST, combining templates and annotation, compiler create an operational model correspond with conceptual structure. With this research, model in GAML was convert into Java syntax, containing species, theirs attributes and simple reflex behaviors . This method has implemented into GAMA in form a plugin to facilitate the process of converting. In the next time, we will made entire structure of model with complex behaviors, skills and linking between multi model.

Acknowledgments. This publication has been made possible through support provided by the IRD-DSF.

References

1. Auslander, J., Philipose, M., Chambers, C., Eggers, S.J., Bershad, B.N.: Fast, effective dynamic compilation. In: Proceedings of the ACM SIGPLAN 1996 Conference on Programming Language Design and Implementation, PLDI 1996, pp. 149–159. ACM, New York (1996)
2. Bebenita, M., Brandner, F., Fhndrich, M., Logozzo, F., Schulte, W., Tillmann, N., Venter, H.: Spur: a trace-based jit compiler for cil. In: Cook, W.R., Clarke, S., Rinard, M.C. (eds.) Proceedings of the 25th Annual ACM SIGPLAN Conference on Object-Oriented Programming Systems, Languages, and Applications, OOPSLA 2010, pp. 708–725. ACM, Reno/Tahoe, Nevada (2010)
3. Benson, T.: UML and XML. Principles of Health Interoperability HL7 and SNOMED. Health Information Technology Standards, pp. 51–70. Springer, London (2012)
4. Bettini, L.: A DSL for writing type systems for xtext languages. In: Proceedings of the 9th International Conference on Principles and Practice of Programming in Java, PPPJ 2011, pp. 31–40. ACM, New York (2011)
5. Bryant, J.: Java syntax. In: Java 7 for Absolute Beginners, pp. 15–33. Apress (January 2011)

6. Chambers, C., Ungar, D., Lee, E.: An efficient implementation of SELF a dynamically-typed object-oriented language based on prototypes. SIGPLAN Not. **24**(10), 49–70 (1989)

7. Gong, J., Cheng, R., Cheung, D.W.: Efficient management of uncertainty in XML schema matching. The VLDB Journal **21**(3), 385–409 (2012)

8. Hassanieh, H., Indyk, P., Katabi, D., Price, E.: Simple and practical algorithm for sparse fourier transform. In: Proceedings of the Twenty-Third Annual ACM-SIAM Symposium on Discrete Algorithms, SODA 2012, pp. 1183–1194. SIAM, Kyoto (2012)

9. Henderson-Sellers, B.: Modelling languages. On the Mathematics of Modelling. Metamodelling, Ontologies and Modelling Languages. SpringerBriefs in Computer Science, pp. 63–74. Springer, Heidelberg (2012)

10. Ishizaki, K., Ogasawara, T., Castanos, J., Nagpurkar, P., Edelsohn, D., Nakatani, T.: Adding dynamically-typed language support to a statically-typed language compiler: performance evaluation, analysis, and tradeoffs. SIGPLAN Not. **47**(7), 169–180 (2012)

11. Jones, J.: Abstract syntax tree implementation idioms. In: Proceedings of the 10th Conference on Pattern Languages of Programs (PLoP2003) (2003)

12. Kerr, A., Diamos, G., Yalamanchili, S.: Dynamic compilation of data-parallel kernels for vector processors. In: Proceedings of the Tenth International Symposium on Code Generation and Optimization, CGO 2012, pp. 23–32. ACM, New York (2012)

13. Koju, T., Tong, X., Sheikh, A.I., Ohara, M., Nakatani, T.: Optimizing indirect branches in a system-level dynamic binary translator. In: Proceedings of the 5th Annual International Systems and Storage Conference, SYSTOR 2012, pp. 5:1–5:12. ACM, New York (2012)

14. Kulkarni, P., Arnold, M., Hind, M.: Dynamic compilation: the benefits of early investing. In: Proceedings of the 3rd International Conference on Virtual Execution Environments, VEE 2007, pp. 94–104. ACM, New York (2007)

15. Liu, Y., Fong, A.S.: Heuristic optimisation algorithm for java dynamic compilation. **6**(4):307–312 (2012)

16. Mernik, M., Heering, J., Sloane, A.M.: When and how to develop domain-specific languages. **37**(4):316–344 (December 2005)

17. Parr, T.J., Quong, R.W.: ANTLR: a predicated-LL(k) parser generator. Software Practice and Experience **25**, 789–810 (1994)

18. Psaila, G.: On the problem of coupling java algorithms and XML parsers (invited paper). In: 17th International Workshop on Database and Expert Systems Applications, 2006. DEXA 2006, pp. 487–491 (2006)

19. Rohl, M., Uhrmacher, A.M.: Flexible integration of XML into modeling and simulation systems. In: Proceedings of the 37th Conference on Winter Simulation, WSC 2005, pp. 1813–1820. Winter Simulation Conference, Orlando (2005)

20. Rohl, M., Uhrmacher, A.M.: Composing simulations from XML-specified model components. In Proceedings of the 38th Conference on Winter Simulation, WSC 2006, pp. 1083–1090. Winter Simulation Conference, Monterey (2006)

21. Spafford, K.L., Vetter, J.S.: Aspen: a domain specific language for performance modeling. In: Proceedings of the International Conference on High Performance Computing, Networking, Storage and Analysis, SC 2012, pp. 84:1–84:11. IEEE Computer Society Press, Los Alamitos (2012)

22. Taillandier, P., Vo, D.-A., Amouroux, E., Drogoul, A.: GAMA: a simulation plat-
    form that integrates geographical information data, agent-based modeling and
    multi-scale control. In: Desai, N., Liu, A., Winikoff, M. (eds.) Principles and Prac-
    tice of Multi-Agent Systems. LNCS, vol. 7057, pp. 242–258. Springer, Heidelberg
    (2012)
23. Tam, D., Wu, J.: Using hardware counters to improve dynamic compilation. Tech-
    nical report (2003)
24. Touraille, L., Traore, M.K., Hill, D.R.C.: A mark-up language for the storage,
    retrieval, sharing and interoperability of DEVS models. In: Proceedings of the
    2009 Spring Simulation Multiconference, SpringSim 2009, pp. 163:1–163:6. Society
    for Computer Simulation International, San Diego (2009)
25. Ueberhuber, C.W.: Scientific modeling. Numerical Computation 1, pp. 1–8.
    Springer, Heidelberg (1997)
26. Vo, D.-A., Drogoul, A., Zucker, J.-D., Ho, T.-V.: A modelling language to represent
    and specify emerging structures in agent-based model. Principles and Practice of
    Multi-Agent Systems. LNCS, vol. 7057, pp. 212–227. Springer, Heidelberg (2012)

MetaAB - A Novel Abundance-Based Binning Approach for Metagenomic Sequences

Van-Vinh Le[1,3]([✉]), Tran Van Lang[2], and Tran Van Hoai[1]

[1] Faculty of Computer Science and Engineering, HCMC University of Technology,
Ho Chi Minh City, Vietnam
vinhlv@fit.hcmute.edu.vn
[2] Institute of Applied Mechanics and Informatics,
Vietnam Academy of Science and Technology, Hanoi, Vietnam
[3] Faculty of Information Technology, HCMC University of Technical Education,
Ho Chi Minh City, Vietnam

Abstract. Metagenomics is a research discipline of microbial communities that studies directly on genetic materials obtained from environmental samples without isolating and culturing single organisms in laboratory. One of the crucial tasks in metagenomic projects is the identification and taxonomic characterization of DNA sequences in the samples. In this paper, we present an unsupervised binning of metagenomic reads, called MetaAB, which can be able to identify and classify reads into groups of genomes using the information of genome abundances. The method is based on a proposed reduced-dimension model that is theoretically proved to have less computational time. Besides, MetaAB detects the number of genome abundances in data automatically by using the Bayesian Information Criterion. Experimental results show that the proposed method achieves higher accuracy and run faster than a recent abundance-based binning approach. The software implementing the algorithm can be downloaded at http://it.hcmute.edu.vn/bioinfo/metaab/index.htm

Keywords: Metagenomics · Binning · Next-generation sequencing · Bayesian information criterion · Genome abundance

1 Introduction

Since microbes are the most diverse forms on Earth, the understanding of them can bring many benefits to human being [1]. Microbial communities have been studied for many years. However, due to experimental limitations, traditional methods only focus on single species in laboratory culture. A drawback of these methods is that 99% percent of microbes cannot be cultured in the laboratory [2]. Moreover, a clone culture cannot represent the true state of affairs in nature since a sample obtained from a microbial community may contain many species which interact with both each other and their habitats [3]. An alternative research trend

© Institute for Computer Sciences, Social Informatics and Telecommunications Engineering 2015
P.C. Vinh et al. (Eds.): ICTCC 2014, LNICST 144, pp. 132–141, 2015.
DOI: 10.1007/978-3-319-15392-6_13

which can overcome the limits of traditional methods is metagenomics. This discipline allows the direct study on genomes from an environmental sample without isolation and cultivation of single organisms. However, it takes many costs to obtain genomic information directly from microbial communities by traditional sequencing technologies (e.g., Sanger sequencing technology). Fortunately, new sequencing technologies (so-called next-generation technologies [4,5]), which can produce millions of reads with small costs, have make metagenomics feasible in practice.

One of the crucial step in a metagenomic project is to classify reads into groups of individual genomes or closely related organisms, which is referred to as *binning problem*. Binning methods can be roughly classified into three main categories: *homology-based, composition-based*, and *abundance-based* methods.

Homology-based approaches classify reads by using alignment tools (e.g., Blast, HMMER) to align DNA sequences directly to reference genomes. Among the approaches, MEGAN [6] maps reads by Blast with the nr database of NCBI (National Center for Biotechnology Information), then it assigns labels for the reads using a technique of lowest common ancestor. CARMA [7] is another homology-based method in which data is aligned with a protein database Pfam by either BLAST or HMMER3 homology searches.

Many binning approaches are known as composition-based methods, which use compositional features (e.g., oligonucleotide frequencies, GC-content) for classification. They can be further divided into two kinds of methods: *supervised* and *unsupervised* methods. Supervised methods [8,9] require reference databases which consist of known taxonomic origin sequences. The supervised methods are shown to perform well in case of full-availability of reference databases. However, the majority of microorganisms on Earth remains undiscovered [10]. This makes the methods may be not efficient in practice. To deal with the lack of reference databases, some unsupervised methods were proposed to perform the classification basing on features extracted from analyzed sequences. MetaCluster 2.0 [11], MetaCluster 3.0 [12] and MCluster [13] are recent algorithms which are based on the signature of frequency distribution of tetra-nucleotides. These approaches are shown to be efficient for long sequences ($\geq$ 800kbp), but get low accuracy for short reads (50-400bp). Furthermore, many approaches do not perform well if the abundance levels of genome in data are very different [11].

Some recent unsupervised approaches can perform on short reads by using the information of genome abundances in data. MetaCluster 5.0 [23] separates reads into three groups of different abundance levels (high, low and extremely low level) and applies further classification strategies to each group. Abundance-Bin [15] and Olga *et al* [16] are two approaches for binning of reads which only reply on the feature of genome abundances. Those approaches group reads into bins that the reads in the same bin belong to genomes of similar abundance levels. Both approaches is based on an assumption that the occurrences of l-mers (with a sufficient value of l) in data follow Poisson distribution, and then an expectation maximization algorithm is used to estimate genome abundances. Another abundance-based binning approach, MarkovBin [14], models nucleotide sequences as a fixed-order Markov chain and classifies them into groups of different genome abundances. However, this method still does not support detecting automatically the number of genome abundance levels in data.

This paper proposes a new abundance-based binning algorithm for metagenomic reads without any reference databases, called MetaAB (i.e., Abundance-based Binning of METAgenomic sequences). The proposed method uses a reduced-dimension model to find maximum likelihood estimates of parameter in a statistical model, which can reduce much computational time comparing with other approaches. Furthermore, by the advantage of the proposed model, we applies a new method of estimating the number of bins in data basing on the Bayesian information criterion.

The following sections of this paper are organized as follows. In section 2, a proposed reduced-dimension model is presented, then it is applied within an algorithm which additionally can detect the number of genome abundance levels in data by using the Bayesian information. Section 3 shows experimental results. The last section provides conclusions and future works.

2   Methods

An abundance of a species is the number of individual of the species within a given area or community. An environmental sample may contain many genomes of species with different abundance levels. This work aims to extract the information of genome abundances in a metagenomic dataset in order to classify reads into bins (or clusters) such that reads in each bins belong to genomes of very similar abundances. The proposed method is based on an observation that l-mer frequencies in reads generated from a genome is proportional to the genome abundance [15,16]. Besides, basing on the study of Lander and Waterman [17], an assumption used in this work is that the number of the occurrences of l-mers in a set of reads from a single genome follows a Poisson distribution, and all l-mers appearing in a metagenomic project are considered as mixture of Poisson distributions. Using the assumption, the proposed method firstly tries to find the maximum likelihood estimate of parameters for the model. It then classifies reads into bins basing on the probability of their l-mers belonging to each components.

2.1   Mixture Model of l-mer Frequencies

Given a metagenome dataset which consists of n reads $R = \{r_1, r_2, \ldots, r_n\}$. Let $w_1, \ldots, w_q$ be a set of l-mers in the dataset. We have a data $\mathcal{X}$ with q observations, where $c(w_i), i = \{1, \ldots, q\}$ is the value of the observation ith (i.e., the number of occurrences of w_i in the dataset). From the above assumption, the distribution of l-mers within each genome g_m is governed by a Poisson distribution with parameter λ_m. The probability function of the number of occurrences of an l-mer w_i coming from the genome g_m is

$$p_m(c(w_i)|\lambda_m) = \frac{\lambda_m^{c(w_i)} e^{-\lambda_m}}{c(w_i)!} \tag{1}$$

Assuming that the dataset consists of k species with different abundance levels, and $c(w_i), i = [1, \ldots, q]$ is independent, identically distributed observations. A finite mixture model of the k components is the convex combination, and its probability density function can be written as

$$p(c(w_i)|\Theta) = \sum_{m=1}^{k} \alpha_m p_m(c(w_i)|\theta_m), \qquad (2)$$

where $\alpha_1, \ldots, \alpha_k$ are the mixing proportions and must satisfy $\sum_{m=1}^{k} \alpha_m = 1, \alpha_m > 0$. Besides, $\Theta = (\alpha_1, \ldots, \alpha_k, \theta_1, \ldots, \theta_m)$ is the set of parameters of the mixture. Each θ_m is the set of parameters of the mth component. In this context of Poisson model, we have $\theta_m \equiv \lambda_m$. The log-likelihood corresponding to the mixture of k components is:

$$\log \mathcal{L}(\Theta|\mathcal{X}) = \log \prod_{i=1}^{q} p(c(w_i)|\Theta) = \sum_{i=1}^{q} \log \left(\sum_{m=1}^{k} \alpha_m p_m(c(w_i)|\lambda_m) \right). \qquad (3)$$

We aim to find the maximum likelihood estimate (MLE) of the parameter Θ, which represents the most likely assignment of the l-mers to the genomes in the dataset.

$$\Theta^* = \arg \max_{\Theta} \log p(\mathcal{X}|\Theta) \qquad (4)$$

We note that this model have been also applied in [15, 18] for different purposes.

2.2   A Reduced-Dimension Model

Regarding the aspect of computational cost, this study modifies the above mixture model for reducing dimension. Firstly, we present the following lemma:

Lemma 1. *Given two l-mers w_i, w_j, and a component m with parameter of λ_m. If $c(w_i) = c(w_j)$, we have $p_m(c(w_i)|\lambda_m) = p_m(c(w_j)|\lambda_m)$.*

Proof. ccording to expression 1, we have

$$p_m(c(w_i)|\lambda_m) - p_m(c(w_j)|\lambda_m) = \frac{\lambda_m^{c(w_i)} e^{-\lambda_m}}{c(w_i)!} - \frac{\lambda_m^{c(w_j)} e^{-\lambda_m}}{c(w_j)!} \qquad (5)$$

$$= 0 \text{ (because } c(w_i) = c(w_j))$$

That means $p_m(c(w_i)|\lambda_m) = p_m(c(w_j)|\lambda_m)$.

Given a set of all l-mers $w_1, \ldots, w_q$ in the dataset R. Sorting the l-mers into b non-empty groups in which all l-mers $w_i, w_j, i \neq j$ in the same group t have the same number of occurrences and are equal to $c_t, t = \{1, \ldots, b\}$ (i.e., $c(w_i) = c(w_j) = c_t$), and $\forall t, s \in \{1, \ldots, b\}, c_t \neq c_s$. Denoting by $nu_t \geq 1, t = \{1, \ldots, b\}$ the number of l-mers in group t. We have

$$q = \sum_{t=1}^{b} nu_t \qquad (6)$$

It is clear that since $nu_t \geq 1$, we always have $b \leq q$.

According to the Lemma 1, two l-mers having the same number of occurrences have the same probability of belonging to components. Thus, the log-likelihood corresponding to the mixture of k components, stated in expression 3, can be reformulated as

$$\log \mathcal{L}(\Theta|\mathcal{X}) = \sum_{t=1}^{b} nu_t \log \left(\sum_{m=1}^{k} \alpha_m p_m(c_t|\lambda_m) \right) \tag{7}$$

In practice, a large proportion of l-mers from the same genomes have the same number of occurrences (i.e., $nu_t \gg 1$). Given the number of l-mers q, the larger value of nu_t it is, the smaller value of b it is (see equation 6). Therefore, by using expression 7, the cost for finding maximum log-likelihood estimate of the parameter Θ can be much reduced.

2.3 Estimating Model Parameters

The Expectation Maximization (EM) algorithm [19] is used to find maximum likelihood estimates of the parameter Θ. The observed data $\mathcal{X}$ is considered to be incomplete data, and the missing data is a set of b labels $\mathcal{Z} = \{z_1, \ldots, z_b\}$ which is associated with the observed data. Each binary vector $z_t = [z_{t1}, \ldots, z_{tk}], t = \{1, \ldots, b\}$, indicates which genome produces the l-mers whose counts are equal to c_t, where $z_{tm} = 1, m = \{1, \ldots, k\}$ if the l-mers whose counts are equal to c_t is from the mth genome, and $z_{tm} = 0$ otherwise. The log-likelihood of the complete data $(\mathcal{X}, \mathcal{Z})$ is

$$\log \mathcal{L}(\Theta|\mathcal{X}, \mathcal{Z}) = \sum_{t=1}^{b} nu_t \sum_{m=1}^{k} z_{tm} \log \alpha_m p(c_t|\lambda_m). \tag{8}$$

In the EM algorithm, the unknown set of parameters $\Theta = (\alpha_1, \ldots, \alpha_k, \lambda_1, \ldots, \lambda_m)$ are randomly initialized. The parameters will be updated after each iteration. We denote by $\Theta^{(s)} = (\alpha_1^{(s)}, \ldots, \alpha_k^{(s)}, \lambda_1^{(s)}, \ldots, \lambda_m^{(s)})$ the set of parameters obtained after s iterations. Each iteration performs the following two steps (the following represents for iteration $s + 1$):

+ **Expectation Step:** Calculate the probability of l-mers whose counts are equal to $c_t, t = \{1, \ldots, b\}$ belonging to species mth given parameter $\Theta^{(s)}$, and c_t:

$$p(z_{tm} = 1|c_t, \Theta^{(s)}) = \frac{\alpha_m^{(s)} p_m(c_t|\lambda_m^{(s)})}{\sum_{v=1}^{k} \alpha_v^{(s)} p_v(c_t|\lambda_v^{(s)})} \tag{9}$$

Denoting $p(z_{tm} = 1|c_t, \Theta^{(s)})$ by π_{tm}, and it is called a posterior probability.

+ **Maximization Step:** In this step, the parameters are updated according to

$$\Theta^{(s+1)} = \arg\max_{\Theta} Q(\Theta, \Theta^{(s)}), \tag{10}$$

where the Q-function is the expectation of the complete data log-likelihood:

$$Q(\Theta, \Theta^{(s)}) = E[log(p(\mathcal{X}, \mathcal{Z}|\Theta))|\mathcal{X}, \Theta^{(s)}]$$

$$= \sum_{t=1}^{b} nu_t \sum_{m=1}^{k} \pi_{tm} log(\alpha_m) + \sum_{t=1}^{b} nu_t \sum_{m=1}^{k} \pi_{tm} log(p_m(c_t|\theta_m)) \quad (11)$$

The parameters can be calculated as follows.

$$\alpha_m^{(s+1)} = \frac{\sum_{t=1}^{b} nu_t \pi_{tm}}{\sum_{t=1}^{b} nu_t}, \quad \lambda_m^{(s+1)} = \frac{\sum_{t=1}^{b} nu_t \pi_{tm} c_t}{\sum_{t=1}^{b} nu_t \pi_{tm}} \quad (12)$$

Once the parameters of the mixture model are estimated. Each read r_j is assigned into a component (or bin) basing on the probability of their l-mers belonging to the components. Denote by f_{im} the probability of an l-mer w_i belonging to bin mth ($i = \{1, \ldots, q, \}, m = \{1, \ldots, k\}$). Choose $t \in \{1, \ldots, b\}$ such that $c(w_i) = c_t$, we set $f_{im} = \pi_{tm}$. Let y_j to indicate in which bin a read r_j is assigned. It is calculated as

$$y_j = \underset{1 \leq m \leq k}{\arg\max} \frac{\prod_{w_i \in r_j} f_{im}}{\sum_{u=1}^{k} \left(\prod_{w_i \in r_j} f_{iu}\right)}. \quad (13)$$

2.4   Binning Algorithm

The pseudocode for the proposed algorithm is provided in Algorithm 1. The occurrences of l-mers in all reads $r_i \in R, i = \{1, \ldots, n\}$ are firstly calculated. In order to find the number of bins in data, we use the Bayesian information criterion. The method is a penalized likelihood approach which was shown to perform well in many fields [21]. A drawback of the BIC is that it takes much computational time to compute. However, the reduced-dimension model proposed in this study makes it applicable. The BIC is defined as BIC $= log\mathcal{L}(\Theta_M^*|\mathcal{X}) - \frac{d}{2}log(q)$ in which, M is the number of components, $\mathcal{L}(\Theta_M^*|\mathcal{X})$ is the maximum likelihood with M components, and d is the numbers of parameters in the mixture model. With this Poisson mixture model, we have $d = 2M - 1$ for a M-finite Poisson mixture model. To compute the maximum likelihood $\mathcal{L}(\Theta_M^*|\mathcal{X})$, the EM algorithm presented above is used. To choose the best model for the l-mers distribution, the EM algorithm is performed iteratively with the different number of components (or bins) m. The model which have the largest BIC value is chosen. The final step of the algorithm is to assign reads into the bins basing on the probability of their l-mers belonging to the bins. Some empty bins in which there are not any reads assigned will be removed.

Note that, after l-mer counts are computed, some untrusted l-mers whose counts do not correctly reflect the genome abundances exist in data are discarded. The unstrusted l-mers may be produced by: (1) l-mers are repeated within each genome; (2) l-mers are shared by different genomes; (3) and sequencing errors which can produce unreal l-mers.

Algorithm 1. Binning algorithm

Input: List of reads R, the number of reads n, the length of l-mers l, the minimum number of bins k_{min}, the maximum number of bins k_{max}

Output: List of bins C, the number of bins k

1: Compute counts of l-mers in R
2: Discard untrusted l-mers
3: $m = k_{min}$
4: **repeat**
5:     Call *EM algorithm* in which the number of components is fixed to m
6:     Compute BIC value BIC_m
7:     $m = m + 1$
8: **until** $m > k_{max}$
9: $BIC_{max} = max(BIC_m), k_{min} \leq m \leq k_{max}$
10: $k = m$, where $BIC_m = BIC_{max}$
11: Assign $r_i \in R, i \in \{1, ..., n\}$ into bins C using Equation (13)
12: Remove empty bins
13: $k = k-$ the number of empty bins

---

3   Experiments Results

In those experiments, the proposed method is compared with AbundanceBin [15] (version 1.01, February 2013) on datasets of both with and without sequencing errors. According to the study in [22], the percentage of common l-mers between microbial genomes is less than 1% when $l \leq 20$. Moreover, AbundanceBin was shown to achieve the best performance with l-mer length of 20. Therefore, we also choose $l = 20$ for those experiments. To evaluate the approaches, two commonly used performance metrics, namely, *precision* and *recall* which are defined in [23] are used. The computer used for the experiments is an Intel Xeon with 20GB RAM running at 2.3 GHz.

3.1   Datasets

Due to the lack of standard metagenomic datasets, simulated datasets are widely used to evaluate the performance of binning algorithms. A tool used for generating metagenomic reads is MetaSim [24] which allows us to select a sequencing model and control considered parameters (e.g., read length, genome coverage, error rate). We simulate metagenomic datasets based on the bacterial genomes which are downloaded from the NCBI (National Center for Biotechnology Information) database. We generate samples which can be classified into two groups. The first group which is denoted by from S1 to S7 contains reads without sequencing errors. The second group denoted by from T1 to T7 contains reads of sequencing errors. The error-free sequencing sequences (with length of 150bp) are created by the exact simulator setting of MetaSim, while error sequencing sequences (with length of 80bp) follow the Illumina error profile with an error rate of 1%. The samples in the two groups (from S1 to S7, and from T1 to T7) have the same the number of species, the number of abundance levels, abundance levels and the list of used species or strains, respectively.

3.2   Results on Error-Free Sequencing Reads

MetaAB firstly is compared with AbundanceBin on the samples from S1 to S7. The parameters of AbundanceBin were set default. Table 1 presents the *precision* and *recall* of the two approaches. It can be seen from the table, by using the BIC, the proposed approach is able to estimate correctly the number of bins for most of the samples (6 out of 7 cases), while AbundanceBin fails to estimate correctly the number of bins for 3 out of 7 cases. Note that each bin consists of reads from one or many species which have similar abundances. In addition, MetaAB can achieve better both *precision* and *recall* for most the tested cases. On computational performance, the proposed approach needs smaller computing time than that of AbundanceBin in many cases, especially the samples of the large number of reads.

Table 1. The *precision* and *recall* of AbundanceBin and MetaAB on samples from S1 to S7

ID	# actual bins	AbundanceBin				MetaAB			
		# bins	Precision	Recall	Running time (s)	# bins	Precision	Recall	Running time (s)
S1	2	2	96.57%	96.57%	**94**	2	96.57%	96.57%	116
S2	3	3	94.9%	95.58%	**305**	3	**95.83%**	**95.58%**	328
S3	3	4	90.72%	86.84%	556	3	**95.4%**	**95.06%**	**483**
S4	4	4	96.96%	96.96%	**745**	4	**97.61%**	**97.08%**	812
S5	4	3	65.43%	**94.69%**	507	4	**85.72%**	85.24%	**489**
S6	5	4	85.54%	**88.41%**	795	5	**86.18%**	77.63%	**782**
S7	6	6	**94.46%**	94.46%	2808	2	73.12%	**99.16%**	2519

3.3   Results on Error Sequencing Reads

Binning approaches should have ability to deal with sequencing errors since there are no any current sequencing technologies which could generate reads without errors. The proposed approach is tested on the datasets with sequencing errors from T1 to T7, and is compared with AbundanceBin. In order to reduce the bad effects of the errors, and for a fair comparison, both approaches are set to discard the l-mers which appear only once from the binning process. Table 2 compares the accuracy and computational time of the two approaches. Obviously, MetaAB can work well with the error sequencing reads and outperforms AbundanceBin for most of the tested samples. The proposed approach can estimate correctly the number of bins in each sample for 5 out of 7 cases, whereas AbundanceBin detects correctly the number of bins for only one sample (sample T1). Because of sequencing errors, AbundanceBin seems to return the estimated number of bins which are much less than the actual ones. This helps it to achieve high *recall* values, but its get very low *precision* for the samples. It is very interesting that MetaAB get higher *precision* than that of AbundanceBin for all the tested samples. Furthermore, the proposed approach is much faster than AbundanceBin.

Table 2. The *precision* and *recall* of AbundanceBin and MetaAB on samples from T1 to T7

ID	# actual bins	AbundanceBin				MetaAB			
		# bins	Precision	Recall	Running time (s)	# bins	Precision	Recall	Running time (s)
T1	2	2	94.6%	94.5%	135	2	**98.04%**	**98.04%**	**107**
T2	3	2	92%	98.52%	315	2	**92.8%**	**99.53%**	**282**
T3	3	1	49.3%	**100%**	1524	3	**96.58%**	96.56%	**422**
T4	4	3	61.22%	**95.39%**	858	4	**94.35%**	93.81%	**643**
T5	4	2	63.55%	**94.25%**	670	4	**71.43%**	71.89%	**417**
T6	5	2	62.72%	89.99%	1630	4	**89.17%**	**91.65%**	**612**
T7	6	2	71.34%	**97.56%**	6789	6	**94.27%**	85.33%	**2224**

4   Conclusion

The development of next-generation sequencing, which allows to produce a mass of data, brings computational challenge in metagenomic projects. This study focuses on the challenge in which a reduce-dimension model is proposed. By taking the advantage of the model, a method of detecting the number of bins in data based on the Bayesian information criterion is applied. Our experiments demonstrates that the proposed approach not only achieves higher accuracy but also consumes less computational time than a recent abundance-based binning approach. In future works, we aim to apply the proposed approach for the improvement of compositional-based binning methods.

Acknowledgments. This research is funded by the Ho Chi Minh city University of Technology (Project code: TNCS-2013-KHMT-10).

References

1. Handelsman, J.: The New Science of Metagenomics: Revealing the Secrets of Out Microbial Planet. The National Academies Press, Washington, DC (2007)
2. Aann, R.I., Ludwig, W., Schleifer, K.H.: Phylogenetic identification and in situ detection of individual microbial cells without cultivation. Microbiol Rev. (1995)
3. Wooley, J.C.: A primer on metagenomics. PloS Computational Biology (2010)
4. Shendure, J., Ji, H.: Next-generation dna sequencing. Nature Biotechnology (2008)
5. Qin, J., Li, R., Wang, J.: A human gut microbial gene catalogue established by metagenomic sequencing. Nature **464** (2010)
6. Huson, D.H.: Megan analysis of metagenomic data. Genome Research (2007)
7. Gerlach, W.: Taxonomic classification of metagenomic shotgun sequences with carma3. Nucleic Acids Research (2011)

8. Diaz, N.N., Krause, L., Goesmann, A., Niehaus, K., Nattkemper, T.W.: Tacoa: Taxonomic classification of environmental genomic fragments using a kernelized nearest neighbor approach. BMC Bioinformatics (2009)

9. Yi, W., et al.: Metacluster-ta: taxonomic annotation for metagenomic databased on assembly-assisted binning. BMC Genomics **15** (2014)

10. Eisen, J.A.: Environmental shotgun sequencing: Its potential and challenges for studying the hidden world of microbes. PLoS Biol. **5**(3) (2007)

11. Yang, B., Peng, Y., Qin, J., Chin, F.Y.L.: MetaCluster: unsupervised binning of environmental genomic fragments and taxonomic annotation. In: ACM BCB (2010)

12. Leung, H.C., Yiu, F.M., Yang, B., Peng, Y., Wang, Y., Liu, Z., Chin, F.Y.: A robust and accurate binning algorithm for metagenomic sequences with arbitrary species abundance ratio. Bioinformatics **27**(11), 1489–1495 (2011)

13. Liao, R., Zhang, R., Guan, J., Zhou, S.: A new unsupervised binning approach for metagenomic sequences based on n-grams and automatic feature weighting. IEEE/ACM Transaction on Computational Biology and Bioinformatics (2014)

14. Nguyen, T.C., Zhu, D.: Markovbin: An algorithm to cluster metagenomic reads using a mixture modeling of hierarchical distributions. In: Proceedings of the International Conference on Bioinformatics, Computational Biology and Biomedical Informatics

15. Wu, Y.W., Ye, Y.: A novel abundance-based algorithm for binning metagenomic sequences using l-tuples. Journal of Computational Biology **18**(3), 523–534 (2011)

16. Tanaseichuk, O., Borneman, J., Jiang, T.: A probabilistic approach to accurate abundance-based binning of metagenomic reads. In: Raphael, B., Tang, J. (eds.) WABI 2012. LNCS, vol. 7534, pp. 404–416. Springer, Heidelberg (2012)

17. Lander, E.S., Waterman, M.S.: Genomic mapping by fingerprinting random clones: a mathematic alanalysis. Genomic (1988)

18. Li, X., Waterman, M.S.: Estimating the repeat structure and length of dna sequences using -tuples. Genome research **13**(8), 1916–1922 (2003)

19. Dempster, A.P., Laird, N.M., Rubin, D.B.: Maximum likelihood from incomplete data via the em algorithm. Journal of the Royal Statistical Society.SeriesB (Methodological) **39**(1), 1–38 (1977)

20. Figueiredo, M.A.T., Jain, A.K.: Unsupervised learning of finite mixture models. IEEE Transactions on Pattern analysis and machine intelligence **24**(3), 381–396 (2004)

21. Hirose, K., Kawano, S., Konishi, S., Ichikawa, M.: Bayesian information criterion and selection of the number of factors in factor analysis models. Journal of Data Science **9**(2), 243–259 (2011)

22. Wang, Y., Leung, H.C., Yiu, S.M., Chin, F.Y.: Metacluster 4.0: a novel binning algorithm for ngs reads and huge number of species. Journal of Computational Biology **19**(2), 241–249 (2012)

23. Wang, Y., Leung, H.C., Yiu, S.M., Chin, F.Y.: Metacluster 5.0: a two-round binning approach for metagenomic data for low-abundance species in a noisy sample. Bioinformatics **28**(18), 356–362 (2012)

24. Richter, D.C., Ott, F., Auch, A.F., Schmid, R., Huson, D.H.: Metasim - a sequencing simulator for genomics and metagenomics. PLoS ONE (2008)

An Application of PCA on Uncertainty of Prediction

Santi Phithakkitnukoon[✉]

Department of Computer Engineering, Faculty of Engineering,
Chiang Mai University, Chiang Mai, Thailand
santi@eng.cmu.ac.th

Abstract. Principal component analysis (PCA) has been widely used in many applications. In this paper, we present the problem of computational complexity in prediction, which increases as more input of predicting event's information is provided. We use the information theory to show that the PCA method can be applied to reduce the computational complexity while maintaining the uncertainty level of the prediction. We show that the percentage increment of uncertainty is upper bounded by the percentage increment of complexity. We believe that the result of this study will be useful for constructing predictive models for various applications, which operate with high dimensionality of data.

Keywords: PCA · Uncertainty · Prediction

1   Introduction

Prediction plays an important role in many applications. It is widely applied in various areas such weather, economic, stock, disaster (e.g. earthquake and flooding), network traffic, and call center forecasting. Several techniques and predictive models have been utilized to generate prediction such as regression analysis, Bayesian networks, Markov model, and neural network. These techniques have different computational costs associated with them. As more predicting event's information is provided, the computational cost (and complexity in some predictive models) increases. Reducing the dimensionality of the input to the predictive model in order to lower the computational cost may also increase the uncertainty of the prediction. To avoid degrading the uncertainty of the predictive model while reducing its computational cost, in this paper we present an application of the PCA method as a solution to our problem.

The rest of this paper is structured as follows. Section 2 carries out the main contribution of this paper. The paper is concluded in section 3 with a summary and an outlook on applying our finding to the future work.

2   Applying PCA to Complexity in Prediction

Prediction is a statement about the future observation. The actual future event does not always occur as its prediction. Hence there is an uncertainty associated with a prediction. The uncertainty of prediction can be measured using information entropy

P.C. Vinh et al. (Eds.): ICTCC 2014, LNICST 144, pp. 142–145, 2015.
DOI: 10.1007/978-3-319-15392-6_14

or Shannon's entropy, which is a measure of uncertainty of a random variable [1] defined by (1).

$$H(X) = -\sum_x p(x)\log_2 p(x), \tag{1}$$

where X is a discrete random variable, $x \in X$, and the probability mass function $p(x) = Pr\{X=x\}$.

Cover, T. M., and J. A. Thomas [2] shows that the uncertainty of prediction of event X given the information Y is less than uncertainty of prediction of event X without given information about event X,

$$H(X \mid Y) < H(X). \tag{2}$$

We can extend (2) to a scenario where there is more one known information about predicting event X. Since conditioning reduces entropy, (2) still holds for multiple given information,

$$H(X \mid Y_1, Y_2, Y_3, ...) < H(X). \tag{3}$$

Inequation (3) tells us that theoretically the more information about event X, the less uncertainty about predicting event X. This implies that one may collect infinite information about event X to make the optimal prediction in the sense of having the least uncertainty.

In practical prediction problem, an infinite dimensional dataset is not available. However, there is a high dimensional dataset in which taking entire data will result a high computational complexity in prediction. It is desired to lower the dimensions of dataset while retaining as much as possible of the characteristics of the dataset in order to reduce the computational complexity in prediction. This can be achieved by applying the Principal Component Analysis (PCA) method.

The PCA is a technique of multivariate analysis. It was first introduced by Pearson [3] in 1901 and developed by Hotelling [4] in 1933. The idea of PCA is to reduce the dimensionality of a dataset while retaining as much as possible of the variation present in the dataset. The PCA method composes transformation matrix from the set of input vectors containing correlated components to another set of vectors containing orthogonal and uncorrelated components. PCA reduces dimension of the dataset by keeping the most relevant information and discarding the statistically less relevant information from the multidimensional dataset. The PCA transformation is based on the autocorrelation matrix which is given by (4).

$$R_{xx} = \frac{1}{n}\sum_{j=1}^{n}\left(X_j X_j^T\right), \tag{4}$$

where n is the number of input vectors, X_j is the jth vector.

Principal components are obtained by arranging eigenvalues corresponding to eigenvectors of matrix R_{xx} in order. The first principal component contains the largest percentage of the variation in the original dataset. The second principal component contains the second largest percentage of the variation in the original dataset and so on. The main idea of PCA is to reduce dimensionality of dataset to first m principal components. I.T. Jollife [5] suggests three types of rule for choosing m; cumulative percentage of total variation, size of variances of principal components, and the scree graph and the log-eigenvalue diagram. Choosing the number of principal components is not in the scope of this paper. Interested readers may find more information from [5].

By choosing the number of principal components m, one can construct a matrix P which is given by (5).

$$P = [P_1 \quad P_2 \quad \ldots \quad P_m],$$

(5)

where P_j is the jth principal component.

The PCA can also be visualized as a simple transformation from one domain to another by projecting original data points onto the new principal component axis where the first principal component contains the largest percentage of the variation in the original data points and so on. Figure 1 shows the original data points from X-Y axis to be projecting onto the principal component axis (PC_1 and PC_2).

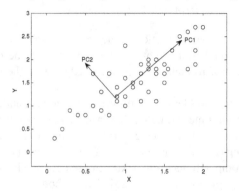

Fig. 1. Example of projection of the data points onto the principal component axis

Since the first principal component contains the largest percentage of the variation in the original dataset, therefore range of the percentage of the variation in the original dataset that the first principal component contains ($\%Var(P_1)$) lies between $100/n\%$ and 100% where n is the dimension of the original dataset.

$$\frac{1}{n} \leq \%Var(P_1) \leq 1 \cdot$$

(6)

The percentage of the variation in the original dataset contained in the first principal component has the maximum value of 100% when the original data points form a straight line. On the other hand, the percentage of the variation in the original dataset contained in the first principal component has the minimum value of $100/n\%$ when the original data points form a perfect sphere cloud where the variation of the original data contained in the first principal component is equal to the variation of the original data contained other principal components. In general, having all features (dimension) of the data equally represent the overall data is very rare.

Given a high n-dimensional dataset to predict event X with the computational complexity of $O(n)$ and uncertainty of $H(X|Y_1, Y_2, ..., Y_n)$, using the PCA method reduces the dimension of the data to n-k while increases the uncertainty to $H(X|P_1, P_2, ..., P_{n-k})$, where P_j is the jth principal component. Thus, the complexity is reduced by $(n$-$k)/n$ % while the uncertainty is increased at most by $(n$-$k)/n$ % since %$Var(P_1)$ has lower bound of $1/n$ and its equality holds if and only of all principal components contain the same variation of the original data (Eq. 6). Since the dimension of the data is reduced to n-k which means n-k principal components are retained, thus

$$\sum_{i=1}^{n-k} \%Var(P_i) \ge \frac{n-k}{n}. \tag{7}$$

This means that by applying PCA, percentage decrement of computational complexity $(\%{\downarrow}C)$ is greater than and equal to the percentage increment of uncertainty $(\%{\uparrow}H)$,

$$\%{\downarrow}C \ge \%{\uparrow}H, \tag{8}$$

which implies that using PCA can reduce the computational complexity of the predictive model while maintaining the uncertainty level of the predicting event as much as possible with its percentage incretion never be more than percentage decrement of complexity.

3   Conclusion

In this paper, we present an application of the PCA in the prediction. We show that the computational complexity of the prediction increases as the dimensionality of the dataset grows and in order to reduce computational complexity in prediction while maintaining the level of the uncertainty of prediction, the PCA method can be applied.

References

1. Shannon, C.E.: A mathematical theory of communication. Bell System Technical Journal **27**, 379–423 and 623–656 (1948)
2. Cover T.M., Thomas, J.A.: Elements of Information Theory. Wiley (1991)
3. Pearson, K.: On lines and planes of closest fit to systems of points in space. Phil. Mag. **2**(6), 559–572 (1901)
4. Hotelling, H.: Analysis of a complex of statistical variables into principal components. J. Educ. Psychol. **24**, 417–441 and 498–520 (1933)
5. Jolliffe, I.T.: Principal Component Analysis. Springer Series in Statistics (2002)

Sensing Urban Density Using Mobile Phone GPS Locations: A Case Study of Odaiba Area, Japan

Teerayut Horanont[1,2,(✉)], Santi Phithakkitnukoon[3,(✉)], and Ryosuke Shibasaki[1]

[1] Department of Civil Engineering, The University of Tokyo, Tokyo, Japan
teerayut@siit.tu.ac.th, shiba@csis.u-tokyo.ac.jp
[2] Sirindhorn International Institute of Technology, Pathum Thani, Thailand
[3] Department of Computer Engineering, Chiang Mai University,
Chiang Mai, Thailand
santi@eng.cmu.ac.th

Abstract. Today, the urban computing scenario is emerging as a concept where humans can be used as a component to probe city dynamics. The urban activities can be described by the close integration of ICT devices and humans. In the quest for creating sustainable livable cities, the deep understanding of urban mobility and space syntax is of crucial importance. This research aims to explore and demonstrate the vast potential of using large-scale mobile-phone GPS data for analysis of human activity and urban connectivity. A new type of mobile sensing data called "Auto-GPS" has been anonymously collected from 1.5 million people for a period of over one year in Japan. The analysis delivers some insights on interim evolution of population density, urban connectivity and commuting choice. The results enable urban planners to better understand the urban organism with more complete inclusion of urban activities and their evolution through space and time.

Keywords: GPS · Mobile sensing · Urban density · Mobile phone locations · Pervasive computing · Urban computing.

1 Introduction

New technology can help cities manage guarantee and deliver a sustainable future. In the past few years, it has become possible to explicitly represent and account for time-space evolution of the entire city organism. Information and communication technology (ICT) has the unique capability of being able to capture the ever-increasing amounts of information generated in the world around us, especially the longitudinal information that enables us to investigate patterns of human mobility over time. Thus, the use of real-time information to manage and operate the city is no longer just an interesting experience but a viable alternative for future urban development.

In this research, the analysis of mobile phone location, namely "Auto-GPS", has been used to serve as frameworks for the variety of measures of effective city planning. More specifically, we explore the use of location information from Auto-GPS to characterize human mobility in two major aspects. First is the commuting statistics and

© Institute for Computer Sciences, Social Informatics and Telecommunications Engineering 2015
P.C. Vinh et al. (Eds.): ICTCC 2014, LNICST 144, pp. 146–155, 2015.
DOI: 10.1007/978-3-319-15392-6_15

second is the city activity, how the change of activities in part of urban space can be detected over times.

In general, a classic travel survey is frequently used to acquire urban connectivity and trip statistics. However, they truly lack of long-term observation and sample size is always the main limitation due to the highly cost and extra processing time. In this paper, we propose a novel approach that takes advantage of anonymous long-term and preciously collected spatial-temporal location generated by Auto-GPS function from ordinary mobile phone users. As of the best of our knowledge, this is the first time that large-scale GPS traces from the mobile phone have been observed and analyzed countrywide for travel behavior research.

To have evidence showing clearly how this would help planning and decision making, we selected one of the major active area in central Tokyo called Odaiba as our study area. Odaiba is a large artificial island in Tokyo Bay, Japan. It was initially built for defensive purposes in the 1850s, dramatically expanded during the late 20th century as a seaport district, and has developed since the 1990s as a major commercial, residential and leisure area. Odaiba is suitable for this analysis since it is isolated from other parts of Tokyo. It provides all urban amenities like a small city including hotels, department stores, parks, museums, office buildings and residential areas.

The rest of the paper is organized as follows: Section 2 outlines related work; Section 3 describes the datasets and the basics of Auto-GPS; Section 4 covers methodology; Section 5 explains the results from our analysis; and Section 6 provides conclusion.

2   Related Work

Location traces from mobile devices have been increasingly used to study human mobility, which is important for urban planning and traffic engineering. Several aspects of human mobility have been exploited. Human trajectories show a high degree of temporal and spatial regularity with a significant likelihood of returning to a few highly visited locations [1]. Despite the differences in travel patterns, there is a strong regularity in our mobility on a regular basis, which makes 93% of our whereabouts predictable [2]. Understanding mobility patterns would yield insights into a variety of important social issues, such as the environmental impact of daily commutes [3].

These recent studies have emphasized on modeling, prediction, and inter-urban analysis of human mobility, but not on the richer context of it such as the engaged activity in the location visited. There are many studies that use GPS records to identify trip trajectories. Most of these works begin with the segmentation of GPS logs into individual trips, usually when there is a significant drop in speed [4][5], or when GPS logs remain in one area for a certain amount of time [6][7].

With the advance of today's ICT technologies, it is possible to realize a sort of socio-technical super-organism to support high levels of collective "urban" intelligence and various forms of collective actions [8]. It therefore becomes our interest in this work, by building on our previous research [9,10], to investigate on how to use large-scale, long-term GPS data from mobile phones to extract valuable urban statistics and to project the real world information.

3   Datasets

There were two datasets used in this study. The main dataset was collected from approximately 1.5 million mobile phone users through a certain mobile service provided by a leading mobile phone operator in Japan. Under this service, handsets provide a regular stream of highly accurate location data, and thereby enable support services that are closely linked with the user's behavior. Technically, an Auto-GPS-enabled handset position is measured within five minutes and sent through a network of registered services (Fig. 1). The data was recorded from August 2010 to October 2011. In order to preserve user privacy, Auto-GPS data was provided in a completely anonymous form to ensure privacy of personal information. It is important to acknowledge that there was some selection bias in this dataset, as participants were limited to users of a specific mobile phone service. The distribution of user type was estimated from 50,000 online surveys and about 2.6 percent (1,356 respondents) replied to use this service.

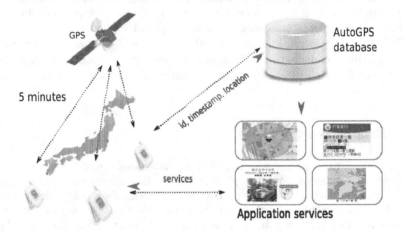

Fig. 1. Flow diagram illustrating the Auto-GPS services supported by Japanese handsets since 2009

Figure 2 shows a graph of the average number of GPS points per day in this dataset. A small sample of the raw data is shown in Fig 3. Each record in the dataset has six-tuple information that includes: User ID, Timestamp, Latitude, Longitude, Error rate, and Altitude. The approximated error rate was identified into three levels: 100 meters, 200 meters, and 300 meters, based on the strength of GPS signal available to the handset.

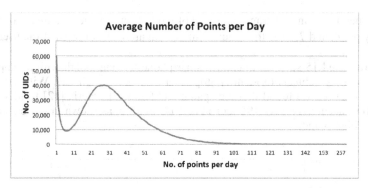

Fig. 2. The average number of GPS points per day is 37, indicating that the users spent approximately three hours traveling each day

Dummy-ID	Time	Latitude	Longitude	Error	Altitude
00862690	2010-08-01 12:01:09	34.69888	135.534146	1	64.00
00862754	2010-08-01 21:10:13	39.703028	141.146445	2	176.94
00886354	2010-08-01 12:48:23	34.33872	135.600167	3	165.73
00862690	2010-08-01 14:46:09	34.709877	135.591781	1	64.00
00169966	2010-08-01 18:19:52	35.534478	140.304336	3	39.64
00169966	2010-08-01 18:24:52	35.527892	140.312319	3	17.83

Fig. 3. A sample of Auto-GPS data that includes an anonymous dummy-id, timestamp, geolocation, error level, and altitude. The error level indicates the strength of the GPS signal available to the handset.

The second dataset is the census data, which was used for validation purpose. The census data was released in 2008, which represents census information for a grid size of one square kilometers. This data was provided by the National-Land Information Office [11].

4   Methodology

Our Auto-GPS data was considered as big data, having a total of 9.2 billion GPS records. Our data was handled and pre-processed using Hadoop./Hive on a computer cluster of six slave nodes. We first processed our Auto-GPS data to estimate the density of people who reside within specific areas (i.e., area population density), more specifically, finding their home locations. First, we extracted the locations of daily rest, or "stay points," for each individual trajectory. Let P represent a set of sequential traces of the user such that $P = \{p(1), p(2), p(3),..., p(i),...\}$ where $p(i)$ is the ith location of the user and $p(i) = \{id, time, lat, lon\}$. A stay point is defined as a series of locations in which the user remains in a certain area for a significant period of time, where distance in space and difference in time between observed points are applied as constrained multi-criteria in the detecting method i.e.,   Distance(p_{start}, p_{end}) < D_{threh} and TimeDiff (p_{start}, p_{end}) > T_{threh}, where D_{threh} and T_{threh} are adjustable parameters;

D_{threh} is the maximum coverage threshold of movement in which an area is considered as a stay point, and T_{threh} is the required minimum amount of time that the user spends in a stay point.

We recruited 15 subjects to carry a smartphone for one month with an application that allowed the subjects to identify stops that they made each day. With this ground truth information, we found that the spatial and temporal criteria [12] to identify stay points most accurately were 196 meters and 14 minutes, as shown in our experimental results in Figs. 4 and 5.

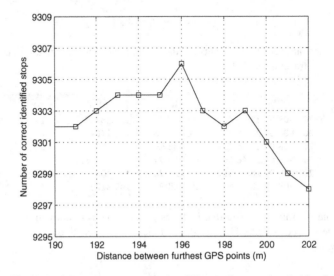

Fig. 4. Stop detection accuracies for different distance threshold values

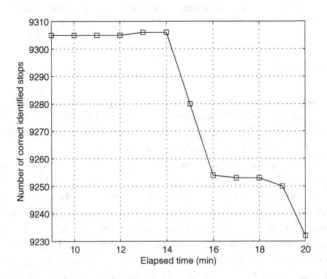

Fig. 5. Stop detection accuracies for different time threshold values

Based on the detected stay points, we estimated home location of each subject as the location with the highest number of stay points between midnight and 6 a.m. This yielded a fairly accurate estimation of home locations, which is comparable ($R^2 = 0.79$) to the population density information of the Census Data provided by the Statistics Bureau, Ministry of Internal Affairs and Communications, as shown in Fig. 6.

According to the result in Fig. 6, we considered our "stay points" to be reliable for our further analysis. The stay points and home locations were used as inputs for calculation of various urban indicators and statistics across different spatial and temporal levels in the next section.

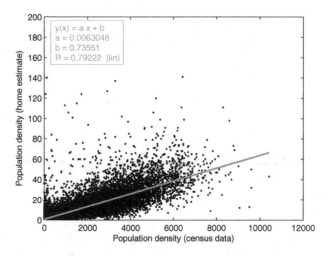

Fig. 6. A comparison of the estimated home locations from the Auto-GPS data against the Census Data of one-square kilometer grids

5   Results

Finding urban descriptive knowledge of the people who use urban spaces is one of the most important information for urban planners. Our first result attempts to explain the origin of people flow. We constructed multiple criteria to define visitors in an area. We used the minimum stay of 30 minutes and excluded people who have home and work location in the area. (Note that work location was derived in a similar way we did for the home location.) The maximum annual visit is set to eight times as it is the third quartile of the entire dataset (Fig. 8). The annual total of visitors to Odaiba area was estimated at 80,463 people from 1.5 million total samples or 5.36% of the population. Figure 7 shows the choropleth map of estimated yearly visitors. As expected, the nearer the prefecture is to the Odaiba area, the more visitors are coming from. There are some exception for the big city such as Nagoya, Osaka, Fukuoka, and Hokkaido where air transport services are operated frequently.

Fig. 7. Estimated annual visitors to Odaiba area by prefecture

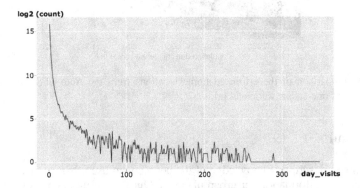

Fig. 8. Count of the number of daily visits to Odaiba area

Figure 9 shows the number of daily visitors to Odaiba area from which it appears that the area is more popular during summer. This is because of the big event arranged by the Fuji Television Network whose station is based in Odaiba. The highest number of visits to Odaiba was on the 14th of August when the Tokyo Bay Grand Fireworks Festival was held. The second most visits were on the Christmas Eve, as the area is known as a dating place. We notice a significant distinct drop in the number of visitors dramatically on 11th March. It was the day when an earthquake of magnitude 9.0 hit Japan in 2011, followed with the "radiation leakage" of two nuclear power plants in Fukushima prefecture. We observed 3 weeks of an abnormal reduction in the number of visits of the area before it returned to normal.

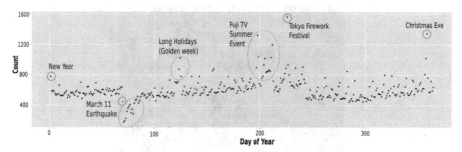

Fig. 9. Detected daily visits to Odaiba area. The magnitude of anomalies can vary greatly between events, and this could lead to composite dominated by a few major events.

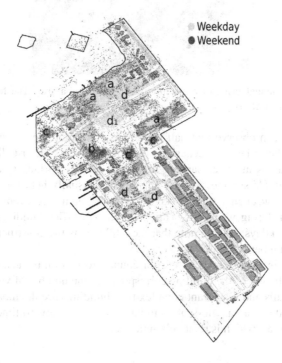

Fig. 10. Comparison of estimated visitor density between weekdays (yellow) and weekends (red)

Next, we visualized how different activities between weekdays and weekend are by overlaying weekdays stay points over the weekends' (Fig. 10). Surprisingly, there are several clusters that highly dominate over each others in particular locations. By incorporating prior knowledge of the area and collection of news, it reveals a clear evidence of how the patterns are created. The locations marked with "a" are complex buildings where shopping malls, hotels, and restaurants are situated. This yields a similar distribution of both weekdays and weekends. The "b" marker is for an open

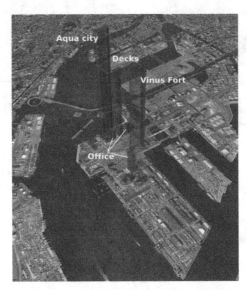

Fig. 11. Detected annual visits of each building in the Odaiba area. The height of building represents the number of visitors.

space where we can observe that half of the areas are more active during the weekends than weekdays. This is because of the special events are usually held only on weekends. The areas in upper part are served as outdoor parking spaces and are the main area of Fuji TV summer events. This event is usually held for three months in the summer both weekends and weekdays. The "c" areas are event spaces that are mainly occupied during weekends. The "d" areas are office buildings that are more active on the weekdays. Please note that the "d_1" area is the construction area during our data collection period.

In addition, Fig. 11 provides the visitor count information in each building for the entire year. The height of the building corresponds to the number of visitors. It is clear that shopping malls and restaurant complex type buildings are the most popular destinations in the Odaiba area. Both of them have approximately 10 times more visitors than the office areas, which is relatively intuitive.

6   Conclusion

This preliminary research explores the potential of using mobile phone GPS locations in a new context and broader advances towards the understanding of today's excessive mobility. The finding of this remarkable dataset is to capture the urban evolution from the real movement of people. The results display the findings of a comprehensive and creative process of the use of Auto-GPS data. Finally, the importance of this research ultimately lies on how it can be practically applied and utilized for future sustainable urban developments.

Acknowledgements. This research carried out under the support of DIAS (Data Integration and Analysis System) by MEXT (Ministry of Education, Culture, Sports, Science and Technology). We would like to thanks ZENRIN Data Com (ZDC) CO., LTD. for archiving the dataset used in this research.

References

1. González, M.C., Hidalgo, C.A., Barabási, A.-L.: Understanding individual human mobility patterns. Nature **458**, 238 (2009)
2. Song, C., Qu, Z., Blumm, N., Barabási, A.-L.: Limits of predictability in human mobility. Science **327**(5968), 1018–1021 (2010)
3. Isaacman, S., Becker, R., Cáceres, R., Kobourov, S., Rowland, J., Varshavsky, A.: A tale of two cities. In: Proceedings of the Eleventh Workshop on Mobile Computing Systems & Applications (2010)
4. de Jong, R., Mensonides, W.: Wearable GPS device as a data collection method for travel research. In: ITS-WP-03-02, Institute of Transport Studies, University of Sydney (2003)
5. Li, Z., Wang, J., Han, J.: Mining event periodicity from incomplete observations. In: Proceedings of the 18th ACM SIGKDD International Conference on Knowledge Discovery and Data Mining (2012)
6. Ashbrook, D., Starner, T.: Using GPS to learn significant locations and predict movement across multiple users. Personal and Ubiquitous Computing **7**, 275–286 (2003)
7. Gong, H., Chen, C., Bialostozky, E., Lawson, C.: A GPS/GIS method for travel mode detection in New York City. Computers, Environment and Urban Systems (2011)
8. Fontana, D., Zambonelli, F.: Towards an infrastructure for urban superorganisms: challenges and architecture. In: IEEE International Conference on Cyber, Physical and Social Computing (2012)
9. Horanont, T., Witayangkurn, A., Sekimoto, Y., Shibasaki, R.: Large-Scale Auto-GPS Analysis for Discerning Behavior Change during Crisis. IEEE Intelligent Systems **28**(4), 26–34 (2013)
10. Horanont, T., Phithakkitnukoon, S., Leong, T.W., Sekimoto, Y., Shibasaki, R.: Weather Effects on the Patterns of People's Everyday Activities: A Study Using GPS Traces of Mobile Phone Users. PLoS ONE **8**(12), e81153 (2013)
11. National-Land Information Office. http://www.mlit.go.jp/kokudoseisaku/gis/index.html (Retrieved January 27, 2013)
12. Zheng, Y., Li, Q., Chen, Y., Xie, X., Ma, W.-Y.: Understanding mobility based on GPS data. In: Proceedings of the 10th ACM International Conference on Ubiquitous Computing (UbiComp 2008), New York, NY, USA, pp. 312–321 (2008)

Co-modeling: An Agent-Based Approach to Support the Coupling of Heterogeneous Models

Nghi Quang Huynh[1]([⊠]), Hiep Xuan Huynh[1],
Alexis Drogoul[2], and Christophe Cambier[2]

[1] DREAM-CTU/IRD, CICT-CTU, Cantho, Vietnam
{hqnghi,hxhiep}@ctu.edu.vn
[2] UMI 209 UMMISCO, IRD, Hanoi, Vietnam
{alexis.drogoul,christophe.cambier}@ird.fr

Abstract. Coupling models is becoming more and more important in the fields where modeling relies on interdisciplinary collaboration. This in particular the case in modeling complex systems which often require to either integrate different models at different spatial and temporal scales or to compare their outcomes. The goal of this research is to develop an original agent-based approach to support the coupling heterogeneous models. The architecture that we have designed is implemented in the GAMA modeling and simulation platform [6]. The benefits of our approach is to support coupling and combining various models of heterogeneous types (agent-based, equation-based, cellular automata) in a flexible and explicit way. It also support the dynamic execution of the models which are supposed to be combined during experiments. We illustrate its use and powerfulness to solve existing problems of coupling between an agent-based model, equation-based model and GIS based model. The outcomes of the simulation of these three models show results compatible with the data observed in reality and demonstrate the interest of our approach for building large, multi-disciplinary models.

Keywords: Models Coupling · Agent-based modeling · Simulation platforms · Land-use change dynamics

1 Introduction

Coupling, anchoring and composing models is more and more common, especially in the field of sustainable development, where researchers tend to work in multidisciplinary setups. Requirements to do so can come from the necessity to integrate different models (for instance, urban and climate models), to compare the outcomes of models used in decision-making processes, to couple models of the same phenomena at different spatial and temporal scales, and so on. Moreover, the questions of the end-users, for which models are initially designed, have become more complex and less focused, forcing modelers to anticipate probable changes in the structure of the models, or to design models in such a way that they can be incrementally modified or experimented in unexpected ways.

© Institute for Computer Sciences, Social Informatics and Telecommunications Engineering 2015
P.C. Vinh et al. (Eds.): ICTCC 2014, LNICST 144, pp. 156–170, 2015.
DOI: 10.1007/978-3-319-15392-6_16

Various solutions have been proposed in the latest years, but they are mostly oriented towards technical approaches to the operational coupling of models (HLA [2], DEVS [19], FMI [1]]), leaving aside the semantic problem of their static or dynamic composition. In particular, there is no way one can provide, let alone revise and reuse, a description of their composition, such as, for instance, the spatial and temporal scales of the models involved, their transfer functions, how they are supposed to be combined during experiments, etc.

In this paper we propose a new approach for the coupling of heterogeneous model developed in a simulation platform Gama. This approaches is tested on a concrete case study of the land use change which is defined every 5 years through a specific methodology: this one is based a land use evaluation according to several environmental (water quantity and quantity, soil type) and socio-economical factors.

In Section 2, we present the definition, problem of coupling model and the existing approaches. In Section 3 we describe our proposed approaches: co-modeling, and how it has been implemented in the GAMA simulation platform. Section 4 provides some results obtained by simulating the coupled model and describes in details the experiments that we have conducted. Finally, Section 5 concludes our ongoing work.

2   Models Coupling

2.1   Definition

In general, the terminology of coupling between models is used when modeler makes some interactions between at least two models which have ability to operate independently [4]. This approaching of coupling can be found when modeler wants to do research on the heterogeneous system with many levels of details and the best approaching model of that system is an association of different existing models. It also occurs when modeler wants to answer a complex question with different existent components that have been made in special objectives. For instance, the question of climate changes (as the general one in ecologies) is a clear example of the necessity to couple different domains or researches from multidisciplinary with different level of spatial and times scales.

A model referencing a heterogeneous systems, is called heterogeneous model, include multiple components, each component is a model or smaller systems, which can operate independently of each other. The coupling of heterogeneous models [8] can be considered as several meaning: it is the connections, the links, and the anchors between models with models. It shows how the models are integrated with each others, how they can interact in coupling context. Models can be coupled themselves with the others in a certain order of space or time to be a system corresponding with the scales in heterogeneous system.

2.2   Type of Coupling

In [7], the authors classify the coupling based on the principle of coupling as following:

– Methods based on a coupling factor (space, time event) or a common element models is identified to the coupling operation. For example the specification language DEVS (Discrete Event System Specification) [19], the DS model [3].
– The methods based on an intermediqate using an interface for coupling the various models. In this category of approaches include the Osiris model [4] for the UrbanSim model[17], the HLA [2] model.
– Methods based on integration where the models are built, modified and adapted to each other to build a new model.

In [4], the authors list the coupling approaches by degree of the coupling:

– The coupling which is based on the establishment of data transmission, is also called a weak coupling, this approach of coupling depends on a solution of technical infrastructure of simulator, if these facilities can support the simulation of models from different platforms.
– The strong coupling describes the coupling between behaviors of models, for the integration between each of them. This type of coupling is often based on the same platform, which provides the capability to import or re-implement one or many parts of existent models.

We choose to categorize the coupling in two type: (1) The coupling which is based on the establishment of data transmission or exchangement values, is also called weak (loosely) coupling. This approach of coupling depends on a solution of technical infrastructure of simulator, if these facilities can support the simulation of models from different platform. This type of coupling contains a set of common data exchange protocol. (2) The strong coupling describes the coupling between behaviors of models.

2.3   Importance of Coupling

Coupling models is a high priority approach which seeks to enhance knowledge and reuse previously validated models, to expect at the same time a lower risk of error and a faster construction of simulation models. Climate forecast, prediction of environmental risks or simulation of urban mechanisms are the relevant examples. For example, the zoning process is defined at 4 administrative levels: National, Provinces, Districts and Communes. Based on this zoning process, a land use planning policy is defined every 5 years through a specific methodology: this one is based a land use evaluation according to several environmental (water quantity and quantity, soil type) and socio-economical factors. However, the land use planning is rarely followed by farmers because of: (1) modifications of the natural conditions, (2) changements in the farmers socio-economic situation or the fact that farmers may prefer to follow other farmers when making their decision of land use change. This scenario leads to the need of coupling models to test hypotheses on the main factors influencing farmer's decisions who taking into account external (physical or economic) factors. The model would be very complex as it touches on many fields providing a lot of factors related to the behaviors of the farmer, the economic and the natural conditions. It is not easy to combine various factors coming from different models.

2.4 Problems

In this paragraph, we generally introduce the existing problems of the coupling activity.

Different Formalism of Coupling. Because coupling models often take place when the modeling carried out with more and more models from many different fields that each one has a particular modeling formalism. Thus, modeler has been lead to the problem of diverting the formalism of coupling models. Nowadays, scientific models usually base on three formalism: model base on differential equation, model base on automata cellular, model base on agent. The three formalism are different naturally in the way that they describe the model and it is the root cause why they have a big difficulty to reuse all in one context.

Spatial and Temporal Scales. While couple models, modeler usually encounter with the needs to change the spatial and temporal level of an object or components of model. This change benefit the diverse representation from one model to other considering their discipline.

Facilitation the Manipulation of Coupling. Most of the current solutions proposed dont support an approach to ease the description of coupling between models. It leaving aside the semantic problem of dynamic composition.

2.5 Existing Approaches

There are three existing popular coupling formalism: High-Level Architecture (HLA) [2] and Discrete Event Systems (DEVS) [19], Functional Mockup Interface [1]).

HLA uses most in humans training to perform tasks and analysis of scenarios in a simulated world. HLA integration the mechanism for the synchronization of simulators whenever they exchange data. The principle of HLA is consider that simulators are assemblies to the Federation. An interface RTI (Runtime Infrastructure) assures the synchronization of exchange between the Federation. HLA is defined by three core elements: the template object model (contains HLA Federation Object Model and HLA Simulation Object Model), the interface specification with Runtime Infrastructure, and HLA rules.

DEVS is a formalism proposed to model discrete event systems with two type of models: model atomic is considered as sub model with contribute parameters (the set of input, output events, sequential states; the time advance, the external/internal transition function and the output function. It helps modeler to specify their models events, set of states, internal and external transition, inputs and outputs), and coupled model which specify by three main set of: atomic models to be coupled, translation function between models, influences between models. The interaction assured by the ports, input and output, which are favorites the modularity.

FMI is an independent approach for model exchange that is support black box model exchange. This standard has been developed to meet the requirements of standardization, availability, easy-of-use, adoption, accompanying documentation and maturity of such an interface. This standard is a promising candidate to become the industrial standard and cross-company collaboration, but it is not suitable too much with white box modeling of the complex system with one modeling language that is not suitable for all requirements in different domains. This approach offers the possibility for deep system understanding by equation-based, object-oriented modeling and symbolic manipulation.

Beside these three common standards, such works have often implemented their own coupling method of spatial, temporal and data on a specific modeling platform. Many researches have been done to couple the models of complex system in multi-discipline: coupling among model different domain (urban - travel [10], environment and pelagic resources [18], community land model to the regional climate [14]). Other researches couple multi models in same domain but in different objective, to show if these objectives represent an important factor that modify or improve in the simulation results and evaluate them [11]. They exchange the data in phase of executions in an order temporal simultaneous one by one or parallel, i.e., in [9] the coupling is called "coupler" who exchange data input and output between models scales. Coupling also has been done by different modeling approaches: coupling hydrodynamic model and individual-based models [12], coupling multi-agent model and GIS [8] [13], coupling of physical models and social models multi-modeling [5].

All these approaches provide mechanisms that allow interaction between several models but they still have following disadvantages:

– In general, these approaches are not very generic and seem to be very difficult to be re-implemented in different domains and contexts.
– There are no consideration of the differences in spatial and temporal scales.
– They do not support to couple the case of heterogeneous models between mathematician, informatics, GIS

3   Co-modeling

We present in this section the methodology we propose to couple multiple models. Then, it has been implemented in the GAMA agent-based modeling and simulation platform [6].

3.1   Conceptual Proposal

We propose to address the problem identified in II.C. with the modeling and simulating of the "co-model" as a contraction of "coupling of models" and "composing of models". The central claim of our approach will be considered a "co-model" as a model, and more specifically an agent-based model, in which the agents wrap one or several instances of the models to couple, with their own life-cycle, operations, collaborations, conflict resolution mechanisms, etc. which will draw from the numerous works already published on multi-agent systems.

In this perspective, a co-model will be a model that captures and represents a particular collaboration between these micro-models, which can be based on existing collaboration schemes between experts, or any other organisation of their contributions. Conversely, this work will allow to consider regular multi-agent based models as very specific implementations of co-models, where agents only wrap models of individuals. Our approaches challenge the first problem of coupling model, by considering agents as models, the different modeling formalisms could be considered as behaviors of agents. Then, it solve the second problem of spatial and temporal scales by inherit the rich existing researches on these difference level of scaling, thus the proposal did not, itself, propose the concrete solution. The inheriting from agent based modeling help modeler to easily manipulate the description of coupling with the declaration behaviors and attributes interaction between agents which are, in fact, models.

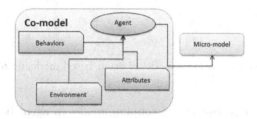

Fig. 1. Co-model extend the concept of agent-based modeling formalism

The figure 1 represent our propose: a comodels agent (in rose) associate with its attributes, behaviors and environment as normal agent, then we attache an concept micro-model to the agent. The agent, now, known theirs micro-models and can easily couple, access, integrate and control them dynamically.

3.2 Computer Implementation

To further clarify the co-modeling methodology, our enrichment enabled GAMA modeling language (GAML) to support the modeler in the development of coupling agent-based models.

We exploit the current meta-model of GAMA in Figure 2. It represents a diagram with three parts: meta-model, model and simulation. The meta-model part describes the meta-model concept of a agent based model in GAMA. These concepts of meta-model use in the model part to specify an agent-based model. The simulation part shows an example of a simulation initialized from the model. The current agent-based modeling platforms rely on a meta-model with the following principal concepts: Agent, Environment, Scheduler, Spatial scale and temporal scale. Agent represents the concept of agent in the model, which also defines a level of organization. Environment support modeling the environment in which agents are situated, i.e., the spatial scale. Scheduler schedules the execution of agents during the simulation, defined the temporal scale. Spatial and temporal scale concepts help modeler to define the spatial scale which is an area that agents can be situated, and temporal scale which defines how agents are scheduled in the simulation. This meta-model is missing a part of representing and manipulating the co-model of our approaches.

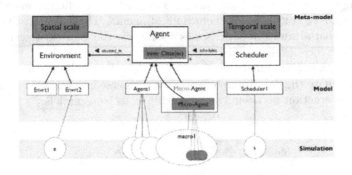

Fig. 2. A simplified meta-model of agent-based modeling platforms

To support the development of coupling model in agent based, we propose an extension of the current meta-model described in [16]. We thus introduce new concepts to do coupling operation. The new concepts micro-model represented as classes in the extended meta-model Figure 3 give an answer to the first two modelers requirement : Entities may define different levels of organization related to specific agents which create the instant the micro-models s experiment. These levels of organization may be hierarchical. The micro-model concepts, attached to Agent, offer the modeler the possibility to define the coupling model for each type of agent. It defines the models on which agents can access and control their schedule in the simulation, i.e., their scheduling frequency and order. These two concepts make the meta-model capable of satisfying the first requirement. Thanks to this concept, the modeler can declare an model as micro-model inside a specific Agent type which can be a normal Agent or the Agent World. The agent World is the top-level agent which is the instant of current model. An instance of the outer Agent type is called co-model while an instance of the inner Agent type is called micro-model. A co-model always maintains a reference to its micro-model and vice versa, the micro-model also know their container, co-model. This concept thus facilitates the modeling of hierarchical organization of levels and the coupling between levels, i.e., the modeling of interaction and data exchanges between levels.

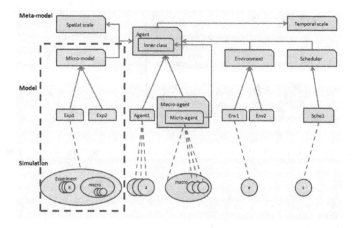

Fig. 3. Extend a simplified version meta-model of current agent-based modeling platforms to support coupling models (changes are in left dot-rectangle)

With our alter on the current meta-model, a co-model in GAMA is represented as model in GAML, which wrap several micro-models. This wrapping is called an importation. In side of current form of importation, all the declarations of the model(s) imported will be merged with those of the current model (in the order with which the import statements are declared, i.e. the latest definitions of global attributes or behaviors superseding the previous ones), we give its an model-identifier to precise the imported model are a micro-model. The co-model is implemented in GAMA with three phases: importation, instantiation and execution. These phases are not presented in the meta-model for the sake of simplicity, but it is controlled by the simulation process of GAMA. A species can thus contain several micro-model representing different coupling that agents of the species can execute. They are executed when the corresponding agents are scheduled by the scheduler. We present these three phase with demonstration by using the three model in figure 4. Model product market gives the values of the products. Model environments contains characteristics and dynamics of soil, water and flooding plots. Model cognitive with agents farmers choose among crops in neighbors that considers economic conditions and their culture.

Importation. This phase is extended from the current type of importation. Normally, the importation will merge all composition of imported models into the main model. We have modify it to accept an identifier of each micro-model importation. This identifier uses as alias name in which modeler decide to reuse the same micro-model with different scenario, they give it different identifier. Figure 5 present an example of importation. The syntax is divide in three part: the keyword "import", the path to existing micro-model, and the identifier, to be used, followed the keyword "as".

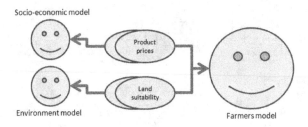

Fig. 4. An example with three models used for coupling approaches

```
10  import "marketProduct.gaml" as myMarket
11  import "SeaLevel.gaml" as mySea
12  import "environmentChange.gaml" as myEnv
```

Fig. 5. Importing model as micro-species

Instantiation. This phase will instantiate agent of micro-model. Modeler can use identifier that they declare in importation phase, to instantiate micro-model with "create" statement. Thus , we have provided to reuse one model many times with "identifier", modeler can initialize the micro-model with different input values as parameters. Figure 6 demonstrate syntax of the instantiation the micro-models with default value of parameters, nothing was declared in statement: keyword create, micro-model's identifier.

```
51   init {
52         create myMarket.marketgrow;
53         create mySea.SaltIntrusion;
54         create myEnv.envChange;
```

Fig. 6. Instantiate agents of micro-species

Execution. Thanks to multi-level modeling in GAMA [16] and our coupling approach, the execution of micro-model carried out by asking micro-model's agent to do step by step of simulation. The syntax is simply semantic as natural language: "ask" micro-model's identifier do step (see Figure 7). Beside, modelers can access all behaviors, attributes of micro-models and do data-exchange between them.

```
167    ask myMarket.marketgrow
168    {
169        do _step_;
170        myself.price_rice <-  priceRice;
171        myself.price_shrimp <- priceShrimp;
172        myself.price_coconut <- priceCoco;
173    }
174
175
176    ask mySea.SaltIntrusion
177    {
178        loop times: 10
179        {
180            do _step_;
181        }
182        myself.envOut <- outParcel;
183    }
```

Fig. 7. Ask agents of micro-species to simulate and exchange data between models

4   Experiments

4.1   Objectives

This part will show the experimentation of our coupling approaches framework by applying the coupling model for Land use change modeling in Thanh Phu district, Ben Tre province. We have 3 scenarios for testing as the reasons of land use change: (1) The farmer changed their land use type following the others based on the increasing of price product; (2) The natural condition changed by the new dike build or operation of the sluice gates to control the salted water effect to decision of farmer; (3) Combine two condition : product prices and salt intrusion. The purpose of the co-models is to show the progressive that how we have solve issues of : Spatial - temporal scales, the coupling entities between models, and the presentation of organization co-models.

4.2   Data Used

The land unit map of Thanh Phu district have done by GIS analysis method UNION the single layers: soil, saline water and flood depth layer. The land unit map are used for determining the properties of land parcel on it. Each farmer have a parcel, each parcel based on a land unit that contains soils type, a land use type, saline level, flood duration and flood depth.

Land unit of Thanh Phu district (Source: My N T H, 2012) analyzing the Land Suitability of the land units for six popular land use types of the district as the 8. The levels of land suitability measure the capacity of the land unit for each land use type: $S1 = 100$.

The three scenarios use the following data structure: it contains the land use type, the area, salt level and land unit type. Land use type is the current type in agriculture of farmers, it can be Annual-crops, Aquaculture, Perennial-fruit, Perennial industrial crop, Rice, Rice Shrimp, 2 Rice 1 Annual-crops. The area of each parcel is in square meter units. Salt level present the level of salt intrusion, begin from 2/1000 to the highest 9/1000.

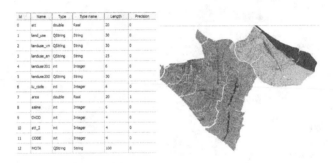

Fig. 8. Input data of Land use model (left) and real map in 2010 (right)

4.3   Scenarios 1 : Coupling with Economic Model

The first scenario, farmers take decisions depend on price of products. The price come from a micro-model which simulate the price change of agriculture product from 2005 to 2010, the data is take from real market and modeled in a mathematical function, ffigure 9 show the value from this model.

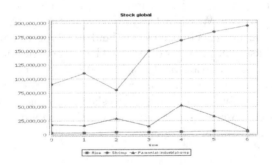

Fig. 9. Market product price in VND simulated from 2005 to 2010

The farmers take decision the best price product that their neighbors have, to change their next land use plan. This scenario reach to show the capability of coupling between mathematical model and agent-based model. At each simulation step, farmers ask economic model to get the price of all products types in that year, then they look in their neighbors to compared the highest benefit to decide the next types of products in next simulation.

Figure 10 show the reality that the product price did not change too much, so the decision of farmers are keeping in their current type of land-use, until the product price have a big change for their benefits.

4.4   Scenarios 2 : Coupling with Environment Model

In this scenario, we couple two models, one define the agriculture activities of farmers on their land unit, other model simulate the salt intrusion where the

Fig. 10. Simulation results when coupling farmer's land-use model with market product model

salt level in the river diffuse to land unit in dry season, and inverse the direction of diffusion in rain season. Then, at each simulation step, farmers look at environment especially soil and water properties effected by salt intrusion. If the salt level of the parcel is too high (over 0.8/1000 units) farmer could not do any other agriculture activities except the aquaculture. If salt level is lower, they can make choice of rice shrimp or other types suitable with salt level. We see the changes in result (Figure 10 black part on the right) compared with the current state (Figure 8 right part).

Fig. 11. Simulation Results when coupling farmer's land-use model with environment model (salt intrusion)

After simulation, the state of land use change show the effect of salt intrusion in two area (black color). These two one is nearest river and take too much salt from river in dry season. The farmers chose to change from rice type to rice shrimp type, which is adopt by higher salt level.

4.5   Scenarios 3 : Coupling with Environment and Economic Model

In the last scenario, we decide to combine these three models together as in Figure 4, to see the effects on the fly of the farmers. They consider both conditions on economic and environment changes beside their desire to maximize income but minimize pollution and risk financial. At each simulation step, the price product and salt intrusion modify attribute land use type, salt level of parcels in progress of changes the agriculture activities. Firstly, if last changed of land use type to Perennial tree, farmer have to wait at least 4 years to other LUT; Secondly, farmers do the Perennial or fruit near their house, their parcel

have to touch the river; Thirdly, They can not do rice, vegetable or fruit inside
the people how are doing shrimp because he dont have fresh water, inversely
they can not do the shrimp inside the rice or fruit. Lastly, the Shrimp type have
to touch river, channel or other shrimp.

Figure 12 show the result which have many change compared with current
state in 2010, it demonstrate the strong effect when we coupling environment
with price product into the land use change.

Fig. 12. Simulation results in case of coupling both environment and socio-economic
model with farmer's land-use

4.6   Verify Results

The simulation of each scenario run with 5 steps, corresponding with 5 years
from 2005 to 2010, and it repeat 5 times to take the average values. We take
the total area of each type of agriculture in 2010 and make a compare chart as
in Figure 13. In this current research we just review on this chart between real
data and simulation results.

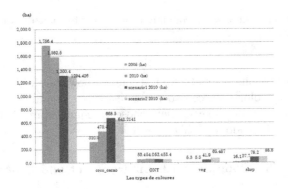

Fig. 13. Total area of products in simulated result comparing with real data in 2010

Current validation cannot compare these consecutive parcel or definitely
position, the neighbors was just moving a little bit which are considered as
no changed... Improvement in our future works will be the applying fuzzy kappa
algorithm [15].

5   Conclusion

This paper has proposed a coupling methodology in multi-agent based modeling, and implemented it to platform GAMA. With this implementation, modeler can easily reuse multi exists models. The current infrastructure allows developers to integrate diversity type of model (multi-agent, mathematical) and also diversity platforms which is in experimental phase supporting R language. In the next research, we will made the validation of coupling model by exploring number of parcels and the distant of right parcel to the simulated parcel.

Acknowledgments. This publication has been made possible through support provided by the IRD-DSF. A special thanks to Quang Chi TRUONG of Land Resource Department - College of Environment and Natural Resources - Can Tho university for supporting data collection in this research.

References

1. Bertsch, C., Ahle, E., Schulmeister, U.: The functional mockup interface - seen from an industrial perspective, 27–33, March, 2014
2. Dahmann, J., Fujimoto, R., Weatherly, R.: The DoD high level architecture: an update. In: Simulation Conference Proceedings, Winter, vol. 1, pp. 797–804 (December 1998)
3. David, D., Payet, D., Botta, A., Lajoie, G., Manglou, S., Courdier, R.: Un couplage de dynamiques comportementales : le modle ds pour l'amnagement du territoire. In: JFSMA 2007, pp. 129–138 (2007)
4. Fianyo, Y. E.: Couplage de modles l'aide d'agents: le systme OSIRIS. PhD thesis, ANRT, Grenoble (2001)
5. Gauthier Quesnel, D.V.: Coupling of physical models and social models: multi-modeling and simulation with VLE. Joint Conference on Multi-Agent Modelling for Environmental Management (CABM-HEMA-SMAGET 2005), Bourg Saint Maurice, France, pp. 21–25 (2005)
6. Grignard, A., Taillandier, P., Gaudou, B., Vo, D.A., Huynh, N.Q., Drogoul, A.: GAMA 1.6: Advancing the Art of Complex Agent-Based Modeling and Simulation. In: Boella, G., Elkind, E., Savarimuthu, B.T.R., Dignum, F., Purvis, M.K. (eds.) PRIMA 2013. LNCS, vol. 8291, pp. 117–131. Springer, Heidelberg (2013)
7. Hassoumi, I.: Approche multi-agent de couplage de modles pour la modmes complexes spatiaux: application l'amnagement de l'espace urbain (ville de touia). PhD thesis, Paris 6 (2013)
8. Huang, H., Wang, L., Zhang, X., Luo, Y., Zhao, L.: Coupling multi-agent model and GIS to simulate pine wood nematode disease spread in ZheJiang province, china, pp. 71430X–71430X-8 (October 2008)
9. Moreira, E., Costa, S., Aguiar, A.P., Cmara, G., Carneiro, T.: Dynamical coupling of multiscale land change models. Landscape Ecology **24**(9), 1183–1194 (2009)
10. Nicolai, T.W., Wang, L., Nagel, K., Waddell, P.: Coupling an urban simulation model with a travel modela first sensitivity test. Computers in Urban Planning and Urban Management (CUPUM), Lake Louise, Canada. Also VSP WP, pp. 11–07 (2011)

11. Rajeevan, M., Nanjudiah, R.: Coupled model simulations of twentieth century climate of the indian summer monsoon. Current Trends in Science, pp. 537–567 (2009)

12. Rochette, S., Huret, M., Rivot, E., Le Pape, O.: Coupling hydrodynamic and individual-based models to simulate long-term larval supply to coastal nursery areas. Fisheries Oceanography **21**(4), 229–242 (2012)

13. Rousseaux, F., Bocher, E., Gourlay, A., Petit, G.: Toward a coupling between GIS and agent simulation: USM, an OrbisGIS extension to model urban evolution at a large scale. In: OGRS 2012 Proceedings, pp. 206–214 (October 2012)

14. Steiner, A.L., Pal, J.S., Rauscher, S.A., Bell, J.L., Diffenbaugh, N.S., Boone, A., Sloan, L.C., Giorgi, F.: Land surface coupling in regional climate simulations of the west african monsoon. Clim. Dyn. **33**(6), 869–892 (2009)

15. van Vliet, J., Hagen-Zanker, A., Hurkens, J., van Delden, H.: A fuzzy set approach to assess the predictive accuracy of land use simulations. Ecol. Model. **261–262**, 32–42 (2013)

16. Vo, D.-A., Drogoul, A., Zucker, J.-D.: Multi-level agent-based modeling: a generic approach and an implementation. In: Barbucha, D., Le, M.T., Howlett, R.J., Jain, L.C. (eds.) KES-AMSTA, vol. 252. Frontiers in Artificial Intelligence and Applications, pp. 91–101. IOS Press (2013)

17. Waddell, P.: UrbanSim: Modeling urban development for land use, transportation, and environmental planning. Journal of the American Planning Association **68**(3), 297–314 (2002)

18. Yez, E., Hormazbal, S., Silva, C., Montecinos, A., Barbieri, M.A., Valdenegro, A., Rdenes, A., Gmez, F.: Coupling between the environment and the pelagic resources exploited off northern chile: ecosystem indicators and a conceptual model (2008)

19. Zeigler, B., Moon, Y., Kim, D., Ball, G.: The DEVS environment for high-performance modeling and simulation. IEEE Computational Science Engineering **4**(3), 61–71 (1997)

Adaptive Distributed Systems with Cellular Differentiation Mechanisms

Ichiro Satoh[✉]

National Institute of Informatics, 2-1-2 Hitotsubashi, Chiyoda, Tokyo 101-8430, Japan
ichiro@nii.ac.jp

Abstract. This paper proposes a bio-inspired middleware for self-adaptive software agents on distributed systems. It is unique to other existing approaches for software adaptation because it introduces the notions of differentiation, dedifferentiation, and cellular division in cellular slime molds, e.g., dictyostelium discoideum, into real distributed systems. When an agent delegates a function to another agent coordinating with it, if the former has the function, this function becomes less-developed and the latter's function becomes well-developed.

1 Introduction

Self-adaptiveness is useful in distributed systems, because their scale and complexity are beyond the ability of traditional management approaches, e.g., centralized and top-down ones. Distributed systems should adapt themselves to changes in their system structures, including network topology, and the requirements of their applications. This paper presents a bio-inspired self-tuning approach for adapting software components that a distributed application consists of without any centralized and top-down management systems. It is characterized in introducing *cellular differentiation* into distributed systems. It is the mechanism by which cells in a multicellular organism become specialized to perform specific functions in a variety of tissues and organs. It is impossible for us to expect what functions software components should have and how computational resources should be assigned to software components. This is because distributed systems are dynamic and may partially have malfunctioned, e.g., network partitioning. Our middleware system aims at building and operating distributed applications consisting of self-adapting/tuning software components, called agents, to differentiate their functions according to their roles in whole applications and resource availability, as just like cells. It involves treating the undertaking/delegation of functions in agents from/to other agents as their differentiation factors. When an agent delegates a function to another agent, if the former has the function, its function becomes less-developed in the sense that it has less computational resources, e.g., active threads, and the latter's function becomes well-developed in the sense that it has more computational resources.

2 Related Work

This section discusses several related studies on software adaptation in distributed systems. One of the most typical self-organization approaches to distributed systems is

© Institute for Computer Sciences, Social Informatics and Telecommunications Engineering 2015
P.C. Vinh et al. (Eds.): ICTCC 2014, LNICST 144, pp. 171–180, 2015.
DOI: 10.1007/978-3-319-15392-6_17

swarm intelligence [2,3]. Although there is no centralized control structure dictating how individual agents should behave, interactions between simple agents with static rules often lead to the emergence of intelligent global behavior. There have been many attempts to apply self-organization into distributed systems, e.g., a myconet model for peer-to-peer network [10], and a cost-sensitive graph structure for coordinated replica placement [4]. Most existing approaches only focus on their target problems or applications but are not general purpose, whereas distributed systems have a general-purpose infrastructure. Our software adaptation approach should be independent of applications. Furthermore, most existing self-organization approaches explicitly or implicitly assume a large population of agents or boids. However, since the size and structure of real distributed systems have been designed and optimized to the needs of their applications, the systems have no room to execute such large numbers of agents.

The aim of resource management strategy is to maximize the profits of both customer agents and resource agents in large datacenters by balancing demand and supply in the market. Several researchers have addressed resource allocation for clouds by using an auction mechanism. For example, Lin et al [5] proposed a mechanism based on a sealed-bid auction. The cloud service provider collected all the users' bids and determined the price. Zhang et al. [12] introduced the notion of spot markets and proposed market analysis to forecast the demand for each spot market.

Suda et al. proposed bio-inspired middleware, called Bio-Networking, for disseminating network services in dynamic and large-scale networks where there were a large number of decentralized data and services [8,11]. Although they introduced the notion of energy into distributed systems and enabled agents to be replicated, moved, and deleted according to the number of service requests, they had no mechanism to adapt agents' behavior unlike ours. As most of their parameters, e.g., energy, tended to depend on a particular distributed system. so that they may not have been available in other systems.[1] Our approach should be independent of the capabilities of distributed systems as much as possible.

The Anthill project [1] by the University of Bologna developed a bio-inspired middleware for peer-to-peer systems, which is composed of a collection of interconnected nests. Autonomous agents, called ants can travel across the network trying to satisfy user requests. The project provided bio-inspired frameworks, called Messor [6] and Bison [7]. Messor is a load-balancing application of Anthill and Bison is a conceptual bio-inspired framework based on Anthill.

3   Basic Approach

This paper introduces the notion of (de)differentiation into a distributed system as a mechanism for adapting software components, which may be running on different computers connected through a network.

Differentiation: When dictyostelium discoideum cells aggregate, they can be differentiated into two types: prespore cells and prestalk cells. Each cell tries to become a

---

[1] For example, they implicitly assumed a quantitative relation between the costs of agent processing and migration, but such a relation depends on individual distributed systems.

prespore cell and periodically secretes cAMP to other cells. If a cell can receive more than a specified amount of cAMP from other cells, it can become a prespore cell. There are three rules. 1) cAMP chemotaxically leads other cells to prestalk cells. 2) A cell that is becoming a prespore cell can secrete a large amount of cAMP to other cells. 3) When a cell receives more cAMP from other cells, it can secrete less cAMP to other cells.

Each agent has one or more functions with weights, where each weight corresponds to the amount of cAMP and indicates the superiority of its function. Each agent initially intends to progress all its functions and periodically multicasts *restraining* messages to other agents federated with it. Restraining messages lead other agents to degenerate their functions specified in the messages and to decrease the superiority of the functions. As a result, agents complement other agents in the sense that each agent can provide some functions to other agents and delegate other functions to other agents that can provide the functions.

Dedifferentiation: Agents may lose their functions due to differentiation as well as be busy or failed. The approach also offers a mechanism to recover from such problems based on dedifferentiation, which a mechanism for regressing specialized cells to simpler, more embryonic, unspecialized forms. As in the dedifferentiation process, if there are no other agents that are sending restraining messages to an agent, the agent can perform its dedifferentiation process and strengthen their less-developed or inactive functions again.

4   Design and Implementation

Our approach is maintained through two parts: runtime systems and agents. The former is a middleware system for running on computers and the latter is a self-contained and autonomous software entity. It has three protocols for (de)differentiation and delegation.

4.1   Agent

Each agent consists of one or more functions, called the *behavior* parts, and its state, called the *body* part, with information for (de)differentiation, called the *attribute* part.

- The body part maintains program variables shared by its behaviors parts like instance variables in object orientation. When it receives a request message from an external system or other agents, it dispatches the message to the behavior part that can handle the message.
- The behavior part defines more than one application-specific behavior. It corresponds to a method in object orientation. As in behavior invocation, when a message is received from the body part, the behavior is executed and returns the result is returned via the body part.
- The attribute part maintains descriptive information with regard to the agent, including its own identifier. The attributes contains a database for maintaining the weights of its own behaviors and for recording information on the behaviors that other agents can provide.

The agent has behaviors $b_1^k, \ldots, b_n^k$ and w_i^k is the weight of behavior b_i^k. Each agent (k-th) assigns its own maximum to the total of the weights of all its behaviors. The W_i^k is the maximum of the weight of behavior b_i^k. The maximum total of the weights of its behaviors in the k-th agent must be less than W^k. ($W^k \geq \sum_{i=1}^{n} w_i^k$), where $w_j^k - 1$ is 0 if w_j^k is 0. The W^k may depend on agents. In fact, W^k corresponds to the upper limit of the ability of each agent and may depend on the performance of the underlying system, including the processor. Note that we never expect that the latter will be complete, since agents periodically exchange their information with neighboring agents. Furthermore, when agents receive no retraining messages from others for longer than a certain duration, they remove information about them.

4.2 Removing Redundant Functions

Behaviors in an agent, which are delegated from other agents more times, are well developed, whereas other behaviors, which are delegated from other agents fewer times, in a cell are less developed. Finally, the agent only provides the former behaviors and delegates the latter behaviors to other agents.

1: When an agent (k-th agent) receives a request message from another agent, it selects the behavior (b_i^k) that can handle the message from its behavior part and dispatches the message to the selected behavior (Figure 2 (a)).

2: It executes the behavior (b_i^k) and returns the result.

3: It increases the weight of the behavior, w_i^k.

4: It multicasts a restraining message with the signature of the behavior, its identifier (k), and the behavior's weight (w_i^k) to other agents (Figure 2 (b)). [2]

The key idea behind this approach is to distinguish between internal and external requests. When behaviors are invoked by their agents, their weights are not increased. If the total weights of the agent's behaviors, $\sum w_i^k$, is equal to their maximal total weight W^k, it decreases one of the minimal (and positive) weights (w_j^k is replaced by $w_j^k - 1$ where $w_j^k = \min(w_1^k, \ldots, w_n^k)$ and $w_j^k \geq 0$). The above phase corresponds to the degeneration of agents.

1: When an agent (k-th agent) receives a restraining message with regard to b_i^j from another agent (j-th) , it looks for the behaviors ($b_m^k, \ldots b_l^k$) that can satisfy the signature specified in the receiving message.

2: If it has such behaviors, it decreases their weights ($w_m^k, \ldots w_l^k$) and updates the weight (w_i^j) (Figure 2 (c)).

3: If the weights ($w_m^k, \ldots, w_l^k$) are under a specified value, e.g., 0, the behaviors ($b_m^k, \ldots b_l^k$) are inactivated.

---

[2] Restraining messages correspond to cAMP in differentiation.

4.3 Invocation of Functions

When an agent wants to execute a behavior, even if it has the behavior, it needs to select one of the behaviors, which may be provided by itself or others, according to the values of their weights.

1: When an agent (k-th agent) wants to execute a behavior, b_i , it looks up the weight (w_i^k) of the same or compatible behavior and the weights ($w_i^j, \ldots, w_i^m$) of such behaviors ($b_i^j, \ldots, b_i^m$).

2: If multiple agents, including itself, can provide the wanted behavior, it selects one of the agents according to selection function ϕ^k, which maps from w_i^k and $w_i^j, \ldots, w_i^m$ to b_i^l, where l is k or $j, \ldots, m$.

3: It delegates the selected agent to execute the behavior and waits for the result from the agent.

The approach permits agents to use their own evaluation functions, ϕ, because the selection of behaviors often depends on their applications. Although there is no universal selection function for mapping from behaviors' weights to at most one appropriate behavior like a variety of creatures, we can provide several functions.

4.4 Releasing Resources for Redundant Functions

Each agent (j-th) periodically multicasts messages, called *heartbeat messages*, for a behavior (b_i^j), which is still activated with its identifier (j) via the runtime system. When an agent (k-th) does not receive any heartbeat messages with regard to a behavior (b_i^j) from another agent (j-th) for a specified time, it automatically decreases the weight (w_i^j) of the behavior (b_i^j), and resets the weight (w_i^k) of the behavior (b_i^k) to be the initial value or increases the weight (w_i^k) (Figure 2 (d)). The weights of behaviors provided by other agents are automatically decreased without any heartbeat messages from the agents. Therefore, when an agent terminates or fails, other agents decrease the weights of the behaviors provided by the agent and if they then have the same or compatible behaviors, they can activate the behaviors, which may be inactivated.

4.5 Increasing Resources for Busy Functions

The approach also provides a mechanism for duplicating agents, including their states, e.g., instance variables, as well as their program codes and deploying a clone at a different VM in IaaS or a runtime system in PaaS. It permits each agent (k-th agent) to create a copy of itself when the total weights ($\sum_{i=1}^{n} w_i^k$) of functions ($b_1^k, \ldots, b_n^k$) provided in itself is the same or more than a specified value. The sum of the total weights of the mother agent and those of the daughter agent is equal to the total weights of the mother agent before the agent is duplicated. The current implementation supports two conditions. The first permits each agent (k-th) to create a clone of it when the total of its weights ($\sum_{i=1}^{n} w_i^k$) is more than its maximal total weight W^k and the second condition is twice that of the total initial weights of the functions. When a busy agent running as a user program in PaaS has no access resources, it allocates resources to the daughter agent via the external control system.

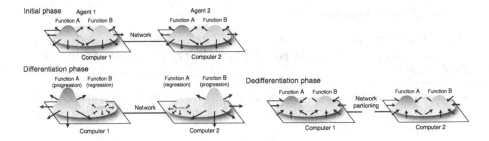

Fig. 1. Differentiation mechanism for software configuration

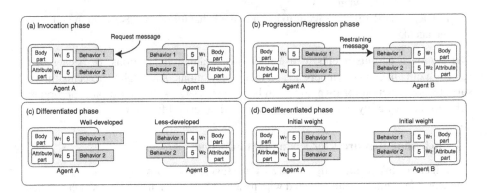

Fig. 2. Differentiation mechanism for agent

5   Experiment

To evaluate our proposed approach, we constructed it as a middleware system with Java (Figure 3), which can directly runs on Java-based PaaS runtime systems or Java VM running on VMs in IaaS, e.g., Amazon EC2. It is responsible for executing duplicating, and deploying agents based on several technologies for mobile agent platforms [9]. It is also responsible for executing agents and for exchanging messages in runtime systems on other IaaS VMs or PaaS runtime systems through TCP and UDP protocols. Each runtime system multicasts heartbeat messages to other runtime systems to advertise itself, including its network address through UDP multicasts.

Adaptation messages, i.e., *restraining* and *heartbeat* messages, are transmitted as multicast UDP packets, which are unreliable. When the runtime system multicasts information about the signature of a behavior in restraining messages, the signature is encoded into a hash code by using Java's serial versioning mechanism and is transmitted as code. Restraining messages for behaviors that do not arrive at agents are seriously affected, because other agents automatically treat the behaviors provided by the senders to be inactive when they do not receive such messages for certain durations. Since our mechanism does not assume that each agent has complete information about all agents, it is even available when some heartbeat messages are lost.

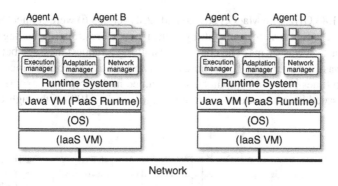

Fig. 3. Runtime system

Application-specific messages, i.e., *request* and *reply*, are implemented through TCP sessions as reliable communications. When typical network problems occur, e.g., network partitioning and node failure during communication, the TCP session itself can detect such problems and it notifies runtime systems on both sides to execute the exception handling defined in runtime systems or agents. The current implementation supports a multiplexing mechanism to minimize communication channels between agents running on two computers on at most a TCP session. To avoid conflicts between UDP packets, it can explicitly change the periods of heartbeat messages issued by agents.

Each agent is an autonomous programmable entity. The body part maintains a key-value store database, which is implemented as a hashtable, shared by its behaviors. We can define each agent as a single JavaBean, where each method in JavaBean needs to access the database maintained in the body parts. Each method in such a JavaBean-based agent is transformed into a Java class, which is called by another method via the body part, by using a bytecode-level modification technique before the agent is executed. Each body part is invoked from agents running on different computers via our original remote method invocation (RMI) mechanism, which can be automatically handled in network disconnections unlike Java's RMI library. The mechanism is managed by runtime systems and provided to agents to support additional interactions, e.g., one-way message transmission, publish-subscription events, and stream communications.

Since each agent records the time the behaviors are invoked and the results are received, it selects behaviors provided in other agents according to the average or worst response time in the previous processing. When a result is received from another agent, the approach permits the former to modify the value of the behavior of the latter under its own control. For example, agents that want to execute a behavior quickly may increase the weight of the behavior by an extra amount, when the behavior returns the result too soon.

6   Evaluation

Although the current implementation was not constructed for performance, we evaluated that of several basic operations in a distributed system where eight computers (Intel

Core 2 Duo 1.83 GHz with MacOS X 10.6 and J2SE version 6) were connected through a giga-ethernet. The cost of transmitting a heartbeat or restraining message through UDP multicasting was 11 ms. The cost of transmitting a request message between two computers was 22 ms through TCP. These costs were estimated from the measurements of round-trip times between computers. We assumed in the following experiments that each agent issued heartbeat messages to other agents every 100 ms through UDP multicasting.

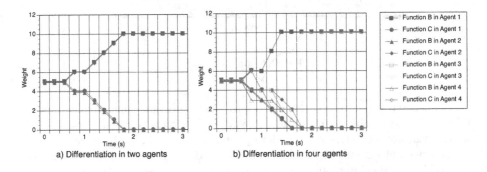

Fig. 4. Degree of progress in differentiation-based adaptation

The first experiment was carried out to evaluate the basic ability of agents to differentiate themselves through interactions in a reliable network. Each agent had three behaviors, called A, B, and C. The A behavior periodically issued messages to invoke its B and C behaviors or those of other agents every 200 ms and the B and C behaviors were null behaviors. Each agent that wanted to execute a behavior, i.e., B or C, selected a behavior whose weight had the highest value if its database recognized one or more agents that provided the same or compatible behavior, including itself. When it invokes behavior B or C and the weights of its and others behaviors were the same, it randomly selected one of the behaviors. We assumed in this experiment that the weights of the B and C behaviors of each agent would initially be five and the maximum of the weight of each behavior and the total maximum W^k of weights would be ten.

Figure 4 presents the results we obtained from the experiment. Both diagrams have a timeline in minutes on the x-axis and the weights of behavior B in each agent on the y-axis. Differentiation started after 200 ms, because each agent knows the presence of other agents by receiving heartbeat messages from them. Figure 4 (a) details the results obtained from our differentiation between two agents. Their weights were not initially varied and then they forked into progression and regression sides. Figure 4 (b) shows the detailed results of our differentiation between four agents and Figure 4 (c) shows those of that between eight agents. The results in (b) and (c) fluctuated more and then converged faster than those in (a), because the weights of behaviors in four are increased or decreased more than those in two agents. Although the time of differentiation depended on the period of invoking behaviors, it was independent of the number of agents. This is important to prove that this approach is scalable.

Our parameters for (de)differentiation were basically independent of the performance and capabilities of the underlying systems. For example, the weights of behaviors are used for relatively specifying the progression/repression of these behaviors.

The second experiment was carried out to evaluate the ability of the agents to adapt to two types of failures in a distributed system (5). The first corresponded to the termination of an agent and the second to the partition of a network. We assumed in the following experiment that three differentiated agents would be running on different computers and each agent had four behaviors, called A, B, C, and D, where the A behavior invokes other behaviors every 200 ms. The maximum of each behavior was ten and the agents' total maximum of weights was twenty. The initial weights of their behaviors (w_B^i, w_C^i, w_D^i) in i-th agent were $(10, 0, 0)$ in the first, $(0, 10, 0)$ in the second, and $(0, 0, 10)$ in the third.

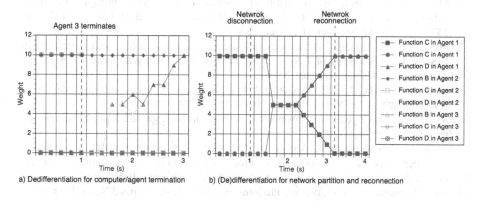

a) Dedifferentiation for computer/agent termination   b) (De)differentiation for network partition and reconnection

Fig. 5. Degree of progress in adaptation to failed agent

7 Conclusion

This paper proposed a framework for adapting software agents on distributed systems. It is unique to other existing software adaptations in introducing the notions of (de)differentiation and cellular division in cellular slime molds, e.g., dictyostelium discoideum, into software agents. When an agent delegates a function to another agent, if the former has the function, its function becomes less-developed and the latter's function becomes well-developed. When agents have many requests from other agents, they create their daughter agents. The framework was constructed as a middleware system on real distributed systems instead of any simulation-based systems. Agents can be composed from Java objects. We are still interesting in reducing the number of messages for adaptation like quorum sensing in cells.

References

1. Babaoglu, O., Meling, H., Montresor, A.: Anthill: a framework for the development of agent-based peer-to-peer systems. In: Proceeding of 22th IEEE International Conference on Distributed Computing Systems (July 2002)
2. Bonabeau, E., Dorigo, M., Theraulaz, G.: Swarm Intelligence: From Natural to Artificial Systems. Oxford University Press (1999)
3. Dorigo, M., Stutzle, T.: Ant Colony Optimization. MIT Press (2004)
4. Herrman, K.: Self-organizing replica placement - a case study on emergence. In: Proceedings of 2nd IEEE International Conference on Self-Adaptive and Self-Organizing Systems (SASO 2007), pp. 13–22. IEEE Computer Society (2007)
5. Lin, W., Lin, G., Wei, H.: Dynamic auction mechanism for cloud resource allocation. In: Proceedings of 10th IEEE/ACM International Conference on Cluster, Cloud and Grid Computing (CCGrid 2010), pp. 591–592 (2010)
6. Montresor, A., Meling, H., Babaoğlu, Ö.: Messor: load-balancing through a swarm of autonomous agents. In: Moro, G., Koubarakis, M. (eds.) AP2PC 2002. LNCS (LNAI), vol. 2530, pp. 125–137. Springer, Heidelberg (2003)
7. Montresor, A., Babaoglu, O.: Biology-inspired approaches to peer-to-peer computing in BISON. In: Proceedings of International Conference on Intelligent System Design and Applications, Oklahoma (August 2003)
8. Nakano, T., Suda, T.: Self-Organizing Network Services With Evolutionary Adaptation. IEEE Transactions on Neural Networks 16(5), 1269–1278 (2005)
9. Satoh, I.: Mobile Agents. In: Handbook of Ambient Intelligence and Smart Environments, pp. 771–791. Springer (2010)
10. Snyder, P. L., Greenstadt, R., Valetto, G.: Myconet: a fungi-inspired model for superpeer-based peer-to-peer overlay topologies. In: Proceedings of 3rd IEEE International Conference on Self-Adaptive and Self-Organizing Systems (SASO 2009), pp. 40–50 (2009)
11. Suda, T., Suzuki, J.: A Middleware Platform for a Biologically-inspired Network Architecture Supporting Autonomous and Adaptive Applications. IEEE Journal on Selected Areas in Communications 23(2), 249–260 (2005)
12. Zhang, Q., Gurses, E., Boutaba, R., Xiao, J.: Dynamic resource allocation for spot markets in clouds. In: Proceedings of 11th USENIX Conference on Hot Topics in Management of Internet, Cloud, and Enterprise Networks and Services (Hot-ICE 2011). USENIX Association (2011)

Slowdown-Guided Genetic Algorithm
for Job Scheduling in Federated Environments

Eloi Gabaldon[✉], Josep L. Lerida, Fernando Guirado, and Jordi Planes

Department of Computer Science, Universitat de Lleida, Lleida, Spain
{eloigabal,jlerida,f.guirado,jplanes}@diei.udl.cat

Abstract. Large-scale federated environments have emerged to meet the
requirements of increasingly demanding scientific applications. However,
the seemingly unlimited availability of computing resources and heterogeneity turns the scheduling into an NP-hard problem. Unlike exhaustive algorithms and deterministic heuristics, evolutionary algorithms have
been shown appropriate for large-scheduling problems, obtaining near optimal solutions in a reasonable time. In the present work, we propose a
Genetic Algorithm (GA) for scheduling job-packages of parallel task in
resource federated environments. The main goal of the proposal is to determine the job schedule and package allocation to improve the application
performance and system throughput. To address such a complex infrastructure, the GA is provided with knowledge based on slowdown predictions for the application runtime, obtained by considering heterogeneity
and bandwidth issues. The proposed GA algorithm was tuned and evaluated using real workload traces and the results compared with a range of
well-known heuristics in the literature.

Keywords: Resource federation · Scheduling · Co-allocation · Genetic
Algorithms · Slowdown-execution predictions

1 Introduction

The computing requirements of scientific applications are continuously growing
as is the amount of data that those applications produce and process. The use of
new and sophisticated infrastructures is necessary to cover these requirements.
One of the earliest infrastructures for covering scientist requirements was the
emergence of cluster systems that integrate a number of standalone computers
together to work as a single system. Later, despite the reduction in resource
costs and the sprawl of infrastructures in organizations and institutions, the
requirements still outweighed the local resources. To overcome the problem, grid
and cluster federation systems have been developed to enable federated resource
sharing logically or physically distributed in different administrative domains.
Nowadays, most of the scientific work-flows and applications are deployed in
these systems due to their high performance and large storage capacity. Recently,
the attention has switched to Cloud computing, a new paradigm for distributed

© Institute for Computer Sciences, Social Informatics and Telecommunications Engineering 2015
P.C. Vinh et al. (Eds.): ICTCC 2014, LNICST 144, pp. 181–190, 2015.
DOI: 10.1007/978-3-319-15392-6_18

computing, which transfers local processing to centralized facilities operated by third-party utilities. This paradigm provides on-demand access to thousands of computers distributed throughout the world, with different levels of services and driven by economies of scale, applicable to completely new problems that are beyond the aim of this work. The present paper is focused on federation systems environment, which will allow to take profit for the idle computing resources present in any organization.

The amount of available computing resources in federated systems, the heterogeneity and co-allocation of tasks between different administrative domains, turns job scheduling into an NP-hard problem.The job scheduling optimization methodologies can be mainly categorized as Deterministic Algorithms (DA) and Approximate Algorithms (AA). DAs [1] can find good solutions among all the possible ones but do not guarantee that the best or the near optimal solution will be found. These methodologies are faster than traditional exhaustive algorithms but inappropriate for large-scale scheduling problems. AAs [2,3] employ iterative strategies to find optimal or near optimal solutions. The Genetic Algorithms (GAs) especially find excellent solutions by simulating nature. Although they are less efficient than deterministic algorithms they can find better solutions for large-scale problems in a reasonable time.

In this paper, we focus on the batch-scheduling optimization of parallel applications in heterogeneous federated environments. Specifically, we design different GAs to minimise the Makespan of parallel batch jobs. The first proposal is to use a random strategy to create the initial population in the initialization stage. The second one uses the knowledge produced by a heuristic based on the estimation of the execution slowdown to guide the GA search process. The model of execution slowdown used by the GA was previously proposed by the authors in [4]. The model envisages the resource heterogeneity and also the contention of the communication links to estimate the execution slowdown. This model is used for objective function evaluation in the proposed GA algorithms.

The reminder of this paper was organized as follows. Section 2 presents related work. The proposed genetic algorithm with its variants are elaborated in Section 3. Section 4 demonstrates the performance analysis and the simulation results for real Workload traces. The conclusions and future work are presented in Section 5.

2   Related Work

The potential benefit of sharing jobs between independent sites in federated environments has been widely discussed in previous research [5,6].However, the resource heterogeneity, data transferring and contention in the communication-links have a large influence on the cost of execution of parallel applications, becoming critical aspects for the exploitation of resources and application performance [7–9]. To improve the performance of co-allocation frameworks many policies and models have been proposed. Mohamed et al. [10] proposed the co-allocation of tasks in resources that are close to the input files with the aim of reducing communication overhead. Jones et al. [8] proposed minimising the communication link usage by maximizing the grouping of tasks in clusters with available resources, but without considering the heterogeneity. The performance of different scheduling strategies using co-allocation based on job queues was analyzed in [6]. This work concludes that unrestricted co-allocation is not recommended and limiting the component sizes of the co-allocated jobs improves performance. The performance for large-scale grid environments was explored in [11,12], concluding that workload-aware co-allocation techniques are more effective at reducing the mean response time and obtaining better load-balance.

Traditional algorithms on job scheduling have in common that jobs are treated individually [1,13]. Allocating jobs without taking into account the rest of the jobs can reduce the performance of future allocations and could decrease overall system performance [14]. More recent research has proposed algorithms that consider later jobs in the queue when making scheduling decisions. Shmueli et al. [14] proposed a backfilling technique in which later jobs are packaged to fill in holes and increase utilization without delaying the earlier jobs. Tsafrir et al. [13] proposed a method to select the most suitable jobs to be moved forward based on system-generated response time predictions. These techniques are based on predetermined order, moving some jobs that accomplish specific deadline requirements forward only on certain occasions. Another point of view had been proposed by Blanco et al. [4], presenting a new technique that tries to schedule the set of jobs in the queue based on the prediction of execution time slowdown.

A common issue in the previous works is that they are based on deterministic heuristics that obtain good results but do not guarantee the best solution. Other techniques based on exhaustive algorithms were explored in the literature [7,15, 16]. However, they are impractical for large-scale environments due to their time cost. Alternatively, approximate techniques, such as Simulated Annealing, Tabu Search, Genetic Algorithms, Particle Swarm, etc., have emerged as effective for complex large-scale environments. Particularly, GA are well known for their good results and robustness and are being applied successfully to solving scheduling problems in a wide range of fields [1,17,18].

Our proposal overcome previous works as it is designed to treat large complete set of jobs identifying their resources allocation, and in case that not enough free resources are available, it also determines the best job execution order that minimizes the global makespan.

3   Genetic Algorithm Meta-Heuristic

A Genetic Algorithm (GA) is a stochastic search heuristic used to find nearly-optimal solutions with the use of nature-based techniques. It starts by creating an initial population of solutions known as individuals, each one encoded using a chromosome. To create a new generation, four steps are performed: ranking the individuals driven by a fitness function, a ranking-based selection, the crossover and the mutation. The algorithm is motivated by the hope that, after several generations, the new population will be better than the older ones.

One of the key decisions in GA is the chromosome design, which represents each individual in the population. In order to reduce the chromosome size, and thus the offspring generation time, the chromosome corresponds to the job order in which the jobs have to be executed. Given a chromosome, the final allocation is decided by a deterministic method described in Algorithm 1. It has shown good results for improving the system overall system performance [4]. The method first searches for the most powerful nodes available lines 2-4, where Power(n) is the computational power of the node n. However, for the parallel jobs, their execution time is denoted by the slowest computational node used. So, some of these powerful nodes will not be used at their full. Then, the heuristic tries to make these nodes free, wich can be achieved by using slower ones without loosing performance in the job execution time lines 5-10.

Algorithm 1.. Allocation Algorithm

Require: $\mathcal{Q}$: Set of jobs
Ensure: $\mathcal{A}$: Set of $(Task, Node)$
1: **for** $Job \in \mathcal{Q}$ **do**
2:     **for** $Task \in Job$ **do**
3:         $\mathcal{A} \leftarrow \mathcal{A} \cup (Task, \text{argmax}_{n \in FreeNodes}(Power(n)))$
4:     **end for**
5:     **for** $(Task, Node) \in \mathcal{A} : Node = \text{argmax}_{(t,n) \in \mathcal{A}}(Power(n))$ **do**
6:         $Node' \in FreeNodes : Power(Node') \geq \min_{(t,n) \in \mathcal{A}}(Power(n))$
7:         **if** $\exists Node'$ **then**
8:             $\mathcal{A} \leftarrow \mathcal{A} \setminus (Task, Node) \cup (Task, Node')$
9:         **end if**
10:     **end for**
11: **end for**

To start the evolutionary process, it is necessary to have an initial population composed of a varied set of chromosomes to facilitate a thorough exploration of the search space. In our first proposal, named *GA-Random*, the chromosomes that make up the initial population are randomly generated by using different permutations of the set of jobs.

Next, the GA uses the heuristic described in Algorithm 1 to allocate the jobs to the computational nodes. If we run out of computational nodes, GA predicts the first job to finish using a execution slowdown model and releases its allocated nodes for the subsequent jobs.

The individuals in the population of each generation are evaluated to score the scheduling solutions. In the present work, such a score depends on the makespan.

The makespan is defined as the elapsed time between the submission of the first job until the finalization of the last one. It is calculated as $\max(F_i) - \min(I_j)$ for all the jobs in the workload, F_i being the time when job i finishes, and I_j being the time when job j starts.

The crossover operator combines the information about the different individuals in the current generation to create new individuals as offspring. First a mask of random binary values is generated. For every position with value 1, the job of the first parent is placed into the offspring. For the missing jobs, the order of the second parent is chosen. Additionally, some parents are not crossed but copied to the next generation.

The selection operator is used to choose which individuals should mate. The population is ordered by using the standard tournament selection algorithm.

Finally, the mutation is the operation used to find new points to evaluate the search space. In our case, a mutation is the swapping of two jobs in a given assignment.

In our second proposal, named *GA-METL*, we decided to add some knowledge into the genetic algorithm to speed-up the search: one of the individuals in the initial population is created by a systematic search solution, based on the heuristic presented in [4] named METL (Minimum Execution Time Loss), that considers heterogeneity and bandwidth contention for predicting the execution slowdown and chooses the job with less time lose for execution. This addition of knowledge helps the GA by starting the search with a good solution in the initial population.

4 Experimentation

In this section we have conducted an experimental study with the aim to determine the best GA parameters. Finally we compared the effectiveness of the GA with other heuristics present in the literature.

An important contribution of our proposals is the ability to obtaining better scheduling solutions by means an effective packing of the jobs in the queue. The package size can have a great impact on the effectiveness of the scheduling algorithm, and by this, first was conducted an experimental study to analyze the performance of the GA proposals for different package sizes.

Figure 1 shows the results of the makespan with bars (primary Y axes) and their time-cost with lines (secondary Y axes) obtained by our proposed meta-heuristics. The package size was ranged from 100 to 1000 jobs. As can be observed, the time cost of both proposals GA-METL and GA-Random, is very similar irrespectively of the package size. Instead, when the number of jobs in the package increases the GA-METL is able to reduce the makespan while for the GA-Random the results worsen. This is because the initial random population needs more iterations to evolve to an adequate solution when the search space increases. These results show that providing the GA with some knowledge (GA-METL) allows to improve the algorithm effectiveness.

Other parameters critical for the effectiveness of the genetic algorithms and directly related with the package size are the number of iterations and the population size. To evaluate how these parameters affect the effectiveness of the proposed algorithms a new experimentation was conducted varying them separately. The package size was fixed to 1000 jobs, the value which provides bigger

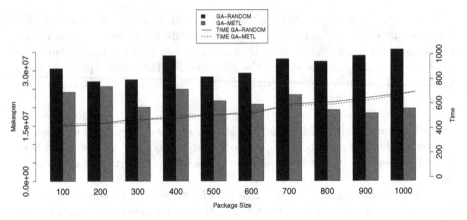

Fig. 1. Method performance for workload of 2000 jobs by package size. Population and Iterations fixed to preliminar values.

differences between GA-Random and GA-METL in the previous experimentation.

Figure 2 shows the results varying the number of iterations from 100 to 500 with the population size fixed to 500. As can be observed, the GA-Random benefits from this increase reducing the makespan. This results show the ability to achieve better solutions when the population evolves. On the other side, the GA-METL that starts with certain knowledge in the initial population produce a significant improvement in makespan. However, the execution times increase largely.

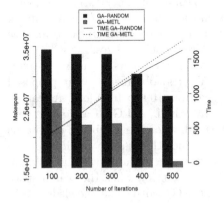

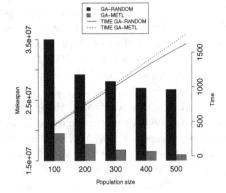

Fig. 2. Performance incrementing the number of iterations when the population size is fixed to 500

Fig. 3. Performance incrementing the population size when the number of iterations is fixed to 500

The results when varying the population size can be seen in Figure 3. In the case of the GA-Random, larger populations allows major number of crossover and mutations obtaining better results. In the other hand, the behavior for the GA-METL algorithm is similar to the above but with much higher gains of makespan, due to the initial knowledge produces faster convergence towards better solutions. As can be seen, the execution time has the same tendency that in the previous experimentation.

Finally, we compared the performance of the GA proposals with diverse heuristics with co-allocation capabilities from the literature. These heuristic are *JPR*, a variant of Naik's heuristic [16], where the tasks are matched with the most powerful available resources to take advantage of the heterogeneity in multi-cluster resources. *CBS* (*Chunk Big Small*) [8], which tries to allocate a "large chunk" (75% of the job tasks) to a single cluster in an attempt to avoid inter-cluster link saturation. Both of them evaluates individual jobs from the workload. We also used the heuristic *METL* (*Minimum Execution Time Loss*) [4], that is able to consider a set of jobs with the aim to minimize the global job execution slowdown based on the available resources. The set of parameters that guide our proposals were adjusted as shown in Table 1, selected by taking a trade-off between the performance improvement and the computational cost according to the previous experimentation.

Table 1. Settings of GA proposals key parameters

Parameter	GA-Random
Num. Iterations	500
Population Size	200
Mutation Frequency	1%
Crossover Frequency	80%

We have evaluated six different workloads {Wk-1,..Wk-6}, composed of 2000 jobs, from the HPC2N. They were evaluated for two different package sizes, small packages (100 jobs) and big packages (1000 jobs). When evaluating the workload with small packages, Figure 4, we can observe that GA-Random proposal obtained better results than the METL technique (by about 20%), even without using extra knowledge in the initial population. This is because the search space is limited being easier to find a better solutions. Furthermore, GA-METL proposal performs better than any other, as it was expected. The single job traditional heuristics, *JPR* and *CBS*, obtained worst results because they scheduled the jobs individually allocating them in the best available resources without taking into account the following jobs in the queue.

The results obtained for big packages are shown in Figure 5. The GA-Random obtained worse results than the experimentation with small package sizes. By contrast, the GA-METL maintained its behavior obtaining in all cases good makespan results. When the size of the packages are huge, the solutions search

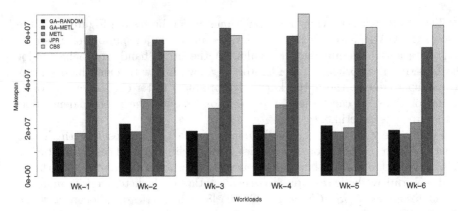

Fig. 4. Makespan results for different workloads composed of 2000 jobs, evaluated with package size of 100

space grew exponentially and both GAs, with the previously chosen parameters, have difficulties to find better results. However, this did not occur with the METL heuristic that was able to obtain good results because its behavior does not depend on the size of the package, and also the best solution it is not guaranteed. In conclusion, to improve the GAs effectiveness for huge packages it is necessary not only to increase the iteration and population parameters but also to redefine the GA functions such as the crossover, mutation, etc.

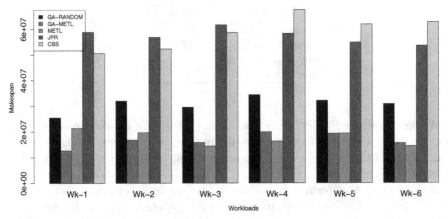

Fig. 5. Makespan results for different workloads composed of 2000 jobs, evaluated with package size of 1000

5   Conclusions

The research for new ways to schedule the jobs in federated resource environments is a critical issue for improving the performance of these systems. We can see that such sophisticated heuristic methods such as the METL heuristic achieve very good results, outperforming other heuristics that only take into account the optimization of a simpler criteria such as computational power, bandwidth, etc. However, these deterministic heuristics have proven to be inappropriate for large-scale and dynamic environments. In this paper, the authors present a GA that obtains better results than the heuristic methods. The results also showed that providing some knowledge to guide the GA gives better performance results, and also helps the algorithm to converge quickly and reduce the time cost. However, when the package size increase largely the GA showed difficulties to find solutions without modifying the configuration parameters.

In a future work, we are interested in exploring new evolutionary functions applied to our GA proposal in order to obtain better results with lower computational cost when evaluating large packages of jobs. We also aim to study different meta-heuristics that have shown good performance for large-scale problems such as Particle Swarm Optimization (PSO), Ant Swarm Optimization (ASO), or hybrid techniques.

References

1. Braun, T.D., Siegel, H.J., Beck, N., Bölöni, L.L., Maheswaran, M.-C., Reuther, A.I., Robertson, J.P., Theys, M.D., Yao, B., Hensgen, D., Freund, R.F.: A comparison of eleven static heuristics for mapping a class of independent tasks onto heterogeneous distributed computing systems. Journal of Parallel and Distributed Computing **61**(6), 810–837 (2001)
2. Kolodziej, J., Xhafa, F.: Enhancing the genetic-based scheduling in computational grids by a structured hierarchical population. Future Generation Computer Systems **27**(8), 1035–1046 (2011)
3. Mathiyalagan, P., Suriya, S., Sivanandam, S.N.: Hybrid enhanced ant colony algorithm and enhanced bee colony algorithm for grid scheduling. Int. J. Grid Util. Comput. **2**(1), 45–58 (2011)
4. Blanco, H., Llados, J., Guirado, F., Lerida, J.L.: Ordering and allocating parallel jobs on multi-cluster systems. In: CMMSE, pp. 196–206 (2012)
5. Ernemann, C., Hamscher, V., Schwiegelshohn, U., Yahyapour, R., Streit, A.: On advantages of grid computing for parallel job scheduling. In: CCGRID, pp. 39–39. IEEE (2002)
6. Bucur, A.I.D., Epema, D.H.J.: Scheduling policies for processor coallocation in multicluster systems. IEEE Transactions on Parallel and Distributed Systems **18**(7), 958–972 (2007)
7. Blanco, H., Lerida, J.L., Cores, F., Guirado, F.: Multiple job co-allocation strategy for heterogeneous multi-cluster systems based on linear programming. The Journal of Supercomputing **58**(3), 394–402 (2011)
8. Jones, W.M., Ligon III, W.B., Pang, L.W., Stanzione Jr., D.C.: Characterization of bandwidth-aware meta-schedulers for co-allocating jobs across multiple clusters. The Journal of Supercomputing **34**(2), 135–163 (2005)
9. Liu, D., Han, N.: Co-scheduling deadline-sensitive applications in large-scale grid systems. International Journal of Future Generation Communication & Networking **7**(3), 49–60 (2014)
10. Mohamed, H.H., Epema, D.H.J.: An evaluation of the close-to-files processor and data co-allocation policy in multiclusters. In: IEEE CLUSTER, pp. 287–298 (2004)

11. Finger, M., Capistrano, G., Bezerra, C., Conde, D.R.: Resource use pattern analysis for predicting resource availability in opportunistic grids. Concurrency and Computation: Practice and Experience **22**(3), 295–313 (2010)
12. Wang, C.-M., Chen, H.-M., Hsu, C.-C., Lee, J.: Dynamic resource selection heuristics for a non-reserved bidding-based grid environment. Future Generation Computer Systems **26**(2), 183–197 (2010)
13. Tsafrir, D., Etsion, Y., Feitelson, D.G.: Backfilling using system-generated predictions rather than user runtime estimates. IEEE Transactions on Parallel and Distributed Systems **18**(6), 789–803 (2007)
14. Shmueli, E., Feitelson, D.G.: Backfilling with lookahead to optimize the packing of parallel jobs. Journal of Parallel and Distributed Computing **65**(9), 1090–1107 (2005)
15. Blanco, H., Guirado, F., Lerida, J.L., Albornoz, V.M.: Mip model scheduling for bsp parallel applications on multi-cluster environments. In: 3PGCIC, pp. 12–18. IEEE (2012)
16. Naik, V.K., Liu, C., Yang, L., Wagner, J.: Online resource matching for heterogeneous grid environments. In: CCGRID, pp. 607–614 (2005)
17. Carretero, J., Xhafa, F., Abraham, A.: Genetic algorithm based schedulers for grid computing systems. International Journal of Innovative Computing, Information and Control **3**(6), 1–19 (2007)
18. Zomaya, A.Y., Teh, Y.-H.: Observations on using genetic algorithms for dynamic load-balancing. IEEE Transactions on Parallel and Distributed Systems **12**(9), 899–911 (2001)
19. Garg, S.K.: Gridsim simulation framework (2009). http://www.buyya.com/gridsim
20. Feitelson, D.: Parallel workloads archive (2005). http://www.cs.huji.ac.il/labs/parallel/workload

Measurement of Cloud Computing Services Availability

Jakub Pavlik, Vladimir Sobeslav[(✉)], and Ales Komarek

Department of Information Technologies, Faculty of Informatics and Management,
University of Hradec Kralove, Rokitanskeho 62,
500 03 Hradec Kralove, Czech Republic
{Jakub.pavlik,vladimir.sobeslav,ales.komarek}@uhk.cz

Abstract. Recently we are witnessing the engagement of cloud computing services such as emails, web services, mobile application, sharing data-stores and many others. Huge number of companies, customers and public institutions are considering the migration to the cloud services. The topical questions behind this effort is the efficiency and measurement of the QoS – Quality of Services of the cloud computing utilisation. This paper is focused on the problematic of measuring and monitoring service availability in Cloud Computing. It deals with the Service-Level Agreement (SLA) monitoring approaches and frameworks. Furthermore it presents a new approach of the cloud service availability monitoring from the client-centric perspective. On the basis of the client-centric approach a new solution was designed, implemented and tested on a sample cloud environment.

Keywords: QoS · SLA · Cloud Computing · Service availability · SLA monitoring

1 Introduction

Cloud Computing creates a new trend in which companies buy IT resources, platforms, and applications as a service. This approach provides multiple economic, technological and functional benefits. But, these are accompanied by new threats, problems and challenges such as security issues, quality of service definition and measuring, responsibility between related parties, service availability, etc. Cloud computing also promises to provide high quality and on-demand services. However, cloud services usually come with various levels of services and performance characteristics which complicate the chances for precise classifications [2]. As shown in Fig. 1, Cloud Computing distinguishes between three basic service models. Cloud service can be the end user software (SaaS), a platform especially used by developers (PaaS), or an infrastructure itself (IaaS) [3]. The goal of Cloud Computing services is to consolidate and optimize existing software and hardware resources and provide automated, on-demand, service-oriented solution with broad network access [4].

Success of these cloud services depends on the required functionality and other characteristics such as availability, respond time, latency, performance, timeliness, scalability, high availability, trust, security, etc. All of these characteristics can be

© Institute for Computer Sciences, Social Informatics and Telecommunications Engineering 2015
P.C. Vinh et al. (Eds.): ICTCC 2014, LNICST 144, pp. 191–201, 2015.
DOI: 10.1007/978-3-319-15392-6_19

covered by the term Quality of Cloud Service (QoCS) which comes from general QoS [5]. QoCS parameters are non-functional definition and properties of cloud service. Hence, it is difficult to assure the accurate evaluation and measuring of QoCS. On the one hand, it solves requirements such as security and trust which are very difficult to evaluate, and on the other hand it resolves the reliability, availability, and performance characteristics. Another problem is the great variety of different cloud providers, as well as the variety of cloud services. Here come the questions of how to evaluate the QoCS and how to ensure its monitoring and compliance.

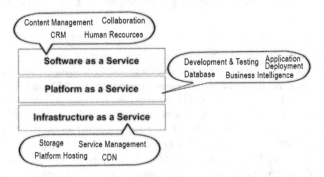

Fig. 1. Cloud services

In practice, QoCS are technical parameters of provided services which are contained and formalized into Service Level Agreements (SLA). SLAs are part of service contracts and are usually agreements between two parties (service provider and customer) which formally define the services. Service contracts use the percentage of service availability as a unit. In practice, today SLAs are not sufficiently accurate and need to be proved and measured. Furthermore, they do not provide guarantees for the availability of services. Rather, the whole process is based on customers' claims of outages or downtime incidents sent to the provider [6]. This paper is a part of a bigger project where the overall goal of the project is to define some nonfunctional aspects, using the Web Ontology Language OWL [7] and focusing on the automatic or semi-automatic generation of cloud service agreements by using ontologies including monitoring, measuring and compliance checking for SLAs. This paper defines a new approach for monitoring, measuring and compliance validation of SLA in Cloud Computing from Client-Centric point of view.

2   Analysis of Existing SLA Monitoring Solutions

This section focuses on SLA in terms of its monitoring and measuring, because only given availability percentage nines (e.g. 99.99%) are not enough for a quality of the cloud service. The goal is also to provide a view on the standard and current SLA monitoring approaches, frameworks or languages which is the cornerstone for designing the future of cloud availability monitoring tools. As [8] describes, the best-known projects for SLA specifications include: RBSLA, SLAng, SLA@SOI, and WSLA. Each of them are briefly specified in the following subsections."

2.1   RBSLA

Rule based SLA is a rule based approach to SLA representation and management which allows separating the contractual business logic from the application logic and enables automated execution and monitoring SLA's specifications. The key features of this concept are: good integration of external data or systems; ECA rules including monitoring intervals, active event monitoring (measurement) functions and executable actions [10]. The whole concept of Rule-based Service Level Management is being built with a computational model based on the ContractLog and the open source rule engine Prova [9].

2.2   SLAng

In addition to RBSLA, SLAng is a language for defining Service Level Agreements that cover needs for Quality of Service [11]. SLAng provides the format for definitions of QoS, responsibility between parties, and language appropriate for automated reasoning systems. The SLAng syntax is obviously an XML schema, specifically a combination of WSDL and BPEL. This approach is based on the Service Provision Reference Model. The nodes are architecture components and edges depict possibilities for SLA between two parties. The structure is divided into three parts: Application tier, Middle tier, and Underlying resources. Thus, the SLA classification distinguishes between Horizontal (different parties with same service) and Vertical SLA (parties on different levels of service) [11].

2.3   SLA@SOI

The SLA@SOI is the largest project related to the SLA field sponsored by leading Industrial, Academic and Research Institutes from around Europe. SLA@SOI "created a holistic view for the management of service level agreements (SLAs) and provides an SLA management framework that can be easily integrated into a service-oriented infrastructure" [12]. This approach is not only about definition of SLA, their measurement, and results, it provides a complex view on the whole area of business. It includes requirements and functions like: predictability and dependability of all components in the processes; holistic SLA management gaining the transparent IT; automated negotiation of SLA between parties.

2.4   WSLA

Last approach of existing SLA concepts is Web service SLA. Even though this is the oldest one, all other approaches mentioned above are based on it [12] [11] [8]. Considering [8], we decided that the best is to thoroughly describe this approach and build our solution on it. Software & Hardware solutions and their service availability have usually a set of specific requirements for availability, reliability, etc. For this purpose,

the Web Service Level Agreement (WSLA) language was created and is used especially for the Web Services domains as SOAP, which "defines assertions of a service
provider to perform a service according to agreed guarantees for IT-level and business
process-level service parameters such as response time and throughput, and measures
to be taken in case of deviation and failure to meet the asserted service guarantees, for
example, a notification of the service customer." [13]. Result of WSLA is an XML
schema forming an abstract language for implementation of the whole SLA management on both consumer and provider side. Detailed description of the SLA and its
structure is not the subject of this paper.

3   Client-Centric Solution

Based on our research, cloud service availability measuring and analysis should be
done from the consumer's perspective (the client-centric approach), automatically and
independently of provider. The following important issues and requirements can be
concluded:

- **Client-centric solution** – should be independent of the provider's infrastructure. Provider's monitoring systems or probes located in their infrastructure should not be used due to inaccuracy of results.
- **Automated solution** – fully automated or semi-automated in order to enable flexible response to changes in cloud services.
- **General and simple solution** – should be standardized and applicable for
  any kind of cloud service such as IaaS, PaaS, or SaaS.

All of these requirements aim to create an agent software for the consumer's machine. We propose three basic approaches or solution designs. Each of them uses
BlackBox detection and monitoring systems. The detection discovers consumer requests for the cloud service and the monitoring gathers data sets (success or fail and
latency). The representation of availability is evaluated by using goodness-of-fit tests
analysis (probability distribution) in the next steps. As shown in Figure 2, the first
solution puts the BlackBox detection and monitoring system in one location between
the consumer machine and the cloud service as a kind of proxy site. The goal is to
analyze direct user's request to the service to decide about availability.

Fig. 2. Solution Approach I

The second approach places the BlackBox on a consumer side, more precisely to
each consumer end machine. The consumer environment is affected by the implementation agent which detects cloud service requests and gathers data about them. Data

are gathered only during consumer communication with cloud service, which actually does not provide accurate service availability, because the consumer only uses the service when he/she needs it. The goal is to provide precise SLA for the whole period of cloud service offering. Another issue is related to service unavailability caused by failure on the consumer side, e.g. internet outage on the consumer side. This means that neither of the mentioned approaches is optimal.

Fig. 3. Solution Approach II

The last approach tries to resolve disadvantages of the previous two approaches. This means to separate BlackBox detection and monitoring into different locations. The detection is done on the consumer's machine by an installed agent which analyzes cloud service requests and provides materials for configuration of remote monitoring. The detection can be carried out by a machine learning process together with network analysis.

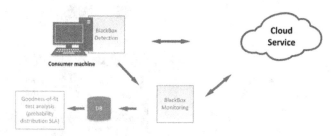

Fig. 4. Solution Approach III

4   Monitoring Solution

Generally, there are two ways how to monitor systems, applications, software, hardware, etc. - Agent-based and Agentless. An Agent-based approach uses a software lite monitoring agents installed directly inside the target monitored system, where specific data is collected and sent to the monitoring server side. In contrast, Agentless approach monitors the systems remotely from the server side, which means that the agents are installed on the monitoring server and not on the target system. An Agent-based approach has more capabilities and power than agentless monitoring solutions and allows more control of the target monitoring configuration. As Figure 4 shows, our solution should work as the Blackbox remote monitoring server. Therefore, Agentless approach is the first requirement which must be fulfilled.

In addition to the Agentless criteria, the monitoring system must be open, flexible, standard and easy to deploy withing enterprise-class. A survey was conducted (with four big customers in the Czech Republic) among IT companies and it was found that the most widely used open source tool is Nagios [14]. Nagios is the Industry Standard in IT Infrastructure Monitoring and it is provided in commercial or open source versions. Its biggest advantage is the large number of existing monitoring plugins that allow virtual monitoring of many entities. The last requirement is the web graphical interface enabling scalable real-time graphing of collected data. This function provides wide range of options to display data in time.

As mentioned above, Nagios meets the requirements of the first two paragraphs, but for graphical function a commercial license is needed and the output is more suitable for classic static infrastructure monitoring than for the purpose in question. Therefore, it was decided to use the open-source project Graphite [15] for scalable real-time graphing and replace Nagios by the open-source monitoring framework Sensu [16], which can reuse existing Nagios plugins. The reason for choosing Sensu instead of Nagios was primarily due to the absolute openness and simplicity. Figure Fig. 5 shows the resulting monitoring architecture where the two above mentioned open-source projects were joined (beyond the standard projects like Apache or RabitMQ).

As mentioned above, the cornerstones of our solution are Sensu and Graphite. The monitoring architecture (Fig. 5) contains following components:

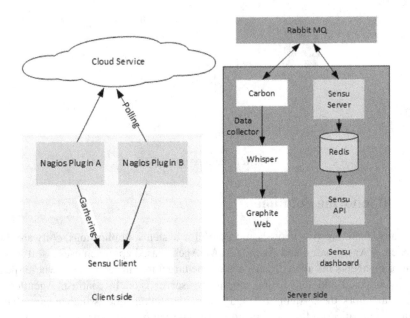

Fig. 5. Monitoring Architecture

Client side - monitoring agents located inside the target system, application, etc. These measure, poll and collect data and send them into monitoring server core. In the current case it is located on the same side (physical or virtual machine) as Server side, because the Agentless approach is used

Sensu server - is responsible for orchestrating check executions, the process of checking results, and event handling. It stores last status of check with details and launches event notifications, which are kept there until resolved. In this solution it is used primarily for scheduling execution and real-time verification of cloud service.

5   Statistical Data Analysis

The main idea of the solution is to be simple, easy to implement, and automatic or semiautomatic. Therefore, all the monitoring checks generate similar data sets. Each of them creates two data types: Availability data - discrete data that can only take certain values. In this case it is value "1" or "0", success or failure. Latency data - continuous data that can take any value within a specific range. In this case it is the response time or latency of our monitoring check given in UNIX time stamp (nanoseconds).

Availability data is almost the same for any cloud service, unlike latency for which response time can be completely different and the similarity among cloud services is almost never the same. The next difference is that the Availability data is always present (except failure of monitoring server), but the Latency data is only present if availability is "1". Otherwise, the latency is useless. This means that the latency analysis is valuable only if the cloud service is available.

We estimated types of probability distribution function using descriptive statistic and graphical methods. Descriptive statistics consists of calculating parameters such as Mean, Median, Maximum, Minimum, Standard Deviation, Variance, Summary, Skewness, and Kurtosis. This led to the finding that availability data distribution is almost always skewed towards the left, which confirms the statement that the median is greater than the mean.

After that several graphical techniques (histograms, empirical cumulative distribution function, Q-Q plot, and density plot) for data analysis were used. These can help to identify the kind of pdf to use to fit the model. They were compared with other theoretical discrete distributions, such as Poisson, Binomial, and others.

Based on the foregoing, it was concluded that the availability of data can be represented by Binomial or Poisson distributions. Both are very similar. Due to the large number of values (N), Binomial distribution looks like a Poisson with the same mean [23]. Poisson distribution is used in the case when p is very small or N is very large. The hypergeometric distribution was also considered, but it was rejected due to the fact that it describes the probability of k successes in n draws without replacement. It is a contrast to Binomial which is with replacement. The availability data is with replacement, because both values can appear more than one time.

This statement is supported by mathematical goodness of fit test using Chi-square testing. Chi-square test is based on comparing empirical frequencies with theoretical frequencies. Theoretical distribution was estimated using the maximum likelihood estimate (MLE), which is naturally implemented in R language. The chi-square test is defined for the hypothesis:

H_0: *the data follows the specified distribution*
H_A: *the data does not follow the specified distribution*
The basic calculation formula is defined as:

$$X^2 = \sum_{i=1}^{k} \frac{O_i - E_i^2}{E_i}$$

where O_i indicates the observed frequency of the number (e.g. number of 0 value) and E_i is the expected frequency of pdf. For any X^2 test, the number of degrees of freedom is given as k-p-1. p is the parameter estimated from the sample data. The hypothesis H_0 is accepted if X^2 is lower than the chi-square percent point function with degrees of freedom and a significance level of α. Each time it is assumed that the significance level is 5%. Asample plot of goodness of fit summary (Fig. 6) can be also drawn. X-axis displays the number of occurrences and Y-axis shows the squared frequencies.

Availability data vs Binomial distribution

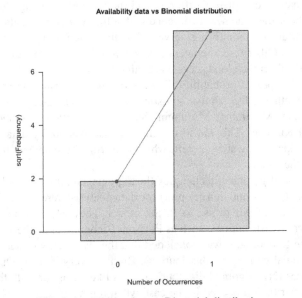

Fig. 6. Availability data vs Binomial distribution

The availability data was described by basic tests, then the pdf and estimated parameters of the model were suggested. The goodness of fit tests were performed and it was decided that the data comes from Binomial distribution. When the probability distribution is known, a specific statistical analysis and tests can be applied. The selection of these tests is based on source [24] which deals with the modeling of binary data.

Correlation or linear regression cannot be conducted to one statistic variable, which is caused by storing latency only in case of successful check. The linear dependency between statistics variables cannot be measured when the availability is zero, due the latency is missing. If H_A is rejected, then the statistical analysis of latency data is run to guarantee a defined cloud service quality. Otherwise, the quality measurement is pointless.

In general, statisticians test if data is normally distributed, because most of the specific tests (t test, z test, F test, ANOVA) assume the normality of data. That is why it was decided to replace the goodness of fit tests with normality tests. Another reason for this was the excessive existing probability distribution (Lognormal, Gamma, Weibull, Exponential, etc.), which would not allow the future automation of the entire solution, because each monitoring check may follow different distribution and it is not possible to cover all existing cases.

At first the graphical evaluation of normality Q-Q was tested. It was a scatter plot comparing the fitted and empirical distribution (availability data) in terms of the dimensional values of the variable. If the data is obtained from normal population, the points should fall approximately along the reference line. Fig. 7 shows that data is not normally distributed.

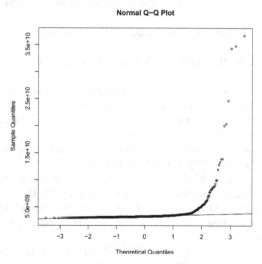

Fig. 7. Normal Q-Q Plot

6   Conclusions

The basic statistical analysis which is automated was conducted and it provided the automatic SLA compliance check for specific time period. The difference between time periods validation was not analyzed and the time series, which can be used for predictive analysis were also not considered. This procedure is simple, but meets all the requirements for the service availability and SLA. Due to this simplicity, it can be easily developed and implemented in future objectives as user request detection tools.

This research shows that the suggested client-centric approach is applicable for deployment in real environment. The questions of measuring and monitoring availability of cloud services remotely were answered and the experiments to find out, what the probability distribution data follows, were conducted. This helps to create very accurate results and moves the availability of cloud services further than just like the number of "nines" usually specified in the SLA document.

Acknowledgment. This work was supported by the project of specific research no. 2103. Faculty of Informatics and Management, University of Hradec Kralove.

References

[1]   Gartner.com.   Gartner   it   glossary   -   cloud   computing   (February   2014). http://www.gartner.com/it-glossary/cloud-computing/

[2]   Wang, S., Liu, Z., Sun, Q., Zou, H., Yang, F.: Towards an accurate evaluation of quality of cloud service in service-oriented cloud computing. Journal of Intelligent Manufacturing, 1–9 (2012)

[3]   Furht, B., Escalante, A.: Handbook of cloud computing. Springer, New York (2010)

[4]   Mell, P., Grance, T.: The NIST definition of cloud computing. NIST Special Publication **800**(145), 7 (2011)

[5]   Stantchev, V.: Performance evaluation of cloud computing offerings, pp. 187–192 (2009)

[6]   Bauer, E., Adams, R.: Reliability and availability of cloud computing. Wiley-IEEE Press, Hoboken, N.J. (2012)

[7]   Rady, M.: Formal Definition of Service Availability in Cloud Computing Using OWL. In: Moreno-Díaz, R., Pichler, F., Quesada-Arencibia, A. (eds.) Computer Aided Systems Theory - EUROCAST 2013. Lecture Notes in Computer Science, vol. 8111, pp. 189–194. Springer, Heidelberg (2013)

[8]   Nie, G.E.X., Chen, D.: Research on Service Level Agreement in Cloud Computing, pp. 39–43 (2012). 10.1007/978-3-642-28744-2_5

[9]   Paschke, A.: rbsla - RBSLA: Rule Based Service Level Agreements Project. http://ibis.in.tum.de/projects/rbsla/ (accessed: March 19, 2014)

[10]   Paschke, A., Bichler, M., Dietrich, J.: ContractLog: An Approach to Rule Based Monitoring and Execution of Service Level Agreements, pp. 209–217 (2005). 10.1007/11580072_19

[11]   Lamanna, D.D., Skene, J., Emmerich, W.: SLAng: A Language for Defining Service Level Agreements, p. 100 (2003). http://dl.acm.org/citation.cfm?id=797134 (accessed: March 19, 2014)

[12]   Wieder, P.: Service level agreements for cloud computing. Springer, New York (2011)

[13]   Ludwig, H., Franck, R.: Web Service Level Agreement (WSLA) Language Specification (2003)

[14]   Nagios.com.: Nagios - The Industry Standard in IT Infrastructure Monitoring and Alerting. http://www.nagios.com/ (accessed: March 19, 2014)

[15]   Graphite.wikidot.com.:   Graphite   -   Scalable   Realtime   Graphing   -   Graphite. http://graphite.wikidot.com/ (accessed: March 19, 2014)

[16]   Heavy Water Operations, L. Sensu | An open source monitoring framework. http://sensuapp.org/ (accessed: March 19, 2014)

[17]   Redis.io. Redis. http://redis.io/ (accessed: March 19, 2014)

[18]   Rabbitmq.com. RabbitMQ - Messaging that just works. http://www.rabbitmq.com/ (accessed: March 19, 2014)

[19] Graphite.readthedocs.org. The Render URL API — Graphite 0.10.0 documentation. https://graphite.readthedocs.org/en/latest/render_api.html (accessed: March 19, 2014)

[20] Karian, Z.A., Dudewicz, E.J.: Handbook of Fitting Statistical Distributions with R. CRC Press, Boca Raton (2011)

[21] Ricci, V.: Fitting distribution with R (2005)

[22] Teaching, C.: Goodness of fit tests (2010)

[23] Collins, J.C.: Binomial Distribution: Hypothesis Testing, Confidence Intervals (CI), and Reliability with Implementation in S-PLUS (2010)

[24] Collett, D.: Modelling Binary Data. Chapman & Hall/CRC, Boca Raton (2003)

[25] Teaching, C.: Hypotesis testing: One sample test (2010)

[26] Lowry, R.: Concepts and Applications of Inferential Statistics (1998)

[27] Fee, K.: Delivering E-Learning: A Complete Strategy for Design, Application and Assessment, 4th Edn. Kogan Page, ISBN:978-0749453978 (2009)

Security Aspects of Cloud Based Mobile Health Care Application

Richard Cimler, Jan Matyska, Ladislav Balik,
Josef Horalek, and Vladimir Sobeslav[✉]

Faculty of Informatics and Management, Department of Information Technologies,
University of Hradec Kralove, Rokitanskeho 62, 50003 Hradec Kralove,
Czech Republic
{richard.cimler,jan.matyska,ladislav.balik,
josef.horalek,vladimir.sobeslav}@uhk.cz

Abstract. As mobile computing has become very common, a new vulnerabilities and security threads appeared. Cloud computing is a new distribution model of services for various technologies and solutions including the mobile applications. Mobile cloud computing benefits from the interconnection of these two areas. This approach brings many assets, but on the other hand, also the security risks and potential problems. This paper discuss security aspects of mobile cloud computing with a focus on the developed health care mobile application using cloud computation services. Personal data about health of the person are one of the most confidential thus need to be secured against different types of threats. Proposed solution is based on the smartphone as a client gathering data and the cloud servers as a computational platform for data storage and analysing.

Keywords: Cloud computing · Security · Mobile application · Health care

1   Introduction

Businesses, government agencies, organizations, and individual consumers are rapidly adopting mobile and cloud computing technologies [2]. This technologies are having a high potential for broadening their development, services, and marketing through information technologies [3] [4]. Securing the personal data is very important part of whole cloud computing concept. General overview of cloud computing security can be found at [5] [6]. Both papers are unique by its complexity and described analysis. Several areas of research and dynamic development of the mobile Cloud computing security are considered. Encryption and key management algorithms, called ad hoc Clouds in [5] are presented as well.

As mentioned in article [5] cloud computing bring various benefits to organizations and users. There are many challenges related to security and privacy in the Cloud environment. It opens up space for research new techniques for security and privacy in mobile Cloud and ad hoc Cloud. This includes a need for a dynamic security model and better crypto (and key management) algorithms that targets different levels of security and privacy for Cloud computing. With the increasing usage of the Cloud

© Institute for Computer Sciences, Social Informatics and Telecommunications Engineering 2015
P.C. Vinh et al. (Eds.): ICTCC 2014, LNICST 144, pp. 202–211, 2015.
DOI: 10.1007/978-3-319-15392-6_20

services it is possible to collect sufficient evidence from the cloud providers on the level of trust on each of their services. This can help the service providers, infrastructure providers, and the end-users to better choose the right services from the ever growing Cloud vendors.

In the paper [13] is described usage of virtualization as a tool for solving security issues of cloud computing using M2M (machine-to-machine) communications. In the M2M computing technologies personal computers, Internet, wireless sensors, and mobile devices are working together. There are many security threats for mobile devices which are the same as for the desktop and server ones. Virtualization technique in M2M communication is described as a way for increasing protection against mobile treats and increase of the performance efficiency.

There are a many benefits of Cloud computing but on the other hand a lot of security risks. Many technologies are connected in the Cloud Computing solutions. Together with its capabilities Cloud Computing inherits capabilities of these technologies but its vulnerabilities as well. It is necessary to understand these vulnerabilities to be able to use cloud computing safely. The article [7] presents the security issues of IaaS, PaaS, and IaaS Cloud models. Issues vary depending on the model and described storage. Similarly presents solutions for Cloud deployment model and comprehensive paper [8] and [9]. In papers [10] [11]we can found, that Cloud Service as a kind of Web Services is based on Internet service, it faces all kinds of security problems because Internet has many inherent safety defects and also exists in other attacks and threats. Therefore the development of Cloud Service depends on its security deeply, and it is a major significance to consensus on the Cloud Service security. Security issues of the cloud based application for mobile devices and usage of different frameworks is discussed in many papers, articles and analyses such as [12] [13].

Modern solution for solving security issues is usage of the frameworks. It also enables to ensure the integrity, secure the data and improves user's identification. Proxy-based multicloud computing framework is introduced at [14]. Several features such as dynamic, on-the-fly collaborations, addressing trust, resource sharing among cloud-based services, privacy issues without pre-established collaboration agreements or standardized interfaces are described in this paper. Another Secured Mobile-Cloud framework is proposed in [15]. Framework is focused on the security of data transmitted between the components of a mobile cloud application. Two aspects are taken into the account: energy consumptions and users options regarding the security level required for private data. Several distributed components deployed in the cloud or on the mobile device are included in the framework. There is proposed a proof of concept of Android prototype as well.

2   Safety of Cloud Computing Application and Services

We can classify user data concerning the state of user's health among one of the most personal data that the user has. For that reason, we have to take into consideration the safety of saved data and pay attention to the risks of individual solutions.

Those problems are in most of the cases not connected to a technical solution. A range of safety risks connected with public Clouds run is not solely technical. Problems connected with cooperation with another subject play a big part here. For example, it is possible to use the situation when the client uses services of supplying company for SaaS. Even if the client verifies the company to find out if it meets the technical requirements, it is reliable, etc., unexpected complications can occur. The company can go bankrupt, it can be merged with another company or bought by another company. Thereafter, our data go to someone else and we cannot influence that. These non-technically orientated issues are the subject of risk management and even though we have to include their risks, they have no direct connection with the operation solution from the technical perspective.

The main technical risk related to public Cloud is a loss of isolation. The isolation is for the run of public Cloud solution absolutely crucial. If the clients run their own service in public Cloud, their operator is obliged to separate their data and processors from other clients even though they share the same hardware. That way the physical disks, processors, RAM memories and network connections are shared and their separation happens in logical layers, in software. The virtualization safety of data storages is very closely connected to that. The user, however, does not have an influence on this operator's environment. The effective protection of application run in Cloud environment resides for the user or operator in a careful selection of the provider and in case that the provider cannot be trusted, it is good to opt for running an own private Cloud.

We have to consider that the run of a private Cloud or a home server does not automatically guarantee a higher safety. This presumption would be possible only in case where we would consider that the operator of the private cloud or home server has unlimited tools or skills for their protection. We would recommend the client to use the services of public Cloud and private Cloud in case that it is convenient to invest resources to building an administration of such solution. When a customer chooses a cloud provider, there are seven general security issues concerning Cloud computing described by Gartner [20]. They include issues like privileged user access which addresses risk of confidentiality disruption. This issue is connected either with data transfers and Cloud service provider. Both are addressed by an application security model and a careful selection of a provider. These risks address most common issues related with cloud-computing oriented solutions. It can be used as a reference for Watchdog implementation same as for general use with any cloud-computing oriented project.

3   Cloud Based Mobile Health Care Application

Modern smartphones are powerful devices with computing performance comparable to personal computers and laptops. Various sensors are embedded into these devices. These sensors are capable of monitoring a lot of different physical quantities which makes smartphones, together with smartphone computation performance, useful devices capable of monitoring and processing information about status of person. It is possible to monitor position of person, not only wide area position using GPS but position of the body towards the earth surface as well. That enables to monitor the occurrence of critical situations such as a fall of the person to the ground. By using an accelerometer and a gyroscope it is also possible to monitor the person's breathing [21]. Further devices can be located in the surrounding area and transmit information from sensors about the condition of the environment. Actuators controlled by the application should adjust the environment in the location according the health status of the monitored person. Based on data from sensors, the application can create also a notification of the alert action – to call an emergency, to create a warning message to relatives or personal doctor.

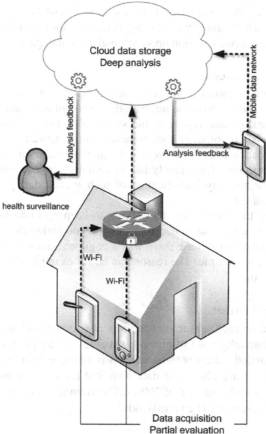

Fig. 1. System scheme

Application named Watch Dog is an application which is being currently created primary to monitor position and activities of the elder people and notify about life threatening situations. Measured data are partly evaluated in the devices in order to find out dangerous situations such as fall of the person. After basic evaluation in the device data are sent to the cloud server where deeper analysis will be running on the long term data. Wi-Fi connection can be used for indoor usage of the system. Data size of transmitted data is optimized also for using device outdoors with technology 3G, GPRS or LTE. Due to deep analysis computation demands it is run in the cloud server and only most critical functions run on the smart phone. System scheme can be seen on Fig.1.

3.1 Client and Server Communication

There is a communication model required for the receiving and processing the data. Client and server communicate based on this model. The basic parameters of the model are data format, frequency of sending data, and amount of data transferred per one transmission and a confirmation upon receival and cataloging.

Data Transmission Frequency

Based on the used application, a frequency of 1 minute seems adequate as the transmission frequency. During this time interval, the client collects data and every minute prepares a data package that is sent to the server. This time interval can be further adjusted, but there is a problem of high communication utilization. One minute interval allows an evaluation even for some life-threatening situations. Of course the one minute interval is too long for a timely identification of critical situations like a respiratory failure. For a timely identification of such events, data processing must be done on the device itself.

The system logs the data locally and allows to keep up to 48 hours of measurements. These data can be send in one transmission containing the data from the last confirmed synchronization in case there was a communication failure or the service was unavailable for some time. The reason can be for example, the lack of mobile or Wi-Fi data connection.

Data Structure and Extent

The data measured on each sensor are send in a raw form to the server. For this type of data, which is basically a set of numeric variables, easily processable structure of ASCI comma-separated values is to be used. It is a simple, convenient and data format. It is expected to use chunks of data with 300 lines, which are generated by a local data collection in the interval of 200ms. The volume final volume of the data for one minute measurement is to be up to 0.5kB.

Confirmation upon Receival and Cataloguing

The system uses round-robin model for the local (the client's database) storage of data. Therefore only a limited amount (fixed amount after the first 48 hours) of data is stored on the client device and the old data is always replaced with the new one. This way, the client's device database never exceeds the size of 72MB and allows to use the application even on less equipped devices. This mechanism makes the application rather usable not only with the always available Wi-Fi connection but also with a connection provided by a mobile network operator, such as GPRS, CDMA, 3G, LTE, etc.

Every line of ASCI coma-separated data is identified with a time stamp which also serves as a unique key in the server's database. The long-term data are stored in a pre-processed and summarized form.

Upon receival, checksum of the data package is always recalculated, so that it is possible to detect any data corruption during transfer. During the server-client communication, the server confirms the reception of the data packages. The server can also request additional retransmission of some data from the last 48 hours. The data are in this case identified by a timestamp.

3.2 Communication Security Model

There is a two-way communication between client and server, which always uses a communication media that are vulnerable to eavesdropping in some way, whether it is using the Wi-Fi or the Internet. It is necessary not only to encrypt the data, but provide additional security features. For that reason, the application uses [16] AAA security model, Authentication, Authorization and Accounting.

AAA – Authentication, Authorization and Accounting

The AAA is a security model, which provides all the basic security features the system needs. AAA model is a widespread standard, therefore it allows interconnection of the application with other already existing services, such as various domain and authentication services. Authentication, in this case, provides user authentication using a username and a password. With these, the user can access both, the web frontend and mobile applications (where the password is saved for user convenience).

Authorization grants an access to user's own data and also the data of other users, if the he owns the permissions. Authorization also includes a verification of used mobile device for data collection, as discussed further. The purpose of Accounting is a collection of usage information, later used for billing purposes and for access logging to identify safety incidents.

Mobile Device Verification

As a part of authorization, the system uses verification of a mobile device that is connected to the user account and is able to upload logged data to the cloud server. To ensure a stronger security, it is not possible to use just any mobile device with the installed application using a username and a password. In order to communicate with the application, the server authenticates also a unique identifier of the device that is generated upon the first run and registered to the user's account. This method can be combined with an IMEI number verification. This security model is similar to the one that some banks use for their smartphone banking.

Transmission of Recorded and Processed Data

HTTPS protocol is used for the transmission of recorded data [16]. It features a complete model of the security based on the use of certificates and it also includes mechanisms for a safe key exchange, symmetric data encryption and hashing methods. The

server, as well as the application, is to support an SSL 3.0, or alternatively TLS encryption.

Data Encryption

Based on focus of the application, it is necessary to provide a high degree of security.
The data are encrypted during the transmission on the level of the application itself
and moreover it is presumed, that only secure communication links will be used. On
the application level, symmetric encryption of AES protocol is to be used. With the
length of a key 256-bit, the sufficient level of security is provided. More secure variant of AES (with a longer key length) can be used, but there is only small amount of
additional security in comparison to higher processing requirements. The encryption
using AES 256-bit protocol is directly implemented in the Java and other major programming languages and therefore its use is simple for the mobile devices.

4   Mobile Application and Type of Cloud Computing Service Models

Modern mobile applications that require efficient platform for recorded data processing very often use remote data processing by means of servers situated in a local
network or in the Internet. These servers then either offer user interface with higher
functionality or they only process the data and send them back.

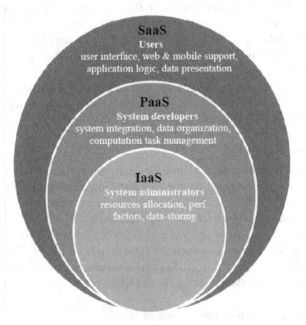

Fig. 2. Cloud computing distribution models

If the concern is an application that needs a remote data processing in order to
work and it can make use of the web access as a platform for visualization of those

processed data, it can be thought about a backend platform in form of Cloud solution. With Cloud solution there is a choice of its form. From the point of view of offered services, there can be distinguished three basic distribution models. See Fig.2.

4.1   Watchdog Cloud Computing Solutions

Watchdog application is able to run in three majorly different solutions. Two of them are purely cloud based, and the third is a small environment oriented.

Public Cloud Run as Service

With Watchdog application, Cloud solution for processing and presenting data (in case of public Cloud) has a form of a software run as a service. User has to log into that application and the application will offer three basic services. First, there is a performance for data processing and processing itself. Second, there is a presentation of processed data. Finally, there is a storage where the processed data are saved.

The advantage of this solution is the already mentioned simplicity of use. The user does not have to care about the infrastructure nor the application. The user only uses the services in accordance with the SaaS model. In contrast, there are all disadvantages of public Clouds. The most important is undoubtedly the safety. Others are limited data control, impossibility to intervene in the form of application, etc.

Private Cloud for Gathered Data Processing

In case of running a Cloud application, we can think about the usual architecture Software as a Service as mentioned above, or about the possibilities of a private Cloud.

Considering the magnitude of the whole solution, it can be spoken about private Cloud only in connection with the organization that operates this service for their clients. If it was a case of one user of this application who runs server application at home for own purposes, we could not be talking about a Cloud solution. In contrast to that, we can imagine a situation where a nursing home with 500 clients runs this service as a private Cloud. Here, a necessary separation of the hardware infrastructure from the very service is put to work. IT staff takes care of the Cloud and the service is consequently used by care assistants and clients.

In case of the private Cloud the risks of security stay but the operator has an absolute control over the data and the form of the application (Open-source solution is expected) with all its positive and negative results (care of the Cloud, data backup, the risk of data mishandling).

Server Run for Independent User

In the case of the situation described above, where one user wants to operate the service only for own use, we cannot talk about Cloud solution but this form of operation is naturally also possible. However, there is a range of limitations and complications that make this solution, in our opinion, the least recommendable. Mobile application itself can evaluate some basic occurrences but primarily it is designed for constant communication with the server. Therefore, it is necessary to arrange either a constant access to the server through Wi-Fi or make the server accessible from the Internet. For domestic use, there are difficulties arising with public addresses, possible use of dynamic DNS records, and also the server security when we cannot assume that an ordinary user will be at the same time a specialist in the server security area.

5   Conclusions

The aim of the paper was to present the security aspects of the utilization of Cloud computing approach in mobile applications in health care environment. Personal data has to be secured thoroughly. The developed mobile application collects data by using the internal sensors of a smart phone. Data are partly evaluated in the device to evaluate critical situation and sent to the server for the deeper analysis. There are more layers utilized for better security of solution. The application is using AAA security model, the server authenticates IMEI of the device and encrypting using SSL 3.0 as well. Data are also encrypted on the application level by the symmetric encryption by means of the AES protocol with the key length of 256-bit.

Three possible cloud computing solution of the developed application has been analysed: Public Cloud run as service, Private Cloud for gathered data processing and Server run for independent user. On the basis of the presented analysis of Cloud computing security issues and mobile health care application, it can be conclude, that this approach brings many assets and challenges at the same time. These problems can be solved by the proposed solution.

Acknowledgment. This work was supported by the project of specific research no. 2101 and 2103. Faculty of Informatics and Management, University of Hradec Kralove.

References

1. Hřebíček, J. a kol.: Scientific computing in mathematical biology, MU (2012). http://www.iba.muni.cz/res/file/ucebnice/hrebicek-vedecke-vypocty.pdf
2. Bureš, V., Otčenášková, T., Čech, P., Antoš, K.: A Proposal for a Computer-Based Framework of Support for Public Health in the Management of Biological Incidents: the Czech Republic Experience. Perspectives in Public Health **132**(6), 292–298 (2012). doi:10.1177/1757913912444260. ISSN: 1757-9139
3. Allan, R.: Cloud and Web 2.0 resources for supporting research (2012). http://tyne.dl.ac.uk/NWGrid/Clouds/
4. Bureš, V., Brunet-Thornton, R.: Knowledge management: the czech situation, possible solutions and the necessity for further research. In: Proceedings of the 6th International Conference on Intellectual Capital and Knowledge Management, McGill University, Montréal, Canada, pp. 95–102 (2009). ISBN: 978-1-906638-45-0
5. Chirag, M., Dhiren, P., Bhavesh, B., Avi, P., Muttukrishnan, R.: A survey on security issues and solutions at different layers of Cloud computing. The Journal of Supercomputing **63**(2), 561–592 (2013). doi:10.1007/s11227-012-0831-5. ISSN: 0920-8542
6. Subashini, S., Kavitha, V.: A survey on security issues in service delivery models of cloud computing. Journal of Network and Computer Applications **34**(1), 1–11 (2011). http://dx.doi.org/10.1016/j.jnca.2010.07.006. ISSN: 1084-8045

7. Hashizume, K., Rosado, D.G., Fernández-Medina, E., Fernandez, E.B.: An analysis of security issues for cloud computing. Journal of Internet Services and Applications **4**(5) (2013). doi: 10.1186/1869-0238-4-5. ISSN: 1867-4828

8. Fernandes Diogo, A.B., Soares Liliana, F.B., Gomes João, V., Freire Mário, M., Inácio Pedro, R.M.: Security issues in cloud environments: a survey. International Journal of Information Security (2013). doi: 10.1007/s10207-013-0208-7. ISSN: 1615-5262

9. Lee, H., Kim, J., Lee, Y., Won, D.: Security issues and threats according to the attribute of cloud computing. In: Kim, T., Stoica, A., Fang, W., Vasilakos, T., Villalba, J.G., Arnett, K.P., Khan, M.K., Kang, B.-H. (eds.) SecTech, CA, CES3 2012. CCIS, vol. 339, pp. 101–108. Springer, Heidelberg (2012). doi:10.1007/978-3-642-35264-5_14. ISSN: 978-3-642-35264-5

10. Weihua, J., Shibing, S.: Research on the security issues of cloud computing. In: Du, Z. (ed.) Intelligence Computation and Evolutionary Computation. AISC, vol. 180, pp. 845–848. Springer, Heidelberg (2013). doi:10.1007/978-3-642-31656-2_115. ISSN: 2194-5357

11. Mouratidis, H., Islam, S., Kalloniatis, Ch., Gritzalis, S.: A framework to support selection of cloud providers based on security and privacy requirements. Journal of Systems and Software **86**(9), 2276–2293 (2013). http://dx.doi.org/10.1016/j.jss.2013.03.011. ISSN: 0164-1212

12. Sujithra, M., Padmavathi, G.: Mobile device security: A survey on mobile device threats, vulnerabilities and their defensive mechanism. International Journal of Computer Applications **56**(14) (2012). doi:http://dx.doi.org/10.5120/8960-3163. ISSN: 09758887

13. Cagalaban, G., Kim, S., Kim, M.: A mobile device-based virtualization technique for M2M communication in cloud computing security. In: Kim, T., et al. (eds.) SecTech, CA, CES3 2012. CCIS, vol. 339, pp. 160–167. Springer, Heidelberg (2012). doi:10.1007/978-3-642-35264-5_23. ISSN: 18650929

14. Singhal, M., Chandrasekhar, S., Ge, T., Sandhu, R., Krishnan, R., Ahn, G.J., Bertino, E.: Collaboration in Multicloud Computing Environments: Framework and Security Issues. Computer **46**(2), 76–84 (2013). ISSN: 0018-9162, WOS:000314943300019

15. Popa, D., Boudaoud, K., Borda, M.: Secure mobile-cloud framework - implementation on the mobile device. Acta Technica Napocensis **54**(4), 7–12 (2013). ISSN: 12216542

16. Wood, J., Aboba, B.: RFC 3539 - Authentication, Authorization and Accounting (AAA) Transport Profile (2003). http://tools.ietf.org/html/rfc3539

17. Singhal, M., Chandrasekhar, S., Ge, T., Sandhu, R., Krishnan, R., Ahn, G.J., Bertino, E.: Collaboration in Multicloud Computing Environments: Framework and Security Issues. Computer **46**(2), 76–84 (2013). ISSN: 0018-9162, WOS:000314943300019

18. Gejibo, S., Mancini, F., Mughal, K.A., Valvik, R., Klungsøyr, J.: Challenges in implementing an end-to-end secure protocol for Java ME-based mobile data collection in low-budget settings. In: Barthe, G., Livshits, B., Scandariato, R. (eds.) ESSoS 2012. LNCS, vol. 7159, pp. 38–45. Springer, Heidelberg (2012)

19. European Union Agency for Network and Information Security. Cloud Computing Risk Assessment — ENISA (2009). http://www.enisa.europa.eu/activities/risk-management/files/deliverables/cloud-computing-risk-assessment

20. Brodkin, J.: Gartner: Seven cloud-computing security risks. Infoworld, 1–3 (2008)

21. Suba, P., Tucnik, P.: Mobile monitoring system for elder people healthcare and AAL. In: Conference on Intelligent Environments, vol. 17, pp. 403–414 (2013). doi:10.3233/978-1-61499-286-8-403

New NHPP SRM Based on Generalized S-shaped Fault-Detection Rate Function

Nguyen Hung-Cuong[✉] and Huynh Quyet-Thang

Department of Software Engineering, School of Information and Communication Technology, Hanoi University of Science and Technology, Hanoi, Vietnam
cuongnh86@gmail.com, thanghq@soict.hust.edu.vn

Abstract. Software reliability modelling (SRM) is a mathematics technique to estimate some measures of computer system that relate to software reliability. One group of existing models is using non-homogeneous Poisson process (NHPP) whose fault-number and failure-rate are constant or time-dependent functions. A few studies have been manipulated S-shaped curve to construct their models. However, those works remain some limitations. In this study, we introduce a new model that is based on a generalised S-shaped curve and evaluate it by real data set. After installing it in real code of Matlab and using MLE method to estimate parameter with a range of initial solution, we prove that our model converge to the most basic model of NHPP group, Goel-Okumoto model.

Keywords: Software Reliability Modelling · Non-Homogeneous Poisson Process · S-shaped curve

1   Introduction

Having a big number of applications in many areas of our life, computer and software technology are being developed day by day. Like other sciences, researchers and developers have to solve a sequence of entangles to improve contribution of their products to human society. One of the biggest problems is to ensure the working state of software system, which is called software reliability and is considered as one characteristic of software quality [3]. Many authors [4,7,12] focus on software reliability modelling (SRM) to model system mathematically, in that they can estimate some characteristics of system as a total number of errors, predicted time of next failure, etc.. NHPP is a stochastic process whose rate parameter is a time-dependent function and is used widely in SRM research with plenty models [7].

We can use a S-shaped curve to mathematically model many natural processes that go to a steady state after an early growth period. Many authors have used this curve to build their model in software reliability modelling research and practice [6,7,9,10]. However, they have to face with two limitations: firstly, function that describes total number of faults of system is unbounded, in other words it approaches to infinity when time approaches infinity; secondly, failure detection rate functions in their study have simple form.

© Institute for Computer Sciences, Social Informatics and Telecommunications Engineering 2015
P.C. Vinh et al. (Eds.): ICTCC 2014, LNICST 144, pp. 212–221, 2015.
DOI: 10.1007/978-3-319-15392-6_21

To improve reality of NHPP SRMs that use S-shaped curve, we try to generalize existing S-shaped curve failure-detection-rate. So when their reality is increased, the complexity of computation also increased. In this study, we introduce a new model whose a failure detection rate function is generalised S-shaped curve. After theoretical computations, we use three materials to install our model: firstly, T project data set of AT&T [1] to apply; secondly, MLE method to estimate parameters; and the last, Matlab to support mathematics computing.

Organization of our paper is: we start by introduction section, we will discuss about NHPP SRM clearly in section 2. Section 3 will show some basic computation about S-shaped curve and apply in NHPP SRM. At the end, section 4 shows experimental results to evaluate our idea and section 5 summarizes our work with extended opinions.

2　NHPP Software Reliability Models

In this section, we will discuss about characteristic of SRMs base on NHPP, Pham [7].

2.1　General NHPP Software Reliability Model Calculation

Let's use some function to describe characteristic of system in Table 1.

Table 1. Characteristic functions of software system

$a(t)$	Total number of faults
$b(t)$	Fault detection rate
$m(t)$	Expected number of fault detected by time t (mean value function)
$\lambda(t)$	Failure intensity

By time t, system have $a(t)$ faults and $m(t)$ faults have been detected so we have $a(t)-m(t)$ remaining faults. With detection rate is $b(t)$, we have relationship among number of faults detected in period Δt, total remaining faults of system and fault detection rate:

$$m(t + \Delta t) - m(t) = b(t)[a(t) - m(t)]\Delta t + o(\Delta t) \tag{1}$$

where $o(\Delta t)$ is infinitesimal value with Δt: $\lim_{\Delta t \to 0} \frac{o(\Delta t)}{\Delta t} = 0$. Let $\Delta t \to 0$, we have:

$$\frac{\partial}{\partial t}m(t) = b(t)[a(t) - m(t)] \tag{2}$$

If t_0 is the starting time of testing process, with initial conditions $m(t_0) = m_0$ and $\lim_{t \to \infty} m(t) = a(t)$, Pham shows that general solution of (2) is [7]:

$$m(t) = e^{-B(t)}\left[m_0 + \int_{t_0}^{t} a(\tau)b(\tau)e^{B(\tau)}d\tau\right] \tag{3}$$

where

$$B(t) = \int_{t_0}^{t} b(s)ds \tag{4}$$

2.2 Existing NHPP SRMs

We have some existing NHPP SRMs shown in Table 2, Goel [2], Pham [7][8][9][10], Ohba [5], Yamada [13][14].

Table 2. Existing NHPP SRMs

Model	$a(t)$	$b(t)$	$m(t)$
Goel Okumoto	a (const)	b (const)	$a(1 - e^{-bt})$
Inflection S-shaped (Ohba)	a (const)	$\frac{b}{1+\beta e^{-bt}}$	$a \times \frac{e^{bt}-1}{e^{bt}+\beta}$
Delayed S-shaped (Yamada)	a (const)	$\frac{b^2 t}{bt+1}$	$a[1 - (1 + bt)e^{-bt}]$
Yamada 1	ae^{at}	b (const)	$\frac{ab}{b+a} \times (e^{at} - e^{-bt})$
Yamada 2	$a(1 + \alpha t)$	b (const)	$a(1 - e^{-bt})(1 - \frac{a}{\beta}) + a\alpha t$
PNZ	$a(1 + \alpha t)$	$\frac{b}{1+\beta e^{-bt}}$	$\frac{a}{1+\beta e^{-bt}}[(1 - e^{-bt})(1 - \frac{a}{\beta}) + at]$
Pham exponential	$ae^{\beta t}$	$\frac{b}{1+ce^{-bt}}$	$\frac{ab}{b+\beta} \times \frac{e^{(\beta+b)t}-1}{e^{bt}+c}$
Pham-Zhang	$c + a(1 - e^{-at})$	$\frac{b}{1+\beta e^{-bt}}$	$\frac{1}{1+\beta e^{-bt}}[(c+a)(1-e^{-bt}) - \frac{ab}{b-a}(e^{-at} - e^{-bt})]$
Pham fault detection dependent parameter	$a(1 + bt)^2$	$\frac{b^2 t}{bt+1}$	$a(bt + 1)(bt + e^{-bt} - 1)$

2.3 Parameter Estimation Using MLE Method

We work with the second data type that records the individual times at which failure occurred. So given data is a set of t_i, or occurrence time of N observed failures. Our model can have some parameter, called θ generally. Using MLE method, we have the following equation that related to each parameter θ is [7]

$$\sum_{i=1}^{N} \frac{\frac{\partial}{\partial\theta}\lambda(t_i)}{\lambda(t_i)} - \frac{\partial}{\partial\theta}m(t_N) = 0 \tag{5}$$

Assump that our model have n parameter $\theta_1, \theta_2, \cdots, \theta_n$, we will have system of n equations with n variables. Solve it, we will get estimated parameter of our model.

2.4   Application of SRM

SRM is a stochastic technique to model a set of occurrence time of failure. After collect those set, known as data set, practitioner will apply one of SRMs to get his MLE system of equations. Solution of this system of equations is a estimator of the set of parameter of system, then we have numeric model. From this model, we can estimate some characteristic measures of software system as a total number of errors, predicted time of next failure, etc.. There are two problem with any SRMs. Firstly, different SRMs have own advantages and limitations, then practitioner have to decide what model will be chosen. Secondly, complex assumptions will make a better functions of model, so estimated measures of system will be better. But we have to face with complex computation when build it, for example system of MLE equations can not be solved manually.

3   Generalised S-shaped Fault-Detection-Rate Function

We will introduce S-shaped function and its computation when applying it into NHPP SRM.

3.1   Generalised S-shaped Function

Consider S-shaped function whose equation is:

$$f(t) = b \times \frac{1 + m \times e^{-\frac{t}{\tau}}}{1 + n \times e^{-\frac{t}{\tau}}} \tag{6}$$

where $m < n$. This function can be described as follows:

1. In early time, its rapid increasing depends on value of m, n and τ.
2. After this period, it goes to constant b: $\lim_{t \to \infty} f(t) = b$.

This function has been widely applied in many science areas, where it describes state of some processes in real life. We have a simple S-shaped function called *sigmoid* in equation (7) where $b = 1$, $m = 0$, $n = 1$, $\tau = 1$ and that is shown in Figure 1.

$$f(t) = \frac{1}{1 + e^{-t}} \tag{7}$$

3.2   Proposed Fault-Detection-Rate Function Base on Generalised S-shaped

As shown before, some existing SRMs used specific type of S-shaped function: Infection S-shaped of Ohba [6]; Pham exponential imperfect [11], PNZ [9] and Pham-Zhang [10] of Pham et al. In those studies, authors use:

$$b(t) = b \times \frac{1}{1 + \beta \times e^{-bt}} \tag{8}$$

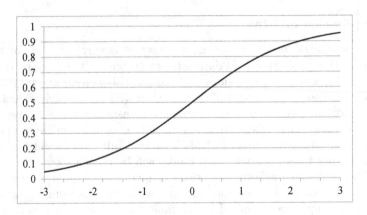

Fig. 1. Sigmoid function

We suggest using generalised S-shaped function as follows:

$$b(t) = b \times \frac{1 + m \times e^{-bt}}{1 + n \times e^{-bt}} \qquad (9)$$

where $0 < m < n < +\infty$, $b > 0$. Obviously, $b(t)$ in (8) is a specific case of equation in (9) when $m = 0$. To evaluate the appearance of m, let $b = 1$ and $n = 1$, consider functions with $m = 0.05$ (with dashed line) and $m = 0.7$ (with normal line) that are presented in Figure 2. From this, we realize that m affect to the initial value and the increment of S-shaped function.

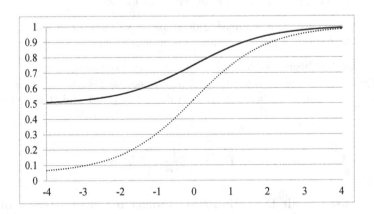

Fig. 2. Effect of parameter m to generalised S-shaped function

Let $k = \frac{m}{n} \Leftrightarrow m = k \times n$, note that $0 < k < 1$, we have:

$$b(t) = b \times \frac{e^{bt} + k \times n}{e^{bt} + n} \qquad (10)$$

So:

$$B(t) = bkt + (1 - k) \times \ln \frac{e^{bt} + n}{1 + n} \qquad (11)$$

And:

$$e^{B(t)} = e^{bkt} \times \left(\frac{e^{bt} + n}{1 + n}\right)^{1-k} \qquad (12)$$

3.3 Calculation of Mean Value Function of NHPP SRMs Base on General S-shaped Fault-Detection-Rate Function

From general solution in (3), substitute (10) and (12) into it, we have:

$$\int_0^t a(\tau)b(\tau)e^{B(\tau)}d\tau = \frac{b}{(1 + n)^{1-k}} \times \int_0^t a(\tau) \times e^{bk\tau} \times \frac{e^{b\tau} + kn}{(e^{b\tau} + n)^k}d\tau \qquad (13)$$

So:

$$m(t) = e^{-bkt} \times (e^{bt} + n)^{k-1} \times b \times \int_0^t a(\tau) \times e^{bk\tau} \times \frac{e^{b\tau} + kn}{(e^{b\tau} + n)^k}d\tau \qquad (14)$$

Equation (15) shows the relationship between mean value function $m(t)$ and fault-number function $a(t)$. Being a basic case of fault-number function, we have:

$$a(t) = a \qquad (15)$$

Substituting (16) into (15) we have:

$$m(t) = a - a \times e^{-bkt} \times \left(\frac{e^{bt} + n}{1 + n}\right)^{k-1} \qquad (16)$$

And

$$\lambda(t) = \frac{ab}{(1 + n)^{k-1}} \times e^{-bkt}(e^{bt} + n)^{k-2}(e^{bt} + kn) \qquad (17)$$

4 Experimental Results

4.1 Data Set

We use the failure data set of Ehrlich [1] to analysis our new SRM. This data set has been widely used in analysing and assessment SRMs. The data is testing data of project T that is developed in AT&T [1]. This system is a network management center that works as a connector between data collectors and operators [1]. Occurrence time of failures after testing period is given as in Table 3 [1]. The *Failure time* column provides exactly when each failure occur. The *Inter-failure time* column provides the length of period between two consecutive errors.

Table 3. AT&T system T project failures data set

Index	Failure time	Inter-failure time
1	5.50	5.50
2	7.33	1.83
3	10.08	2.75
4	80.97	70.89
5	84.91	3.94
6	99.89	14.98
7	103.36	3.47
8	113.32	9.96
9	124.71	11.39
10	144.59	19.88
11	152.40	7.81
12	166.99	14.60
13	178.41	11.41
14	197.35	18.94
15	262.65	65.30
16	262.69	0.04
17	388.36	125.67
18	471.05	82.69
19	471.50	0.46
20	503.11	31.61
21	632.42	129.31
22	680.02	47.60

4.2 Installing Environment

Our calculation is deployed in Thinkpad personal machine with technical information as follows:

- Processor Intel(R) Core(TM) i5-2410M CPU @2.30 GHz, 4.00 GB memory.
- Window 7 Professional Service Pack 1 operating system.
- Matlab R2012a stand alone version.

4.3 Parameter Estimation

Our new SRM has 4 parameter a, b, k and n. From equation (5), with derivation computations of $m(t)$ and $\lambda(t)$ in Appendix, we have system of 4 MLE equations. Those parameter can be estimated based on value of t_i of data set T that described in the first sub-section. Because this system of equations can not be solved primary, we need to use the support of Matlab tool.

We estimate parameters using `fsolve()` function of Matlab to solve MLE system of equations. Because there can have more than 1 solution, we use this Matlab statement with an array of initial solutions as:

- Initial solution vector begins from
  `[a,b,k,n]=[24,0.01,0.1,1]`

- Next initial solution vector of [a,b,k,n] is
  [a+1,b+0.01,k+0.1,n+1]
- To initial solution vector
  [a,b,k,n]=[50,0.99,0.9,30]

Furthermore, optimset()options is set to:

- 'MaxFunEvals'=1000000
- 'MaxIter'=1000

After 721710 loop instances, we have only one solution:

$$[a*,b*,k*,n*]=[23.7451,0.00341519,1.0,0.0].$$

From this calculation, we confirm that using MLE method to estimate parameters, our model will converge on Goel-Okumoto SRM with mean value function:

$$m(t) = a(1 - e^{-bt}) \tag{18}$$

From existing result, Pham [7] indicates that G-O SRM have good prediction value when comparing with other SRMs.

5   Conclusions and Future Works

In this paper, we have proposed new SRM by generalising existing S-shaped curve. Authors applied S-shaped functions in their and have many result. Based on the advantages of this curve, we expand their work by using generalised S-shaped function. However, the increment of reality of this generalising will make the computation more complex.

When apply our new model in real failure data set about project T of AT&T, with the computation support of Matlab, the result shows that this new SRM will converge to the most basic SRM, Goel-Okumoto.

For the further works, like any SRMs, let consider non-zero initial debugging time to get a better estimators. In addition, fault-number function of our model is constant, so some better time-dependent fault-number functions should be considered. The last extended idea is using other parameter estimations to get the set of parameters.

Appendix: Derivation Computations of $m(t)$ and $\lambda(t)$

We have some mathematics computations as follows:

- Derivation of $m(t)$ in each variables a, b, k and n:

$$\frac{\partial}{\partial a} m(t) = 1 - e^{-bkt} \times \left(\frac{e^{bt} + n}{1 + n}\right)^{k-1} \tag{19}$$

$$\frac{\partial}{\partial b}m(t) = \frac{b \times e^{-bkt}}{(1+n)^{k-1}} \times (e^{bt}+n)^{k-2} \times (e^{bt}+kn) \qquad (20)$$

$$\frac{\partial}{\partial k}m(t) = -a \times e^{-bkt} \times \left(\frac{e^{bt}+n}{1+n}\right)^{k-1} \times \left[\ln\left(\frac{e^{bt}+n}{1+n}\right) - bt\right] \qquad (21)$$

$$\frac{\partial}{\partial n}m(t) = e^{-bkt} \times (k-1) \times (e^{bt}+n)^{k-2} \times \frac{e^{bt}-1}{(n+1)^k} \qquad (22)$$

- Derivation of $\lambda(t)$ in each variables a, b, k and n:

$$\frac{\partial}{\partial a}\lambda(t) = \frac{b \times e^{-bkt}}{(1+n)^{k-1}} \times (e^{bt}+n)^{k-2} \times (e^{bt}+kn) \qquad (23)$$

$$\frac{\partial}{\partial b}\lambda(t) = \frac{-a \times e^{-bkt}}{(1+n)^{k-1}} \times (e^{bt}+n)^{k-3} \times \left[kn^2(bkt-1)\right.$$
$$\left. + ne^{bt}(3bkt-k-bt-1) + e^{2bt}(bt-1)\right] \qquad (24)$$

$$\frac{\partial}{\partial k}\lambda(t) = \frac{ab \times e^{-bkt}}{(1+n)^{k-1}} \times (e^{bt}+n)^{k-2}$$
$$\times \left[n - bte^{bt} - bknt + (e^{bt}+kn) \times \ln\left(\frac{e^{bt}+n}{1+n}\right)\right] \qquad (25)$$

$$\frac{\partial}{\partial n}\lambda(t) = \frac{-ab \times e^{-bkt}}{(1+n)^k} \times (k-1) \times (e^{bt}+n)^{k-3}$$
$$\times \left[e^{bt}(kn-n-2) + e^{2bt} - kn\right] \qquad (26)$$

So:

$$\frac{\frac{\partial}{\partial a}\lambda(t)}{\lambda(t)} = \frac{1}{a} \qquad (27)$$

$$\frac{\frac{\partial}{\partial b}\lambda(t)}{\lambda(t)} = \frac{kn^2(bkt-1) + e^{2bt}(bt-1)}{-b(e^{bt}+n)(e^{bt}+kn)} + \frac{ne^{bt}(3bkt-k-bt-1)}{-b(e^{bt}+n)(e^{bt}+kn)} \qquad (28)$$

$$\frac{\frac{\partial}{\partial k}\lambda(t)}{\lambda(t)} = \frac{(e^{bt}+kn) \times \ln\left(\frac{e^{bt}+n}{1+n}\right) - bte^{bt} + n - bknt}{e^{bt}+kn} \qquad (29)$$

$$\frac{\frac{\partial}{\partial n}\lambda(t)}{\lambda(t)} = \frac{-(k-1)\left[e^{bt}(kn-n-2) + e^{2bt} - kn\right]}{(1+n)(e^{bt}+n)(e^{bt}+kn)} \qquad (30)$$

Acknowledgments. This research was supported partly by The National Foundation for Science and Technology Development (NAFOSTED) under Grant 102.03-2013.39: Automated verification and error localization methods for component-based software.

The authors would like to thank Dr. Nguyen Thanh-Hung in Hanoi University of Science and Technology about his helpful comment; Le Yen, Hung-Cuong's colleague, about mathematical checking in early time of our work.

References

1. Ehrlich, W., Prasanna, B., Stampfel, J.: Determining the cost of a stop-test decision (software reliability). IEEE Software **10**(2), 33–42 (1993)
2. Goel, A.L., Okumoto, K.: Time-dependent error-detection rate model for software reliability and other performance measures. IEEE Transactions on Reliability **28**(3), 206–211 (1979)
3. Jung, H.-W., Kim, S.-G., Chung, C.-S.: Measuring software product quality: A survey of iso/iec 9126. IEEE Software **21**(5), 88–92 (2004)
4. Lyu, M.R., et al.: Handbook of software reliability engineering, vol. 3. IEEE Computer Society Press, CA (1996)
5. Ohba, M, Yamada, S.: S-shaped software reliability growth models. In: International Colloquium on Reliability and Maintainability, 4 th, Tregastel, France, pp. 430–436 (1984)
6. Ohba, M.: Software reliability analysis models. IBM Journal of Research and Development **28**(4), 428–443 (1984)
7. Pham, H.: System software reliability. Springer (2006)
8. Pham, H.: An imperfect-debugging fault-detection dependent-parameter software. International Journal of Automation and Computing **4**(4), 325–328 (2007)
9. Pham, H., Nordmann, L., Zhang, Z.: A general imperfect-software-debugging model with s-shaped fault-detection rate. IEEE Transactions on Reliability **48**(2), 169–175 (1999)
10. Pham, H., Zhang, X.: An nhpp software reliability model and its comparison. International Journal of Reliability, Quality and Safety Engineering **4**(03), 269–282 (1997)
11. Pham, L., Pham, H.: Software reliability models with time-dependent hazard function based on bayesian approach. IEEE Transactions on Systems, Man and Cybernetics, Part A: Systems and Humans **30**(1), 25–35 (2000)
12. Xie, M., Dai, Y.-S., Poh, K.-L.: Computing system reliability: models and analysis. Springer (2004)
13. Yamada, S., Ohba, M., Osaki, S.: S-shaped software reliability growth models and their applications. IEEE Transactions on Reliability **33**(4), 289–292 (1984)
14. Yamada, S., Osaki, S.: Software reliability growth modeling: Models and applications. IEEE Transactions on Software Engineering **12**, 1431–1437 (1985)

Enhancement of Innovation Co-creation Processes and Ecosystems Through Mobile Technologies

Tracey Yuan Ting Wong, Gabrielle Peko, and David Sundaram[✉]

Department of Information Systems and Operations Management,
University of Auckland, Auckland, New Zealand
won074@aucklanduni.ac.nz, {g.peko,d.sundaram}@auckland.ac.nz

Abstract. The process of value creation was traditionally driven almost exclusively within the firm. The role of the consumer was seen only at the end of the product development process. However, as the emergence of the Internet and its related technologies resulted in greater product variety there was a need for accelerating the innovation process. The concept of co-creation has been presented as a highly valuable trend and the next progression in open innovation. While extensive research has been conducted on innovation co-creation between firms and consumers, a coherent understanding of its application in the mobile environments has not been achieved. This paper explores the general evolution of the innovation co-creation paradigm and the opportunities mobile technologies bring in further developing this. An innovation co-creation framework is proposed along with a roadmap that provides a more detailed understanding of how to implement the components to realise the necessary innovation co-creation ecosystem.

Keywords: Innovation · Co-creation · Consumers · Mobile technology

1 Introduction

The success of an enterprise lies in the development of new products to meet consumer demands, and delivering them profitability in the marketplace. Innovation is one of the primary ways firms can differentiate their products from the competition and thus retain sustainable growth. By creating the perception that no substitutes are available, this strategy allows firms to compete in areas other than price [14]. In the past, many organisations have been able to survive with very limited amounts of innovation. They focused on simply updating products to a minimum level that maintains their competitiveness in the market. However, due to factors such as changes in consumer tastes, ever-shortening product lifecycles, competitive movements, technological advances, and globalisation, there is an increased need for firms to improve their response to changing markets. According to a survey conducted by Accenture, two-thirds of executives identified innovation as one of the five most critical factors required for companies to succeed and sustain a competitive advantage. However, the same survey found that only one in eight executives feel strongly that their companies excel at achieving innovation. While most firms today put high priority on creating

© Institute for Computer Sciences, Social Informatics and Telecommunications Engineering 2015
P.C. Vinh et al. (Eds.): ICTCC 2014, LNICST 144, pp. 222–232, 2015.
DOI: 10.1007/978-3-319-15392-6_22

innovative products and services, how they should go about finding the best source of innovation is still lacking [17].

Benkler [2] argues that the best innovative solutions lie not within firms, but within consumers. A survey conducted by the Economist Intelligence Unit [4] suggests that consumers are becoming increasingly important sources of innovation across all regions, industries, and company sizes. Skills and insights from the ultimate users of the output help firms develop relevant products that closely mirror consumer needs. By taking full advantage of the collective creative power in both current and potential consumers, firms have the potential to lead existing markets and create new ones, in a short period of time. Innovation co-creation has recently been gaining popularity among businesses as a fundamental source of competitive advantage. While the idea of creating two-way dialogues with key stakeholders has been around for some time, the availability of powerful web-based tools makes it relatively easier to start conversations and gather input rapidly from a large number of participants. Many of the world's leading companies, such as LEGO, Starbucks and Nike, are actively using innovation co-creation platforms and communities to engage directly with consumers to access new ideas [16]. These enabling tools have predominantly been isolated to the traditional desktop environment. The emergence of mobile technologies presents great challenges and opportunities for the creation of business value [3]. Mobile technologies have provided users with the ability to communicate with other parties and access information from anywhere and at any time. One significant outcome of this increased empowerment is that consumers now desire to play a greater role in their interactions with companies [7]. As a result, there is the question of how the development of mobile technologies will transform the enterprise and its consumer-centric processes such as innovation co-creation.

With mobile technologies continuing to significantly transform the ways in which a firm can interact with their consumers, they have the potential to increase participation in innovation co-creation processes. However, there is little in the existing literature that provides guidance on how to achieve this. This study seeks to address this gap through answering the following research questions: What is the process of innovation co-creation? What is the ecosystem necessary for effective innovation co-creation? How could this ecosystem be enhanced with the adoption of mobile technologies?

2   The Innovation Co-creation Process

This section discusses the key concepts of innovation co-creation to establish the necessary theoretical background and context for answering the research questions. In this section we will review the process of innovation co-creation. Then in the following section we will explore the literature on achieving the required ecosystem for innovation co-creation.

Traditionally, the innovation process was linear and sequential, with firms developing new ideas internally before testing them in the market. Consumers were passive participants in the innovation process, only acting as validators at the end stages of the product development lifecycle [10]. However, the process of innovation has changed. In the late 1980s, the societal process of individualisation arose when consumers started expressing their preferences through consumption choices. Firms became consumer-centric to appeal to these individual needs, with the offering of customised goods and services. Also, distribution channels and logistics changed in order for firms to deliver products faster and at the location desired by the consumer.

The emergence of Web 2.0 around 2006 was another important development that facilitated co-creation. The Internet became a global interconnected platform of web applications, and enabled people to create and change content. Consumers now have larger choice sets due to the increased ability to exchange information and opinions, to adapt their own perceptions and behaviour, and to define brands on their own. While consumers could customise products depending on the extent to which a firm's production chain allowed it, there were limited or no channels going back into the firm. This made adaptive or generative learning difficult to achieve [19].

The concept of co-creation transformed the traditional closed innovation process into a parallel and open one [6]. Today's new products must satisfy multiple consumer needs in terms of quality, function and price to be successful. To achieve this, innovation activities must take place simultaneously, with information being processed from various sources at the time products are conceived and designed. Linear innovation models that undertake tasks in a step-by-step manner are inappropriate for this purpose [13]. Co-creation allows the transformation of the traditional production chain into a dynamic network where consumers and firms continuously interact with each other and exchange knowledge. Co-creation can be found in all stages of the innovation process, including idea generation, design, engineering, and test and launch. In innovation co-creation, consumers actively engage with the firm at all stages of the product development lifecycle [12]. They are able and willing to provide ideas for new goods and services that fulfil needs not yet met by the market or are better than what is currently being offered. In addition, they are now able to easily communicate these ideas to the firm using the Internet [7]. By being important influencers as well as a main source of innovative ideas, consumers are now considered a main source of value creation and competitive advantage [19].

3   The Innovation Co-creation Ecosystem

Prahalad and Ramaswamy [15] argue that a space of potential co-creation experiences in which individuals jointly create value at multiple points of interaction must be established as the foundation of co-creation. The success of co-creation is focused on the quality of consumer-firm interactions. Participants need to initiate rich dialogues among themselves to exchange and generate knowledge to realise shared objectives. Therefore, it is essential to offer an open and transparent environment where participants feel comfortable and have the right capabilities to contribute their input. Current technologies for supporting remote collaboration are mainly desktop-based, which constrains the users to be close to their desktop computers in order to be updated on each other's statuses and progress. Furthermore, consumers have traditionally lacked the technical skills and capabilities required for effective innovation co-creation. This in turn restricts their ability to participate effectively in new product development processes.

The Internet and related technologies have played a vital role in enabling innovation co-creation. Firms can use virtual environments as an effective platform to greatly enhance their connectivity with consumers in a cost-effective manner and involve them as true partners throughout the new product development process [11]. As a ubiquitous network, the Internet has also made it possible to communicate to a large group of people as well as engage in rich conversation with particular individuals regardless of location or timezone [20]. The literature suggests that good results from co-creation are generally caused by frequency, direction, and depth of the interactions. With features such as extended reach, enhanced interactivity, increased speeds, and great flexibility, virtual environments can meet these aspects for effective innovation co-creation. Firms can use Web 2.0 technologies to collaborate with consumers and create open innovation platforms. With the interactivity features, they have the ability to coordinate discussions, reach a higher number of people faster, and synchronise group tasks. Participants can contribute to discussions and decision making when they have the time to do it, and without the need to send and resend e-mails.

Some firms currently use social networking platforms such as Facebook and Twitter to directly connect and interact with parties outside of organisational boundaries such as consumers. Social networking allows the accumulation of knowledge that can be searched and shared with like-minded communities [20]. By interacting with consumers through social networking tools, firms have the ability to gain access to the free flow of ideas and understand their customers without face-to-face interaction. Social networking tools facilitate the ability to influence the perception of the firm through improved relationships with consumers and innovation [20].

Jarche [8] suggested a model that illustrates the role of social networks in driving innovation. The model emphasizes that firms must first become open and transparent in order to be more innovative. It also emphasizes that knowledge is shared and diverse points of view are accepted to increase opportunities to participate in co-creation tasks. While participants have to be continuously sharing knowledge in their communities, the roles of the firm and consumer are not defined in this model. With no mention of two-way dialogues, the idea that firms cannot work in silos for effective new product development is not clear.

4   Exploration of Mobile Technologies

This section will begin by reviewing the features of mobile technologies that have been used in collaboration processes. Next, we explore the potential impacts of mobile technologies on both firms and consumers in how they work with each other. Finally, we will discuss the potential of mobile technologies to improve consumer engagement. Due to today's fast-paced world and the ability of the Internet to connect people worldwide, participants of innovation co-creation tend to be distributed and rarely situated in fixed locations most of the time. There is a need for a way to allow these members to collaborate with each other even when they are commuting. Mobile technologies have the potential to enable firms and consumers with the ability to not only keep in the loop on what has been done, but also to input ideas and give feedback anytime, anywhere with just their mobile devices. By extending activities into the wireless medium, mobile technologies allow users to have constant access to information. This in turn provides greater flexibility in communication, information sharing, and collaboration. In comparison to traditional forms of collaboration, mobile technologies offer several unique features: portability, reachability, localisation, identification, accessibility. Over the past decade, the continuing spread of mobile technology adoption has had a significant impact on the way firms and consumers do business with each other in terms of people, process, and technology.

Enterprise mobility can solve unique business problems by taking the business process to the consumers, who add rich content to business information [18]. From the consumer's perspective, mobilisation means higher quality service and thus increased consumer satisfaction. The proliferation of mobile technologies has led to a profound change in the way people communicate, collaborate, and make decisions. The success of customer relationship management (CRM) lies in the ability of the firm to communicate continuously with consumers on an individual level and provide differentiated value. It is also important to provide CRM activities through channels that consumers are also interested in using to interact with the firm. Mobile technologies can be used to manage the coordination of consumer interactions and relationships. Wind et al. [22] suggest that digital channels can create unique and positive experiences for consumers.

5   Problems, Issues and Requirements

An extensive literature review has resulted in the identification of four problems.

1. Lack of distinction between innovation co-creation and crowdsourcing – There is a huge focus on social networking tools in most literature related to innovation co-creation, but they only talk about using it for crowdsourcing purposes and not innovation co-creation as defined earlier in this dissertation.

2. Lack of research on increasing transparency to information – Meaningful dialogue is difficult to achieve if consumers do not have the same access to information.

3. Lack of research on how to set up an open platform – Innovation co-creation requires an open platform which can be accessed by both the firm and consumers.

4. Lack of research on balancing freedom and control – Co-creation should be an open process to foster an environment where varied inputs, ideas, and perspectives can be generated [5]. On the other hand, there needs to be defined structures and procedures that enable the effective coordination and filtering of ideas [1], [21].

To solve the problems of innovation co-creation and address their related issues, a set of requirements have been proposed to achieve this.

1. Commitment – Successful innovation co-creation in virtual environments is dependent on stimulating participant involvement. In order to achieve effective dialogue, it is important to carefully select the appropriate consumers who participate in co-creation tasks [15].

2. Learning – Firms need to be able to rapidly and efficiently respond to the input provided by consumers [9].

3. Engagement – The overall success of co-creation does not rely upon a single encounter between the firm and consumers. Co-creation is an ongoing effort involving synergies of all co-creation instances [1].

4. Prescriptions – There is generally a lack of research that provides support on how to set up the required open platform for innovation co-creation.

5. Connectivity – Increasing access to co-creation platforms enhances the frequency, direction, and depth of interactions [9], [15].

6. Flexibility – To find the right balance between freedom and control, flexible user protocols set up by participants can be used that determine the rules of engagement and can be constantly revised over time based on the experiences [15].

6   Innovation Co-creation Framework

In this section, a framework for innovation co-creation using mobile technologies with three levels of abstraction is proposed. To understand what innovation co-creation is, Figure 1 shows an abstract representation of an innovation co-creation ecosystem based on the three components suggested in Section 3: frequency, direction, and depth. Based on the literature review, increasing the extent to which all these aspects are achieved is crucial to improving innovation co-creation in virtual environments. Not only must there be a high number of conversations that take place over time, but they must also involve the exchange of rich and relevant information.

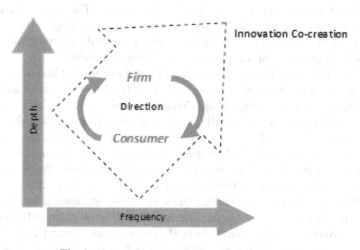

Fig. 1. Abstract innovation co-creation framework

Furthermore, firms must treat consumers as equal partners in the innovation co-creation process. While we increase the frequency and depth of interactions, a balance of exchanges in the form of two-way dialogues between involved parties must be achieved over time. As shown in Figure 2, this framework can then be viewed on a more detailed level in terms of how each of the three components can be realised.

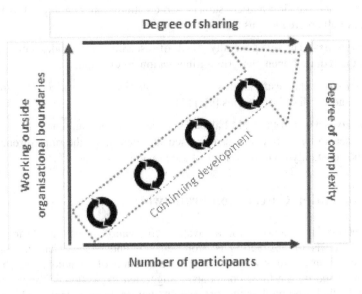

Fig. 2. Innovation co-creation ecosystem framework

Increasing the number of participants and degree of sharing enhances the frequency of interactions, while working outside organisational boundaries and increasing the degree of complexity enhances the depth of interactions. The greater the extent to which the four aspects are achieved and the more two-way dialogues that take place over time, the higher the level of continuous new product development. This in turn improves the chances of innovation co-creation being successful.

A high level technical framework that could support our abstract framework and eco-system framework is illustrated in Figure 3. Essentially at the lowest level are Network Services that take care of transport, signaling, provisioning, etc. These in turn support Collaboration Services such as workflow, real time messaging, real time dataflow, authoring, recording, playback, session management, scheduling, calendaring, knowledgebase management, database management, content management, etc. Collaborative services in turn become the base for co-creation applications that support activities such as brainstorming, inspiring, creation, drafting, curating, decision support, email, bulletin boards, social networks, forums, etc. These applications together support the entire spectrum of same time same place as well as different place and different time co-creation activities. These applications need to be accessible on devices such as desktops, laptops, smart boards and smart mobile devices for a variety of participants within organisations as well as outside organizational boundaries.

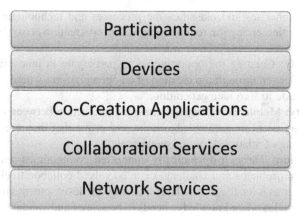

Fig. 3. Innovation co-creation technical framework

7   Innovation Co-creation Roadmap

This section will discuss a generalised roadmap with four stages on how to achieve and maintain the required innovation co-creation framework. We need to establish an environment of processes and technologies that allow direct and immediate communication between co-creation participants. It is important for firms to go through similar steps that will be proposed as it ensures that the required frequency, direction, and depth of interactions will be achieved for innovation co-creation. Figure 4 shows a roadmap for innovation co-creation. Based on the literature review, four steps are required to implement the required enablers, capabilities, and characteristics for initiating and continuing innovation co-creation. Each iteration of the cycle involves a series of two-way rich dialogues which increase the extent to which innovation co-creation can be achieved.

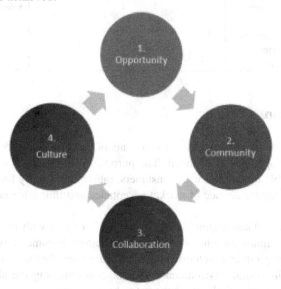

Fig. 4. Innovation co-creation roadmap

Table 1 summarises and classifies the processes and technologies that form the roadmap for implementing the required innovation co-creation ecosystem.

1. Opportunity: Creating the opportunities to participate in innovation co-creation. This can be achieved through the creation of an open platform where multiple connections can be made to start idea generation.

2. Community: Mobile technologies initiate the interaction between potential participants. Allowing users to acknowledge input and prove that they are listening facilitates the building of relationships and engagement.

3. Collaboration: Through dynamically connected communities with the most appropriate users, problems and challenges can be solved collaboratively. Mobile technologies can act as a feedback mechanism during the development and testing phases of innovation cycles when knowledge needs to be shared and validated.

4. Culture: The result is a changed organisational culture of increased sharing and creativity. By opening up the firm to key influencers of the brand or product, this prompts employees to see new perspectives that may trigger new ideas and new strategic directions.

Table 1.   Innovation co-creation ecosystem roadmap

	Opportunity ⇨	Community ⇨	Collaboration ⇨	Culture
To increase	Number of participants	Working outside organisational boundaries	Degree of sharing Degree of complexity	
Process	• Listen to all	• Engage with many	• Develop with some	• Validate ideas
Technology	• Design technology to support open platform • Configure and implement platform	• Locate user • Connect with user	• Transfer data	• Test and monitor performance • Verify technology

8   Conclusion

As consumers are no longer just passive recipients of goods and services, their role in new product development has changed. The purpose of innovation co-creation is to allow firms to enable innovation with consumers, rather than simply for them. Consequently, there is a higher chance of market acceptance and thus a lower risk of failed projects.

The Internet and related technologies have provided firms with the ability to implement distributed innovation practices where consumers become active participants throughout the new product development process. However, the challenges of managing communities in virtual environments without compromising the ability to share resources and create active dialogues have yet to be overcome.

Mobile technologies provide participants with the enhanced information and network for innovation co-creation. They offer the greatest power to contribute ideas and select components that should be incorporated into the new product offering. By offering an open platform that is jointly maintained by the firm and consumers, they have the potential to accelerate internal business processes and improve consumer relations.

References

1. Bartl, M.: Co-creation 360 (2009). http://www.michaelbartl.com/co-creation/wp-content/uploads/Co-Creation_360.pdf (accessed 30 October 2012)
2. Benkler, Y.: The Wealth of Networks: How Social Production Transforms Markets and Freedom. Yale University Press, New Haven (2006)
3. Creeger, M.: ACM CTO roundtable on mobile devices in the enterprise. Communications of the ACM **54**(9), 45–53 (2011)
4. Economist intelligence unit. The digital company 2013: how technology will empower the customer (2008). http://www.pwc.com/gx/en/technology/assets/digital_co_1.pdf (accessed 3 November 2012)
5. Enkel, E., Gassmann, O., Chesbrough, H.: Open R&D and open innovation: Exploring the phenomenon. R&D Management **39**(4), 311–316 (2009)
6. Hagel, J., Brown, J.S.: Creation nets: harnessing the potential of open innovation. Journal of Service Science **1**(2), 27–40 (2008)
7. Hoyer, W.D., Chandy, R., Dorotic, M., Krafft, M., Singh, S.S.: Consumer cocreation in new product development. Journal of Service Research **13**(3), 283–296 (2010)
8. Jarche, H.: Social networks drive innovation (2011). http://www.jarche.com/2011/09/social-networks-drive-innovation/ (accessed 11 November 2012)
9. Lusch, R., Vargo, S.: Service-dominant logic: a guiding framework for inbound marketing. Marketing Review St. Gallen **6**, 5–10 (2009)
10. Maklan, S., Knox, S., Ryals, L.: New trends in innovation and customer relationship management: a challenge for market researchers. International Journal of Market Research **50**(2), 221–240 (2008)
11. Nambisan, S., Nambisan, P.: How to profit from a better 'virtual customer environment'. MIT Sloan Management Review **49**(3), 53–61 (2008)
12. O'Hern, M.S., Rindfleisch, A.: Customer co-creation: a typology and research agenda. Review of Marketing Research **6**, 84–106 (2010)
13. Parthasarthy, R., Hammond, J.: Product innovation input and outcome: moderating effects of the innovation process. Journal of Engineering and Technology Management **19**(1), 75–91 (2002)
14. Porter, M.E.: Competitive Strategy: Techniques for Analyzing Industries and Competitors. Free Press, New York (1998)
15. Prahalad, C.K., Ramaswamy, V.: Co-creating unique value with customers. Strategy & Leadership **32**(3), 4–9 (2004)
16. Ramaswamy, V.: Co-creation of value – towards an expanded paradigm of value creation. Marketing Review St. Gallen **26**(6), 11–17 (2009)
17. Rau, C., Neyer, A., Möslein, K.M.: Innovation practices and their boundary-crossing mechanisms: a review and proposals for the future. Technology Analysis & Strategic Management **24**(2), 181–217 (2012)

18. Sheedy, T.: Make mobility standard business practice (2010). http://www.computerweekly.com/opinion/Make-mobility-standard-business-practice (accessed 15 October 2012)
19. van Dijk, J.: The effects of co-creation on brand and product perceptions (2011). http://issuu.com/joycediscovers/docs/msc_thesis_joycevandijk_public (accessed 30 October 2012)
20. van Zyl, A.S.: The impact of social networking 2.0 on organisations. The Electronic Library **27**(6), 906–918 (2009)
21. Whitla, P.: Crowdsourcing and its application in marketing activities. Contemporary Management Research **8**(1), 15–18 (2009)
22. Wind, Y., Mahajan, V., Gunther, R.E.: Convergence Marketing: Strategies for Reaching the New Hybrid Consumer. Prentice-Hall, Englewood Cliffs (2002)

Design and Implementation
of Sustainable Social Shopping Systems

Claris Yee Seung Chung$^{(\boxtimes)}$, Roman Proskuryakov, and David Sundaram

Department of Information Systems and Operations Management,
University of Auckland, Auckland, New Zealand
{yee.chung,d.sundaram}@auckland.ac.nz, rpro3000@gmail.com

Abstract. Sustainability is one of the most often discussed topics in our society. Although no one argues that individuals are the main players in changing society and the environment, individuals have always been treated as just actors and decision makers who transform the organizational, societal, national, and/or global sustainability practices. However, our fundamental belief is that individual and personal sustainability are at the heart of organizational and societal sustainability. One of the key activities that humans undertake that has an overwhelming influence on the economic, environmental, and health facets of their life is shopping. In this paper, we explore the possibility of using the concepts and principles of decision-making, habit formation, social networks, and benchmarking to influence consumer behavior towards sustainable shopping. We propose a framework and architecture for Sustainable Social Shopping Systems. We are in the process of prototyping and implementing them in the context of a purely online supermarket.

Keywords: Sustainability · Social shopping · Decision-making · Consumer behavior · Transformation · Habit formation · Wellbeing · Health · Finance · Environment

1   Introduction

"How can we live well?" is a question that has been asked through the ages. A burgeoning self-management $13 billion industry has grown around trying to answer this question [1]. In addition, the recent proliferation of smart device technologies has made the self-management industry to broaden its services to the web and mobile applications [2]. Individuals can now manage their lives easily as they can access their daily life data from web services and mobile applications. Despite the increase in the so-called "self-improvement/self-management" apps and web services, recent research and consumers have started to question the efficiency and effectiveness of the web services and apps. For instance, 26% of users reported to have used health apps only once [8]. A key reason for their failure could be that they have overlooked the behavioral side of individuals' activities, decisions, habit formation and transformation. To be sustainable, individuals need to create balance among physical and spiritual values, thoughts, actions and behaviors [7]. This means that these web

© Institute for Computer Sciences, Social Informatics and Telecommunications Engineering 2015
P.C. Vinh et al. (Eds.): ICTCC 2014, LNICST 144, pp. 233–242, 2015.
DOI: 10.1007/978-3-319-15392-6_23

services and mobile applications also should support the various dimensions of an individual's life allowing the prioritization of various aspects in accordance with situations [3–6]. To support true sustainability, it is crucial to identify human activities, which can change our behaviors to be sustainable. Shopping is a household activity that has an overwhelming influence on individuals' sustainability as it has close relationships with financial, health, philosophical and environmental values, and is often carried out by individual's habitual behaviors [9, 10].

This paper proposes Sustainable Social Shopping as a pathway to individual sustainability, by synthesizing concepts, models, processes, and frameworks from sustainability, shopping, social shopping, decision-making, and habit formation. This paper reviews the literature related to individual sustainability, shopping, online shopping, sustainable shopping, and social shopping. After that, the paper suggests concepts, models, framework and architectural components for the design of Sustainable Social Shopping Systems. Finally a prototypical implementation of a sustainable social shopping system in terms of the process and system views will be described.

2   Individual Sustainability

"Sustainability" was initially outlined by the World Commission on Environment and Development Report in 1987 and gained international momentum in 1992 Rio de Janeiro Earth Summit which was sponsored by the United Nations [11]. Since "Sustainability" and "Sustainable development" became a global buzzword, the concept has been studied and discussed in many academic disciplines. In general terms, the concepts of "Sustainability" have been approached and developed by incorporating ecological and environmental issues at the organizational level. However, to achieve true sustainability, researchers and policy makers had also recognized the social and economic dimensions of sustainability and sustainable development. This encouraged organizations to manage integrated and balanced performances of economic, environmental and social aspects. These three key performance indicators is now known as the Triple Bottom Line (TBL). TBL encourages organizations to take the driving seat for "People, planet and profits" to be sustainable [12]. TBL brings the idea that people are an important factor to consider in order to make our society sustainable. Ordinary individuals are the real decision makers for sustainable development [13], as they are responsible for understanding and improving awareness of sustainability, and decide whether to adapt their attitudes and behaviors for sustainable development within different roles of their lives, for instance, as an individual or a family member [14]. More and more individuals are becoming aware of the importance of sustainability and they tend to engage with choices that contribute to positive changes and happiness [15]. We synthesize these ideas and propose a model of sustainability where the individual is at the heart of a sustainable society (Fig. 1).

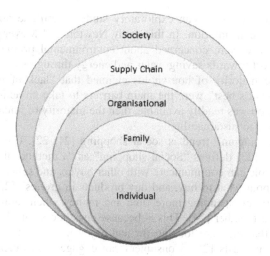

Fig. 1. Level of Sustainability

3   Shopping, Sustainable Shopping and Social Shopping

Shopping is a decision-making process that people or households make on a daily basis [16]. Many people do shopping like a mundane task, but it is an activity that influences not only individual or household life patterns, but also business production and distribution processes, and even the national economy [9]. At the individual household level, shopping affects people's lives from financial and health considerations to philosophical values. At the organizational or global level, shopping directly influences the businesses' profits, and thus indirectly has an effect on the entire economy and the global environment. Also shopping is the activity that can bring fundamental changes in our life, because it is habitual and often reflects life values [9].

When "Sustainability" became one of the biggest tasks to address solutions for the good of the public, researchers and policy makers focused on individuals and household shopping activities while businesses and organizations tried to transform themselves to meet sustainability regulations and policies. Sustainable shopping, sustainable consumption, green consumption and many similar terminologies were conventionally used in various articles to explain how shopping activities can lead the ecological sustainability of the world [10, 16–18].

The idea of sustainable consumption emerged at the 1992 Rio Earth Summit, and the action plan for sustainable development was endorsed by 179 heads of state [16]. Taking this into consideration, sustainable shopping concept has been used in the context of environmental issues, in particular concepts that included bringing changes in consumer's quality of life. Jackson suggests that sustainable consumption does "not only involve changes in consumer behavior and lifestyle" but is also achieved through improvements in efficiency [19]. Therefore it is worthwhile to consider several concepts related to shopping for supporting true sustainability.

Firstly, sustainable shopping concept needs to be considered. Although sustainable shopping has been promoted strategically by government level agencies, it is a daunting task to make families and individuals to shop in a sustainable manner [17].

Newton and Meyer conducted an exploratory study of attitude and action gap in household resource consumption. In this study Newton and Meyer found that most Australian households were concerned about environmental problems and strongly showed their support towards saving water and energy through sustainable consumption. However the majority of households claimed that "lack of information" and "can't work out what's best" were the main barriers to take an action [20]. In other words, if information was readily available, then the majority of households would be willing to contribute to sustainability.

Another recent shopping trend is social shopping [21, 22]. Cambridge Business English Dictionary [23] defines "Social shopping" as "a method of shopping on the internet where people can communicate with other buyers and sellers to discuss products, get advice about what to buy, and buy products in groups" [23]. In a shopping context, consumers are spending more time and money when family or friends are doing the shopping together [24]. This is because consumers can share and get opinions on products that they are looking for and enjoy interactions with other people who have similar interests [25]. Consumers can engage with others through social shopping features, e.g. share purchases on their social network services, and then often form their social presence by interdepending, connecting and responding to shopping behaviors within their relationships [26]. Social shopping is rapidly gaining attention and popularity from the marketplace, because communication and interaction are key elements in the success of eCommerce [27].

Table 1. Keywords frequency in leading IS Journal and in Google Scholar (2000-2014)

IS Journal	Sustainability	Sustainable Consumption	Shopping	Sustainable Shopping	Social	Social Shopping	Sustainable Social Shopping
Information Systems Research	1	0	164	0	371	0	0
MIS Quarterly	16	0	140	0	864	0	0
Journal of Management Information Systems	3	0	163	0	434	0	0
Information Systems Journal	0	0	62	0	208	0	0
European Journal of Information Systems	2	0	98	0	312	0	0
Communications of the ACM	13	0	740	0	1,330	0	0
IS Journal Total	35	0	1,367	0	3,519	0	0
Google Scholar Across Disciplines	997K	16.2K	1,200K	201	451K	1.7K	0

Sustainable shopping and online social shopping are mutually sustaining concepts that could be leveraged to support individual sustainability. However, no studies or practical solutions have been attempted, to combine these readily available concepts and mechanisms as a solution for individual sustainability. This became more obvious when key words related to "Sustainability", "Social", and "Shopping" were analyzed in six leading Information Systems journals for the last 14 years [28] and searched for in Google Scholar. While many articles have been found with each key word separately, a distinct lack of research interest has been apparent when combining concepts from these key words in the Information Systems discipline. A Google Scholar search across disciplines shows that there is research interest when combining any two from these key words, however there is no single matching article returned when the three key words of "sustainable social shopping" were combined (Table 1). In the next section, we propose Sustainable Social Shopping Systems (SSSS) as a means by which we can practically support individuals to become more sustainable and ultimately transform their lives.

4   Foundation of Sustainable Social Shopping Systems

Sustainable social shopping system (SSSS) is an online shopping cart system that provides insightful information to help consumers to be sustainable. Unlike an ordinary online shopping cart system, SSSS will provide at least three life dimensions information (financial, health and environmental aspects) in an integrated manner. In SSSS consumers will get two types of information for each life dimension. In a product detail and selection page, consumers will get notified on sustainability information for that specific product; in a shopping confirmation page, current overall shopping information for sustainability, and historical shopping information, of three life dimensions are given for comparison or future reference. Information for each life dimension will be guided by either commonly adapted method or government regulations. For example, information about health dimension in the selection page will be shown in traffic lights color code manner (green, amber and red), based on the UK guideline to creating a front of pack (FoP) nutrition label for pre-packaged products sold through retail outlets [29]. To be sustainable, integrated and balanced information should be offered to consumers. It was clearly shown in interviews conducted by Young et al. [30], that 30% of UK consumers were very concerned about environmental issues. However, interviewees pointed out "lack of information" of environmental and social performance of products and producers were the main barriers to action. Therefore SSSS can be a very attractive system for both consumers and eCommerce businesses, as it not only supports individual sustainability, but also has the potential of becoming a promising business model.

Traditionally, multiple cognitive steps were broadly adapted to understand consumers' behavior in marketing studies [31]. For example, when consumers make a purchase of an item, they often follow the five-stage buying decision process model, which involves need recognition, information search, evaluation, purchase decision and post-purchase behavior [32, 33]. Also shopping can be understood as a habitual decision making process [20] because customers purchase products based on their daily life routine. Therefore this paper proposes the Sustainable Social Shopping System based on purchase decision model and habit model. According to Duhigg, habit is formed through a three-step loop; cue, routine and reward (Fig. 2) [34]. On a large scale, SSSS follows the habit model, but each step is incorporated with the details of the buying decision processes. Under the cue step, the need recognition stage begins with intrinsic and extrinsic stimuli like craving feeling, time based needs or commercial promotions. In the routine step, information search, evaluation and purchase decision stages are processed. In the reward step, post-purchase behavior stage is carried out and this step will feed the cue step again. Customers will experience these three steps through online shopping, and over time they will form a habit relating to shopping online. To support individuals' sustainable transformation, SSSS needs to provide prompt features for steps and stages that will inspire them to become sustainable.

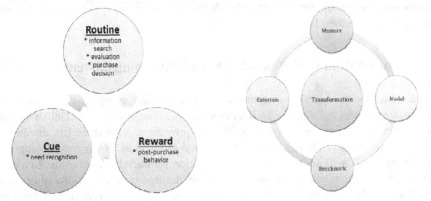

Fig. 2. Decision Making and the Cue-Routine-Reward Cycle

Fig. 3. A Framework for Individual Sustainability Transformation

In order to support individual's sustainability, SSSS should be able to provide insightful multi-dimensional information through the entire shopping process. However, there is no current framework that embraces all these concepts, models and processes completely. The ultimate goal of Sustainable Social Shopping System is helping individuals to transform their lives to be sustainable. As most individuals' current status is strongly engaged with inputs, the first step of transformation is to "measure" these inputs. This is followed by understanding these inputs through "models" tested by "benchmarking" (setting goals and meeting them), and finally "transformation" is achieved. "Entertain" is an element that entails "Transformation". While the process of measure, model, and benchmark may seem onerous there is a possibility that transformation could also be approached and achieved through gamification features, social features, and ultimately entertainment. For example, customers can share products that they want to purchase via social network and discuss about it with information provided by SSSS. While they are sharing their opinions about products and reaching a purchase decision together, individuals influence others and are influenced in turn by others too (Fig.3).

5   A Prototypical Sustainable Social Shopping Systems

Due to the prevailing use of mobile devices in these days [35], online shopping through mobile devices has become common [36]. In order to meet current consumers' trend, SSSS has a tablet-friendly design. Basically the system consists of 5 pages: Featured, Search, Statistics, Cart, and Profile.

5.1   Featured and Product Selection Pages

Featured page includes new and noteworthy products and packages, which stand out in the market and are potentially attractive to the user. A product or a package appearing in the featured page is a result of a process run by a sophisticated recommendation engine. Featured page infrastructure is flexible, which means sections (like Top-Charts, Social Choice etc.) are easily altered and updated. This page also shows the pre-defined shopping list (Fig.4). Within this page, customers can click into a detailed product information page and multi-dimensional information will be provided to help with individuals' sustainability practices (Fig. 5).

Fig. 4. Pre-defined Shopping List Page   **Fig. 5.** Product Selection Page

5.2   Search and Statistics

Search page provides basic search functionality for the user to be able to find products, categories of products or packages (Fig. 6). The statistics page is responsible for aggregating transactional data, produced by the user, and presenting useful information acquired from this data to the user in three dimensions (Health, Finance, and Environmental Footprint). This page is designed to let the user understand his/her online shopping behavior as well as the level of personal sustainability (Fig. 7).

Fig. 6. Search Page   **Fig. 7.** Statistics Page

5.3   Cart and Profile Pages

All chosen products will be shown on the Cart page. Unlike the ordinary shopping system, it will show sustainability information and provide social shopping features (Fig. 8). Profile page includes user's basic personal information such as (name, username, billing information). The user will be able to log in using existing social networks; there is also provision to log into additional fitness social networks, which will later provide more useful information about health dimension of the user's sustainability status (Fig. 9).

Fig. 8. Cart Page   **Fig. 9.** Profile Page

6   Future Research Directions

The individuals' life spectrum is broad. Therefore, identifying human activities that influence multiple life facets and ultimately their sustainability is important. From the literature review, we identified shopping as a potential area for improving the sustainability of individuals. However we also recognized that there is sparse research on sustainable shopping and almost no research on sustainable social shopping. To address this lacuna we have developed a Sustainable Social Shopping System (SSSS). SSSS will predict and recommend products to customers based on customers' specific circumstances, preferences and shopping history. Sustainability information on three life dimensions (finance, health and environment) will be provided in an integrated manner for assisting shoppers. Currently we are working on integrative models and recommendation algorithms. Parameters/KPIs for the three dimensions are heterogeneous, thus *integrative models* for understanding interrelationships between the data need to be developed. Based on these models, *prediction/suggestion/recommendation algorithms* also need to be developed. The data is currently sourced from product suppliers, government regulations and studies from expert organizations. However, in order to support a holistic individual sustainability, the system also needs to be flexible to incorporate other aspects of life dimensions and connect to a larger variety of data from outside sources in the future.

References

1. Pierleoni, A.: Do self-help books work? (2013). http://www.suntimes.com/lifestyles/mindbody/18103274-423/do-self-help-books-work.html
2. McKendrick, J.: Decision making on the go. http://www.teradatamagazine.com/v11n01/Features/Decision-Making-on-the-Go/
3. Christensen, C.M., Allworth, J., Dillon, K.: How Will You Measure Your Life?. Harper Business, London (2012)
4. Csikszentmihalyi, M.: Flow: The Psychology of Optimal Experience. Harper Perennial, New York (1991)
5. Csikszentmihalyi, M.: Finding Flow: The Psychology of Engagement with Everyday Life. Basic Books, New York (1997)
6. Seligman, M.E.P.: Flourish: A Visionary New Understanding of Happiness and Well-being. Free Press, New York (2011)
7. Pappas, E.C.: Individual sustainability: preliminary research. In: 2013 IEEE Frontiers in Education Conference, pp. 1631–1636. IEEE (2013)
8. iHealthBeat: Mobile Health Apps Popular, but Efficacy in Question, Experts Say (2011). http://www.ihealthbeat.org/articles/2011/3/22/mobile-health-apps-popular-but-efficacy-in-question-experts-say
9. Young, C.W., Quist, J., Green, K.: Strategies for sustainable shopping, cooking and eating for 2050 – suitable for europe. In: International Sustainable Development Research Conference (2000)
10. Gilg, A., Barr, S., Ford, N.: Green Consumption or Sustainable Lifestyles? Identifying the Sustainable Consumer. Futures **37**, 481–504 (2005)
11. Marshall, J.D., Toffel, M.W.: Framing The Elusive Concept of Sustainability: A Sustainability Hierarchy. Environ. Sci. Technol. **39**, 673–682 (2005)
12. Elkington, J.: Enter the triple bottom line. In: Henriques, A., Richardson, J. (eds.) The Triple Bottom Line: Does It All Add Up, pp. 1–16. Capstone Publishing, Oxford (2004)
13. Schmidheiny, S.: Changing Course: A Global Business Perspective on Development and the Environment. MIT Press, Cambridge (1992)
14. Starik, M.: Toward a Multi-level, Multi-Systems Approach to Sustainability Governance and Outcomes : An Essay. Innov. Manag. Policy Pract. **6**, 167–169 (2004)

15. Venhoeven, L., Bolderdijk, J., Steg, L.: Explaining the Paradox: How Pro-Environmental Behaviour can both Thwart and Foster Well-Being. Sustainability **5**, 1372–1386 (2013)
16. Seyfang, G.: Shopping for Sustainability: Can Sustainable Consumption Promote Ecological Citizenship? Env. Polit. **14**, 290–306 (2005)
17. Jones, P., Hillier, D., Comfort, D.: Shopping for Tomorrow: Promoting Sustainable Consumption within Food Stores. Br. Food J. **113**, 935–948 (2011)
18. Quist, J., Toth, K.S., Green, K.: Shopping, cooking and eating in the sustainable household. In: Greening of Industry Network Conference. pp. 1–10 (1998)
19. Jackson, T.: Readings in Sustainable Consumption. In: The Earthscan reader in sustainable consumption, pp. 1–27. Earthscan, London (2006)
20. Newton, P., Meyer, D.: Exploring the Atitudes-Action Gap in Household Resource Consumption: Does Environmental Lifestyle Segmentation Align With Consumer Behaviour? Sustainability **5**, 1211–1233 (2013)
21. Tedeschi, B.: Like Shopping? Social Networking? Try Social Shopping (2006). http://www.nytimes.com/2006/09/11/technology/11ecom.html?_r=0
22. Grange, C., Benbasat, I.: Online social shopping: the functions and symbols of design artifacts. In: The 43rd Hawaii International Conference on System Sciences – 2010, pp. 1–10. IEEE (2010)
23. Cambridge Business English Dictionary: English Definition of "Social Shopping." http://dictionary.cambridge.org/dictionary/business-english/social-shopping
24. Sommer, R., Wynes, M., Brinkley, G.: Social Facilitation Effects in Shopping Behavior. Environ. Behav. **24**, 285–297 (1992)
25. Pfeiffer, J., Benbasat, I.: Social influence in recommendation agents: creating synergies between multiple recommendation sources for online purchase. In: European Conference on Information Systems, Barcelona, Spain (2012)
26. Biocca, F., Harms, C., Gregg, J.: The networked minds measure of social presence: pilot test of the factor structure and concurrent validity. In: 4th Annual International Workshop on Presence, Philadelphia, PA (2001)
27. Rayport, J., Jaworski, B.: Introduction to E-Commerce. McGraw-Hill, New York (2001)
28. Peffers, K., Ya, T.: Identifying and evaluating the universe of outlets for information systems research: Ranking the journals. J. Inf. Technol. Theory Appl. **5**, 63–84 (2003)
29. Department of Health: Guide to Creating a Front of Pack (FoP) Nutrition Label for Prepacked Products Sold through Retail Outlets (2013). www.dh.gsi.gov.uk
30. Young, W., Hwang, K., McDonald, S., Oates, C.J.: Sustainable Consumption: Green Consumer Behaviour when Purchasing Products. Sustain. Dev. **18**, 20–31 (2010)
31. Comegys, C., Hannula, M., Vaisanen, J.: Longitudinal Comparison of Finnish and US Online Shopping Behaviour Among University Students: The Five-stage Buying. J. Targeting, Mes. Anal. Mark. **14**, 336–356 (2006)
32. Kotler, P., Kelle, K.L.: Marketing Management. Prentice Hall, Upper Saddle River (2006)
33. Kotler, P., Amstrong, G.: Marketing: An Introduction. Prentice Hall, Upper Saddle River (2005)
34. Duhigg, C.: The Power of Habit. Why We Do What We Do and How to Change. Random House LLC, London (2012)
35. Lenhart, A., Purcell, K., Smith, A., Zickuhr, K.: Social Media & Mobile Internet Use Among Teens and Young Adults, Washington (2010)
36. Li, Y.-M., Yeh, Y.-S.: Increasing Trust in Mobile Commerce through Design Aesthetics. Comput. Human Behav. **26**, 673–684 (2010)

Developing Method for Optimizing Cost of Software Quality Assurance Based on Regression-Based Model

Vu Dao-Phan[(⊠)], Thang Huynh-Quyet, and Vinh Le-Quoc

School of Information and Communication Technology,
Hanoi University of Science and Technology, Hanoi, Vietnam
dpvu@moet.edu.vn, thanghq@soict.hust.edu.vn, vinhlq199@gmail.com

Abstract. In this paper we present a method for Optimizing Cost of Software Quality Assurance base on Regression-based Model proposed by Omar AlShathry [1,2]. Based on the regression-based model, regression analysis to estimate the number of defects in software, we propose an optimal method for software quality assurance based on the constraint conditions using linear programming techniques. The results of a detailed analysis of the theoretical and empirical models are presented and evaluated.

Keywords: Regression-based Model · Software Quality · Optimizing Cost

1   Introduction

In the software development process, the project manager is always interested in three constraints: cost, schedule and quality since the models above cannot accurately determine the trade-off between the constraints. The software cost estimation models such as COCOMO [4] and COQUALMO [4,5], the software quality process standards such as ISO 9126 [5] used to predict the development effort, defect estimation and quality assessment software will be built. However, models based on data analysis of many previous software projects may encounter difficulties for an organization to adjust the fit of the model. Moreover, these models do not show the balance issues between three software constraints.

Cost of software quality (CoSQ) won the major concern of the project managers because it has been estimated that approximately 40% of the software budget is not reasonably used in the defect discovery and removal process [1]. The regression model provides the project managers with ability to control investment capital to ensure software quality by implementing optimization techniques based on the data manipulation of historical projects [1,2]. In addition, based on the model, the project managers and QA practitioners can handle and deal with unforeseen difficulties related to the software development process [3,4]. It also brings out the best solution for quality assurance decisions for the project managers and QA practitioners to deal with budget shortages, reduced schedule or to achieve goals such as minimum quality cost, successful defect removal [5]. Based on the Regression-based Model [1,2], we present

© Institute for Computer Sciences, Social Informatics and Telecommunications Engineering 2015
P.C. Vinh et al. (Eds.): ICTCC 2014, LNICST 144, pp. 243–253, 2015.
DOI: 10.1007/978-3-319-15392-6_24

our approach to develop a method for optimizing the cost of Software Quality Assurance: using classification of software phases into products based on the available risk level; using data storage of quality assurance techniques to store detailed information about the quality assurance activities; using improved matrix containing defects to help accurately determine the efficiency of defect removal of the applied quality assurance techniques. We proposed also to apply the least squares algorithm into linear regression to estimate the number of defects in software. The paper also presents an optimal model which applies linear planning problem to generate optimal solutions for quality assurance plan based on the defined constraint conditions. To build testing software, we studied to install Simplex Algorithm and use LINDO API library [7] to solve the problem in the optimization model.

The content of the paper is presented as follows: Section 2 introduces Regression-based Model in details; Section 3 presents the proposed method; Section 4 provides the results of experimental settings and evaluates the results; Section 5 presents the final conclusion and the development direction of the research.

2   Regression-Based Model

Theoretical regression-based model includes two main components [1,2]: regression analysis and computation to find optimal solutions for quality assurance costs. Regression analysis including 2 processes: data collection and analysis. Figure 1 describes the process of modeling activities. The estimation calculation of the costs as input for Linear programming problem, combined with the known boundary conditions to obtain the output is an optimal solution for software quality assurance plan. Before collecting data, it is necessary to go through the phase classification process of the artifacts into the specific risks. Figure 2 describes the model overview including the phase classification process of the artifacts into the specific risks and quality assurance activities in each phase.

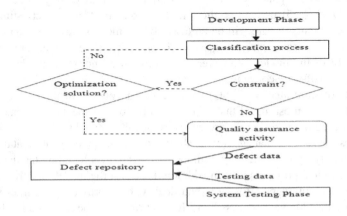

Fig. 1. Work-flow of the Quality Model [9]

Through the two processes mentioned above, the data model will be stored and processed in database, which helps make decisions for projects in the future. To estimate costs, the model bases on the data of the projects in the past but only gets from a single organization, storing and analyzing data generated from the quality assurance activities of the organization. After product sorting process, the quality assurance group stores all the data related to the details of the product. The details include: phase, phase size, type of artifacts, size, and rate of products. In each phase, the input data consist of two interconnected boards: the type of products of each phase and the QA techniques assigned to each product as follows: the cover of each technique, the number of defects found and the number of defects overlooked corresponding to each technique.

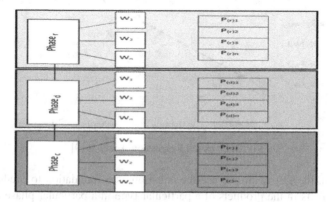

Fig. 2. Model overview [9]

The proposed model that improved defect containment matrix is used to analyze the effectiveness of the technique in order to verify, to validate and to monitor operations and then to detect and remove the defects at each phase. Throughout the development process, the project managers can analyze the effectiveness of quality assurance techniques as a whole for each development phase. Matrix plays an important role in the process of collecting and analyzing data.

$$DRE = \frac{Number\ of\ defects\ found}{Total\ defects} \tag{1}$$

The process of data analysis group of variables associated with each analysis, thereby determining the relationship between them. The analysis principle bases on the average values of the variables and the regression analysis. To build the decision support system based on the variables in the model, it is necessary to determine the relationship between the number of defects in each product and the size of the work product. The relationship can be in two forms: linear relationship and non-linear relationship. Many studies have shown that the growth of software size tends to increase the number of defects [1,2,8,9]. To increase the accuracy of the model, it is supposed that there is always a linear relationship between the size and the total number of defects found. The goal of linear regression analysis for a set of data points is to solve the following equation denoting the best-fit trend line between those data points:

$$y = m*x + b$$

Where: y is a number of defects in a work product; x is a size of work product; m is the slope-intercept between the two variables x, y; b is a constant.

After the regression analysis, we obtain a line graph of the values of two variables (x, y) connecting the number of defects with the size of the software work product:

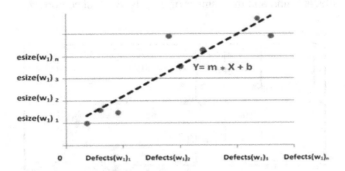

Fig. 3. Proposed Regression Analysis [9]

Since then, the QA team can use the equation as a foundation to predict the total estimated defects in the products of a particular type in a particular phase of the software development lifecycle.

Least squares method to determine the parameters of m and b:

For the data set $\{(x_1, y_1),\ldots,\{(x_n, y_n)\}$, we need to determine the linear equation $y = m*x + b$ so that the expectation $E(m,b)$ achieves the smallest value using the formula [9]:

$$E(m, b) = \sum_{n=1}^{N}(y_n - (mx_n + b^2))^2 \tag{2}$$

For the boundary value, when $|m|$ and $|b|$ are larger the $E(m,b)$ is the greater, it should not need to consider the boundary value.

The goal is to find the values of m and b to obtain the smallest $E(m,b)$.

We calculate the differential for each component of m and b [9]:

$$\frac{\partial E}{\partial m} = \sum_{n=1}^{N} 2(y_n - (mx_n + b)(-x_n))$$

$$\frac{\partial E}{\partial b} = \sum_{n=1}^{N} 2(y_n - (mx_n + b))$$

Rewriting the equation:

$$\left(\sum_{n=1}^{N} x_n^2\right) * m + \left(\sum_{n=1}^{N} x_n\right) * b = \sum_{n=1}^{N} x_n y_n$$

$$\left(\sum_{n=1}^{N} x_n\right) * m + \left(\sum_{n=1}^{N} 1\right) * b = \sum_{n=1}^{N} y_n$$

The above equations can be expressed as a matrix M:

$$\begin{pmatrix} \sum_{n=1}^{N} x_n{}^2 & \sum_{n=1}^{N} x_n \\ \sum_{n=1}^{N} x_n & \sum_{n=1}^{N} 1 \end{pmatrix} \begin{pmatrix} m \\ b \end{pmatrix} = \begin{pmatrix} \sum_{n=1}^{N} x_n y_n \\ \sum_{n=1}^{N} y_n \end{pmatrix}$$

Calculate the determinant of the matrix M:

$$detM = N^2 * \frac{1}{N} \sum_{n=1}^{N} (x_n - \bar{x})^2 \tag{3}$$

If the different values x_i with $i = \overline{1,N}$ then $detM$ is always different from 0. Then it easily calculates the matrix (m,b) by multiplying the right-hand side matrix with the inverse matrix of the left-hand side coefficient matrix.

As a result we obtain a formula to calculate the parameters m and b [1,2]:

$$b = \left(\sum_{n=1}^{N} x_n{}^2 * \sum_{n=1}^{N} y_n - \sum_{n=1}^{N} x_n y_n * \sum_{n=1}^{N} x_n \right) / detM \tag{4}$$

$$m = \left(N * \sum_{n=1}^{N} x_n y_n - \sum_{n=1}^{N} x_n * \sum_{n=1}^{N} y_n \right) / detM \tag{5}$$

$$detM = \left(N * \sum_{n=1}^{N} x_n{}^2 - \sum_{n=1}^{N} x_n * \sum_{n=1}^{N} x_n \right) \tag{6}$$

The computational complexity of the algorithm in the worst case is $O(n^3)$.

3   A Proposed Method for Optimizing Cost

3.1   The Optimization Model Structure

The proposed model as the basis for the process of making decisions for QA activities includes three interrelated components: (1) Estimated number of defects is detected and ignored; (2) Cost and time of a QA technical and (3) Cost incurred due to defects overlooked. The number of defects detected by QA p technique is the estimated number of defects found in the product w that depends mainly on the value of the experience derived from the regression analysis process of the past projects and the estimated size of the final product [9]:

$$eD_w = I_w * \text{esize}(w) \tag{7}$$

Among them: Iw is the defect infection rate of each KLOC in product w of phase x; esize(w) is the estimated size of product w. We have the formula to estimate the total number of defects found in phase x [9]:

$$N_x^{found} = \sum_{w \in W} \sum_{p \in P} \beta(p) * eD_w * DRE_p \quad (8) \tag{8}$$

With DRE_p is the value of the defect removal effectiveness of QA p technique; β_p is the coverage of the QA p technique compared with the overall size of the product in a quality assurance activities. Overall condition: $\sum_{p \in P} \beta(p) \leq 100\%$. Total number of defects overlooked in phase x [9]:

$$N_x^{escaped} = \sum_{w \in W} \sum_{p \in P} \beta(p) * eD_w * (1 - DRE_p) \tag{9}$$

Costs and effort are divided into two parts: the cost to implement a QA technique and costs to remove the defect found. To estimate the time and effort implementing quality assurance techniques, it should use parameters t_p: the average execution time of an application technique QA $p \in P$ for the product $w \in W$. This value is retrieved from the model data source. Unit of measurement is time standard compared to size (hour/FP), and $size_w$: the size of the product.

Total execution time for the entire phase [9]:

$$Ext_x = \sum_{w \in W} \sum_{p \in P} \beta(p) * size_w * t_p \tag{10}$$

Execution cost is calculated by: $Exc_p = Lr* Ext_p$ \hfill (11)

Where: Lr is the coefficient of worker, Ext_p is the amount paid to quality assurer in a unit of time.

The defect removal cost of the technique QAp is:

$$Rc_p = \beta_p * eD_w* DRE_p* C_p^{removal} * Lr \tag{12}$$

Where: $C_p^{removal}$ is the cost to remove a defect originating from a product $w \in W$ in phase $x \in X$ by technique QA $p \in P$.

Cost arising from defects overlooked by the activities is the cost to eliminate defects overlooked in the development phases and is detected in the test phase:

$$Esc_p = \beta_p * eD_w* (1 - DRE_p)* C_w^{escaped} * Lr \tag{13}$$

With: $C^{escaped}$ is incurred cost for each defect overlooked.

In some cases of the high-risk products, the project managers can apply a combination of at least two QA techniques simultaneously to reduce infection rate of defects in the next phases.

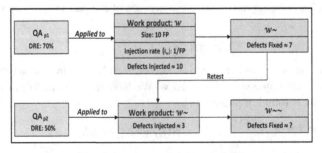

Fig. 4. Combining QA Practices [9]

The variable λ is the probability so that the technique QA p_2 finds the defects which are different from the defects detected by p_1.

The number of defects detected after applying consecutive combination p_1-p_2 [9] is as follows:

$$N_w^{found} = \beta_{p1} * eD_w * \text{DRE}_{p1} + \beta_{p2} * eD_w * (1 - \text{DRE}_{p1}) * \lambda_{p1-p2} \tag{14}$$

The cost saving from quality assurance activities is the cost of applying one paid QA technique in the testing phase in order to evaluate the cost-effectiveness of two potential QA plans in terms of cost saving in the future compared with the current estimated cost. Cost savings [9]:

$$Sc_p = \beta_p * eD_w * \text{DRE}_p * C^{escaped} \tag{15}$$

The overall cost is:

$$Total\ development\ cost = The\ cost\ of\ product\ development$$
$$+ The\ cost\ of\ quality \tag{16}$$

The cost of product development can be estimated by COCOMO model.

Return on investment is as follows: $ROI = \dfrac{Value}{Cost}$ \hfill (17)

Among them: *value* is the savings cost of fixing defects found in the testing phase; *cost* is equals the effort of both executing the QA practice and fixing defects found.

Return on investment *ROI* of all QA techniques applied to product *w*:

$$ROI_w = \frac{\sum_{p \in P} Scp - (\sum_{p \in P} Scp + Rcp + Esp)}{\sum_{p \in P}(Excp + Rcp + Esp)} \tag{18}$$

3.2   An Optimization Method

The input conditions for the optimization problem in the model consist of three parts: type of optimization, objective function and constraints. Optimization type in the present case, we need to solve the optimization problem with minimum cost, which is equivalent to achieving the desired DRE value with minimum cost. QA costs include 3 categories: execution cost, elimination cost and incurred cost. It is necessary to consider the sides of the QA costs. Therefore, optimization type is to minimize the overall costs generated by QA process undertaken by any QA technique distribution. The objective function is synthesized from the types of costs: execution cost, execution time, execution cost, defect removal cost and incurred cost. From that we can calculate the overall cost function as follows:

$$TotalCost_{x,y,z} = Exc_p(x,y,z) + Rc_p(x,y,z) + Esc_p(x,y,z) \tag{19}$$

The constraints established by the project managers: the defect removal effectiveness value of the desired DRE, the coverage of the QA techniques, execution cost. Linear programming method is used to solve the optimization problem in the model of the form [7,8].

4   Experiments and Evaluation

4.1   The Testing

The model is mainly aimed at medium and big sized projects which often have development period from 8 months to 1 year. The model needs to collect data from over 20 software projects of an organization to develop the data source before being used as a decision support system for quality assurance plans. For testing data of the model, the organizations should have verification and validation activities (V&V).

4.2   Experimental Software Development

The programmed model is simulated by JAVA language in Netbeans IDE and in Windows 7 64 bit operating system environment. The model uses LINDO API providing the means for software developers to integrate optimization into their programs [6,7]. LINDO API is designed to solve many optimization problems including the linear programming problem. LINDO API represents discrete matrix to store the coefficient matrix in the model. It represents the matrix through 3 or 4 vectors.

4.3   The Experimental Results

Typical Case Study of Experiment: Company X applies the regression-based model to manage and control QA activities. After applying the model to some software projects, they were able to develop a significant data source containing QA data of all QA activities of the projects in the past.

Input Data: Data are classified and analyzed to fit the model, to help define the necessary values for the parameters in the model.
Company X launches a new software project and applies the software model for accurate estimation of the expected outputs of the QA plans applied for the project.
Project P with estimated size: 20000 KLOC, development period: 2 months, labor: 3000 persons/ month.

After product sorting process: document making phase has FP 100 product sizes at high-risk level (the important specification).

Applying the regression-based model, infection rate of the high-risk products is predicted, I = 0.4 defects/FP.

Available 3 QA techniques that can be applied in a total of 9 techniques have been applied to the same type of product in the previous projects.

The project managers can set constraints such as the value of defect removal effectiveness (DRE) for the 3 desired QA techniques applied is $\overline{DRE} = 60\%$, and the total coverage of all three techniques is 100%. That means that all products with the specific risks will be checked and maintained the defect removal effectiveness to be 60% with minimal cost.

Table 1. Details of the QA technique applied in the project of Company X

Scenario-based reading technique		Ad-hoc-based reading technique		Checklist-based reading technique	
Variable	Value	Variable	Value	Variable	Value
DRE	75%	DRE	69%	DRE	50%
$C_p^{removal}$	(3 h/defect)	$C_p^{removal}$	(2.5 h/defect)	$C_p^{removal}$	(1 h/defect)
Ext	2 (h/FP)	Ext	0.5 (h/FP)	Ext	1 (h/FP)
$C_p^{escaped}$	40 (h/FP)	$C_p^{escaped}$	40 (h/FP)	$C_p^{escaped}$	40 (h/FP)

Results Using the Optimization Model

X, Y, Z are respectively three techniques: scenario-based reading techniques, ad-hoc reading, checklist-based reading.

With 3 QA techniques above, through linear regression data analysis, we will estimate the number of defects at specific risk level which may occur in project P. Then, to find solutions to ensure software quality with optimizing cost as Linear programming problem, we apply Simplex Optimization Method to obtain the optimization solution:

Find min $(Total.Eff + Total.Esc)_{X,Y,Z}$ // Total labor effort + The total overlooked cost
With assumptions: $\beta_x + \beta_y + \beta_z = 100\%$ $\overline{DRE} = 60\%$

After implementing the Simplex Optimization Method by LINDO API, we obtain the optimization solution with the lowest cost ~ \$15,189.47

This cost can be achieved with weights for 3 QA techniques applied respectively:

TechWeightX: $\beta_x = 0\%$ TechWeightY: $\beta_y \approx 53\%$ TechWeightZ: $\beta_z \approx 47\%$

4.4   Evaluation of the Method

Advantages: The regression-based model plays a role as a decision support system combined with the calculation formula to estimate the number of defects infected in the products or the entire development phase of software life cycle. It compares the effectiveness and appropriateness of the different software quality assurance techniques to a specific quality assurance activity in a software organization. Calculating the execution cost and time, defect removal cost of a quality assurance plan. Bringing out the best solution for quality assurance plan based on the three constraints: costs, quality and time. Assessing the quality assurance plan is based on ROI.

Disadvantages: The model only applies linear relation to estimate the number of defects without taking into account the non-linear relation. The linear attribute is only precise if the software development process is stable and the factors that may affect the number of defects are reduced. Functional system is mainly based on the interaction between each development phase of software life cycle and the system testing phase. The process of quantifying values of the model such as defect removal effectiveness, defect increased coefficient, eliminate cost, etc. is based on the links between data generated from quality assurance activities in the development phases and the system testing phase. The model is imprecise due to not taking into account the mutual correlation between the phases of the software life cycle (the previous phases and the next phases). The model should be evaluated based on the actual data from software projects in the same development organization to build a stable and reliable source of data. This process will consume a lot of time.

5   Conclusions and Future Research

We have introduced a regression-based model optimizing cost for software quality assurance using the collected data on the quality assurance activities, studying classification options of software phases into the products based on the available risk level, introducing data storage resources of quality assurance techniques to store detailed information about the quality assurance activities. The improved matrix containing defects will enable us to accurately determine the defect removal effectiveness of quality assurance techniques applied. We also presented theoretical and empirical evaluation of the model. Through the results, it can be stated that the regression-based model optimizing cost for software quality assurance can provide the optimization solution for quality assurance plan based on the defined constraint conditions. The identified result is an optimizing cost value for the quality assurance activities and quality assurance plan accordingly.

However, the model only applies linear relation for estimating the number of defects without taking into account the non-linear relationship, which may be inaccurate due to not taking into account the mutual correlation between the phases of the life cycle, between the previous phases and the next phases. The model should be evaluated based on the actual data from software projects in the same development organization to develop a stable and reliable source of data. This process must consume a lot of time.

Some possible development directions are specifically recommended. Firstly, we should apply the algorithm to handle data, including non-linear relation between the product size and the number of defects detected. Secondly, we study the correlation between the development phases of the software life cycle to increase the accuracy of the model when the quality assurance activities in later development phases can detect and remove defects in the previous phases. Thirdly, we should propose decision support process based on risk: the quality assurance methods are linked to the level of risk associated with them. Each defect can be assigned a found probability value which characterizes the probability of detecting defects in the system testing phase.

References

1. Alshathry, O., Janicke, H.: Optimizing software quality assurance. In: 2010 IEEE 34th Annual on Computer Software and Applications Conference Workshops (COMPSACW), pp. 87–92 (2010)

2. AlShathry, O.: Operational profile modeling as a risk assessment tool for software quality techniques. In: 2014 International Conference on Computational Science and Computational Intelligence (CSCI), vol. 2, pp. 181–184, 10–13 March 2014
3. Lazic, L., Kolasinac, A., Avdic, D.: The software quality economics model for software project optimization. World Scientific and Engineering Academy and Society (WSEAS) 8(1), January 2009
4. Jones, C.: Estimating Software Costs: Bringing Realism to Estimation, 2nd edn. McGraw-Hill, New York (2007)
5. Alshathry, O., Helge, J., Hussein, Z., Abdulla, A.: Quantitative quality assurance approach. In: NISS 2009 International Conference (2009)
6. Kan, S.: Metrics and Models in Software Quality Engineering, 2nd edn. Addison Wesley (2000)
7. Lindo System Inc., Optimization Modeling with LINGO, 6th edn. Lindo System Inc. (2006)
8. Moore, D., McCabe, G.: Introduction to the Practice of Statistics. W. H. Freeman and Co., London (2003)
9. AlShathry, O.: A Regression-based Model for Optimizing Cost of Software Quality Assurance, De Montfort University (2010)

Un-normlized and Random Walk Hypergraph Laplacian Un-supervised Learning

Loc Hoang Tran[1(✉)], Linh Hoang Tran[2], and Hoang Trang[3]

[1] Computer Science Department/University of Minnesota, Minneapolis, USA
tran0398@umn.edu
[2] ECE Department/Portland State University, Portland, USA
linht@pdx.edu
[3] Ho Chi Minh City University of Technology-VNU HCM
Ho Chi Minh City, Vietnam
hoangtrang@hcmut.edu.vn

Abstract. Most network-based clustering methods are based on the assumption that the labels of two adjacent vertices in the network are likely to be the same. However, assuming the pairwise relationship between vertices is not complete. The information a group of vertices that show very similar patterns and tend to have similar labels is missed. The natural way overcoming the information loss of the above assumption is to represent the given data as the hypergraph. Thus, in this paper, the two un-normalized and random walk hypergraph Laplacian based un-supervised learning methods are introduced. Experiment results show that the accuracy performance measures of these two hypergraph Laplacian based un-supervised learning methods are greater than the accuracy performance measure of symmetric normalized graph Laplacian based un-supervised learning method (i.e. the baseline method of this paper) applied to simple graph created from the incident matrix of hypergraph.

Keywords: Hypergraph Laplacian · Clustering · Un-supervised learning

1 Introduction

In data mining problem sceneries, we usually assume the pairwise relationship among the objects to be investigated such as documents [1,2], or genes [3], or digits [1,2]. For example, if we group a set of points in Euclidean space and the pairwise relationships are symmetric, an un-directed graph may be employed. In this un-directed graph, a set of vertices represent objects and edges link the pairs of related objects. However, if the pairwise relationships are asymmetric, the object set will be modeled as the directed graph. Finally, a number of data mining methods for un-supervised learning [4] (i.e. clustering) and semi-supervised learning [5,6,7] (i.e. classification) can then be formulated in terms of operations on this graph.

However, in many real world applications, representing the set of objects as undirected graph or directed graph is not complete. Approximating complex relationship as pairwise will lead to the loss of information. Let us consider classifying a set of

© Institute for Computer Sciences, Social Informatics and Telecommunications Engineering 2015
P.C. Vinh et al. (Eds.): ICTCC 2014, LNICST 144, pp. 254–263, 2015.
DOI: 10.1007/978-3-319-15392-6_25

genes into different gene functions. From [3], we may construct an un-directed graph in which the vertices represent the genes and two genes are connected by an edge if these two genes show a similar pattern of expression (i.e. the gene expression data is used as the datasets in [3]). Any two genes connected by an edge tend to have similar functions. However, assuming the pairwise relationship between genes is not complete, the information a group of genes that show very similar patterns of expression and tend to have similar functions [8] (i.e. the functional modules) is missed. The natural way overcoming the information loss of is to represent the gene expression data as the hypergraph [1,2]. A hypergraph is a graph in which an edge (i.e. a hyperedge) can connect more than two vertices. However, the clustering methods for this hypergraph datasets have not been studied in depth. Moreover, the number of hyperedges may be large. Hence this leads to the development of the clustering method that combine the dimensional reduction methods for the hypergraph dataset and the popular hard k-mean clustering method. Utilizing this idea, in [1,2], the symmetric normalized hypergraph Laplacian based un-supervised learning method have been developed and successfully applied to zoo dataset. To the best of our knowledge, the random walk and un-normalized hypergraph Laplacian based un-supervised learning methods have not yet been developed and applied to any practical applications. In this paper, we will develop the random walk and un-normalized hypergraph Laplacian based un-supervised learning methods and apply these two methods to the zoo dataset available from UCI repository.

We will organize the paper as follows: Section II will introduce the definition of hypergraph Laplacians and their properties. Section III will introduce the un-normalized, random walk, and symmetric normalized hypergraph Laplacian based un-supervised learning algorithms in detail. In section IV, we will apply the symmetric normalized graph Laplacian based un-supervised learning algorithm (i.e. the current state of art network based clustering method) to zoo dataset available from UCI repository and compare its accuracy performance measure to the two proposed hypergraph Laplacian based un-supervised learning algorithms' accuracy performance measures. Section V will conclude this paper and the future directions of research of these methods will be discussed.

2   Hypergraph Definitions

Given a hypergraph $G=(V,E)$, where V is the set of vertices and E is the set of hyper-edges. Each hyper-edge $e \in E$ is the subset of V. Please note that the cardinality of e is greater than or equal two. In the other words, $|e| \geq 2$, for every $e \in E$. Let $w(e)$ be the weight of the hyper-edge e. Then W will be the $R^{|E|*|E|}$ diagonal matrix containing the weights of all hyper-edges in its diagonal entries.

2.1   Definition of Incidence Matrix H of G

The incidence matrix H of G is a $R^{|V|*|E|}$ matrix that can be defined as follows

$$h(v,e) = \begin{cases} 1 \ if \ vertex \ v \ belongs \ to \ hyperedge \ e \\ 0 \ otherwise \end{cases}$$

From the above definition, we can define the degree of vertex v and the degree of hyper-edge e as follows

$$d(v) = \sum_{e \in E} w(e) * h(v, e)$$

$$d(e) = \sum_{v \in V} h(v, e)$$

Let D_v and D_e be two diagonal matrices containing the degrees of vertices and the degrees of hyper-edges in their diagonal entries respectively. Please note that D_v is the $R^{|v|*|v|}$ matrix and D_e is the $R^{|e|*|e|}$ matrix.

2.2   Definition of the Un-normalized Hypergraph Laplacian

The un-normalized hypergraph Laplacian is defined as follows

$$L = D_v - HWD_e^{-1}H^T$$

2.3   Properties of L

1. For every vector $f \in R^{|V|}$, we have

$$f^T L f = \frac{1}{2} \sum_{e \in E} \sum_{\{u,v\} \subseteq E} \frac{w(e)}{d(e)} (f(u) - f(v))^2$$

2. L is symmetric and positive-definite
3. The smallest eigenvalue of L is 0, the corresponding eigenvector is the constant one vector 1
4. L has $|V|$ non-negative, real-valued eigenvalues $0 \leq \lambda_1 \leq \lambda_2 \leq \cdots \leq \lambda_{|V|}$

Proof:

1. We know that

$$\frac{1}{2} \sum_{e \in E} \sum_{\{u,v\} \subseteq E} \frac{w(e)}{d(e)} (f(u) - f(v))^2$$

$$= \frac{1}{2} \sum_{e \in E} \sum_{\{u,v\} \subseteq E} \frac{w(e)}{d(e)} (f(u)^2 + f(v)^2 - 2f(u)f(v))$$

$$= \sum_{e \in E} \sum_{u,v \in V} \frac{w(e)}{d(e)} (f(u)^2 - f(u)f(v)) h(u, e)h(v, e)$$

$$=$$

$$\sum_{e \in E} \sum_{u \in V} w(e)f(u)^2 h(u, e) \sum_{v \in V} \frac{h(v, e)}{d(e)} - \sum_{e \in E} \sum_{u,v \in V} \frac{w(e)}{d(e)} f(u)f(v)h(u, e)h(v, e)$$

$$= \sum_{e \in E} \sum_{u \in V} w(e)f(u)^2 h(u, e) - \sum_{e \in E} \sum_{u,v \in V} \frac{w(e)}{d(e)} f(u)f(v)h(u, e)h(v, e)$$

$$= \sum_{u \in V} f(u)^2 \sum_{e \in E} w(e)h(u, e) - \sum_{e \in E} \sum_{u,v \in V} \frac{w(e)}{d(e)} f(u)f(v)h(u, e)h(v, e)$$

$$= \sum_{u \in V} f(u)^2 d(u) - \sum_{e \in E} \sum_{u,v \in V} \frac{w(e)}{d(e)} f(u)f(v)h(u, e)h(v, e)$$

$$= f^T D_v f - f^T HWD_e^{-1}H^T f$$

$$= f^T (D_v - HWD_e^{-1}H^T)f$$

$$= f^T L f$$

2. L is symmetric follows directly from its own definition.

Since for every vector $f \in R^{|V|}$, $f^T L f = \frac{1}{2} \sum_{e \in E} \sum_{\{u,v\} \subseteq E} \frac{w(e)}{d(e)} (f(u) - f(v))^2 \geq 0$. We conclude that L is positive-definite.

3. The fact that the smallest eigenvalue of L is 0 is obvious.

Next, we need to prove that its corresponding eigenvector is the constant one vector 1.

Let $d_v \in R^{|V|}$ be the vector containing the degrees of vertices of hypergraph G, $d_e \in R^{|E|}$ be the vector containing the degrees of hyper-edges of hypergraph G, $w \in R^{|E|}$ be the vector containing the weights of hyper-edges of G, $1 \in R^{|V|}$ be vector of all ones, and $one \in R^{|E|}$ be the vector of all ones. Hence we have

$$L1 = (D_v - HWD_e^{-1}H^T)1 = d_v - HWD_e^{-1}d_e = d_v - HWone = d_v - Hw = d_v - d_v = 0$$

4. (4) follows directly from (1)-(3).

2.4   The Definitions of Symmetric Normalized and Random Walk Hypergraph Laplacians

The symmetric normalized hypergraph Laplacian (defined in [1,2]) is defined as follows

$$L_{sym} = I - D_v^{-\frac{1}{2}} HWD_e^{-1} H^T D_v^{-\frac{1}{2}}$$

The random walk hypergraph Laplacian (defined in [1,2]) is defined as follows

$$L_{rw} = I - D_v^{-1} HWD_e^{-1} H^T$$

2.5   Properties of L_{sym} and L_{rw}

1. For every vector $f \in R^{|V|}$, we have

$$f^T L_{sym} f = \frac{1}{2} \sum_{e \in E} \sum_{\{u,v\} \subseteq E} \frac{w(e)}{d(e)} \left(\frac{f(u)}{\sqrt{d(u)}} - \frac{f(v)}{\sqrt{d(v)}} \right)^2$$

2. λ is an eigenvalue of L_{rw} with eigenvector u if and only if λ is an eigenvalue of L_{sym} with eigenvector $w = D_v^{\frac{1}{2}} u$

3. λ is an eigenvalue of L_{rw} with eigenvector u if and only if λ and u solve the generalized eigen-problem $Lu = \lambda D_v u$

4. 0 is an eigenvalue of L_{rw} with the constant one vector 1 as eigenvector. 0 is an eigenvalue of L_{sym} with eigenvector $D_v^{\frac{1}{2}} 1$

5. L_{sym} is symmetric and positive semi-definite and L_{sym} and L_{rw} have $|V|$ non-negative real-valued eigenvalues $0 \leq \lambda_1 \leq \cdots \leq \lambda_{|V|}$

Proof:

1. The complete proof of (1) can be found in [1].
2. (2) can be seen easily by solving

$$L_{sym}w = \lambda w \Leftrightarrow \left(I - D_v^{-\frac{1}{2}}HWD_e^{-1}H^T D_v^{-\frac{1}{2}}\right)w = \lambda w$$

$$\Leftrightarrow D_v^{-\frac{1}{2}}\left(I - D_v^{-\frac{1}{2}}HWD_e^{-1}H^T D_v^{-\frac{1}{2}}\right)w = \lambda D_v^{-\frac{1}{2}}w$$

$$\Leftrightarrow D_v^{-\frac{1}{2}}w - D_v^{-1}HWD_e^{-1}H^T D_v^{-\frac{1}{2}}w = \lambda D_v^{-\frac{1}{2}}w$$

Let $u = D_v^{-\frac{1}{2}}w$, (in the other words, $w = D_v^{\frac{1}{2}}u$), we have

$$L_{sym}w = \lambda w \Leftrightarrow u - D_v^{-1}HWD_e^{-1}H^T u = \lambda u$$
$$\Leftrightarrow (I - D_v^{-1}HWD_e^{-1}H^T)u = \lambda u$$
$$\Leftrightarrow L_{rw}u = \lambda u$$

This completes the proof.

3. (3) can be seen easily by solving

$$L_{rw}u = \lambda u \Leftrightarrow (I - D_v^{-1}HWD_e^{-1}H^T)u = \lambda u$$
$$\Leftrightarrow D_v(I - D_v^{-1}HWD_e^{-1}H^T)u = \lambda D_v u$$
$$\Leftrightarrow (D_v - HWD_e^{-1}H^T)u = \lambda D_v u$$
$$\Leftrightarrow Lu = \lambda D_v u$$

This completes the proof.

4. First, we need to prove that $L_{rw}1 = 0$.

Let $d_v \in R^{|V|}$ be the vector containing the degrees of vertices of hypergraph G, $d_e \in R^{|E|}$ be the vector containing the degrees of hyper-edges of hypergraph G, $w \in R^{|E|}$ be the vector containing the weights of hyper-edges of G, $1 \in R^{|V|}$ be vector of all ones, and $one \in R^{|E|}$ be the vector of all ones. Hence we have

$$L_{rw}1 = (I - D_v^{-1}HWD_e^{-1}H^T)1$$
$$= 1 - D_v^{-1}HWD_e^{-1}d_e$$
$$= 1 - D_v^{-1}HWone$$
$$= 1 - D_v^{-1}Hw$$
$$= 1 - D_v^{-1}d_v$$
$$= 0$$

The second statement is a direct consequence of (2).

5. The statement about L_{sym} is a direct consequence of (1), then the statement about L_{rw} is a direct
consequence of (2).

3   Algorithms

Given a set of points $\{x_1, x_2, \dots, x_n\}$ where n is the total number of points (i.e. vertices) in the hypergraph $G=(V,E)$ and given the incidence matrix H of G.

Our objective is to partition these n points into k groups.

Random walk hypergraph Laplacian based un-supervised learning algorithm

First, we will give the brief overview of the random walk hypergraph Laplacian based un-supervised learning algorithm. The outline of this algorithm is as follows

1. Construct D_v and D_e from the incidence matrix H of G
2. Compute the random walk hypergraph Laplacian $L_{rw} = I - D_v^{-1}HWD_e^{-1}H^T$
3. Compute all eigenvalues and eigenvectors of L_{rw} and sort all eigenvalues and their corresponding eigenvector in ascending order. Pick the first k eigenvectors $v_2, v_3, \dots, v_{k+1}$ of L_{rw} in the sorted list. k can be determined in the following two ways:
   a. k is the number of connected components of L_{rw} [4]
   b. k is the number such that $\frac{\lambda_{k+2}}{\lambda_{k+1}}$ or $\lambda_{k+2} - \lambda_{k+1}$ is largest for all $2 \le k \le n$
4. Let $V \in R^{n*k}$ be the matrix containing the vectors $v_2, v_3, \dots, v_{k+1}$ as columns.
5. For $i = 1,..,n$, let $y_i \in R^{1*k}$ be the vector corresponding to the i-th row of V.
6. Cluster the points y_i for all $1 \le i \le n$ with k-means clustering method.

Un-normalized hypergraph Laplacian based un-supervised learning algorithm

Next, we will give the brief overview of the un-normalized hypergraph Laplacian based un-supervised learning algorithm. The outline of this algorithm is as follows

1. Construct D_v and D_e from the incidence matrix H of G
2. Compute the un-normalized hypergraph Laplacian $L = D_v - HWD_e^{-1}H^T$
3. Compute all eigenvalues and eigenvectors of L and sort all eigenvalues and their corresponding eigenvector in ascending order. Pick the first k eigenvectors $v_2, v_3, \dots, v_{k+1}$ of L in the sorted list. k can be determined in the following two ways:
   a. k is the number of connected components of L [4]
   b. k is the number such that $\frac{\lambda_{k+2}}{\lambda_{k+1}}$ or $\lambda_{k+2} - \lambda_{k+1}$ is largest for all $2 \le k \le n$
4. Let $V \in R^{n*k}$ be the matrix containing the vectors $v_2, v_3, \dots, v_{k+1}$ as columns
5. For $i = 1,..,n$, let $y_i \in R^{1*k}$ be the vector corresponding to the i-th row of V
6. Cluster the points y_i for all $1 \le i \le n$ with k-means clustering method

Symmetric normalized hypergraph Laplacian based un-supervised learning algorithm

Next, we will give the brief overview of the symmetric normalized hypergraph Laplacian based un-supervised learning algorithm which can be obtained from [1,2]. The outline of this algorithm is as follows

1. Construct D_v and D_e from the incidence matrix H of G
2. Compute the symmetric normalized hypergraph Laplacian $L_{sym} = I -$
   $$D_v^{-\frac{1}{2}} H W D_e^{-1} H^T D_v^{-\frac{1}{2}}$$
3. Compute all eigenvalues and eigenvectors of L_{sym} and sort all eigenvalues and their corresponding eigenvector in ascending order. Pick the first k eigenvectors $v_2, v_3, \ldots, v_{k+1}$ of L_{sym} in the sorted list. k can be determined in the following two ways:
   a. k is the number of connected components of L_{sym} [4]
   b. k is the number such that $\frac{\lambda_{k+2}}{\lambda_{k+1}}$ or $\lambda_{k+2} - \lambda_{k+1}$ is largest for all $2 \leq k \leq n$
4. Let $V \in R^{n*k}$ be the matrix containing the vectors $v_2, v_3, \ldots, v_{k+1}$ as columns
5. For $i = 1, \ldots, n$, let $y_i \in R^{1*k}$ be the vector corresponding to the i-th row of V
6. Cluster the points y_i for all $1 \leq i \leq n$ with k-means clustering method

At step 6 of the above three algorithms, k-means clustering method is used for simplicity and is not discussed. Next, the k-mean clustering methods will be discussed. The k-mean clustering method is considered the most popular method in clustering field [4]. The k-mean clustering method can be completed in the following four steps:

1. Randomly choose k initial cluster centers (i.e. centroids).
2. For every feature vector, associate it with the closest centroid.
3. Recalculate the centroid for all k clusters.
4. Repeat step 2 and step 3 until convergence.

In the other words, the k-mean clustering method is trying to minimize the objective function

$$J = \sum_{j=1}^{k} \sum_{i=1}^{n} r_{ij} \|F(i,:) - c_j\|^2$$

In the above formula, c_j is the centroid of the cluter j. $F(i,:)$ is the i-th feature vector. The matrix R is defined as follows

$$r_{ij} = \begin{cases} 1 \ if \ feature \ vector \ i \ belongs \ to \ cluster \ j \\ \quad\quad\quad 0 \ otherwise \end{cases}$$

Moreover, we can also easily see that

$$J = trace(\sum_{j=1}^{k} \sum_{i \in j} (F(i,:) - c_j)^T (F(i,:) - c_j))$$

Finally, the current state of the art network based clustering method (i.e. the symmetric normalized graph Laplacian based un-supervised learning method) can be completed in the following steps.

1. Compute the symmetric graph Laplacian L_{g-sym}: $L_{g-sym} = I - D^{-\frac{1}{2}} W D^{-\frac{1}{2}}$.

2. Compute all eigenvalues and eigenvectors of L_{g-sym} and sort all eigenvalues and their corresponding eigenvector in ascending order. Pick the first k eigenvectors $v_2, v_3, \ldots, v_{k+1}$ of L_{g-sym} in the sorted list. k can be determined in the following two ways:

   a. k is the number of connected components of L_{g-sym} [4]

   b. k is the number such that $\frac{\lambda_{k+2}}{\lambda_{k+1}}$ or $\lambda_{k+2} - \lambda_{k+1}$ is largest for all $2 \le k \le n$

3. Let $V \in R^{n*k}$ be the matrix containing the vectors $v_2, v_3, \ldots, v_{k+1}$ as columns.

4. Compute the new matrix $U \in R^{n*k}$ from V as follows

$$u_{ij} = \frac{v_{ij}}{\sqrt{\sum_l v_{il}^2}}$$

5. For $i = 1, \ldots, n$, let $y_i \in R^{1*k}$ be the vector corresponding to the i-th row of U.

6. Cluster the points y_i for all $1 \le i \le n$ with k-means clustering method.

The way describing how to construct W and D will be discussed in the next section.

4   Experiments and Results

Datasets
In this paper, we used the zoo data set which can be obtained from UCI repository. The zoo data set contains 100 animals with 17 attributes. The attributes include hair, feathers, eggs, milk, etc. The animals have been classified into 7 different classes. Our task is to embed the animals in the zoo dataset into Euclidean space by using random walk and un-normalized hypergraph Laplacian Eigenmaps and by using the symmetric normalized graph Laplacian Eigenmaps. We embed those animals into Euclidean space by using the eigenvectors of the graph Laplacian and hypergraph Laplacians associated with the 7 (i.e. number of classes) smallest eigenvalues different from 0. Finally, the k-mean clustering method is applied to the transformed dataset.

There are three ways to construct the similarity graph from the incident matrix H of zoo dataset:

    a.   The ε-neighborhood graph: Connect all animals whose pairwise distances are smaller than ε.

    b.   k-nearest neighbor graph: Animal i is connected with animal j if animal i is among the k-nearest neighbor of animal j or animal j is among the k-nearest neighbor of animal i.

    c.   The fully connected graph: All animals are connected.

In this paper, the similarity function is the Gaussian similarity function

$$w_{ij} = s(H(i,:), H(j,:)) = \exp\left(-\frac{d(H(i,:), H(j,:))}{t}\right)$$

In this paper, t is set to 10 and the 3-nearest neighbor graph is used to construct the similarity graph from the zoo dataset. This describes how we construct W of the simple graph. D is the diagonal matrix and its i-th element is defined as follows:

$$d_i = \sum_j w_{ij}$$

Experiments and Results

In this section, we experiment with the above proposed un-normalized and random walk hypergraph Laplacian based un-supervised learning methods (i.e. hypergraph spectral clustering) and the current state of the art method (i.e. the symmetric normalized graph Laplacian based un-supervised learning method) which is spectral clustering method in terms of accuracy performance measure. The accuracy performance measure Q is given as follows

$$Q = \frac{True\ Positive + True\ Negative}{True\ Positive + True\ Negative + False\ Positive + False\ Negative}$$

All experiments were implemented in Matlab 6.5 on virtual machine. The accuracy performance measures of the above proposed methods and the current state of the art method is given in the following table 1

Table 1. Accuracies of the two proposed methods and the current state of the art method

Accuracy Performance Measures (%)		
Graph (symmetric normalized)	Hypergraph (random walk)	Hypergraph (un-normalized)
89.43	94.86	93.71

From the above table, we recognized that the accuracy of the random walk hypergraph Laplacian method is slightly better than the accuracy of the un-normalized hypergraph Laplacian method. Interestingly, the accuracies of the two proposed hypergraph Laplacian methods are significantly better than accuracy of the current state of the art method.

5   Conclusion

We have proposed the detailed algorithms the two un-normalized and random walk hypergraph Laplacian based un-supervised learning methods applying to the zoo dataset. Experiments show that these two methods greatly perform better than the unnormalized graph Laplacian based un-supervised learning method since these two methods utilize the complex relationships among points (i.e. not pairwise relationship). These two methods can also be applied to digit recognition and text classification. These experiments will be tested in the future. Moreover, these two methods can not only be used in the clustering problem but also the ranking problem. In specific, given a set of genes (i.e. the queries) involved in a specific disease such as leukemia which is my future research, these two methods can be used to find more genes involved in leukemia by ranking genes in the hypergraph constructed from gene expression data. The genes with the highest rank can then be selected and checked by biology experts to see if the extended genes are in fact involved in leukemia. Finally, these selected genes will be used in cancer classification.

Recently, to the best of my knowledge, the un-normalized hypergraph p-Laplacian based un-supervised learning method has not yet been developed. This method is worth investigated because of its difficult nature and its close connection to partial differential equation on hypergraph field.

References

1. Zhou, D., Huang, J., Schölkopf, B.: Beyond Pairwise Classification and Clustering Using Hypergraphs Max Planck Institute Technical Report 143. Max Planck Institute for Biological Cybernetics, Tübingen, Germany (2005)
2. Zhou, D., Huang, J., Schölkopf, B.: Learning with Hypergraphs: Clustering, Classification, and Embedding. In: Schölkopf, B., Platt, J.C., Hofmann, T. (eds.) Advances in Neural Information Processing System (NIPS), vol. 19, pp. 1601–1608. MIT Press, Cambridge (2007)
3. Tran, L.: Application of three graph Laplacian based semi-supervised learning methods to protein function prediction problem. CoRR abs/1211.4289 (2012)
4. Luxburg, U.: A Tutorial on Spectral Clustering Statistics and Computing 17(4), 395–416 (2007)
5. Zhu, X., Ghahramani, Z.: Learning from labeled and unlabeled data with label propagation Technical Report CMU-CALD-02-107, Carnegie Mellon University (2002)
6. Zhou, D., Bousquet, O., Lal, T.N., Weston, J., Schölkopf, B.: Learning with Local and Global Consistency. In: Thrun, S., Saul, L., Schölkopf, B. (eds.) Advances in Neural Information Processing Systems (NIPS), vol. 16, pp. 321–328. MIT Press, Cambridge (2004)
7. Tsuda, K., Shin, H.H., Schoelkopf, B.: Fast protein classification with multiple networks. Bioinformatics (ECCB 2005) 21(Suppl. 2), ii59–ii65 (2005)
8. Tran, L.: Hypergraph and protein function prediction with gene expression data. CoRR abs/1212.0388 (2012)

Graph Based Semi-supervised Learning Methods Applied to Speech Recognition Problem

Hoang Trang[1] and Loc Hoang Tran[2(✉)]

[1] Ho Chi Minh City University of Technology-VNU HCM
Ho Chi Minh City, Vietnam
hoangtrang@hcmut.edu.vn
[2] Computer Science Department/University of Minnesota, Minneapolis, USA
tran0398@umn.edu

Abstract. Speech recognition is the important problem in pattern recognition research field. In this paper, the un-normalized, symmetric normalized, and random walk graph Laplacian based semi-supervised learning methods will be applied to the network derived from the MFCC feature vectors of the speech dataset. Experiment results show that the performance of the random walk and the symmetric normalized graph Laplacian based methods are at least as good as the performance of the un-normalized graph Laplacian based method. Moreover, the sensitivity measures of these three semi-supervised learning methods are much better than the sensitivity measure of the current state of the art Hidden Markov Model method in speech recognition problem.

Keywords: Semi-supervised learning · Graph laplacian · Speech recognition · MFCC

1 Introduction

Two of the most noticeable areas of machine learning research are supervised and unsupervised learning. In supervised learning, a learner tries to obtain a predictive model from explicitly labeled training samples. However, in unsupervised learning, a learner tries to mine a descriptive model from unlabeled training samples. Recently, interest has increased in the hybrid problem of learning a predictive model given a combination of both labeled and unlabeled samples. This revised learning problem, commonly referred to as semi-supervised learning, rises in many real world applications, such as text and gene classification [1,2,3,4,5], because of the freely available of unlabeled data and because of the labor-intensive effort and high time complexity to obtain the explicitly labeled data. For example, in text classification, excessive work is required to manually label a set of documents for supervised training while unlabeled documents are available in abundance. It is normal, in this case, to try to exploit the existence of a large set of unlabeled documents and to lessen the number of labeled documents required to learn a good document classifier. Similarly, in the problem of predicting gene function from microarray data and sequence information, the experiments needed to label a subset of the genes are normally very costly to conduct. As a result, there exist only a few hundred labeled genes out of the population of thousands.

© Institute for Computer Sciences, Social Informatics and Telecommunications Engineering 2015
P.C. Vinh et al. (Eds.): ICTCC 2014, LNICST 144, pp. 264–273, 2015.
DOI: 10.1007/978-3-319-15392-6_26

Although it is a challenging problem, semi-supervised learning offers acceptable promise in practice that many algorithms have been suggested for this type of problem in the past few years. Among these algorithms, graph based learning algorithms have become common due to their computational efficiency and their effectiveness at semi-supervised learning. Some of these graph based learning algorithms make predictions directly for a target set of unlabeled data without creating a model that can be used for out-of-sample predictions. This process is called transductive learning. Such algorithms avoid many of the requirements of traditional supervised learning and can be much simpler as a result. However, other approaches to semi-supervised learning still create a model that can be used to predict unseen test data.

In this paper, we will present the graph based semi-supervised learning methods, derive their detailed regularization framework, and apply these methods to automatic speech recognition problem. To the best of our knowledge, this work has not been investigated. Researchers have worked in automatic speech recognition for almost six decades. The earliest attempts were made in the 1950's. In the 1980's, speech recognition research was characterized by a shift in technology from template-based approaches to statistical modeling methods, especially Hidden Markov Models (HMM). Hidden Markov Models (HMM) have been the core of most speech recognition systems for over a decade and is considered the current state of the art method for automatic speech recognition system [6]. Second, to classify the speech samples, a graph (i.e. kernel) which is the natural model of relationship between speech samples can also be employed. In this model, the nodes represent speech samples. The edges represent for the possible interactions between nodes. Then, machine learning methods such as Support Vector Machine [7], Artificial Neural Networks [8], or nearest-neighbor classifiers [9] can be applied to this graph to classify the speech samples. The nearest-neighbor classifiers method labels the speech sample with the label that occurs frequently in the speech sample's adjacent nodes in the network. Hence neighbor counting method does not utilize the full topology of the network. However, the Artificial Neural Networks, Support Vector Machine, and graph based semi-supervised learning methods utilize the full topology of the network. Moreover, the Artificial Neural Networks and Support Vector Machine are supervised learning methods.

While nearest-neighbor classifiers method, the Artificial Neural Networks, and the graph based semi-supervised learning methods are all based on the assumption that the labels of two adjacent speech samples in graph are likely to be the same, SVM does not rely on this assumption. Graphs used in nearest-neighbor classifiers method, Artificial Neural Networks, and the graph based semi-supervised learning method are very sparse. However, the graph (i.e. kernel) used in SVM is fully-connected.

In the last decade, the normalized graph Laplacian [2], random walk graph Laplacian [1], and the un-normalized graph Laplacian [3, 5] based semi-supervised learning methods have successfully been applied to some specific classification tasks such as digit recognition, text classification, and protein function prediction. However, to the best of our knowledge, the graph based semi-supervised learning methods have not yet been applied to automatic speech recognition problem and hence their overall sensitivity performance measure comparisons have not been done. In this paper, we will apply three un-normalized, symmetric normalized, and random walk graph Laplacian based semi-supervised learning methods to the network derived from the speech samples. The main point of these three methods is to let every node of the graph iteratively propagates its label information to its adjacent nodes and the process is repeated until convergence [2].

We will organize the paper as follows: Section 2 will introduce graph based semi-supervised learning algorithms in detail. Section 3 will show how to derive the closed form solutions of normalized and un-normalized graph Laplacian based semi-supervised learning from regularization framework. In section 4, we will apply these three algorithms to the network derived from speech samples available from the IC Design lab at Faculty of Electricals-Electronics Engineering, University of Technology, Ho Chi Minh City. Section 5 will conclude this paper and discuss the future directions of researches of this automatic speech recognition problem utilizing hypergraph Laplacian.

2   Algorithms

Given a set of feature vectors of speech samples $\{x_1, \dots, x_l, x_{l+1}, \dots, x_{l+u}\}$ where $n = l + u$ is the total number of speech samples in the network, define c be the total number of words and the matrix $F \in R^{n*c}$ be the estimated label matrix for the set of feature vectors of speech samples $\{x_1, \dots, x_l, x_{l+1}, \dots, x_{l+u}\}$, where the point x_i is labeled as sign(F_{ij}) for each word j ($1 \le j \le c$). Please note that $\{x_1, \dots, x_l\}$ is the set of all labeled points and $\{x_{l+1}, \dots, x_{l+u}\}$ is the set of all un-labeled points. The way constructing the feature vectors of speech samples will be discussed in Section IV.

Let $Y \in R^{n*c}$ the initial label matrix for n speech samples in the network be defined as follows

$$Y_{ij} = \begin{cases} 1 \ if \ x_i \ belongs \ to \ word \ j \ and \ 1 \le i \le l \\ -1 \ if \ x_i \ does \ not \ belong \ to \ word \ j \ and \ 1 \le i \le l \\ 0 \ if \ l + 1 \le i \le n \end{cases}$$

Our objective is to predict the labels of the un-labeled points $x_{l+1}, \dots, x_{l+u}$. We can achieve this objective by letting every node (i.e. speech sample) in the network iteratively propagates its label information to its adjacent nodes and this process is repeated until convergence.

Let W represents the network.

Random walk graph Laplacian based semi-supervised learning algorithm
In this section, we slightly change the original random walk graph Laplacian based semi-supervised learning algorithm can be obtained from [1]. The outline of the new version of this algorithm is as follows

1. Form the affinity matrix W. The way constructing W will be discussed in section IV.
2. Construct $S_{rw} = D^{-1}W$ where $D = diag(d_1, d_2, \dots, d_n)$ and $d_i = \sum_j W_{ij}$
3. Iterate until convergence
    $F^{(t+1)} = \alpha S_{rw} F^{(t)} + (1 - \alpha)Y$, where α is an arbitrary parameter belongs to [0,1]

4.   Let F^* be the limit of the sequence $\{F^{(t)}\}$. For each word j, label each speech samples x_i ($l + 1 \leq i \leq l + u$) as sign(F^*_{ij})

Next, we look for the closed-form solution of the random walk graph Laplacian based semi-supervised learning. In the other words, we need to show that

$$F^* = \lim_{t \to \infty} F^{(t)} = (1 - \alpha)(I - \alpha S_{rw})^{-1} Y$$

Suppose $F^{(0)} = Y$, then

$$\begin{aligned}
F^{(1)} &= \alpha S_{rw} F^{(0)} + (1 - \alpha) Y \\
&= \alpha S_{rw} Y + (1 - \alpha) Y \\
F^{(2)} &= \alpha S_{rw} F^{(1)} + (1 - \alpha) Y \\
&= \alpha S_{rw}(\alpha S_{rw} Y + (1 - \alpha) Y) + (1 - \alpha) Y \\
&= \alpha^2 S_{rw}^2 Y + (1 - \alpha)\alpha S_{rw} Y + (1 - \alpha) Y \\
F^{(3)} &= \alpha S_{rw} F^{(2)} + (1 - \alpha) Y \\
&= \alpha S_{rw}(\alpha^2 S_{rw}^2 Y + (1 - \alpha)\alpha S_{rw} Y + (1 - \alpha) Y) + (1 - \alpha) Y \\
&= \alpha^3 S_{rw}^3 Y + (1 - \alpha)\alpha^2 S_{rw}^2 Y + (1 - \alpha)\alpha S_{rw} Y + (1 - \alpha) Y
\end{aligned}$$

$$\cdots$$

Thus, by induction,

$$F^{(t)} = \alpha^t S_{rw}^t Y + (1 - \alpha) \sum_{i=0}^{t-1} (\alpha S_{rw})^i Y$$

Since S_{rw} is the stochastic matrix, its eigenvalues are in $[-1,1]$. Moreover, since $0 < \alpha < 1$, thus

$$\lim_{t \to \infty} \alpha^t S_{rw}^t = 0$$

$$\lim_{t \to \infty} \sum_{i=0}^{t-1} (\alpha S_{rw})^i = (I - \alpha S_{rw})^{-1}$$

Therefore,

$$F^* = \lim_{t \to \infty} F^{(t)} = (1 - \alpha)(I - \alpha S_{rw})^{-1} Y$$

Now, from the above formula, we can compute F^* directly.

The original random walk graph Laplacian based semi-supervised learning algorithm developed by Zhu can be derived from the modified algorithm by setting $\alpha_i = 0$, where $1 \leq i \leq l$ and $\alpha_i = 1$, where $l + 1 \leq i \leq l + u$. In the other words, we can express $F^{(t+1)}$ in matrix form as follows

$$F^{(t+1)} = I_\alpha S_{rw} F^{(t)} + (I - I_\alpha) Y, \text{ where}$$
I is the identity matrix and

$$I_\alpha = \begin{bmatrix} 0 & \cdots & 0 & & & \\ \vdots & \ddots & \vdots & & 0 & \\ 0 & \cdots & 0 & & & \\ & & & 1 & \cdots & 0 \\ & & 0 & \vdots & \ddots & \vdots \\ & & & 0 & \cdots & 1 \end{bmatrix} \text{ (I_α is the diagonal matrix)}$$

Normalized graph Laplacian based semi-supervised learning algorithm

Next, we will give the brief overview of the original normalized graph Laplacian based semi-supervised learning algorithm can be obtained from [2]. The outline of this algorithm is as follows

1. Form the affinity matrix W
2. Construct $S_{sym} = D^{-\frac{1}{2}}WD^{-\frac{1}{2}}$ where $D = diag(d_1, d_2, ..., d_n)$ and $d_i = \sum_j W_{ij}$
3. Iterate until convergence
   $F^{(t+1)} = \alpha S_{sym}F^{(t)} + (1-\alpha)Y$, where α is an arbitrary parameter belongs to $[0,1]$
4. Let F^* be the limit of the sequence $\{F^{(t)}\}$. For each word j, label each speech samples x_i ($l+1 \le i \le l+u$) as $sign(F^*_{ij})$

Next, we look for the closed-form solution of the normalized graph Laplacian based semi-supervised learning. In the other words, we need to show that

$$F^* = \lim_{t\to\infty} F^{(t)} = (1-\alpha)(I - \alpha S_{sym})^{-1}Y$$

Suppose $F^{(0)} = Y$, then

$$F^{(1)} = \alpha S_{sym}F^{(0)} + (1-\alpha)Y$$
$$= \alpha S_{sym}Y + (1-\alpha)Y$$
$$F^{(2)} = \alpha S_{sym}F^{(1)} + (1-\alpha)Y$$
$$= \alpha^2 S_{sym}^2 Y + (1-\alpha)\alpha S_{sym}Y + (1-\alpha)Y$$
$$F^{(3)} = \alpha S_{sym}F^{(2)} + (1-\alpha)Y$$
$$= \alpha^3 S_{sym}^3 Y + (1-\alpha)\alpha^2 S_{sym}^2 Y + (1-\alpha)\alpha S_{sym}Y + (1-\alpha)Y$$

$$...$$

Thus, by induction,

$$F^{(t)} = \alpha^t S_{sym}^t Y + (1-\alpha)\sum_{i=0}^{t-1}(\alpha S_{sym})^i Y$$

Since $D^{-\frac{1}{2}}WD^{-\frac{1}{2}}$ is similar to $D^{-1}W$ which is a stochastic matrix, eigenvalues of $D^{-\frac{1}{2}}WD^{-\frac{1}{2}}$ belong to $[-1,1]$. Moreover, since $0<\alpha<1$, thus

$$\lim_{t\to\infty} \alpha^t S_{sym}^t = 0$$

$$\lim_{t\to\infty}\sum_{i=0}^{t-1}(\alpha S_{sym})^i = (I - \alpha S_{sym})^{-1}$$

Therefore,

$$F^* = \lim_{t\to\infty} F^{(t)} = (1-\alpha)(I - \alpha S_{sym})^{-1}Y$$

Now, from the above formula, we can compute F^* directly.

Un-normalized graph Laplacian based semi-supervised learning algorithm

Finally, we will give the brief overview of the un-normalized graph Laplacian based semi-supervised learning algorithm [3]. The outline of this algorithm is as follows

1. Form the affinity matrix W
2. Construct $L = D - W$, where $D = diag(d_1, d_2, ..., d_n)$ and $d_i = \sum_j W_{ij}$
3. Compute closed form solution $F^* = \gamma(L + \gamma I)^{-1}Y$, where γ is any positive parameter
4. For each word j, label each speech samples x_i $(l + 1 \leq i \leq l + u)$ as $sign(F_{ij}^*)$

The closed form solution F^* of un-normalized hypergraph Laplacian based semi-supervised learning algorithm will be derived clearly and completely in Regularization Framework section.

3   Regularization Frameworks

In this section, we will develop the regularization framework for the normalized graph Laplacian based semi-supervised learning iterative version. First, let's consider the error function

$$E(F) = \left\{ \frac{1}{2} \sum_{i,j=1}^{n} W_{ij} \left\| \frac{F_i}{\sqrt{d_i}} - \frac{F_j}{\sqrt{d_j}} \right\|^2 \right\} + \gamma \sum_{i=1}^{n} \|F_i - Y_i\|^2$$

In this error function $E(F)$, F_i and Y_i belong to R^c. Please note that c is the total number of words, $d_i^{(k)} = \sum_j W_{ij}^{(k)}$, and γ is the positive regularization parameter. Hence

$$F = \begin{bmatrix} F_1^T \\ \vdots \\ F_n^T \end{bmatrix} \text{ and } Y = \begin{bmatrix} Y_1^T \\ \vdots \\ Y_n^T \end{bmatrix}$$

Here $E(F)$ stands for the sum of the square loss between the estimated label matrix and the initial label matrix and the smoothness constraint.

Hence we can rewrite $E(F)$ as follows

$$E(F) = trace\left(F^T(I - S_{sym})F\right) + \gamma trace((F - Y)^T(F - Y))$$

Our objective is to minimize this error function. In the other words, we solve

$$\frac{\partial E}{\partial F} = 0$$

This will lead to

$$(I - S_{sym})F + \gamma(F - Y) = 0$$
$$F - S_{sym}F + \gamma F = \gamma Y$$
$$F - \frac{1}{1+\gamma}S_{sym}F = \frac{\gamma}{1+\gamma}Y$$
$$\left(I - \frac{1}{1+\gamma}S_{sym}\right)F = \frac{\gamma}{1+\gamma}Y$$

Let $\alpha = \frac{1}{1+\gamma}$. Hence the solution F^* of the above equations is

$$F^* = (1 - \alpha)(I - \alpha S_{sym})^{-1}Y$$

Also, please note that $S_{rw} = D^{-1}W$ is not the symmetric matrix, thus we cannot develop the regularization framework for the random walk graph Laplacian based semi-supervised learning iterative version.

Next, we will develop the regularization framework for the un-normalized graph Laplacian based semi-supervised learning algorithms. First, let's consider the error function

$$E(F) = \left\{\frac{1}{2}\sum_{i,j=1}^{n} W_{ij}\|F_i - F_j\|^2\right\} + \gamma\sum_{i=1}^{n}\|F_i - Y_i\|^2$$

In this error function $E(F)$, F_i and Y_i belong to R^c. Please note that c is the total number of words and γ is the positive regularization parameter. Hence

$$F = \begin{bmatrix} F_1^T \\ \vdots \\ F_n^T \end{bmatrix} \text{ and } Y = \begin{bmatrix} Y_1^T \\ \vdots \\ Y_n^T \end{bmatrix}$$

Here $E(F)$ stands for the sum of the square loss between the estimated label matrix and the initial label matrix and the smoothness constraint.

Hence we can rewrite $E(F)$ as follows

$$E(F) = trace(F^T LF) + \gamma trace((F - Y)^T(F - Y))$$

Please note that un-normalized Laplacian matrix of the network is $L = D - W$. Our objective is to minimize this error function. In the other words, we solve

$$\frac{\partial E}{\partial F} = 0$$

This will lead to

$$LF + \gamma(F - Y) = 0$$
$$(L + \gamma I)F = \gamma Y$$

Hence the solution F^* of the above equations is

$$F^* = \gamma(L + \gamma I)^{-1}Y$$

4 Experiments and Results

In this paper, the set of 4,500 speech samples recorded of 50 different words (90 speech samples per word) are used for training. Then another set of 500 speech samples of these words are used for testing the sensitivity measure. This dataset is available from the IC Design lab at Faculty of Electricals-Electronics Engineering, University of Technology, Ho Chi Minh City. After being extracted from the conventional MFCC feature extraction method, the column sum of the MFCC feature matrix of the speech sample will be computed. The result of the column sum which is the R^{26*1} column vector will be used as the feature vector of the three graph Laplacian based semi-supervised learning algorithms.

There are three ways to construct the similarity graph from these feature vectors:

    a.   The ε-neighborhood graph: Connect all speech samples whose pairwise distances are smaller than ε.

    b.   k-nearest neighbor graph: Speech sample i is connected with speech sample j if speech sample i is among the k-nearest neighbor of speech sample j or speech sample j is among the k-nearest neighbor of speech sample i.

    c.   The fully connected graph: All speech samples are connected.

In this paper, the similarity function is the Gaussian similarity function

$$s\big(f(:,i),f(:,j)\big) = \exp\left(-\frac{d(f(:,i),f(:,j))}{t}\right),$$

where $f(:,i)$ is the feature vector of speech sample i.

In this paper, t is set to 10^6 and the 5-nearest neighbor graph is used to construct the similarity graph from this dataset.

In this section, we experiment with the above three methods in terms of sensitivity measure. All experiments were implemented in Matlab 6.5 on virtual machine. The sensitivity measure Q is given as follows

$$Q = \frac{True\ Positive}{True\ Positive + False\ Negative}$$

True Positive (TP), True Negative (TN), False Positive (FP), and False Negative (FN) are defined in the following table 1

Table 1. Definitions of TP, TN, FP, and FN

		Predicted Label	
		Positive	Negative
Known Label	Positive	True Positive (TP)	False Negative (FN)
	Negative	False Positive (FP)	True Negative (TN)

In these experiments, parameter α is set to 0.85 and $\gamma = 1$. For this dataset, the table 2 shows the sensitivity measures of the three methods and HMM method (i.e. the current state of the art method of speech recognition application) applying to network for 50 words.

Table 2. Comparisons of symmetric normalized, random walk, and un-normalized graph Laplacian based methods and HMM method

Sensitivity Measure (%)			
Normalized	Random Walk	Un-normalized	HMM (8 states, 4 mixtures)
97.60%	97.60%	97.60%	89%

The following figure 1 shows the sensitivity measures of the conventional HMM method and the three graph Laplacian based semi-supervised learning methods:

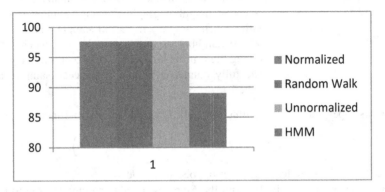

Fig. 1. Sensitivity measures of the three graph based semi-supervised learning methods and conventional HMM method

From the above table 2 and figure 1, we recognized that the symmetric normalized and un-normalized graph Laplacian based semi-supervised learning methods slightly perform better than the random walk graph Laplacian based semi-supervised learning method. Moreover, these three graph Laplacian based semi-supervised learning methods outperform the current state of the art HMM method in speech recognition problem since the graph based semi-supervised learning methods utilize the "relationship" among all speech samples in the datasets (i.e. the kernel's definition) to build the predictive model.

5   Conclusions

The detailed iterative algorithms and regularization frameworks for the three normalized, random walk, and un-normalized graph Laplacian based semi-supervised learning methods applying to the speech recognition problem have been developed. These three methods are successfully applied to this problem (i.e. classification problem). Moreover, the comparison of the sensitivity performance measures for these three methods and the current state of the art HMM method has been done.

Moreover, these three methods can not only be used in classification problem but also in ranking problem. Given a set of genes (i.e. the queries) involved in a specific disease (for e.g. leukemia), these three methods can also be used to find more genes involved in the same disease by ranking genes in gene co-expression network (derived from gene expression data) or the protein-protein interaction network or the integrated network of them. The genes with the highest rank then will be selected and then checked by biologist experts to see if the extended genes in fact are involved in the same disease. These problems are also called biomarker discovery in cancer classification.

Finally, to the best of our knowledge, the normalized, random walk, and un-normalized hypergraph Laplacian based semi-supervised learning methods have not been applied to the speech recognition problem. These methods applied to the speech recognition problem are worth investigated since [10] have shown that these hypergraph Laplacian based semi-supervised learning methods outperform the graph Laplacian based semi-supervised learning methods in text-categorization and letter recognition tasks.

Acknowledgement. This work is funded by the Ministry of Science and Technology, State-level key program, Research for application and development of information technology and communications, code KC.01.23/11-15.

References

1. Zhu, X., Ghahramani, Z.: Learning from labeled and unlabeled data with label propagation. Technical Report CMU-CALD-02-107, Carnegie Mellon University (2002)
2. Zhou, D., Bousquet, O., Lal, T.N., Weston, J., Schölkopf, B.: Learning with local and global consistency. In: Thrun, S., Saul, L., Schölkopf, B. (eds.) Advances in Neural Information Processing Systems (NIPS), vol. 16, pp. 321–328. MIT Press, Cambridge (2004)
3. Tsuda, K., Shin, H.H., Schoelkopf, B.: Fast protein classification with multiple networks. Bioinformatics (ECCB 2005) **21**(Suppl. 2), ii59–ii65 (2005)
4. Tran, L.: Application of three graph Laplacian based semi-supervised learning methods to protein function prediction problem. CoRR abs/1211.4289 (2012)
5. Tran, L.: The Un-normalized graph p-Laplacian based semi-supervised learning method and protein function prediction problem. In: Huynh, V.N., Denoeux, T., Tran, D.H., Le, A.C., Pham, B.S. (eds.) KSE 2013, Part I. AISC, vol. 244, pp. 23–35. Springer, Heidelberg (2014)
6. Rabiner, L., Juang, B.H.: Fundamentals of speech recognition, 507 pp. AT&T (1993)
7. Ganapathiraju, A.: Support vector machines for speech recognition. Diss. Mississippi State University (2002)
8. Marshall, A.: Artificial Neural Network for Speech Recognition, 2nd Annual Student Research Showcase (2005)
9. Labiak, J., Livescu, K.: Nearest neighbor classifiers with learned distances for phonetic frame classification. In: Proceedings of Interspeech (2011)
10. Zhou, D., Huang, J., Schölkopf, B.: Learning with hypergraphs: clustering, classification, and embedding. In: Schölkopf, B., Platt, J.C., Hofmann, T. (eds.) Advances in Neural Information Processing System (NIPS), vol. 19, pp. 1601–1608. MIT Press, Cambridge (2007)

Updating Relational Databases
with Linguistic Data Based on Hedge Algebras

Le Ngoc Hung[1], Vu Minh Loc[2(✉)], and Hoang Tung[3]

[1] Sai Gon University, Ho Chi Minh City, Vietnam
lengochungsg291958@gmail.com
[2] Gia Dinh University of Information Technology, Ho Chi Minh City, Vietnam
vuminhloc@gmail.com
[3] Dong Nai University, Bien Hoa, Vietnam
tungaptechbd@gmail.com

Abstract. Relational Databases (DB) with linguistic data based on hedge algebras (HA) were introduced, following this approach, data manipulation (include linguistic data) is simpler and more efficient, practical than the other one. On this basis, in this paper, we will present the update operations on relational databases with linguistic data based on HA. Update operations are built by mean of semantically quantifying mapping (SQM) and similarity relation of depth k, where k is the length of a linguistic value that belongs to the values domain of an attribute.

Keywords: Hedge algebras · Relational databases with linguistic data · Semantically quantifying mapping · Similarity relation of depth k · Clear key · Mixture key · Fuzzy key

1 Introduction

Updating and querying are major issues in databases. Continuing success in building theory database models following approaches such as: fuzzy set theory, possibility theory, extended possibility theory ... data updating problem has been studied. However, the results of these studies have not been reached practical requirements. In the fuzzy relational database model with linguistic attributes based on HA, universe U of its attributes is a set that includes two type of subsets, the first subset type contains classical attributes and the second subset contains attributes that are considered as linguistic variables. Linguistic and real values are adopted by linguistic variables.

In HA we have notions: semantically quantifying mapping, smallest neighboring of depth k and similarity interval of depth k. By these notions, we can unify data type of real and linguistic value to manipulate with fuzzy data becoming easy. This is facility that enables us to build update operations on relation databases with linguistic data.

The paper is organized as follows: in section 2, some basic concepts about HA will be introduced. Section 3 deals with relation databases with linguistic data based on HA. In section 4 update operations, the major problem in this paper, will be studied. Some conclusions will be given in Section 5.

© Institute for Computer Sciences, Social Informatics and Telecommunications Engineering 2015
P.C. Vinh et al. (Eds.): ICTCC 2014, LNICST 144, pp. 274–291, 2015.
DOI: 10.1007/978-3-319-15392-6_27

2   Some Basic Concepts

Definition 2.1 [1]

Let $AX = (X, G, C, H, \leq)$ be a linear complete hedge algebras (ComLin-HA), a mapping fm: $X \to [0, 1]$ is called a fuzziness measure (abbreviated fm) of terms belong to X if:

1. $fm(c^-) + fm(c^+) = 1$ and $\sum_{h \in H} fm(hu) = fm(u)$, with $\forall\, u \in X$, in this case fm called complete.

2. With the constants 0, W and 1: $fm(0) = fm(W) = fm(1) = 0$;

3. With $\forall\, x, y \in X, \forall\, h \in H$, $\dfrac{fm(hx)}{fm(x)} = \dfrac{fm(hy)}{fm(y)}$, this ratio does not depend

any $fm(x)$, $fm(y)$. and it is the fuzziness measure of hedge h, denoted by $\mu(h)$.

Clause 2.1 [1]

For each fuzziness measure on X fm, the following statements are true:

1. $fm(hx) = \mu(h)fm(x)$, with $\forall\, x \in X$;
2. $fm(c^-) + fm(c^+) = 1$;
3. $\sum_{-q \leq i \leq p, i \neq 0} fm(h_i c) = fm(c)$, $c \in \{c^-, c^+\}$;
4. $\sum_{-q \leq i \leq p, i \neq 0} fm(h_i x) = fm(x)$;
5. $\sum_{-q \leq i \leq -1} \mu(h_i) = \alpha$ và $\sum_{-q \leq i \leq -1} \mu(h_i) = \beta$, α, $\beta > 0$ and $\alpha + \beta = 1$.

Definition 2.2 [1]

A sign function: $X \to \{-1, 0, 1\}$ is a mapping which is defined recursively as follows: with h, h' $\in$ H and $c \in \{c^-, c^+\}$ then

1. Sign(c-) = -1, Sign(c+) = +1,
2. Sign(hc) = - Sign(c) if h is negative w.r.t c, where as Sign(hc) = + Sign(c);
3. Sign(h'hx) = - Sign(hx), if h'hx $\neq$ hx and h' is negative w.r.t h; Sign(h'hx) = + Sign(hx) if if h'hx $\neq$ hx and h' is positive w.r.t h
   Sign (h'hx) = + Sign (hx), if h'hx $\neq$ hx and h' is negative w.r.t h;
4. Sign (h'hx) = 0 if h'hx = hx.

Definition 2.3 [1]

Let $AX = (X, G, C, He, \Sigma, \Phi, \leq)$ be a ComLin-HA

A mapping φ: X → [0, 1] is called semantically quantifying mapping (abbreviated as SQM) of AX, the following affirms are true:

1. φ is mapped 1-1 from X on [0, 1] and maintain order on the X. With $\forall$ x, y $\in$ X, x < y $\Rightarrow$ φ(x) < φ(y) and φ(0) = 0, φ(1) = 1, với 0, 1 $\in$ c;

2. $\forall$ x $\in$ X, φ(Φx) = infimum φ(H(x)) and φ(Σx) = supremum φ(H(x)).

Definition 2.4 [1, 3- 4]

fm is the fuzziness measure on X. a mapping φ: X → [0, 1], induced by fm on X, is defined as follows:

1. φ(W) = θ = fm(c⁻), φ(c⁻) = θ - αfm(c⁻) = βfm(c⁻), φ(c⁺) = θ + αfm(c⁺);

2. $\varphi(h_jx) = \varphi(x) + Sign(h_jx)\{ \sum_{i=Sign(j)}^{j} fm(h_ix) - \omega(h_jx)fm(h_jx) \}$; with j $\in$

{j: -q $\leq$ j $\leq$ p và j $\neq$ 0} (*) and $\omega(h_jx) = \frac{1}{2}[1 + Sign(h_jx)Sign(h_ph_jx)(\beta - \alpha)] \in$

{α, β};

3. φ(Φc⁻) = 0, φ(Σc⁻) = θ = φ(Φc⁺), φ(Σc⁺) = 1, with every j like (*), φ(Φh$_j$x) =

$$\varphi(x) + Sign(h_jx)\{ \sum_{i=Sign(j)}^{j-Sign(j)\frac{1+Sgn(h_jx)}{2}} \mu(h_i)fm(x) \}$$

$$\varphi(\Sigma h_jx) = \varphi(x) + Sign(h_jx)\{ \sum_{i=Sign(j)}^{j-Sign(j)\frac{1-Sgn(h_jx)}{2}} \mu(h_i)fm(x) \}$$

3   Relational Database with Linguistic Data Based on Hedge Algebra

3.1   The Basic Ideas for Building the Databases with Linguistic Data Based on Hedge Algebras

Authors in [1, 3-4] have built a relational database model with language data based on HA as follows:

Relational database schema with linguistic data DB = {U, R$_1$, R$_2$, ..., R$_m$, Const}, U = {A$_1$, ... A$_n$} is attribute universe; R$_i$ are relational schemas; Const is a set of data constraint on DB. Each R$_i$ may contain two attribute groups, first group is normal attributes (classical attributes), the remaining groups is linguistic attributes.

Each linguistic attribute can be viewed as a linguistic variable that its value domain are linguistic values constitutes an HA mixed with set of real values. If A$_i$ is a linguistic attribute then its value domain is D(A$_i$) = LDom (A$_i$) $\cup$ DA$_i$, in which, LDom (A$_i$) is a set of linguistic values and the D$_{Ai}$ is a set of real values.

In addition, according to [4] the value domain of linguistic attribute can also receive value types such as interval values, undefined values, missing values, uncertain values, unknown values. These values can be transformed to unify with linguistic data in one data type. In this paper, we do not deal with these data types mentioned above.

Linguistic and real data type can be unified by mean of semantically quantifying mapping and similar relation of depth k. Based on this, a linguistic value x belong to linguistic values domain of a linguistic attribute, can be expressed through two semantic components:

- *The first one* is a semantic value which belong to the real domain DA, it is just the value of $v(x)$ (v is a semantically quantifying mapping).
- *The second one* is a finite set of fuzziness-intervals-based neighborhoods.

Along with the concept of similar interval of depth k, S_k, we can build equal and matching operation of depth k to compare not only between two linguistic values also between linguistic value and real value.

Similar relation of depth k based on equivalence classes, S_k, composed from D(A) permitting us to build matching operation on the databases. With x, y in D(A), we call "x similar to y at depth k or x $=_k$y" if smallest neighborhoods of them located into same equivalence class of depth k.

We can construct equivalence classes, S_k, as follows:

Denote: k* is a positive integer that is maximum length of each value in D(A).

|x| ≤ k* is the length of linguistic values x, put j = | x |, $T_k(x)$ is fuzziness interval of depth k that contain x by mean of mapping φ.

X_k is the set of linguistic values of length k, U is the universe of attributes belong to the database.

    a. If k = j: $O_{min, k}(x) = T_{k+1}(h_{-1}x) \cup T_{k+1}(h_1x)$;

    b. If 1≤ k < j: $O_{min, k}(x) = T_j(x)$;

    c. if j + 1 ≤ k ≤ k*: $O_{min, k}(x) = T_{k+1}(h_lx) \cup T_{k+1}(h_{l'}x)$, with l, l' $\in$ {-q, p}.

Put H_1 is subset of strong hedges, H_2 is subset of weak hedges, $H_1 = \{h_i, h_{-j} \mid 1 \leq i \leq [p/2], 1 \leq j \leq [q/2]\}$, H2 = $\{h_i, h_{-j} \mid [p/2] \leq i \leq p, [q/2] \leq j \leq q\}$.

Put $I_{k+1}(H_n) = \{T_{k+1}(h_iy) \mid y \in X_k, h_i \in H_n\}$, with n = 1, 2. Two intervals $T_{k+1}(x)$ and $T_{k+1}(y)$ in $I_{k+1}(H_n)$ are called interconnected exist intervals belong to $Ik_{+1}(H_n)$ consecutive ranging from $T_{k+1}(x)$ to $Tk_{+1}(y)$. This relationship will compose $I_{k+1}(H_n)$ into interconnected components.

Denote C be the set of similarity intervals of depth k of linguistic value x, C is defined as follows:

With $I_{k+1}(H_1) = \{T_{k+1}(h_iy) \mid y \in X_k, h_i \in H_1\}$, C = $\{T_{k+1}(h_iy) \mid h_i \in H_1\}$

With $I_{k+1}(H_1) = \{T_{k+1}(h_iy) \mid y \in X_k, h_i \in H_2\}$, Suppose that $X_k = \{x_s \mid s = 0, ..., m-1\}$ of m elements are arranged in the sequence so that $x_i \leq x_j$ if and only if i ≤ j. Denote $H_2^- = H_2 \cap H^-$ and $H_2^+ = H_2 \cap H^+$. Clusters generated from fuzziness intervals $Ik_{+1}(H_2)$ has the following three categories:

    a. Cluster on the left x_0: $\{T_{k+1}(h_ix_0) \mid h_i \in H_2^+\}$.

    b. Cluster on the right x_{m-1}: $\{T_{k+1}(h_ix_{m-1}) \mid h_i \in H_2^+\}$.

    c. Clusters in between x_s and x_{s+1} with s = 0, ..., m-2.; depends on $Sgn(h_px_s)$ and $Sgn(h_px_{s+1})$:

$C = \{T_{k+1}(h_i x_s), T_{k+1}(h'_j x_{s+1}) \mid h_i \in H_2^+, h'_j \in H_2^-\}$, if $Sgn(h_p x_s) = +1$ and $Sign(h_p x_{s+1}) = +1$;

$C = \{T_{k+1}(h_i x_s), T_{k+1}(h'_j x_{s+1}) \mid h_i \in H_2^+, h'j \in H_2^+\}$, if $Sgn(h_p x_s) = +1$ and $Sign(h_p x_{s+1}) = +1$;

$C = \{T_{k+1}(h_i x_s), T_{k+1}(h'_j x_{s+1}) \mid h_i \in H_2^-, h'_j \in H_2^-\}$, if $Sgn(h_p x_s) = +1$ and $Sign(h_p x_{s+1}) = +1$;

$C = \{T_{k+1}(h_i x_s), T_{k+1}(h'_j x_{s+1}) \mid h_i \in H_2^-, h'_j \in H_2^+\}$, if $Sgn(h_p x_s) = +1$ and $Sign(h_p x_{s+1}) = +1$.

Set the all clusters C is denoted ©.

Definition 3.1 [5]

Each $C \in$ ©, similarity interval of depth k that correspond to C is:

$$S_k(C) = \cup \{T_{k+1} \mid T_{k+1} \in C\}$$

Clause 3.1 [5]

Let AX be a ComLin-HA of the attribute A, H^+ and H^- have at least two element, the fuzziness quantifying parameters are determined following the definition 2.4. We have:

a. For each k, $\{S_k(u) \mid u \in X \cup C\}$ are uniquely identified and it's a partition of interval $[0, 1]$

b. For each x, $u \in X \cup C$, if $\varphi(x) \in S_k(u)$ then $O_{min, k}(x) \subseteq S_k(u)$

Definition 3.2 [1]

Let AX be a ComLin-HA and fm is the fuzziness measurer. Suppose that φ_A is SQM on AX with each k that $1 \leq k \leq k^*$, S_k is similarity relationship of depth k on DA. Then, with two arbitrary tuples t, s on U, t[A] and s[A] on the value domain has been called the equal level k, denoted by $t[A] =_{fm, k} s[A]$ or $t[A] =_k s[A]$, if there exists a equivalence class $S_k(u)$ of S_k so that $O_{min, k}(t[A]) \subseteq S_k(u)$ and $O_{min, k}(s[A]) \subseteq S_k(u)$.

To be able to compare two values in the value domain of linguistic attribute as well as compare the value of two tuples on a set of attributes we have the following two definitions:

Definition 3.3 [1]

Suppose that t and s are two tuples in the U. We write $t[A_i] =_{\varphi, k} s[A_i]$ and they are called equal in depth k, if the following conditions are true:

1. If $t[A_i], s[A_i] \in D_{A_i}$ then $t[A_i] = s[A_i]$;

2. If only one of the two tuples t[Ai] or s [Ai] is the linguistic data, assume that t [Ai] then $s[A_i] \in S_k(t[A_i])$;

Definition 3.4 [1]

Assume t, s the same as in definition 3.2, then

1. We write $t[A_i] <_{\varphi, k} s[A_i]$, if $S_k(t[A_i]) < S_k(s[A_i])$;
2. We write $t[A_i] >_{\varphi, k} s[A_i]$, if $S_k(t[A_i]) > S_k(s[A_i])$;
3. We write $t[A_i] \leq_{\varphi, k} s[A_i]$, if $t[A_i] =_{\varphi, k} s[A_i]$ or $S_k(t[A_i]) < S_k(s[A_i])$ and $t[A_i] \geq_{\varphi, k} s[A_i]$, if $t[A_i] =_{\varphi, k} s[A_i]$ or $S_k(t[A_i]) > S_k(s[A_i])$.

Thus, a relational database with linguistic data, will be built with above ideas , they allow us to deploy this type of databases by following reasons:

- The way to build models of a relational database with linguistic data based on hedge algebras   very simple, but the ability to capture, as well as the performed actions with linguistic information is effective;
- Data in the linguistic attributes of the database has been unified into one data type that should be very favorable for manipulation;
- Linguistic data in real applications usually only the maximum length is 3 and the number of these linguistic values are commonly used is not greater, therefore it's not too complex to build a series of elements of a Linguistic attribute;
- It is not difficult to construct a sequence of similarity intervals of depth k (Sk) to the linguistic values, based on a sequence of this intervals that manipulation with data become simple.

3.2   Fuzzy Functional Dependencies (FFD)

Authors in [3] presented general issues and complete information about FFD, we recall some of the concepts, definitions important about FFD:

Let A is a linguistic attribute of the relational database with linguistic data, it will be combined with a set of similarity relationships k_A, this relationship is to define a concept of the fuzziness uncertain equal in level k_A and the denoted $=_{k(A)}$, $0 \leq k_A \leq k_A$, k_A is the maximum length of terms over A.

$K : U \rightarrow N$ (N is the set of positive integers) is a function of parts, it is defined on the set $X \subseteq U$ and assigned to each linguistic attribute A is a positive integer $K(A)$ satisfies conditions $k_A \geq K(A) = k_A > 0$.

As so $K = \{k_A : A \in X\}$; if exists $K = \{k_A : A \in X\}$ and exists $K' = \{k'_A : A \in X$ and write $K_X \geq K'_X$ if $K_A \geq K'_A$ for all $A \in X$.

With $X \subseteq U$, we say that two tuples of t, s on U are equal with the similarity level K, and write $t[X] =_K s[X]$, if we have $t[A] =_{K(A)} s[A]$, for all $A \in X$.

Definition 3.3 [3]

With DB is a relational database with linguistic data and R(U) is a relational schema of DB. With any expression $f = X \rightarrow_K Y$ format called a level K fuzziness dependencies K (K-FFD), X, Y $\subseteq$ R and K is a similarity level to the previous definition $XY = X \cup Y$, and its semantics are interpreted as follows:

a relation any r(R), f is called satisfies r if

$(\forall\ t, s \in r)\ (t[X] =_K s[X]) \Rightarrow t[Y] =_K s[Y])$

In this case we also say that the relationship r satisfied $X \rightarrow_K Y$ or $X \rightarrow_K Y$ be true on r.

Offers by [3] we have axiomatic system for case fuzziness function depends as following:

K1(Reflexivity): if $Y \subseteq X$ then $X \rightarrow_K Y$

K2(Subsumption): if $X \rightarrow_K Y$ then $X \rightarrow_{K*} Y$, with every $K*$ on XY so that $K*_X \geq K_X$ and $K*_Y \leq K_Y$.

K3(Augmentation):   if $X \rightarrow_K Y$ then $XZ \rightarrow_{K \vee K*(Z)} YZ$, with all $Z \subseteq U$ and with all $K*$ on Z so that $K*_{Y \cap Z} \leq K_{Y \cap Z}$, where $XZ = X \cup Z$. and $YZ = Y \cup Z$.

K4 (TransitivIty): if $X \rightarrow_K Y$, $Y \rightarrow_{K*} Z$ then $X \rightarrow_{K \vee K*} Z$, with $K*_Y \leq K_Y$ with $X \subseteq U$ and t, s are two tuples in U, we write $t[X] \leq_K s[X]$, if with any $\forall A \in X$ we always have $t[A] \leq_{K_A} s[A]$.

Definition 3.4 [10]

Let R(U) be a relational shema, relation r on R. $X, Y \subseteq U$ are two set of attributes. We can say r satisfy monotonically increasing fuzzy function dependencies X determine Y at depth k, abbreviated $X^+ \rightarrow_K Y$ in r, if we have: $\forall\ t, s \in r$, $t[X] \leq_K s[X] \Rightarrow t[Y] \leq_K s[X]$.

Definition 3.5 [10]

Let R(U) be a relational shema, relation r on R. $X, Y \subseteq U$ are two set of attributes. We can say r satisfy monotonically decreasing fuzzy function dependencies X determine Y at depth k, abbreviated $X^+ \rightarrow_K Y$ in r, if we have: $\forall\ t, s \in r$, $t[X] \leq_K s[X] \Rightarrow t[Y] \geq_K s[X]$.

Definition 3.6

Let R(U) is a relational schema, F be FFD on U, K are called key of R(U) if and only if the two following conditions are simultaneously satisfied:

1. $K \rightarrow_K U$
2. Do not exists $K' \subset K$ so that $K' \rightarrow_K U$.

4   Update Operations

If we resolve the problem of updating on fuzzy databases successfully, we can build significant factual applications. Fuzzy databases with other approaches such as similar relation, possibility theory, extended possibility theory, ... show many limits in capturing, presenting and storing fuzzy data (see [5], [7]). So, the ability to deploy applications of these model are low because of this reason. With HA, we have concept of semantically quantifying mapping, smallest neighboring of depth k and similarity interval of depth k. We can use these concepts to build matching operation, based on this operation, we will build updating operations on databases with linguistic.

As stated above, a relational databases with linguistic data includes two attribute groups, the first group are the classical attributes, the second group are linguistic attributes as linguistic variables.

In fact, the value of linguistic data in linguistic attributes do not usually have greater than 3 of length, for instance, we consider a linguistic attribute to store information describing the new or old status of a product. The values of this attribute can be "very new", "very very new " ... or "old", "very old", "very very old". The values like "very very very very new" ... that is not factual. Thus, we suppose that linguistic attribute values that has the length is always less than or equal to 3.

We distinguish three types of relational schema with linguistic data, including: relational schema with linguistic data has clear key (the key includes only classical attributes), mixture key (the key includes classical attributes and linguistic attributes) and fuzzy key (the key only includes linguistic attributes).

As we known, the update operations that include insert, modify and delete operations. Now, we'll study these operations on databases with linguistic data.

Let R (U, F) is a relational schema, in which, U is the universe of attributes, F = F = $F_1 \cup F_2$. With F_1 is the set of FFD by definition 3.3, F_2 is the set of monotonically increasing (decreasing) fuzzy function dependencies by the definitions 3.4 and 3.5. Let $U = A_1 \ldots A_n$, $U = U_1 \cup U_2$, $U_1 = A_1 \ldots A_m$ are classical attributes and $U_2 = A_{m+1} \ldots A_n$ are the linguistic attributes.

4.1   Insert Operation

Insert operation is understood as executed by adding tuple t into a relation r(R). Tuple t will be inserted into r, if t satisfies the data constraint on r, concretely, t must satisfy the FFD in F. These FFD in F are divided into two groups, first group, F_1 and second group, F2, as mentioned above.

Tuple t will be inserted into r(R) if t can be passed two checks: check t if satisfies F_1 and check if t satisfies F_2 ? and another problem of insert operation to consider: tuple t as mentioned above, before it is inserted into r(R), first, we needs to check t satisfies F_1? For each s $\in$ r(R), this check is actually check to see t and s have the same key at depth k or not. Thus, when we check to see whether there's the same key between t and s, if we do not specify clearly which of k that is matching, we will have to make even a lot of operations to insert t in the database. This case will become very complicated when r(R) has the large of tuples. So, it's necessary to specify what is the depth of k clearly. With the things that we discussed above, insert operation can be done as follows:

Insertion can be divided into three cases corresponding to three types of relational schema:

- In the first case: insertion in the relation scheme that has the clear key
- In the second case: insertion in the relation scheme has the mixture key
- In the third case: insertion in the relation scheme has The fuzzy key

4.1.1   Insert Operation in the Relational Schema that Has the Clear Key

Check Data Constraint with F_1

This check is tested to verify that tuple t be duplicated the key with any tuple in r or not. It is done the same as in the classical relational schema. If the tuple t satisfied key constraint then it will continue to be tested with data dependencies F_2 with depth k, otherwise tuple t will not be inserted into r (R).

Check Data Constraint with F_2

If F_2 exist, we will use them to check if the tuple t satisfy the condition in definition 3.4 or 3.5, if tuple t satisfy these conditions then t will be inserted into r.

4.1.2   Insert Operation in the Relational Schema that Has the Mixed Key

The examination of data constraint in this case more complicated than the first case. The key of relational schema in this case = group of classical attributes (X) $\cup$ group of fuzzy attributes (Y).

Check Data Constraint with F_1

For each $s \in r$ if $s(key) = t(key) \Leftrightarrow s(X) = t(X)$ (1) and $s(Y) =_K t(Y)$ (2).

The examination (1) is simple because of the comparison between two real values. Suppose (1) is correct, the remaining problem is to check (2).

To be able to check (2) we must perform the following steps:

- Build similarity intervals of depth k_{Ai} of the values $\in$ Dom (Ai) with $A_i \in Y$;

- If with $\forall A_i \in Y$ that $t[A_i] \in S_{k_{Ai}} (s[A_i])$ then testing (2) is correct, that mean tuple t will do not be inserted onto r (R) (because the same key), in contrast, tuple t will be checked with the group of F_2 (if available).

Check Data Constraint with F2

This check is done the same as the first case.

To facilitate tracking of data values in a relation with mixtures key or fuzzy key, each relation need to be supplemented attribute of depth k that contains the set of values of matching of depth k_{Ai}. Each value corresponds to a tuple in relation database to indicate the participating of this tuple in relation databases following the certain matching of depth k.

For example, we have the following relation:

K	A	B
3, 2	a_1	b_2
2, 2	a_2	b_2

In the above relation, we can see the first tuple, $t_1<a_1, b_2>$ is inserted into relation by matching of depth k = {3, 2}.

4.1.3   Insert Operation in the Relational Schema that Has the Fuzzy Key

Check Data Constraint with F_1

Verifying duplicate key in this case is the same as case 2, because the relational schema's key do not include classical attributes.

Check with F_2 Data Constraint with F_2

It's implemented as two above cases.

4.2   The Delete Operation

Executing this operation is accompanied by the delete condition to identify the tuples should be deleted, keep in mind if this condition is not accompanied by any conditions then all of the tuples in the relation will be deleted. Delete condition is actually a classical query, fuzzy query or both of all; With a fuzzy query, based on HA, we can convert to a classical query of depth k. We can distinguish three case of delete conditions:

Case 1:
The delete condition do not include linguistic attributes (classical query). We can handle this case same as in classical databases.

Case 2:
The delete condition that has includes linguistic attributes (include both fuzzy query and classical query)

This case, the delete condition has the form: $\forall\, t \in$ r, t (delete condition) = true $\Leftrightarrow$ $(t[X_1] \,\partial\,$ value$_1)$ θ $(t[X_2] \,\partial\,$ value$_2)$ ... θ $(t[X_u] \,\partial\,$ value$_u)$ θ $t[Y_1] \,\partial_{k_1}$ fvalue$_1)$ θ $(t[Y_2] \,\partial_{k_2}$ fvalue$_2)$...$\theta(t[Y_v] \,\partial_{k_v}$ fvalue$_v)$ is true; in which $X_i \in U_1$ (i=1...u), $Y_j \in U_2$ (j = 1 ... v); θ is the AND or OR operations; ∂ is one equation =, $\leq$, $\geq$, $\neq$, > and <.

The tuple t satisfies two condition groups simultaneously, the first ones, tuple t must be satisfied on set of $X_i \in U_1$ (i=1...u), the second ones, tuple t must be satisfied on set of $Y_j \in U_2$ (j = 1 ... v).

The first condition group was processed same as the classical databases, second condition group we will use methods (*) below to process.

(1). Build list V_i of level k_{Yi} similarity intervals, S_{kYi} in Dom (Yi) with $Y_i \in U_2$

(2). For each t $\in$ r:

- Calculate similarity intervals $S_{k_{Y_i}}$ (t$[Y_i]$);

- Calculate $O_{min,\, k_i}$ (fvalue$_i$), fvaluei is a linguistic values;

- Verify whether value of logical expression t$[Y_1] \,\partial_{k_1}$ fvalue$_1)$ θ $(t[Y_2] \,\partial_{k_2}$ fvalue$_2)$...$\theta(t[Y_v] \,\partial_{k_v}$ fvalue$_v)$ is true or not?

4.3   The Modify Operation

Modify operation to be made through the processing of the two conditions, first condition is used to determine tuples which be modified with matching of depth k in r (denoted X, $X \subseteq r$, assume X has m elements), the second condition is the condition that $\forall t \in X$ after modified data be satisfied.

So, the modify operation in nature is to delete tuples that it satisfies the condition 1 (in X) and insert new tuples that it satisfies the condition 2 into r. We will study two methods for handling this condition.

Processing Conditions 1

Condition 1 of modify operation is the same as delete condition, so we can apply again the way of condition processing of the delete operation above.

Processing Conditions 2

The result after condition 1 processed is understood as extracting X from r, further work can be described as follows: extract tuple t_i $(i = 1, ..., m)$ form X and edit the values on some attributes of the t_i so that it satisfies conditions 2 and finally insert t_i into r.

The problem is that how do we modify the value of some attributes of t_i? we would classify the attributes of t_i that its values be modified into two groups:

The first group: comprises the classical attributes group
The modifying the value of this group is the same as in the classic.
The second group: consists of linguistic attributes
Modifying the value of this group is not simple, it's usually classified into the following cases:

Case 1
A real value will be modified to another real value equal to a linguistic value of depth k.

For example: in a employee salary management database, we have the request: "Look for employees with relatively *rather young age* and their contributions at same level to raise their salary up to *quite high* ".

Suppose that with matching operation of depth k = 2, an employee's salary level at 2.0 belong to *rather low* level, now, we need to modify this salary level become to linguistic value at *rather high*. This modify operation is called modifying a real value become to another real value other that it is similarity of depth k with a linguistic value.

In general, we will process this case as follows:

real c value is converted to real b value, that it is similarity of depth k with x linguistic values.

if a' = $\varphi(x)$, b is similarity to with x of depth k ($\forall k \leq k^*$). Thus, in this case the c value will be changed to a' = $\varphi(x)$.

Case 2
A linguistic value will be replaced by a purely linguistic values, such as "rather good" replaced by "good"

To proceed this case, a linguistic value x will be modified to become a linguistic value y, easily, we replace string represented x by string represented y.

Case 3
Linguistic values x will be modified to a linguistic values y, with condition: $y = x \, \partial \, z$, ∂ is a operation of arithmetic and z is a numeric value.

This case occurs when the condition 2 (increasing or decreasing value) that require the values of a specific attribute of tuples to satisfy the condition. Some linguistic values of attributes (remained values) will also have to change its value to the corresponding to the numeric value.

For example, suppose that we have the condition 2 on an attribute A of a database as follows:

"Increase values (for tuples that satisfy the first condition) of attribute A up to 15%" (#). How can we solve this query if the values of A do not include linguistic values but also include real values ? We cannot perform this operation $y = x \, \partial \, z$ because x and y are linguistic values.

To solve this problem, we propose approximate solution for this case as follows:

We will modify the "core" of linguistic values x, $\varphi(x)$ become to fvalue so that fvalue = $\varphi(x) \, \partial \, z$. Next, we will review a series of similar intervals at level k for any k $\leq$ k* of values of attribute domain which we are considering to determine what similarity intervals of depth k fvalue belong to, if fvalue $\in S_k(x')$ then x will be modified become to y.

4.4   Some Examples about Databases with Linguistic Values

Example 1

Let's consider relational shema R_1(SffCode, Fullname, Recowork, Reward) store information about bonus for staffs in a company. Sffcode: Staff code; Reworkco: review work completion.

r(R1)			
SffCode	**Fullname**	**Recowork**	**Reward**
A001	Nguyen Van Phu	More Good	More High
A002	Truong Phi Qua	Poor	Rather Low
A003	Huynh Phu Hao	8.5	More High
A004	Bang Quan	Very Good	300
A005	Banh Tien Len	2	More Low
A006	Bui The Gian	Very very good	Very High

Recowork and Reward are two linguistic attributes with agreement Dom(Recowork) = [0, 10] (review work completion get values from 0 to 10 points) with generated elements of {Poor, Good }, **H**= {Rather, Possible }, **H** $^+$ = {More, Very} the Dom (Reward) = [0, 500] (Reward get the values from 0 to 500 million) are linguistic variables with generated elements of {Low, High}, **H⁻** = {Rather, Possible}, **H⁺** = {More, Very}

For attribute Recowork: Put fm(Poor) = 0.35 fm(Good) = 0.65; μ(Possible) = 0:15, μ(Rather) = 0.25 μ(More) = 0.2, μ(Very) = 0.4.

For attribute Reward: Put fm(Low) = 0:55, fm(High) = 0:45; μ(Possible) = 0:15, μ(Rather) = 0.25 μ(More) = 0.2, μ(Very) = 0.4.

On R we identify set F of FFD as follows:

[StffCode]→$_K$[Funame], two attributes StffCode and Funame are classical one, so FFD fuzzy return the common dependencies:

[SffCode] → [Funame]   (1);
[StffCode] →$_K$[Recowork]   (2);
[StffCode] →$_K$[Reword]   (3);

These FFD are valid with k > 0.

StffCode is the key of R_1

With every attributes belong to R3, suppose k* = 3.

Example 2

R_2 (Antiqes, Techpater, Seprice) store   information   about   the stock character   of antique shops. Antiqes: Antiques Name; Techpater: Technical Parameter; Seprice: Sale Price.

r (R_2)			
Depth of K	**Antiqes**	**Techpater**	**Seprice**
2, 2	Bowl	Rather Good	More High
1, 2	Bowl	Good	Low
3, 2	Plate	Very Good	High
3, 2	Big jar	Possible Good	Rather High
3, 2	Vase	Rather Poor	Rather High
3, 3	Cup	Very Poor	Rather High
3, 2	Big jar	4.5	Very Low

Attribute Techpater is a linguistic variable with Dom(Techpater) = [0, 10] and two generated elements of {Good, Poor}

H⁻ = {Rather, Possible}, H⁺ = {more very}. Put fm (Poor) = 0.45, fm(Good) = 0.55; μ(Possible) = 0.15, μ(Rather) = 0.25, μ(more) = 0.2, μ(very) = 0.4.

- Attribute SaPrice is a linguistic variable with Dom(SaPrice) = [500, 100000] (from 500 USD to 100000 USD)

With two generated elements of {Low , High}. H⁻ = {Rather, Possible } , H⁺ = {More,Very}. Put fm(Low) = 0.4, fm (High) = 0.6, μ(Possible) = 0.15, μ(Rather) = 0.25, μ(More) = 0.2, μ(Very) = 0.4.

Review set F of FFD on R_2 include:

[Antiqes] [Techpater]→$_K$SaPrice (5);

The Key on R_2 be [Antiqes] [Techpater];

With every attributes in R_3 . Suppose k* = 3

Example 3

R₃(Brd, Impri , Stus, Sapri) of a database about sale the old and new garments. Brd: Brand; Impri: Import price; Stus: Status, Sapri: Sale Price.

r(R3)				
Depth of K	Brd	Impri	Stus	Sapri
2, 2, 2	Good	7000	Rather Old	Rather High
1, 1, 1	Rather Poor	Very Low	Old	17000

- Attribute Brd is a linguistic variable with Dom (Brd) = [0, 10] and two generated elements of {Good, Poor}, H^- = {Rather, Possible}, H^+ = {More, Very}.

Put fm (Poor) = 0.45, fm (Good) = 0.55; μ(Possible) = 0.15, μ(Rather) = 0.25, μ(More) = 0.2, μ(Very) = 0.4.

- Attribute Impri is a linguistic variable Dom (Impri) = [5000, 150000] (from 150000 VND to 5000 VND). With two generated elements of {Low , High}, H^- = {Rather, Possible} , H^+ = {More, Very}.

Put fm (Low) = 0.4, fm (High) = 0.6; μ(Possible) = 0.15, μ(Rather) = 0.25, μ(More) = 0.2, μVery) = 0.4.

- Attribute Stus is a linguistic variable with Dom (Tinhtrang) = [0, 10] and two generated elements {Old, New},

H^- = {Rather, Possible}, H^+ = {More, Very}.

Put fm (Old) = 0.4, fm (New) = 0.6; μ(Possible) = 0.15, μ(Rather) = 0.25, μ(More) = 0.2, μ(Very) = 0.4.

- Attribute Sapri is a linguistic variable Dom (Sapri) = [10000, 500000] (from 10000 VND to 500000 VND). With two generated elements of {Low, High}, H^- = {Rather, Possible} H^+ = {More,Very}.

Put fm(Low) = 0.4, fm (High) = 0.6; μ(Possible) = 015, μ(Rather) = 0.25, μ(More) = 0.2, μ(Very) = 0.4.

Review:

F is a set of FFD on R₃ include:

[Brd] [Impri] [Stus] →ₖ[Sapri] (6).

The Key of R₃ is [Brd] [Impri] [Stus].

With every attributes in R₃, suppose k* = 3

Next, we will present the update on three schemas R₁, R₂, R₃. schemes are distinguished by their nature of key. The key of R₁ only include clear attributes, the key of R₂ include mixed attributes (clear and fuzzy); the key of R₃ only include fuzzy attributes.

Insert Operation

Suppose we have the following requirements:

① Inserting tuple t = <"A008", "Phuong Nam Ngang", "Poor", "Rather Low"> on relations r (R₁);

② Inserting tuple p = <"Vase", 5.0, "Rather high"> on relations r (R_2) with matching level between p and the tuples in relation is $K_{Techpater, Sapri}$ = {1, 1};

③ Inserting tuple q = <"Rather Good", 150000, " Rather Old", "230000"> with level matching between p and tuples of the relationship is $K_{Impri, Stus}$ = {1, 1}.

With the Request ①

This case a tuple is inserted into the relational schema with its key only include classical attributes. Tuple t is inserted into r(R_1) if t satisfy the FFDs:

t satisfied FFDs: (1), (2), (3) and also satisfied monotonically increasing FFD (4).

Conclusion: t is inserted r(R1)

r(R1) after tuple t is inserted as follows:

SffC ode	Fullname	Recowork	Reward
A001	Nguyen Van Phu	More Good	More High
A002	Truong Phi Qua	Poor	Rather Low
A003	Huynh Phu Hao	8.5	More High
A004	Bang Quan	Very Good	300
A005	Banh Tien Len	2	More Low
A006	Bui The Gian	Very very good	Very High
A008	*Phuong Nam Ngang*	*Good*	*Rather Low*

With the Request ②

This is insert operation on relational schema that its key contains mixed between fuzzy attribute and classical ones.

Check p satisfies for FFD (5)?

For each s ∈ r(R2), we need to check p and s having same value ? that mean p and s simultaneously satisfy FFD (5)?

Case p[Antiqes] = s[Antiqes], we need to check   p [Techpater] =$_1$ s[Techpater]?

If p[Antiqes] ≠ s[Antiqes], we conclude p and s satisfy with (5).

If ∃ s ∈ r so that key(p) =$_k$ key(s), we will conclude p does not satisfy (5) and obviously p can not be inserted on r(R_2).

Concretely, with the p as above, p[Antiqes] = "Big jar", this value is different from all value in attribute Antiqes of tuples in r(R_2) except tuple 4 (s_4) and tuple 7 (S_7). So, we just check if   p[Techpater] =$_1$ s_4 [Techpater]   then   p[Saprice] =$_1$ s_4 [Saprice] ? (~)

And if p [Techpater] =$_1$ s_7[Techpater] then p[Saprice] =$_1$ s_7 [Saprice]? (~ ~).

Consider (~): With the matching of depth k = 1, S_1(possible good) = T_1(possible good) = ((φ(Fine) + α.fm(Fine)) - fm (Possible good), φ(Fine) + α.fm(Fine))] = (0:45

+ 0.4 * 0:55 to 0:15 * 0:55, 0:45 + 0:55 * 0.4] = (0:45, 0.67], it mean interval (4.5, 6.7] on the reference value domain. S_4 [Techpater] = 5.0 $\in$ S_1[Possible good) so p[Techpater] $=_1 s_4$[Techpater]. Now we consider p[Sapri] $=_1 s_4$[Sapri]?

p[Sapri] = "high" = s_4[Sapri] so (~) is correct, mean p correct with the s_4, so p will not be inserted on $r(R_2)$ and we do not need to consider (~ ~).

Conclusion: The tuple p is not inserted into relations $r(R_2)$ at matching of depth $K_{Techpater, Sapri}$ = { 1, 1}. Relations $r(R_2)$ remain status.

With the Request ③

This is case that relational schema has only fuzzy key.

Check for each s $\in$ r(R3) if s and q satisfy (6)?

With first tuple (s_1): we have s_1[Impri] $\neq$ q[Impri], so the value of key are different on s_1 and q, that mean they satisfies (6)

With second tuple (s2): We have S_1(very low) = [0 +5, fm (very low) * (150000 - 5000) +5] = [5000, 0.4 * 0.4 * 145000 +5000] = [5000, 28200], to replace q [Impri] = 150000 $\notin$ S_1(very low), so q[Impri] $\neq_1 s_1$[Impri], from this, we have value of key on s_2 and q are different, that mean they satisfy (6).

Conclusion: q will be inserted into $r(R_3)$ and $r(R_3)$ after insert tuple q as follows:

Level K	Brd	Impri	Stus	Sapri
2, 2, 2	Good	7000	Rather Old	Rather High
1, 1, 1	Rather Poor	Very Low	Old	17000
1, 1, 1	*Rather Good*	*150000*	*Old*	*23000*

Delete Operation

Suppose that we have the following requirements:

- "Delete from r(R1) tuples which have "poor" Brd and the depth of k at $k_{Recowork}$ =1 (when we apply delete condition" ④;

Deletion condition includes linguistic attribute which can be formulated as t[Recowork]$=_1$"Poor". We have: S_1(Poor) = (1.4, 2.6] and easily see that on relation $r(R_1)$ tuple 2 (s_2) and tuple 5 (s_5) will be deleted, because s_2[Recowork] and s_5[Recowork] belong to S_1(Poor).

Relation $r(R_1)$ after delete:

SffCode	Fullname	Recowork	Reward
A001	Nguyen Van Phu	More Good	More High
A003	Huynh Phu Hao	8.5	More High
A004	Bang Quan	Very Good	300
A006	Bui The Gian	Very very good	Very High

Modify Operation

Suppose we have the following requirements:

- " With relations r(R1) find all persons who have "very good" recowork, then modified their Reward level become "High" (the matching operation of depth k=2) (5)

Consider the Requirements (5)

Condition 1: All tuples t satisfying this condition, they must have t [Recowork] $=_2$"Very Good". we have S_3(Very Good) = ((1 - fm (Very Good) + fm (Rather Very Good), 1-fm (Very Very Good)] * 10 = (8.1, 9.0]; we have tuples 3 and 4 of r(R_1) will be modified values.

Condition 2: With tuple 3 (s_3), value of attribute Reward satisfied. With tuple 4th (s_4), we have s_4[Reward] = 300 $\notin$ S_2(More High). We have φ(More High) = 1 - fm (Very High) - bfm(More High) = 0.71, so, φ(300) will be replaced by φj(More High), corresponding to the value of reference domain is 0.71 * 500 = 355.

Relation r(R_1) after modified as required (5):

SffCode	Fullname	Recowork	Reward
A001	Nguyen Van Phu	More Good	More High
A002	Truong Phi Qua	Poor	Rather Low
A003	Huynh Phu Hao	8.5	More High
A004	Bang Quan	Very Good	355
A005	Banh Tien Len	2	More Low
A006	Bui The Gian	Very very good	Very High

5   Conclusion

In this paper, we present updating operations on relational databases model with linguistic data based on hedge algebra, included the operations insert, delete and modify. Insert operation is proposed for the three relational schema types, including relational schema with clear key, with fuzzy key and key including clear attributes and fuzzy one; delete operation is done entirely due the delete condition is determined based on the idea converting a fuzzy query become to a clear query with the similar level k; modify operation to be carried out through the delete and insert operation.

With hedge algebras we have some concepts: SQM mapping, fuzziness-intervals-based neighborhoods of a point, k-equality "$=_k$" which enable us to build updating operations on relational databases based on hedge algebras more conveniently than on the other one.

References

1. Ho, N.C., Wechler, W.: Hedge algebras: An algebraic approach to structures of sets of linguistic domains of linguistic truth variable. Fuzzy Sets and Systems 35(3), 281–293 (1990)
2. Ho, N.C., Lan, V.N.: Hedge algebras: an algebraic approach to domains of linguistic variables and their applicability
3. Ho, N.C.: Fuzzy Relational Database with Linguistic Data – Part II: Fuzzy Functional Dependencies, Fuzzy Sets and Systems
4. Ho, N.C.: Linguistic Databases: Relational Model and Hedge-Algebra-Based Linguistic Data Semantics
5. Ho, N.C., Vinh, L.X., Hao, N.C.: Unifying and building similar relation in linguistic databases by Hedge algebras. Journal of Computer and Cybernetics, T.25, S.4, 314–332
6. Nakata, M., Murai, T.: Updating under integrity constraints in fuzzy databases. In: Proc. Sixth IEEE Conf. on Fuzzy Systems (FUZZ-IEEE 1997), Barcelona, pp. 713–719. IEEE (1997)
7. Raiju, K.V.S.V.N., Majumdar, A.K.: Fuzzy functional dependencies and lossless join decomposition of fuzzy relational database system. ACM Trans. Databases Syst. 13, 129–166 (1988)
8. Ma, Z.M., Yan, L.: Updating Extended Possibility – Based Fuzzy Relational Databases. International Journal of Intelligent Systems 22, 237–258 (2007)
9. Bahar, Ozgun, Yazici, Adnan: Normalization and Lossless Join Decomposition of Similarity-Based Fuzzy Relational Databases. Internationnal Journal of Intelligent Systems 19, 885–917 (2004)
10. Ho, N.C., Hao, N.C.: Monotonically functional independencies in fuzzy databases based on hedge algebras. Journal of Computer and Cybernetics, T.24, S.1 (2008)

Primacy of Fuzzy Relational Databases
Based on Hedge Algebras

Le Ngoc Hung[1] and Vu Minh Loc[2(✉)]

[1] Sai Gon University, Ho Chi Minh City, Vietnam
lengochungsg291958@gmail.com
[2] Gia Dinh University of Information Technology, Ho Chi Minh City, Vietnam
vuminhloc@gmail.com

Abstract. Databases (DB) based on fuzzy set (FST), possibility (PT) and extended possibility theory (EPT)…which have many problems that need to be discussed in capturing, representing, storing and manipulating with fuzzy data because these approaches have difficulty implementing. Fuzzy relational databases based on hedge algebras (HA) have approach naturally. So, we will not worry about representing, storing and manipulating fuzzy data. In this paper we will investigate fuzzy relational database based on hedge algebras to clarify three primacies of which: easy to present, update and query data.

1 Introduction

About twenty years ago, prof. Nguyen Cat Ho discovered that linguistic variable domain have computing structure and after that built Hedge Algebras (HA) successfully (see [1]). HA is a new approach to implement more effective on some "hot" fields now such that fuzzy control, fuzzy reason, collect fuzzy knowledge and fuzzy databases…

DB is a field that has been applied in fact widely and deeply and so scientists are very interested in it. Many cases in fact, human have to store and handle fuzzy information. For this reason, fuzzy databases are user's urgent requirement beside classical databases. As mentioned above, the scientists have developed many approaches to fuzzy databases because they desire to implement fuzzy application as soon as possible. In that approaches, EPT emerged as the best approach, however, it has not reached the desired results yet. Concretely, in EPT, data values of fuzzy attribute domain are possibility distributes and must associate with resemblance relations. This idea in theory seems to be optimal, but when we deploy this model that will encounter obstacles. Regardless of aspect of the "rather hard" in capturing the semantics of fuzzy data, just focus on the fuzzy data representation, we'll see, what will we do with a database consists of many attributes and (or) tuples? The answer is that we have to build the resemblance relation table that has a lot of columns and rows (up to hundred or thousand …). It is very bulky and not factual.

Fuzzy databases based on hedge algebras having better capturing, presenting, storing and manipulating method than the others because hedge algebras capture fuzzy data naturally and it is flexible enough to represent the inherent natural meaning of

P.C. Vinh et al. (Eds.): ICTCC 2014, LNICST 144, pp. 292–305, 2015
DOI: 10.1007/978-3-319-15392-6_28

fuzzy data. Furthermore, HA is a rich math structure enough to build the tools for manipulating with fuzzy data effectively.

The rest of this paper will be organized as follows: Section 2 will represent the basis concepts of HA, Section 3 will represents the fuzzy database model based on HA, Section 4, Section 5 and Section 6 respectively will present the advantages of the approach based on HA in three aspects, representing, querying and updating data, section 7 is the conclusion of the article.

2   Some Definitions in HA

Definition 2.1 [1]

The Hedge Algebra is denoted by $AX = (X, G, H, \leq)$, where X is a value domain of a linguistic variable.

- G is the set of generators and constants, $G = (0, c^-, w, c^+, 1)$, where 0, w, 1 are constants expressing the smallest element, the largest element and the neutral element in X; c^- and c^+ are the negative generator and positive generator.

- H is the set of hedges that is considered as the unary operations acting on each term in X, $H = H^- \cup H^+$. $H^+ = \{h_1,..., h_p\}$ and $H^- = \{h_{-1}, ..., h_{-q}\}$, $p, q > 1$ are the set of positive hedges and set of negative hedges respectively. They are ordered as follows $h_1 <...< h_p$ và $h_{-1} < ...< h_{-q}$.

($\leq$) relation is induced from semantic relations on X. We call each linguistic value x of X is a term in the hedge algebra. If the set X and H is the linear ordering, then $AX = (X, G, H, \leq)$ called linear hedge algebra.

Example 2.1

Let's consider linguistic variable "speed", this linguistic variable can receive the linguistic values that are terms such as *fast, slow, very slow, rather fast, very fast, rather slow* ... and they constitute values domain of speed variable.

In here, with the order relation induced from the natural semantics as follows: very slow < rather slow < slow < rather fast < fast < very fast. Thus, we have the HA: G= $\{0, c^- = slow, w, c^+ = fast, 1\}$; $H = \{h^- = possible, h^+ = very\}$.

Fast, slow, very slow, rather fast, very fast, rather slow are terms in X.

Definition 2.2 [2]

$AX = (X, G, C, H, \leq)$ is a HA.

A mapping $f_m: X \to [0, 1]$ is called a fuzziness measure (abbreviated fm) of the terms in X if:

1. $fm(c^-) + fm(c^+) = 1$ and $\sum_{h \in H} fm(hu) = fm(u)$, with $\forall u \in X$; in this case, fm is called complete.

2. With constants 0, W and 1 we have $fm(0) = fm(W) = fm(1) = 0$;

3. With $\forall$ x, y $\in$ X, $\forall$h $\in$ H, $\dfrac{fm(hx)}{fm(x)} = \dfrac{fm(hy)}{fm(y)}$, this ratio does not depend on

fm (x), fm(y). It is fuzzy measure of h and denoted by $\mu(h)$.

Clause 2.2 [2]

Each fuzziness measure fm on X, the following assertions are true:

1. $fm(hx) = \mu(h)fm(x)$, với $\forall$ x $\in$ X;
2. $fm(c^-) + fm(c^+) = 1$;
3. $\sum_{-q\le i\le p, i\ne 0} fm(h_i c) = fm(c)$, c$\in${$c^-,c+$};
4. $\sum_{-q\le i\le p, i\ne 0} fm(h_i x) = fm(x)$;
5. $\sum_{-q\le i\le -1}\mu(h_i) = \alpha$ and $\sum_{-q\le i\le -1}\mu(h_i) = \beta$,$\alpha,\beta > 0$ and $\alpha+\beta=1$.

Definition 2.3 [2]

A Sign function: X $\rightarrow$ {-1, 0, 1} is a mapping defined recursively as follows: for h, h ' $\in$ H and c $\in$ {c-, c +}:

1. $Sign(c^-) = -1$, $Sign(c^+) = +1$;
2. Sign (hc) = - Sign (c), if h is negative for c, in contrast to Sign (hc) = + Sign (c);
3. Sign (h'hx) = - Sign (hx), if h'hx $\ne$ hx and h' is negative for h;Sign (h'hx) = + Sign (hx), if h'hx $\ne$ hx and h' is positive for h;
4. Sign (h'hx) = 0 if h'hx = hx.

Definition 2.4 [2]

AX = (X, G, C, He, $\Sigma\Phi$, $\le$) is a HA(complete linear hedge algebra).

A mapping υ: X $\rightarrow$ [0, 1] is called semantic quantitative mapping (abbreviated SQM) of AX, the following assertions are true:

1. υ is the 1 - 1 mapping from X on [0, 1] and maintain order on X. With $\forall$ x, y $\in$ X, x <y $\Rightarrow\upsilon(x) <\upsilon$ (y) and υ (0) = 0, υ (1) = 1, with 0, 1 $\in$ c;
2. $\forall$ x $\in$ X, υ (Φ x) = infimum υ (H (x)) and υ (Σ x) = supremum υ (H (x)).

Definition 2.5 [2, 4, 5]

With fm is a fuzziness measure on X, A mapping υ: X $\rightarrow$ [0, 1] induced by fm on X that is defined as follows:

1. $\upsilon(W) = \theta = fm(c^-)$, $\upsilon(c^-) = \theta - \alpha fm(c^-) = \beta fm(c^-)$, $\upsilon(c^+) = \theta + \alpha fm(c^+)$;

$2. \upsilon(h_j x) = \upsilon(x) + \text{Sign}(h_j x)\{ \sum_{i=\text{Sign}(j)}^{j} fm(h_i x) - \omega(h_j x) fm(h_j x) \}$; with $j \in$

$\{j: -q \leq j \leq p \text{ and } j \neq 0\}(*)$ and $\omega(h_j x) = \dfrac{1}{2}[1 + \text{Sign}(h_j x)\text{Sign}(h_p h_j x)(\beta - \alpha)] \in$

$\{\alpha, \beta\}; 1+\text{Sgn}(hjx)\, j-\text{Sign}(j)1-\text{Sgn}(hj\, x)\, j-\text{Sign}(j);$

$3.\ \upsilon(\Phi c^-) = 0,\ \upsilon(\Sigma c^-) = \theta = \upsilon(\Phi c^+),\ \upsilon(\Sigma c^+) = 1,\ \forall j \text{ like } (*),$

$$\upsilon(\Phi h_j x) = \upsilon(x) + \text{Sign}(h_j x)\{ \sum_{i=\text{Sign}(j)}^{j-\text{Sign}(j)\frac{1+Sgn(h_j x)}{2}} \mu(h_i)\, fm(x) \}$$

$$\upsilon(\Sigma h_j x) = \upsilon(x) + \text{Sign}(h_j x)\{ \sum_{i=\text{Sign}(j)}^{j-\text{Sign}(j)\frac{1-Sgn(h_j x)}{2}} \mu(h_i)\, fm(x) \}$$

3   Fuzzy Relational Databases Approach Based on Hedge Algebra

Under this approach, a relational database schema with fuzzy data is a set DB = {U, $R_1, R_2, ..., R_m$, Const}, here, U = $A_1, ... A_n$ is the universe of properties; R_i is a relational schema; Const is a set of data constraints on the DB.

Each R_i can include two attribute groups, the first group contains the common attributes (classical attributes), the second group contain the fuzzy attributes. Each fuzzy attribute can be viewed as a linguistic variable and value domain of which contains linguistic values (they constitute a hedge algebra) and real values. If A_i is the fuzzy attribute then the value domain of it is $D(A_i)$ = FDom $(A_i) \cup DA_i$ in which FDom (A_i) is a set of linguistic values, DA_i is the set of normal real values.

FDom (A_i) can receive fuzzy data in common types as follows:

Type 1: fuzzy linguistic data (a very young age)

Type 2: data of interval (the age of a man in (20, 30))

Type 3: undefined data (do not know a student that has a phone number or not?)

Type 4: missing data (my boss will pay me salary but do not know exactly the figure of salary)

Type 5: data is a limited set of certain values (ages is in{31, 33, 35})

Type 6: "do not know" (unknown) data (they have been married but do not know if they have children or not)

To perform comparative operations among fuzzy terms, we have to establish a method of converting semantic representation of linguistic values to the corresponding values over the field of real numbers.

First, we will study the method of representing fuzzy data of type 1, this method will be the basis for representing other type of fuzzy data.

Suppose that attribute A is associated with a ComLin-HA AX = (X, G, C, He, $\Sigma\Phi$, $\leq$) and FDom(A) is a finite subset of X. Set d = k (A), is the maximum length of the terms in FDom (A).With fm is the fuzziness measure given of AX. So set of J_k, k = 1, ..., d, and SQM υ induced from fm can be determined.

Based on the structure of ComLin-HAS, all $x \in$ linguistic data FDom (A) can be expressed through two semantic components:

(1) a semantic value from the domain of DA;

(2) a finite set of neighbors based on fuzzy intervals.

The first semantic component is determined easily since it is just the value $\upsilon_A(x)$.

To determine the second semantic component more difficult, suppose that x is presented as follows: $x = k_{m-1} \ldots k_1 c$, $c \in G$, which means that it has m length. Second semantic component of x is a semantic neighbor systems denoted $Neig^d_{fm}(x)$, here $d = k(A) \geq m$ and fm is a fuzziness measure that was given. For each k, $1 \leq k \leq d$, neighbor of x in $Neig^d_{fm}(x)$ will be determined based on the adjacent k-intervals and is called the k-level neighbor.

To define this concept, we need some concepts as follows:

Denote $H_1 = \{h_i, h_{\cdot j} \in H: 1 \leq i \leq [p/2] \ \& \ 1 \leq j \leq [q/2]\}$ includes "weak" hedges and $H_2 = \{h_i, h_{\cdot j} \in H: [p/2] < i \leq p \ \& \ [q/2] < j \leq q\}$ includes "strong" hedges and $INT_k(H_n) = \{\mathfrak{I}_k(h_i y) \in J_k: y \in X_{k-1}, h_i \in H_n\}$, n = 1, 2. Obviously, $INT_k(H_1) \cap INT_k(H_2) = \varnothing$ và $INT_k(H_1) \cup INT_k(H_2) = J_k$ is the set of all k-intervals.

Two intervals $\mathfrak{I}_k(x)$ and $\mathfrak{I}_k(y)$ in $INT_k(H_n)$ are called the connected if there is a string of consecutive k-level fuzziness intervals belong $INT_k(H_n)$ to interconnect $\mathfrak{I}_k(x)$ and $\mathfrak{I}_k(y)$.

In this case, $\mathfrak{I}_k(x)$ is called connected in $INT_k(H_n)$ with every points in $\mathfrak{I}_k(y)$.

Denote k* is a positive integer number that refer to the maximum length of every values on D(A); $|x| \leq k^*$ is the maximum length of linguistic values of x, put j = $|x|$; $\mathfrak{I}(x)$ is a interval of level k contain x through υ mapping; X_k is the set of linguistic values of k-length; U is a universe of attributes in the databases.

  a. If k = j: $O_{min, k(x)} = \mathfrak{I}_{k+1}(h_{-1}x) \cup \mathfrak{I}_{k+1}(h_1 x)$;

  b. If $1 \leq k < j$: $O_{min, k(x)} = \mathfrak{I}_j(x)$;

  c. If $j + 1 \leq j \leq k^*$: $O_{min, k(x)} = \mathfrak{I}_{k+1}(GCP) \cup \mathfrak{I}_{k+1}(h_{l'}x)$, with l, l' $\in \{-q, p\}$.

Put H_1 is the set of "weak hedges" and H_2 is the set of "strong hedges". Concretely, $H_1 = \{h_i, h_j \mid 1 \leq i \leq [p/2], 1 \leq j \leq [q/2]\}$, $H_2 = \{\{h_i, h_j \mid [p/2] \leq i \leq p, [q/2] \leq j \leq q\}$.

Put $I_{k+1}(H_n) = \{\mathfrak{I}_{k+1}(h_i y) \mid y \in x_k, h_i \in H_n\}$, with n = 1, 2.

Every two intervals $\mathfrak{I}_{k+1}(x)$ and $\mathfrak{I}_{k+1}(y)$ in $I_{k+1}(H_n)$ are called connected to each other if existing the $I_{k+1}(H_n)$ interrupted intervals from $\mathfrak{I}_{k+1}(x)$ to $\mathfrak{I}_{k+1}(y)$. This relation decompose $I_{k+1}(H_n)$ to connected components.

Denote C is cluster of k-level similar intervals with linguistic values x, C will be determined as follows: with $I_{k+1}(H_1) = \{\mathfrak{I}_{k+1}(h_i y) \mid y \in X_k, h_i \in H_1\}$ put C = $\{\mathfrak{I}_{k+1}(h_i y) \mid h_i \in H_1\}$.

With $I_{k+1}(H_1) = \{J_{k+1}(h_i y) \mid y \in X_k, h_i \in H_2\}$, assuming $X_k = \{x_s \mid s = 0, \ldots, m-1\}$ consist of m elements be arranged in a sequence so that $x_i < x_j$ if i < j

$H_2^- = H_2 \cap H^-$ and $H_2^+ = H_2 \cap H^+$. The clusters are generated of the fuzziness intervals of $I_{k+1}(H_2)$ with the following three types:

  a. Clusters on the left x_0: put C:= $\{\mathfrak{I}_{k+1}(h_i x_0) \mid h_i \in H_2^+\}$.

  b. Clusters of the right x_{m-1}: put C:= $\{\mathfrak{I}_{k+1}(h_i x_{m-1}) \mid h_i \in H_2^+\}$.

  c. Clusters in between x_s and x_{s+1} with s = 0, ..., m-2 dependent on SGN ($h_p x_s$) and the Sgn ($h_p x_s + 1$):

$C = \{\mathcal{I}_{k+1}(h_i x_s),\ \mathcal{I}_{k+1}(h'_j x_{s+1})\ |\ h_i \in H_2^+,\ h'_j \in H_2^-\}$, if $Sgn(h_p x_s) = +1$ and $Sign(h_p x_{s+1}) = +1$;

$C = \{\mathcal{I}_{k+1}(h_i x_s),\ \mathcal{I}_{k+1}(h'_j x_{s+1})\ |\ h_i \in H_2^+,\ h'j \in H_2^+\}$, if $Sgn(h_p x_s) = +1$ and $Sign(h_p x_{s+1}) = +1$;

$C = \{\mathcal{I}_{k+1}(h_i x_s),\ \mathcal{I}_{k+1}(h'_j x_{s+1})\ |\ h_i \in H_2^-,\ h'_j \in H_2^-\}$, if $Sgn(h_p x_s) = +1$ and $Sign(h_p x_{s+1}) = +1$;

$C = \{\mathcal{I}_{k+1}(h_i x_s),\ \mathcal{I}_{k+1}(h'_j x_{s+1})\ |\ h_i \in H_2^-,\ h'j \in H_2^+\}$, if $Sgn(h_p x_s) = +1$ and $Sign(h_p x_{s+1}) = +1$.

Set of All cluster C is denoted ©.

Definition 3.1

Each $C \in ©$, we determine the interval at k-level corresponding to C as follows:

Put $S_k(C) = \cup\ \{\mathcal{I}_{k+1}\ |\ \mathcal{I}_{k+1} \in C\}$;

The interval representation of other fuzzy data types will be represented as follows:

Type 2: Each interval value [a, b] is represented by a set contain [a, b]. we have $\theta_{min,k}(x)$ ([a, b]) = {[a, b]} because [a, b] is not fuzzy data, with $\forall\ k \leq k^*$ and $Neig^d_{fm}(x) = \{[a, b]\}$.

Type 3: Each value will represent by the $\varnothing$ set, so $\theta_{i,k}(inapplicable) = \{\varnothing\}$, with $\forall\ k \leq k^*$ and $Neig^d_{fm}(inapplicable) = \{\varnothing\}$.

Type 4: Each value of this data type can receive any value in attribute domain. For this view, $\theta_{min,k}(missing) = \{[a, b]\ |\ a \in D_A\}$, with $\forall\ k \leq k^*$ and $Neig^d_{fm}(missing) = \{[a, b]\ |\ a \in D_A\}$.

Type 5: Each value of this data type can receive any value in $P \subseteq D_A$ but do not know exactly. Similar to type 4, $\theta_{i,k}(P) = \{[a, b]\ |\ a \in P\}$, $\forall k \leq k^*$ and $Neig^d_{fm}(P) = \{[a, b]\ |\ a \in P\}$.

Type 6: Each value of this data type can be considered as combination of data type 4 and data type 5. So, $Neig^d_{fm}(unknown) = \{\varnothing, [a, b]\ |\ a \in D_A\}$.

Clause 3.1 [2]

For AX is a linear complete hedge algebra of attribute A, H^+ and H^- have at least two hedges, the fuzziness quantitative parameters defined by definition 2.4. We have:

a. For each k, $\{S_k(u)\ |\ u \in X \cup C\}$ is determined uniquely and is a partition of [0, 1]

b. For all x, u $\in X \cup C$, if $\varphi(x) \in S_k(u)$ then $O_{min,\ k}(x) \subseteq S_k(u)$.

Definition 3.2 [2]

For linear complete HA, AX and the fuzziness measure, fm. Suppose that φ_A is a quantitative semantic function on AX and for each k, where $1 < k < k^*$, S_k is k-level similar relation on D_A. Meanwhile, with two tuples t and s on U, the two values t[A] and s[A] on the value domain are called k-level equal that denoted by t[A] = $_{fm, k}$ s[A] or t[A] = $_k$ s[A], if existing a equivalence class $S_k(u)$ of S_k so that $O_{min, k}(t[A]) \subseteq S_k(u)$ and $O_{min, k}(s[A]) \subseteq S_k(u)$.

Definition 3.3 [2]

With t and s are two tuples on U. We write t[A_i] = $_{v, k}$s[A_i] (k-level equal) if the following conditions are true:

1. If t[A_i], s[A_i] $\in$ D_{A_i} then t[A_i] = s[A_i];

2. If only one of two t[A_i] or s[A_i] is linguistic data, assume that t[A_i], then s[A_i] $\in$ $S_k(t[A_i])$.

To be able to compare the two values in the domain of a linguistic attribute as well as comparing the value of the two tuples on a set of attributes we have the following two definitions:

Definition 3.4 [2]

With two tuples t, s as in definition 3.2:

1. if $S_k(t[A_i]) < S_k(s[A_i])$ then t[A_i] $<_{v, k}$s[A_i] ;
2. If $S_k(t[A_i]) > S_k(s[A_i])$ then t[A_i] $>_{v, k}$s[A_i] ;
3. t[A_i] = $_{v, k}$s[A_i] or $S_k(t[A_i]) < S_k(s[A_i])$ then t[Ai] £u, ks[Ai];
   if t[A_i] = $_{v, k}$s[A_i] or $S_k(t[A_i]) > S_k(s[A_i])$ then t[A_i]$\geq_{v, k}$s[A_i].

Example 3.1

Let's consider the schema in a fuzzy database of garment shop, R_1= {Itemcode, Brand, Importprice, Status, Saleprice }.

We have Brand, Importprice, Status, Saleprice are fuzzy attributes, itemcode was common attribute.

Table 1. The instance of R_1

Itemcode	Importprice	Status	Saleprice
A001	5	Rather old	Rather High
Q001	Very low	Old	17
A002	9	New	High
A003	8	Possible New	13

4   Primacy in Presenting Fuzzy Data

It can be said that data representation is a key factor that determine the meaning, feasibility and value of a database model because data representation will facilitate or block the construction of data manipulation operations and manipulation operations decide queries issue as well as update database.

In [11] summarize five common approaches to represent fuzzy data as follows:

Table 2. Summarize five common approaches to representing fuzzy data

Approach	Grade of membership	Values of attributes	Elements of domain
Fuzzy relation	*		
Similarity relation		*	
Possibility		* *	
Extended Possibility		* * *	* * *
Aggregation	* *	* *	

Note, the more * appearing, the more database model spreading. Thus, the database model based on extended possibility emerges as a best model.

The basic idea of the fuzzy relational database model based on extended possibility as follows: relation r on the relational schema R_i is a subset of the $\Pi(D_1) \times \Pi(D_2) \times \ldots \Pi(D_n)$, $\Pi(D_i)$ is the possibility distributions on the value domain D_i of the attribute A_i. So every n tuple will have the form $(\pi_{A_1}, \pi_{A_2} \ldots \pi_{An})$ with $\pi_{Ai} \in \Pi(D_i)$. Besides, each R_i is combined with a resemblance

If a relation consist a lot of tuples (hundreds of, thousands or even tens of thousands of tuples ....), it's clear which showed weaknesses of data representation problem under this model because all fuzzy values of each attribute, therefore it will be "wordy" and "downright frustrating" when to express a fuzzy value . For example, to express the age of the person belongs interval "from 30 to 40 years old" people can apply part of possibilities is {0.8/30, 0.7/31... 0.1/40}, Conspicuously, if fuzzy value interval is greater than the its express chain will be longer and more complex. Additionally, with each relational schema included m attribute will have m tables of two-dimensional (otherwise known as the two-dimensional matrix), each table used to represent close relationship between elements under range of values of a properties.

Such a data representation in scalability theoretical approaches (more general fuzzy set theory) complex which will lead to the complexity of data manipulation operations.

Two matching basic operations with fuzzy data included semantics inclusion operations and semantically equivalent operations that proposal [6] and some other documents shall be determined as follows:

$$SID_\alpha(\pi_A, \pi_B) = \sum_{i,j=1}^{n} \min_{u_i, u_i \in U \text{ và } Res_{\Pi}(u_i, u_i) \geq \alpha} (\pi_B(u_i), \pi_A(u_j)) \Big/ \sum_{i=1}^{n} \pi_B(u_i) \ (\#)$$

and

$$SED_\alpha(\pi_A, \pi_B) = \min(SID_\alpha(\pi_A, \pi_B), SID_\alpha(\pi_B, \pi_A)) \ (\# \#)$$

In that, $SID_\alpha(\pi_A, \pi_B)$, $SED_\alpha(\pi_A, \pi_B)$respectively semantics inclusion measure and semantic equivalent measure of between the two possibility distribute π_A, π_B; Res denote closely relationship

Obviously, data representation in efficient leads to complex of operations for data matching.

The representation of fuzzy data in fuzzy databases by hedge algebra approach very natural and simple but very true to the inherent nature of the fuzzy data exist in the real world. Fuzzy data representation in this way is called "correct name" and understand the "true nature" because it was "obtained directly" from spec database when the user's observation and quantification of fuzzy data, so it may says, has not where which fuzzy data representation yet more simple and more brief.

For example, when surveying the material world consideration in any context, the observed object are evaluated as "small" or "very small"...That assessment is essentially fuzzy quantification is represented by fuzzy terms - the fuzzy data representation by hedge algebra approach - in the fuzzy database.

Such back to the above example to represents one's age ranged from 30 to 40, just use term " rather young" in that "rather" be a hedge and "young" be a generate element belong to a hedge algebra which is defined before.

Like that represents fuzzy data of simple and it's also simple when manipulating fuzzy data. By semantics quantitative mapping v(x), terms x from its fuzzy representations will be moved into fuzzy interval - semantics neighboring of x, it's as a topological included v(x) - semantics value x via mapped v(.) still ensures that the inherent semantics order. This allows us to build similar relationships level k between fuzzy terms, from which building operations "$=_k$", "$\leq_k$", "$\geq_k$", "$\neq_k$" to manipulate with fuzzy data easily available form and content like operations in relational database environment classics.

5   Primacy in Data Queries

The design goal of these databases is intended to serve for data query. Query data on the fuzzy relational database was difficult and almost cannot be done for the queries not is built according the hedge algebra approach because The design goal of these databases are intended to serve for data query. Query data on the fuzzy relational database was difficult and almost cannot be done for the queries not is built according the hedge algebra approach because it's very complex for manipulation of matching operations.

We review follow scalability theoretical approach on the example 3.1. Relation R above will be transformed into the following table:

Itemcode	Importprice	Status	Saleprice
A	{0.3/2;0.7/3;0.5/4}	{0.8/2;0.7/3;0.6/4}	{1.0/5}
Q	{1.0/9}	{0.3/5;0.7/6;0.8/7}	{0.3/6;0.6/7;0.7/6}
A	{1.0/58}	{0.4/5;0.7/6;0.5/7}	{1.0/71}

Suppose now we need to make the query "find items priced high" (Query number 2).

To perform this query, we performances a fuzzy term "priced high" as a possibility distribution, then indicates a threshold α which to the tuples satisfy the query conditions.

Next we have to browse through the tuples in the relations and to compute the SED follow the Formula (#, #......)

And in the computing process we have to reference the threshold at each table corresponds closely related......too so complex and not friendly!

At another query "Find items priced lower high" (Ex.1) with this query was almost impossible to accomplish because the comparison operations "less than" or "greater than" between two distribution capabilities are difficult to define.

On the contrary, for queries on the fuzzy relational database which follow the hedge algebra approach, things become much easier can confirm it meets most of fuzzy queries. Indeed, by the matching operations is constructed based on the "k level of close relations", a query in a fuzzy relational database follow the hedge algebra approach can be transformed into classic query (Theorem 3.2, 3.3 and 3.4).

Now we consider the database given by following table:

Example 5.1. The database as in Example 3.1 on Hedge algebra approach

Itemcode	Importprice	Status	Saleprice
A	Very low	Old	5
Q	9	New	High
A	58	Possible New	71

The Importprice and Saleprice properties are linguistic variables with Dom (Importprice), Dom (Saleprice) defined on the same interval [1, 100] (from \$ 1 to \$ 100).

The Hedge Algebra corresponding is defined with the following parameters

Elements generated: {low high | low <high}, negative hedges H¯= {possible, rather | possible < Rather}, positive hedges H^+ = {more, very | more< very}

Put fm(low) = 0.4, fm(High) = 0.6; μ(possible) = 0.15, μ(Rather) = 0.25, μ(more) = 0.2, μ(very) = 0.4.

The status property is a linguistic variable with Dom (status) is defined of over interval [0, 10]

The Hedge Algebra corresponding is defined with the following parameters

Elements generated: {Old, New | Old < New},

Negative hedges H¯= {Possible, Rather | possible < Rather}, positive hedges H^+ = {more, very | more< very}

Put fm(Old) = 0.4, fm(New) = 0.6; m(possible) = 0.15, m(Rather) = 0.25, m(more) = 0.2, m(very) = 0.4.

With query (Ex.1), we will do the following:

Suppose the query is done with the same rate k = 2;

$\upsilon_{saleprice, r}$ (high) = fm (low) + fm (high) * α = (0.4 + 0.6 * 0.4) * (100-1) = 63.36;

$\theta_{2,Importprice, r}$ (high) = $\mathcal{S}_r$(Possible high) $\cup \mathcal{S}_r$(rather high) = ((fm (high) - μ (possible) fm (high)), (fm (high) + μ (more) fm (high)] = (0.6 - 0:15 * 0.6, 0.6 + 0.2 * 0.6] * (100-1) = (50.49, 71.28]

see, t3 [Saleprice] = 71 $\in \theta_{2, Saleprice, r}$ (high) and thus the tuple second t2, and tuple 3rd, t3 satisfy the query conditions.

With query (Ex. 2) was easily accomplished thanks to the results of the query above and theorems. The first tuple, t1, with t1 [Saleprice] = 5, $\theta_{2, Importprice, r}$ (5) = [5, 5] $< \theta_{2,Importprce, r}$ (high) first tuple is inferred as a result of query

Through this example, we see that the queries on the fuzzy relational database which is done base on hedge algebra approach with simple manipulation but with high efficiency.

6   Primacy in Updating Data

Fuzzy database model, only really practical applications when we solve radically the problem updated. It's "depending on the way the fuzzy data semantic is represented in databases and on which concepts of the comparison between the data of different types, including fuzzy data, can be defined" [18]. Fuzzy database model approach based on hedge algebra enables unified data type in fuzzy attributes by taking into concept of level k similar relationships. It's has made the data manipulation becomes simpler very much by the alternative approaches. The unified fuzzy data on each property makes for fuzzy data manipulation similar to the traditional data manipulation. This advantage is the basis for we can build update operations.

In order to show the advantages of the approach based on hedge algebra for the updating fuzzy database we again compare it with fuzzy database update problems follows scalability theoretical approach.

In general, the update solutions approached based on scalability theory which the authors the article made, in our opinion, have not been resolved even on issue theoretically. The following shows its weakness

First, let's insert only be done with prerequisite condition the key must to be certain (the key include only certain properties), zoning such conditions, clearly it's diminish the meaning of fuzzy database.

Second, if to transfer the scheme becomes which has its normal form higher 2NF then "insertion strategy" will "There's no meaning" because it has become insert operate in the classic relational schema.

Third, the delete operations done based on the query, but as analyzed above, queries are made in this model unfavorable, as thus infer the delete operation not be smooth implementation .

Fourth, repair operation done through two of operations insertion and deletion so it will not has been well implementation.

The following examples show the superiority of the update data operations in the fuzzy database relational model which the approach based on hedge algebra.

Example 6.1

Reconsider example 3.1.

Itemcode	Importprice	Status	Saleprice
A	Very low	Old	5
Q	9	New	High
A	58	Possible new	71

Pack all the tuples in the relations r [R1], respectively t1, t2 and t3. In the relational schema exists

FFDs R1: f = { Importprice, Status } →ₐSaleprice

With the updated requirements:

-To Add (insert) tuple of p = <A, 3.5, old, 7> in relations (CN1).
-To Remove (deletion) the tuples has saleprice smaller "rather high" out of relationship (CN2).
-To repair the value of saleprice of the tuples has value at importprice from "very low" to "low" (CN3)

With the request: CN1

I need to check to see p satisfied f ?
Since p [Importprice] = 3 ≠ (t2 [Importprice] and t3 [Importprice]), so we check if p [Importprice] =ₐt1 [very low]?.

We have $v_{\text{Imporprice, r}}$ (low) = β * fm (low) = 0.6 * 0.4 * 10 = 2.4; $\theta_{2, r}$ (low) = $\Im_r$(Rather low) $\cup \Im_r$(Possible low) = ($v_{\text{Importprice , r}}$ (low) - fm (Rather low), $v_{\text{Importprice, r}}$ (low) + fm (Possible low)] = ((2.4 - 0.2 * 0.4, 2.4 * 0.4 + 0:15]) * 10 = (1.6, 3]. 3.5 ∉ (1.6, 3]

So p [Importprice ≠₂ t1 [very low], infer p {Importprice, Status other level 2 with t1} {Importprice , Status}, {Importprice t2, and t3} Status {Importprice, Status}

Conclusion: p satisfied FFDs f, thus p is inserted into the above system.
Result after inserted:

Itemcode	Importprice	Status	Saleprice
A	Very low	Old	5
Q	9	New	High
A	58	Possible new	71
A	3.5	Old	7

With the request CN2

The tuples are deleted, which will been satisfied with (Ex.2), that is, the first tuple in relation R will be deleted.
Result after Deletion:

Itemcode	Importprice	Status	Saleprice
Q	9	New	High
A	58	Possible new	71

With the request CN3

The tuple satisfy the repair condition was the first tuple, t1 = <Very old, old, 5>, we have 2 q, r (low) = (1.6, 3]. t1 [Importprice] = 5, so it is changed becomes the value belong to (1.6, 3], and the value is proposed u GIANHAP, r (low) = 2.4.

Result after Deletion:

Itemcode	Importprice	Status	Saleprice
A	Very low	Old	2.4
Q	9	New	High
A	58	Possible new	71

7   Conclusion

It's been several years, fuzzy databases with different approaches have tried to resolve the problems in capturing, representing and manipulating fuzzy detain order to approach practical applications, but results is seem to be hard to reach because theories is not tune to practice.

HA was built to open new approach to fuzzy databases effectively. By natural way to capture the meaning of fuzzy data – linguistic term, we can say that HA is flexible and strong enough to represent fully fuzzy data meaning.

Order to process linguistic terms, a linguistic value x can present by two semantic elements, first, semantic value of x through a sematic quantitative mapping v, second, family of neighbors based on fuzzy intervals of x. From this base can build similar relation level k on the domain which was embedded in HA of fuzzy attribute This relation determine update operators which allow us to manipulate on fuzzy values effectively. This determines primacy of fuzzy databases based on HA considering aspects following as representing, querying, updating fuzzy data. This paper analyzed and evaluated to provide outlook onto primacy of fuzzy databases based on HA.

References

1. Ho, N.C., Wechler, W.: Hedge algebras: An algebraic approach to structures of sets of linguistic domains of linguistic truth variable. Fuzzy Sets and Systems 35(3), 281–293 (1990)
2. Ho, N.C., Lan, V.N.: Hedge Algebras – An Oder – based Structure of Terms – Domains: An Algebraic Approach to Human Reasoning
3. Ho, N.C., Lan, V.N.: Hedge algebras: an algebraic approach to domains of linguistic variables and their applicability
4. Nguyen, C.H.: Fuzzy Relational Database with Linguistic Data – Part II: Fuzzy Functional Dependencies, Fuzzy Sets and Systems

5. Ho, N.C.: Linguistic Databases: Relational Model and Hedge-Algebra-Based Linguistic Data Semantics
6. Nakata, M., Murai, T.: Updating under integrity constraints in fuzzy databases. In: Proc. Sixth IEEE Conf. on Fuzzy Systems (FUZZ-IEEE 1997), pp. 713–719. IEEE, Barcelona (1997)
7. Raiju, K.V.S.V.N., Majumdar, A.K.: Fuzzy functional dependencies and lossless join decomposition of fuzzy relational database system. ACM Trans. Databases Syst. **13**, 129–166 (1988)
8. Ma, Z.M., Yan, L.: Updating Extended Possibility – Based Fuzzy Relational Databases. International Journal of Intelligent Systems **22**, 237–258 (2007)
9. Bahar, O., Yazici, A.: Normalization and Lossless Join Decomposition of Similarity-Based Fuzzy Relational Databases. International Journal of Intelligent Systems **19**, 885–917 (2004)
10. Ho, N.C., Loc, V.M., Tung, H., An, N.T.: Fuzzy functional dependencies in fuzzy relational databases with linguistic data. Journal of Science and Technology (Viet Nam) **51**(2), 137–152 (2013)
11. Bouchon – Meunier, B., Thuan, H., Ha, D.T.: Fuzzy logic and application (Vietnamese book)

Reducing Impurities in Medical Images Based on Curvelet Domain

Vo Thi Hong Tuyet[✉] and Nguyen Thanh Binh

Faculty of Computer Science and Engineering,
Ho Chi Minh City University of Technology, Ho Chi Minh City, Vietnam
vothihongtuyet.dhbk@gmail.com, ntbinh@cse.hcmut.edu.vn

Abstract. Medical image quality greatly affects the diagnostic process. Most of the tasks of increasing the quality of medical images are deblurring or denoising process. These tasks are the difficult problems in medical image processing because they must keep edge features. In the cases, the medical images that have blur combined with noise are a more difficult problem. In this paper, we proposed a method for reducing impurities in medical images based on curvelet domain. The proposed method uses curvelet coefficient combined with augmented lagrangian function to denoising combined with deblurring in medical images. For evaluating the results of the proposed method, we have compared the results with the other recent methods available in literature.

Keywords: Deblurring · Denoising · Curvelet transform · Augmented lagrangian method · Medical image.

1 Introduction

In medical fields, image becomes a useful tool for specialists. For medical images, there are many types of medical images such as plain X-ray, computed tomography (CT), nuclear medicine imaging, ultrasound, magnetic resonance imaging (MRI), etc. Most of medical images have blur, noise or pair because of many reasons such as [4] machine specification, surroundings, etc. Noise in images always makes the undesirable appearance, but the noise can cover and reduce or lose the visibility of certain features within the image. Increasing the quality of medical images becomes difficult problem for image processing.

In the past, many methods are proposed to improve the quality of images: wavelet transform [1], discrete wavelet transform (DWT) [2, 3], … Although DWT is a powerful tool signal and image analysis but it has three serious disadvantages [4]: shift sensitivity, poor directionality and lack of phase information. Several methods have provided solutions for decreasing these disadvantaged such as: contourlet transform [5], nonsubsampled contourlet transform [6, 7], ridgelet transform [8, 9], curvelet transform [10, 11], etc. The results were significantly improved when using the above methods for denosing or deblurring.

The curvelet transform, a new X-let transform multiscale transforms, is like the wavelet transform, but it has directional parameters, and contains elements with a

© Institute for Computer Sciences, Social Informatics and Telecommunications Engineering 2015
P.C. Vinh et al. (Eds.): ICTCC 2014, LNICST 144, pp. 306–319, 2015
DOI: 10.1007/978-3-319-15392-6_29

very high degree of directional specificity. The results of curvelet transform for denoising are good. In case that the medical images have noise combined with blur, the results of the above methods in some cases are not good.

Stanley [12] proposed augmented lagrangian method for deblurring or denoising. This method has given the good results, special for deblurring or denoising, but in case of blur and noise pair, this is a difficult problem. To handle this problem, deblurring process with blur and noise pair is applied.

In this paper, we proposed a method for reducing impurities in medical images based on curvelet domain. The proposed method uses curvelet coefficient combined with augmented lagrangian function to denoising combined with deblurring in medical images. For evaluating the results of the proposed method, we have compared the results with the other recent methods available in literature such as DWT [2], curvelet transform [10] and augmented lagrangian [12]. For performance measure, we have used Peak Signal to Noise ratio (PSNR) and Mean Square Error (MSE) and it has shown that the present method yields far better results.

The rest of the paper is organized as follows: in section 2, we described the basic of curvelet transform and augmented lagrangian functions; details of the proposed method are given in section 3; the results of the proposed method are presented in section 4 and our conclusions in section 5.

2   Background

2.1   Curvelet Transform

As the above mentioned, DWT has three serious disadvantages [4]: shift sensitivity, poor directionality and lack of phase information. The curvelet transform has provided solutions for decreasing these disadvantages.

Curvelets [10] are better than wavelet based transform in case of representing edges and other singularities along curves. Curvelets can be translated and dilated, similar to wavelet transform. At first decomposing the image into subbands, a curvelet's curve is displayed with width $\approx$ length^2. After decomposing, each scale is analyzed by a local ridgelet transform.

Similar to ridgelets, curvelets occur at all scales, locations, and orientations. However, while ridgelets have global length and variable widths, curvelets in addition to a variable width have a variable length and so does a variable anisotropy.

In wavelet transform, dyadic subbands are $[2^s, 2^{s+1}]$. But with discrete curvelet transform, the subbands have the nonstandard form $[2^{2s}, 2^{2s+2}]$. The basic process of the digital realization for curvelet transform is given as follows [10, 11]:

(i) Subband Decomposition. The image f is decomposed into subbands

$$f \mapsto (P_0 f, \Delta_1 f, \Delta_2 f, ...)$$

(ii) Smooth Partitionning. Each subband is smoothly windowed into "squares" of an appropriate scale (of sidelength ~2-s)

$$\Delta_s f \mapsto (w_Q \Delta_s f)_{Q \in Q_s}$$

where w_Q is a collection of smooth window localized around dyadic squares:

$$Q = [k_1 / 2^s, (k_1 + 1) / 2^s] \times [k_2 / 2^s, (k_2 + 1) / 2^s]$$

(iii) Renormalization. Each resulting square is renormalized to unit scale

$$g_Q = (T_Q)^{-1}(w_Q \Delta_s f), \qquad Q \in Q_S$$

(iv) Ridgelet Analysis. Each square is analyzed via the discrete ridgelet transform.

In this definition, the two dyadic subbands $[2^{2s}, 2^{2s+1}]$ and $[2^{2s+1}, 2^{2s+2}]$ are merged before applying the ridgelet transform.

2.2   Augmented Lagrangian Method

Stanley[12] proposed a algorithm which minimizes a total variation optimization problem for spatial-temporal data. This algorithm uses an augmented lagrangian method to solve the constrained problem. A linear shift invariant imaging system is modeled as [12]: $g = Hf + \eta$, where $f \in \mathbb{R}^{MN \times 1}$ is a vector denoting the unknown (potentially sharp) image of size M x N, $g \in \mathbb{R}^{MN \times 1}$ is a vector denoting the observed image, $\eta \in \mathbb{R}^{MN \times 1}$ is a vector denoting the noise, and the matrix $H \in \mathbb{R}^{MN \times MN}$ is a linear transformation representing convolution operation.

And the goal of image restoration is from the observed image g, algorithms will recover f. Two problems are considered as:

minimize$_f$ $\frac{\mu}{2}\|Hf - g\|^2 + \|f\|_{TV}$, which is known as the TV/L2 minimization

and

minimize$_f$ $\mu\|Hf - g\|_1 + \|f\|_{TV}$, which is known as the TV/L1 minimization.

With equations, μ is a regularization parameter. The idea of the augmented lagrangian method is to find a saddle point and the alternating direction method (ADM) can be used.

3   The Proposed Method

Medical images, which have blur combined with noise, are very difficult to increase the quality of medical image process. In this section, we propose a new approach for image deblurring, with blur combined with noise pair that based on curvelet Transform combined with augmented lagrangian method.

In the proposed method, we divide image processing with blur combined with noise pair into two processes: denoising and deblurring. The proposed method includes two processes. The proposed method can be summarized as follows:

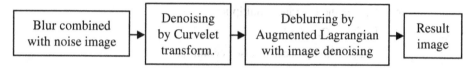

Fig. 1. The process of proposed method

Firstly, medical image denoising. The medical input images are the blur combined with noise images, we use curvelet transform for denoising the image, curvelet's process is as follows [10]:

1) apply the à trous algorithm with scales and set $b_1 = b_{min}$
2) for $j = 1, ..., j$ do
   a. partition the subband w_j with a block size b_j and apply the digital ridgelet transform to each block;
   b. if j modulo 2 = 1 then $b_{j+1} = 2b_j$;
   c. else $b_{j+1} = b_j$

The sidelength of the localizing windows is doubled at every other dyadic subband. After this step, the input images had become image denoising.

Secondly, medical image deblurring. The blur combined with noise images have removed noise in curvelet domain in the above steps. However, the blur in images are not removed more. To remove the blur, we use augmented lagrangian for the output images, which output from the previous steps.

In here, we use augmented lagrangian TV/L2 algorithm [12] to remove the blur.

The problem that we solve in TV/L2 minimization is $\min\limits_{f} imize \ \frac{\mu}{2}\|Hf - g\|^2 + \|f\|_{TV}$

The idea of augmented lagrangian [12] is to find a saddle point of L(f, u, y); then, they use the alternating direction method (ADM) to solve f-subproblem and u-subproblem, with f-subproble and u-subproblem are considered as [12]:

$$f_{k+1} = \arg\min\limits_{f} \frac{\mu}{2}\|Hf - g\|^2 - y_k^T(u_k - Df) + \frac{\rho_r}{2}\|u_k - Df\|^2$$

$$u_{k+1} = \arg\min\limits_{u} \|u\|_1 - y_k^T(u - Df_{k+1}) + \frac{\rho_r}{2}\|u - Df_{k+1}\|^2$$

where ρ_r is a regularization parameter, y is the Lagrange multiplier, u = Df. Algorithm of TV/L2 can be summarized as follows [12]:

(i) Input: vector denoting the observed image and convolution matrix.
(ii) Input: regularization parameter, the isotropic total variation.
(iii) Set parameter with value default for $\rho_r = 2$.
(iv) Compute the matrices of the first-order forward finite difference operators along the horizontal, vertical and temporal directions.
(v) With not coverge do:

   - Solve the f-subproblem.
   - Solve the u-subproblem.

- Update the Lagrange multiplier.
- Update ρ_r.
- Check convergence, if false is continue.

4   Experiments and Results

In this section, we apply the procedure described in section 3 and achieving superior performance in our deblurring experiments as demonstrated in this section. For performance evaluation, we compare the results of the proposed method based on the curvelet transform combined with Augmented Lagrangian (CT-AL) with the other methods such as Discrete Wavelet Transform (DWT), Curvelet Transform (CT) and Augmented Lagrangian method (AL).

We test the above methods in a medical image dataset. This dataset includes different images of the sizes: 256 x 256, 512 x 512. The types of blurs are used Gaussian and Motion combined with Gaussian or Speckle noises which were added to these medical images. Hard thresholding is applied to the coefficients after decomposition in curvelet domain. All of the above methods are done on the same images at similar scale.

The quality of images is inproved by comparison with the value of Mean Square Error (MSE) and Peak Signal-to-Noise Ratio (PSNR). The MSE is defined as:

$$MSE=\sqrt{\frac{1}{NxN}\sum_{i=1}^{N}\sum_{j=1}^{N}(x_{i,j}-y_{i,j})^2}$$

where x is the image which has blur and noise; y is the image result and N x N is the size of the image. The PSNR is used as the measure of the quality of the reconstruction of the image deblurring or denoising, defined as:

$$PSNR=20\log_{10}(\frac{MAX_1}{MSE})$$

where MAX_1 is the maximum pixel value of the image. The proposed method compared with DWT, CT, and AL method by the MSE and PSNR values. The smaller the value of MSE is, the better it is. The higher the value of PSNR is, the better it is. The images dataset includes more than 1000 medical images. In here, we show some test cases.

Figure 2 shows the deblurring of blur combined with noise image by Gaussian blur and Gaussian noise with our proposed method. Figure 3 shows the deblurring of blur combined with noise image by Gaussian blur and Speckle noise with our proposed method.

From Figure 2 and Figure 3 we see that the result of the proposed method is better than the other methods. Figure 4 and Figure 5 show the plot of PSNR, MSE values of different image deblurring methods corrupted with Gaussian blur combined with Gaussian noise.

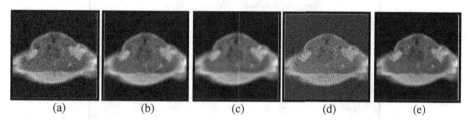

Fig. 2. Blur and noise image with Gaussian blur with Gaussian noise and deblurred images by different methods.
(a) Blur and noise image (PSNR = 21.6304 db). (b) Deblurred image by DWT (PSNR = 28.7178 db). (c) Deblurred image by CT (PSNR = 29.5102 db). (d) Deblurred image by AL (PSNR = 21.8365 db). (e) Deblurred image by CT-AL (PSNR = 30.1838 db).

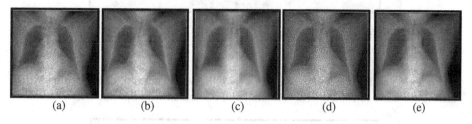

Fig. 3. Blur and noise image with Gaussian blur with Speckle noise and deblurred images by different methods.
(a) Blur and noise image (PSNR = 23.3928 db). (b) Deblurred image by DWT (PSNR = 24.8552 db). (c) Deblurred image by CT (PSNR = 25.6510 db). (d) Deblurred image by AL (PSNR = 23.9808 db). (e) Deblurred image by CT-AL (PSNR = 26.1718 db).

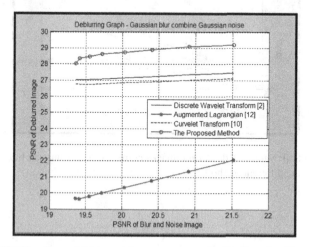

Fig. 4. Plot of PSNR values of deblurred images corrupted with Gaussian blur combined with Gaussian noise using different methods

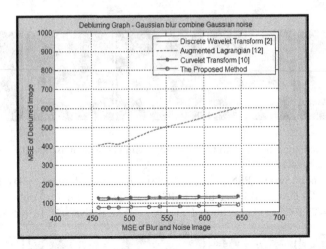

Fig. 5. Plot of MSE values of deblurred images corrupted with Gaussian blur and Gaussian noise using different methods

Figure 6 and Figure 7 show the plot of PSNR, MSE values of different image deblurring methods corrupted with Gaussian blur combined with Speckle noise.

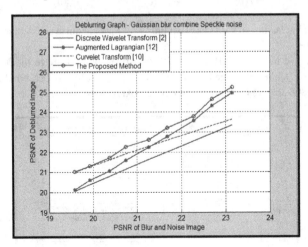

Fig. 6. Plot of PSNR values of deblurred images corrupted with Gaussian blur combined with Speckle noise using different methods

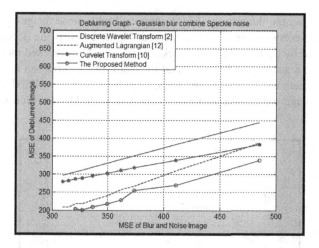

Fig. 7. Plot of MSE values of deblurred images corrupted with Gaussian blur combined with Speckle noise using different methods

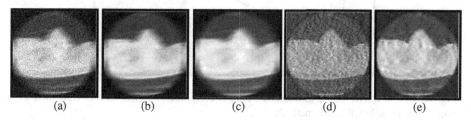

          (a)   (b)   (c)   (d)   (e)

Fig. 8. Blur and noise image with Motion blur corrupted with Gaussian noise and deblurred images by different methods.

(a) Blur and noise image (PSNR = 17.7757 db). (b) Deblurred image by DWT (PSNR = 20.0554 db). (c) Deblurred image by CT (PSNR = 20.2554 db). (d) Deblurred image by AL (PSNR = 16.9942 db). (e) Deblurred image by CT-AL (PSNR = 20.5285db).

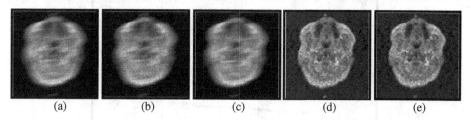

          (a)   (b)   (c)   (d)   (e)

Fig. 9. Blur and noise image with Motion blur corrupted with Speckle noise and deblurred images by different methods.

(a) Blur and noise image (PSNR = 19.8879 db). (b) Deblurred image by DWT (PSNR = 19.8937 db). (c) Deblurred image by CT (PSNR = 19.9248 db). (d) Deblurred image by AL (PSNR = 24.3089 db). (e) Deblurred image by CT-AL (PSNR = 24.7597 db).

Figure 8 shows the deblurring of blur combined with noise image by Motion blur and Gaussian noise with our proposed method. Figure 9 shows the deblurring of blur and noise image by Motion blur and Speckle noise with our proposed method.

From Figure 8 and Figure 9 we see that the result of the proposed method is better than the other methods. Figure 10 and Figure 11 show the plot of PSNR, MSE values of different image deblurring methods corrupted with Motion blur and Gaussian noise.

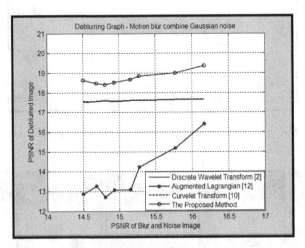

Fig. 10. Plot of PSNR values of deblurred images corrupted with Motion blur combined with Gaussian noise using different methods

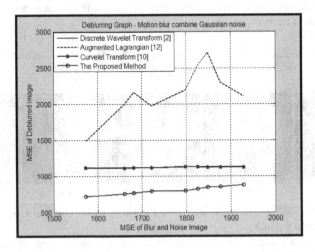

Fig. 11. Plot of MSE values of deblurred images corrupted with Motion blur combined with Gaussian noise using different methods

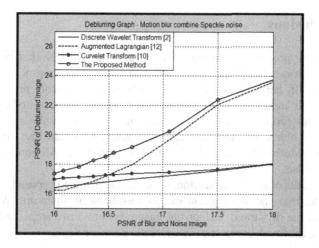

Fig. 12. Plot of PSNR values of deblurred images corrupted with Motion blur combined with Speckle noise using different methods

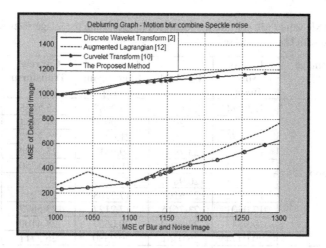

Fig. 13. Plot of MSE values of deblurred images corrupted with Motion blur combined with Speckle noise using different methods

Figure 12 and Figure 13 show the plot of PSNR, MSE values of different image deblurring methods corrupted with Motion blur and Speckle noise.

In the above figures, it is well observed that the proposed method performs better than Discrete Wavelet Transform, Curvelet Transform and Augmented Lagrangian method. We show some results in appendix.

5   Conclusions

In this paper, we propose deblurring for medical images in case that image has blur combined with noise. The proposed method is to divide into two processes: denoising and deblurring. In here, we use curvelet transform for denoising process; then, we apply augmented lagrangian method to remove blur into the result of image denoising. We test this proposed method in medical images. The results are very good in pairs: Gaussian blur combined with Gaussian noise, Gaussian blur combined with Speckle noise, Motion blur combined with Gaussian noise, Motion blur combined with Speckle noise.

From the results of the above section, we conclude that the proposed method works well and better than the other recent methods available in literature. With these results, we think the division of deblurring image pairs into two steps, and the attempt to improve the quality in every step will give the good results.

Appendix

Table A1. PSNR values (dB) of different denoised images using the image sizes with Gaussian blur combined with Gaussian noise

Test Image	Image Size	Blur & Noisy Image	DWT[2]	Augmented Lagrangian [12]	Curvelet Transform [10]	Proposed Method
1		22.9244	25.8099	23.7983	25.5685	**26.5559**
2		22.2133	24.2929	22.9969	24.3754	**25.3269**
3		21.0976	24.8965	21.6440	25.2272	**26.1492**
4		19.4362	23.7983	19.9117	23.9008	**25.0569**
5	256 x 256	18.2394	25.1596	18.1658	25.1750	**25.6090**
6		16.9048	20.9809	17.3390	20.7117	**21.6296**
7		17.5342	23.6197	17.7768	23.5211	**24.5133**
8		17.0701	23.7615	17.2127	23.5877	**24.3908**
9		19.9343	27.0370	20.0527	28.4109	**28.8235**
10		20.0474	26.0461	20.2580	26.2711	**27.2532**
11		29.1889	34.1455	30.3814	33.7877	**35.4287**
12		24.5894	25.868	26.4690	25.5396	**27.5126**
13		23.1588	24.3679	25.1043	24.0030	**26.1835**
14		26.6912	32.1044	27.6333	31.6351	**33.7255**
15	512 x 512	26.2812	32.2987	27.0246	31.8528	**33.6101**
16		22.9881	24.8190	24.7584	24.4512	**26.7523**
17		22.8137	24.9043	24.3170	24.5046	**26.5185**
18		24.0391	28.3583	25.1259	27.9272	**30.4065**
19		23.5482	29.3542	24.1043	29.0079	**30.3145**
20		20.5393	29.0540	20.6704	29.2314	**30.0370**

Table A2. PSNR values (dB) of different denoised images using the image sizes with Gaussian blur combined with Speckle noise

Test Image	Image Size	Blur & Noisy Image	DWT [2]	Augmented Lagrangian [12]	Curvelet Transform [10]	Proposed Method
1		25.3317	26.2724	26.9356	25.9678	**27.3101**
2	256 x 256	23.6729	23.8157	24.7394	24.5437	**25.4935**
3		26.5841	26.5859	28.6510	26.5935	**28.7674**
4		23.0049	23.2379	23.9696	24.0989	**25.1103**
5		22.3268	24.3122	22.7326	25.5115	**25.8778**
6		19.1728	20.1243	19.9501	20.9859	**21.8423**
7		21.7705	22.4099	22.7529	24.5911	**25.5676**
8		20.7059	21.9209	21.3406	24.7097	**25.5628**
9		25.5202	25.6334	25.7726	25.8730	**25.9703**
10		27.7495	28.0029	30.0571	28.6791	**31.0672**
11		27.5376	28.2788	27.8823	29.6975	**29.9848**
12		23.3779	24.9436	24.6555	25.3136	**26.8313**
13		22.6507	22.8481	24.2205	23.1493	**24.5772**
14		27.0762	27.5978	27.5625	28.5009	**28.7954**
15	512 x 512	31.1310	31.4597	33.0762	32.0104	**34.0305**
16		24.0044	24.1745	26.1215	24.3156	**26.4488**
17		24.0804	24.2322	26.0170	24.4191	**26.2889**
18		26.3336	26.7466	27.9941	27.0914	**28.7282**
19		26.8237	27.1567	27.5356	27.8142	**28.5943**
20		25.7610	26.0674	26.0722	26.9874	**27.2278**

Table A3. PSNR values (dB) of different denoised images using the image sizes with Motion blur combined with Gaussian noise

Test Image	Image Size	Blur & Noisy Image	DWT [2]	Augmented Lagrangian [12]	Curvelet Transform [10]	Proposed Method
1		20.6283	24.5833	18.3993	24.5046	**25.1109**
2		19.6985	21.8751	18.4899	22.0335	**23.2947**
3		16.6634	20.1343	14.3206	20.7545	**21.3162**
4		18.7020	21.3746	17.4078	21.4380	**23.5657**
5	256 x 256	20.0156	24.5744	17.3834	24.5559	**25.2453**
6		17.3715	18.8926	17.0862	18.8816	**20.5954**
7		18.3267	19.8430	18.1566	19.8492	**22.7888**
8		19.1747	20.6569	19.8055	20.6399	**23.7520**
9		23.7832	27.1146	22.1617	27.1975	**29.1118**
10		22.7712	24.2517	23.3973	24.2842	**27.2143**
11		24.3067	28.8253	22.3026	28.7308	**31.1969**
12		20.0452	21.5405	20.5063	21.5046	**24.4124**
13		18.2509	19.2933	19.7132	19.2843	**22.7128**
14	512 x 512	21.8895	25.3906	20.4410	25.3813	**28.6708**
15		22.0630	26.7441	19.8375	26.7041	**29.1133**
16		17.9709	19.4733	18.5724	19.4318	**23.0173**
17		17.9843	19.5816	18.2576	19.5591	**22.7241**

Table A3. *continued*

18		19.7384	22.9871	18.1821	22.9640	**25.9907**
19		20.4899	24.5673	18.4405	24.5432	**26.5373**
20		21.0241	26.4155	18.2516	26.4521	**28.0329**

Table A4. PSNR values (dB) of different denoised images using the image sizes with Motion blur combined with Speckle noise

Test Image	Image Size	Blur & Noisy Image	DWT [2]	Augmented Lagrangian [12]	Curvelet Transform [10]	Proposed Method
1		23.2239	23.9372	24.6089	23.9313	**25.5673**
2		21.0064	21.0957	22.2576	21.5293	**23.1924**
3		21.7457	21.8367	23.0025	22.2514	**24.1839**
4		19.2673	19.4222	20.8222	19.9200	**22.0299**
5	256 x 256	17.8965	20.0387	16.1796	20.9946	**21.9860**
6		13.1633	15.0743	10.8040	16.0336	**16.5820**
7		12.5757	14.4820	10.8717	16.3005	**17.3208**
8		16.0558	16.5649	18.7345	16.8521	**21.2138**
9		24.7997	24.8311	27.6666	24.9057	**28.0803**
10		20.5104	21.0270	20.3254	22.1575	**23.3486**
11		25.3272	25.6067	26.4289	26.0485	**28.0667**
12		19.5076	19.8676	22.7892	19.9695	**24.0304**
13		17.6062	17.6547	22.0296	17.7410	**22.2915**
14		23.1467	23.2775	25.7503	23.4773	**26.6989**
15	512 x 512	23.8223	24.1072	24.8569	24.6375	**26.1031**
16		17.5181	17.5862	22.1037	17.6776	**22.5206**
17		17.7036	17.7615	22.0898	17.8653	**22.4803**
18		21.1085	21.2521	24.0262	21.3906	**24.7144**
19		22.2176	22.3451	24.3521	22.5821	**25.2422**
20		23.0288	23.2136	22.5770	23.7427	**23.7650**

References

1. Strang, G.: Wavelets and dilation equations: A brief introduction. SIAM Review **31**(4) (1989)
2. Edwards, T.: Discrete Wavelet Transforms: Theory and Implementation (1992)
3. Kociolek, M., Materka, A., Strzelecki, M., Szczypínski, P.: Discrete Wavelet transform – derived features for digital image texture analysis. In: Proc. of International Conference on Signals and Electronic Systems, pp. 163–168 (2001)
4. Binh, N.T., Khare, A.: Image Denoising, Deblurring and Object Tracking, A new Generation wavelet based approach. LAP LAMBERT Academic Publishing (2013)
5. Do, M.N., Vetterli, M.: The contourlet transform: an efficient directional multiresolution image representation. IEEE Trans. Img. Processing, 2091–2106 (2005)
6. da Cunha, A.L., Zhou, J., Do, M.N.: Nonsubsampled Contourlet Transform: Theory, Design, and Applications. IEEE Trans. Img. Proc, 3089–3101 (2005)
7. da Cunha, A.L., Zhou, J., Do, M.N.: Nonsubsampled Contourlet Transform: Filter design and applications in denoising (2006)

8. Candes, E.J.: Ridgelets: Theory and Applications. Stanford University (1998)
9. Zhang, B.J., Fadili, M., Starck, J.L.: Wavelets, ridgelets and curvelets for poisson noise removal. IEEE Transactions on Image Processing, 1093–1108 (2008)
10. Starck, J.L., Candès, E.J., Donoho D.L.: The curvelet transform for image denoising. IEEE Trans. Image Processing, 670–684 (2002)
11. Binh, N.T., Khare, A.: Multilevel threshold based image denoising in curvelet domain. Journal of Computer Science and Technology, 632–640 (2010)
12. Chan, S.H., Khoshabeh, R., Gibson, K.B., Gill, P.E., Nguyen, T.Q.: An Augmented Lagrangian Method for Total Variation Video Restoration. IEEE Trans. Image Process. **20**(11), 3097–3111 (2011)
13. Khare, A., Tiwary, U.S.: A new method for deblurring and denoising of medical images using complex wavelet transform. IEEE (2005)
14. Ruikar, S.D., Doye, D.D.: Wavelet Based Image Denoising Technique. International Journal of Advanced Computer Science and Applications **2**(3) (2011)
15. Candes, E.J., Demanet, L., Donoho, D.L., Ying, L.: Fast Discrete Curvelet Transforms. Multiscale Modeling and Simulation **5**, 861–899 (2006)
16. Lina, J.M., Mayrand, M.: Complex Daubechies Wavelets. Journal of Applied and Computational Harmonic Analysis **2**, 219–229 (1995)

Increasing the Quality of Medical Images Based on the Combination of Filters in Ridgelet Domain

Nguyen Thanh Binh[1], Vo Thi Hong Tuyet[1(✉)], and Phan Cong Vinh[2]

[1] Faculty of Computer Science and Engineering,
Ho Chi Minh City University of Technology, Ho Chi Minh City, Vietnam
ntbinh@cse.hcmut.edu.vn, vothihongtuyet.dhbk@gmail.com
[2] Faculty of Information Technology, Nguyen Tat Thanh University,
Ho Chi Minh City, Vietnam
pcvinh@ntt.edu.vn

Abstract. In many fields, images become a tool that contains data such as medical images. However, the image not only has blur or noise, but also has blur and noise pair. The aim of deblurring and denoising image is to remove blur and noise detail but this process helps keep edges features and its information. In this paper, we have proposed a method for increasing the quality of medical images based on the combination of filters in ridgelet domain. The proposed method uses ridgelet transform combined with Bayesian thresholding for denoising process and uses Wiener filter for deblurring process in ridgelet domain. For demonstrating the superiority of the proposed method, we have compared the results with the other recent methods available in literature.

Keywords: Deblurring · Denoising · Bayesian thresholding · Wiener filter · Ridgelet transform

1   Introduction

Most of images not only have noise but also have blur. This problem reduces the quality of images and difficulty for viewers. Especially, for medical images, they have blur, noise or pair that influences diagnostic process of medical specialists because a small detail in a medical image is very useful for treatment process. The goal of denoising and debluring is to remove noise and blur details from the corrupted image while maintaining edge features. In the past, many methods are proposed to increase the quality of images such as wavelet transform methods [1], Discrete Wavelet Transform (DWT) [2] method, etc. Although DWT is a powerful tool for this task, however, it has serious disadvantages such as lack information, shift-sensitivity [3] and poor directionality [5]. Several papers have proposed solutions for reducing these disadvantages. In case blur or noise visible in medical image, Wiener filter [8] has given good results in some cases. However, the area of image denoising is hard work and still a great challenge.

© Institute for Computer Sciences, Social Informatics and Telecommunications Engineering 2015
P.C. Vinh et al. (Eds.): ICTCC 2014, LNICST 144, pp. 320–331, 2015
DOI: 10.1007/978-3-319-15392-6_30

In this paper, we have proposed a method for increasing quality of medical images based on the combination of filters in ridgelet domain. The proposed method uses ridgelet transform combined with Bayesian thresholding for denoising process and uses Wiener filter for deblurring process in ridgelet domain. For demonstrating the superiority of the proposed method, we have compared the results with the other recent methods available in literature such as ridgelet transform [3] and Wiener filter [8]. For performance measure, we have used Peak Signal to Noise ratio (PSNR) and Mean Square Error (MSE) and it has shown that the present method yields far better results.

The rest of the paper is organized as follows: in section 2, we described the basic of ridgelet transform, and the principle of Bayesian thresholding and Wiener filter; details of the proposed method are given in section 3; the results of the proposed method are presented in section 4 and our conclusions in section 5.

2   Background

2.1   The Ridgelet Transform

Ridgelets have been recently applied in the image processing application [10], [11], [12]. The theory of ridgelets was developed by Candes [13]. In that work, Candes showed that one could develop a system of analysis based on the ridge functions:

$$\psi_{a,b,\theta}(x, y) = a^{-1/2}\psi((x\cos(\theta) + y\sin(\theta) - b)/a)$$

and the function is constant along the lines: $x\cos(\theta) + y\sin(\theta) = const.$
He introduced a continuous ridgelet transform:

$$R_f(a,b,\theta) = <\psi_{a,b,\theta}(x), f>$$

with a reproducing formula and a Parseval relation. He showed the construction of frames, giving stable series expansions in terms of a special discrete collection of ridge functions. The approach was general, and gave ridgelet frames for functions in $L_2[0, 1]^d$ in all dimensions $d \geq 2$.

Let i be the triple (j, ℓ, k) where the indices run as follows:

$$i \in \ell := \left\{(j, \ell, k), j, k \in Z, j \geq j_0, \ell \in \Lambda_j\right\}$$

and define the collection of discrete ridgelets $\psi_i(x)$ as

$$\psi_i(x) = 2^{j/2}\psi(2^j u_i^T x - k), \quad i \in \ell$$

where j is the ridge scale, k is the ridge location, i is the angular scale and ℓ is the angular location.

The range of the parameter ℓ is scale dependent as it depends on j. Ridgelets are directional and the interesting aspect is the discretization of the directional variable u; this variable is sampled at increasing resolution so that at scale j.

The 2-D continuous ridgelet transform in R^2 can be defined as follows. First define a smooth wavelet function $\psi: R \rightarrow R$ satisfying the admissibility condition given by:

$$\int_{-\infty}^{\infty} \frac{|\psi(\varepsilon)|^2}{|\varepsilon|^2} d\varepsilon < \infty ,$$

where ψ is the Fourier transform of ψ.

The bivariate ridgelet $\psi_{a,b,\theta} : R^2 \rightarrow R^2$ is defined by $\psi_{a,b,\theta}(x, y)$ and the function is constant along the lines $xcos(\theta) + ysin(\theta) = const$. The ridgelet values for the continuous image $f(x, y)$ is given by:

$$Rf(a,b,\theta) = \iint f(x, y)\psi_{a,b,\theta}(x, y)dxdy$$

In short, the ridgelet transform is the application of a 1-D wavelet transform to the slice of the Radon transform where the angular variable θ is constant and t is varying [14]. This means the ridgelet coefficients $Rf(a, b, \theta)$ are given by the analysis of the Radon transform via,

$$Rf(t,\theta) = \int Rf(t,\theta)a^{-1/2}\psi((t-b)/a)dt$$

where $\Psi_{a,b}(t) = a^{-1/2}\Psi((t-b)/a)$ is a 1-D wavelet transform.

To make the ridgelet transform discrete, the Radon transform as well as the wavelet transform have to be discrete. The discrete wavelet transform is well defined but the same cannot be said about the discrete Radon transform. There are many ways to make the Radon transform discrete [15].

The ordinary ridgelet transform can be achieved as follows [16]:

(i)   Compute the 2D Fast Fourier Transform (FFT) of the image.
(ii) Substitute the sampled values of Fourier transform obtained on the square lattice with sampled values on a polar lattice.
(iii) Compute the 1D inverse FFT on each angular line.
(iv) Perform the 1D scale wavelet transform on the resulting angular lines in order to obtain the ridgelet coefficients.

2.2   Bayesian Thresholding

Most of the existing thresholding procedures are essentially minimax. They do not take into account some specific properties of a concrete object in which we are interested. Now, we specify a prior distribution on the wavelet coefficients within a Bayesian framework [17]. Bayesian thresholding's idea is median of thresholdings.

The estimate noise variance σ and signal variance δ can be obtained by equation[19]:

$$\sigma = \left(\frac{median\left(\left|w_{i,j}\right|\right)}{0.6745} \right)^2$$

$$\delta^2 = \max\left(\frac{1}{MxN} \sum_{t=1}^{M}\sum_{j=1}^{N} w_{t,j}^2 - \sigma^2, 0 \right)$$

where $w_{i,j}$ is the lowest frequency coefficient after the transformation, MxN is the sub-band's size.

There are two thresholdings: hard and soft thresholding. In hard thresholding, the important coefficients remain unchanged while the important coefficients are reduced by the absolute threshold value in the soft thresholding.

2.3   Wiener Filter

The filters may be summarized as follows [8]:

(i)   Mean-square value of the estimation error.
(ii) Expectation of the absolute value of the estimation error.
(iii) Expectation of third or higher powers of the absolutely value of the estimation error.

The Wiener deconvolution method has widespread uses in image deconvolution applications, as the frequency spectrum of most of visual images is fairly well behaved and may be estimated easily. One of the most widely used restoration techniques is the Wiener filter. Assuming white Gaussian noise, Wiener filter in the Fourier domain will be calculated by equation [8]:

$$W = \frac{R(\omega) * S_{pp}(\omega)}{\left|R(\omega)\right|^2 S_{pp}(\omega) + \sigma n^2}$$

where $S_{pp}(\omega)$ is the power spectrum of the input projection and σn^2 is the variance of the Gaussian noise.

We compute the Wiener restoration filter and minimize issues associated with divisions by equation [8]:

$$G(k,1) = \frac{H*(k,1)}{\left|H(k,1)\right|^2 + S\_u(k,1)/S\_x(k,1)}$$

$$G(k,1) = \frac{H*(k,1)S\_x(k,1)}{\left|H(k,1)\right|^2 + S\_x(k,1) + S\_u(k,1)}$$

where S_u is the signal power spectrum and S_x is the noise power spectrum.

3   The Proposed Method

Deblurring medical images is very difficult for image processing. Special with medical images consist of blur and noise pair. In this section, we propose an approach for medical image deblurring based on ridgelet transform using Bayesian thresholding combined with Wiener filter for medical images in case of blur combined with noise pair image.

In our proposed, we divide image processing with blur combined with noise pair into two processes: denoising and deblurring processes. The proposed method includes two periods: ridgelet coefficients computation with Bayesian thresholding for denoising, and Wiener filter for deblurring. The proposed method is used as figure 1:

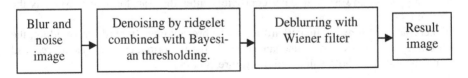

Fig. 1. The process of proposed method

Firstly, the input is the blur and noise image, we use ridgelet for image denoising. The process for image denoising is as follows:

(i) Estimate noise variance.

(ii) Calculate the ridgelet coefficients.

(iii) Based on these coefficients to filter along rows with low and high sub-band, and columns with low sub-band.

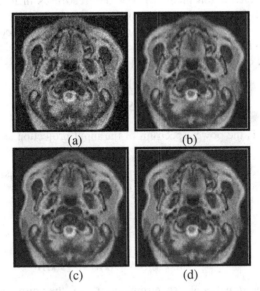

Fig. 2. Noise image with Gaussian noise and denoising images by different methods. (a) Noise image (PSNR = 21.5064 db). (b) Denoising image by Bayesian thresholding (PSNR = 27.9002 db). (c) Denoising image by ridgelet transform (PSNR = 28.1641 db). (d) Denoising image by ridgelet combined with Bayesian thresholding (PSNR = 28.3362 db).

Bayesian thresholding is also the composition in ridgelet transform. We calculate median thresholding and show the result based on new thresholding. With Bayesian thresholding, after calculating the thresholds based on sigmahat, we continue to reconstruct the image.

If the value of pixel details coefficients is less than thresholding then the result is 0. Else, the result is array Y, where each element of Y is 1 if the corresponding element of pixel is greater than zero, 0 if the corresponding element of pixel equals zero, -1 if the corresponding element of pixel is less than zero. After this period, the input image has become image denoising.

Figure 2 shows the denoising of noise image in case Gaussian noise with Bayesian thresholding in ridgelet domain. From figure 2, we see that the result of the method – ridgelet combined with Bayesian thresholding - is better than the other methods such as Bayesian thresholding and ridgelet method. Therefore, this method gives the good result for denoising period.

Secondly, the blur in the image is not removed. In order to remove the blur, we use Wiener filter for the above image result in the previous period.

4   Experiments and Results

In this section, we apply the procedure described in section 3 and achieved superior performance in our deblurring experiments as demonstrated in this section. For performance evaluation, we compare the results of the proposed method based on ridgelet transform combined with Bayesian thresholding and Wiener filter with the other methods such as ridgelet transform and Wiener Filter. We test the result in medical image datasets, this dataset includes different image sizes: 256x256, 512x512.

Gaussian and Motion types are used to blur. In addition, Gaussian noise is added to these images. Hard thresholding is applied to the coefficients after decomposition in ridgelet domain. All of the above methods are done on the same images at similar scale.

The quality of the image is improved by comparison with the value of Mean Square Error (MSE) and Peak Signal-to-Noise Ratio (PSNR). The MSE defined as:

$$MSE=\sqrt{\frac{1}{NxN}\sum_{i=1}^{N}\sum_{j=1}^{N}(x_{i,j}-y_{i,j})^2}$$

where x is the image which has blur and noise, y is the image result and NxN is the size of the image. PSNR is used as the measure of the quality of the reconstruction of image deblurring or denoising, defined as:

$$PSNR=20\log_{10}(\frac{MAX_1}{MSE})$$

where MAX_1 is the maximum pixel value of the image. The proposed method will be compared with ridgelet transform and Wiener filter method by the MSE and PSNR values. The smaller the value of MSE is, the better it is. The higher the value of PSNR is, the better it is. We test so many medical images. In here, we show some test cases.

Figure 3 shows the deblurring of blur and noise image by Gaussian blur and Gaussian noise with our proposed method. Figure 4 shows the deblurring of blur and noise image by Motion blur and Gaussian noise with our proposed method.

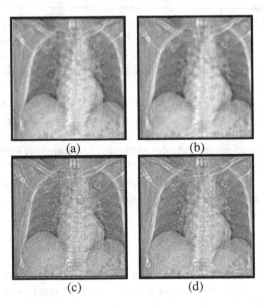

(a)   (b)

(c)   (d)

Fig. 3. Denoising and deblurring images by different methods in the case Gaussian blur combine with Gaussian noise in image.
(a) Blur and noise image (PSNR = 26.4899 db). (b) Deblurred image by Ridegelet Transform (PSNR = 26.5783 db). (c) Deblurred image by Wiener filter (PSNR = 28.1759 db). (d) Deblurred image by RT-BT-WF (PSNR = 28.4001 db).

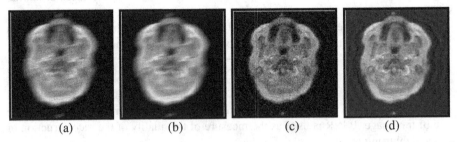

(a)   (b)   (c)   (d)

Fig. 4. Denoising and deblurring images by different methods in case Motion blur is combined with Gaussian noise in image.
(a) Blur and noise image (PSNR = 21.5308 db). (b) Deblurred image by ridegelet transform (PSNR = 21.8387 db). (c) Deblurred image by Wiener filter (PSNR = 22.6385 db). (d) Deblurred image by proposed method (PSNR = 25.3566 db).

From figure 3 and figure 4, we see that the results of the proposed method are better than the other methods. Figure 5 and figure 6 show the plot of PSNR, MSE values of different image deblurring methods corrupted with Gaussian blur combined with Gaussian noise.

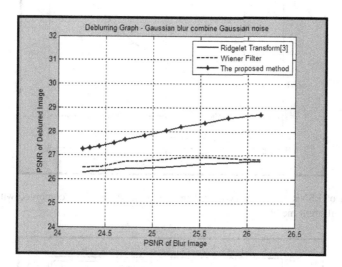

Fig. 5. Plot of PSNR values of deblurred images with Gaussian blur combined with Gaussian noise using different methods

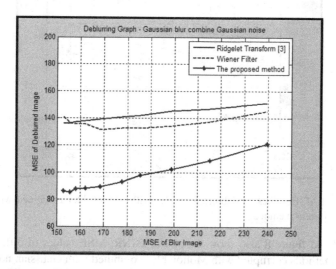

Fig. 6. Plot of MSE values of deblurred images with Gaussian blur combined with Gaussian noise using different methods

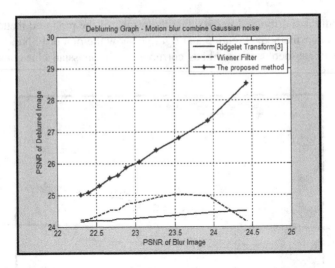

Fig. 7. Plot of PSNR values of deblurred images with Motion blur combined with Gaussian noise using different methods

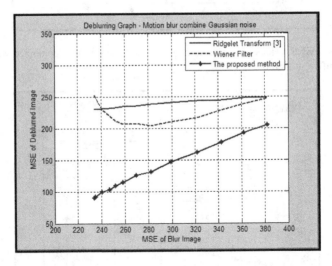

Fig. 8. Plot of MSE values of deblurred images with Motion blur combined with Gaussian noise using different methods

Figure 7 and figure 8 also show the plot of PSNR, MSE values of different image deblurring methods corrupted with Motion blur combined with Gaussian noise.

In these figures, it is well observed that the proposed method performs better than Wiener filter and ridgelet transform method.

5   Conclusions

In this paper, we propose a method for deblurring images for blur combined with noise image pair. The proposed method is divided into two processes: denoising and deblurring. Firstly, we denoise images based on combining ridgelet transform with Bayesian thresholding. Then, we apply Wiener filter for deblurring into denoising image. We test with Gaussian blur combined with Gaussian noise pair and Motion blur combined with Gaussian noise pair in medical image dataset. From the results of the above section, we conclude that the proposed method works well and better than the other recent methods available in literature. With this idea, we think the combination methods can upgrade the quality of image blurring and noising in case of denoising and deblurring.

Appendix

Table A1. PSNR Values (dB) of different denoised images using the image sizes with Gaussian blur combined with Gaussian noise

Test Image	Image Size	Blur & Noisy Image	Ridgelet Transform [3]	Wiener filter	Proposed Method
1		26.4899	26.5783	28.1759	**28.4001**
2		24.9402	25.0515	20.9087	**25.1534**
3		27.1148	27.2895	25.3263	**28.4104**
4		26.9914	27.2757	25.7539	**28.6007**
5	256 x 256	25.1912	25.3753	21.2920	**25.6060**
6		21.7783	21.8618	21.4116	**23.0959**
7		26.3854	26.6870	26.3591	**28.9273**
8		25.7983	26.6906	26.9004	**28.5674**
9		31.0315	33.3208	27.4723	**33.6087**
10		28.3717	29.4430	29.6220	**31.3085**
11		30.9153	33.4346	26.8820	**33.7170**
12		24.6946	25.2133	26.2104	**27.4562**
13		23.3097	23.7127	24.0278	**26.1523**
14		29.0223	31.3864	28.1622	**32.9868**
15	512 x 512	29.7922	31.9072	26.9748	**32.9882**
16		23.6980	23.9378	24.2840	**27.1048**
17		22.8516	24.2431	24.8694	**26.1611**
18		25.5965	27.7678	27.0068	**30.1564**
19		26.0585	29.2006	27.4821	**30.1255**
20		24.9059	30.2079	26.9002	**30.3653**

Table A2. PSNR Values (dB) of different denoising images using the image sizes with Motion blur combined with Gaussian noise

Test Image	Image Size	Blur & Noisy Image	Ridgelet Transform [3]	Wiener filter	Proposed Method
1	256 x 256	24.3540	24.9051	24.8830	**25.0513**
2		22.1404	22.4044	18.5093	**23.3762**
3		21.5308	21.8387	22.6385	**25.3566**
4		20.9264	21.7559	19.3466	**23.6520**
5		22.9106	24.8598	22.7247	**25.3682**
6		18.3682	18.9366	19.1854	**20.6690**
7		19.1375	19.9172	21.1649	**21.9766**
8		19.7133	20.7100	21.5687	**22.5267**
9		23.9735	27.1204	24.6441	**28.1680**
10		22.0956	24.0654	24.0284	**24.7623**
11	512 x 512	27.7823	28.9289	20.4775	**31.3731**
12		21.3390	21.5874	21.3583	**24.9890**
13		19.1648	19.3289	18.7874	**23.3077**
14		24.7470	25.5131	21.7559	**29.4172**
15		25.8007	26.9125	20.8364	**30.0084**
16		19.2751	19.5024	19.3169	**23.5513**
17		18.9320	19.6084	19.9875	**22.3136**
18		20.7517	22.9811	21.8471	**24.3939**
19		19.6183	24.4411	21.8352	**22.9961**
20		19.8857	26.1292	21.9116	**23.8552**

References

1. Strang, G.: Wavelets and dilation equations: A brief introduction. SIAM Review **31**(4) (1989)
2. Edwards, T.: Discrete Wavelet Transforms, Theory and Implementation (1992)
3. Candes, E.J.: Ridgelets: Theory and Applications, Ph.D. thesis, Stanford University (1998)
4. Khare, A., Tiwary, U.S.: A new method for deblurring and denoising of medical images using complex wavelet transform. IEEE (2005)
5. Khare, A., Tiwary, U.S.: Symmetric Daubechies Complex Wavelet Transform and its application to denoising and deblurring. WSEAS Transactions on Signal Processing **2**, 738–745 (2006)
6. Kociolek, M., Materka, A., Strzelecki, M., Szczypínski, P.: Discrete wavelet transform – derived features for digital image texture analysis. In: Proc. Of International Conference on Signals and Electronic Systems, pp. 163–168 (2001)
7. Sitara, K., Remya, S.: Image deblurring in bayesian framework using template based blur estimation. The International Journal of Multimedia & Its Applications (IJMA) **4**(1) (2012)
8. Tsai, D.: Introduction of Wiener Filter, Graduate Institute of Electronics Engineering, Nation Taiwan University, Taipei, Taiwan, ROC
9. Binh, N.T., Khare, A.: Image denoising - deblurring and Object Tracking, a new generation wavelet based approach. LAP LAMBERT Academic Publishing (2013)

10. Lina, J.M., Mayrand, M.: Complex Daubechies Wavelets. Journal of Applied and Computational Harmonic Analysis **2**, 219–229 (1995)
11. Donoho, D.L.: Orthonormal ridgelets and linear singularities, Tech. Report, Department of Statistics, Stanford University (1998)
12. Candès, E.J.: Monoscale ridgelets for the representation of images with edges, Dept. Statist., Stanford Univ., Stanford, CA, Technical Representation (1999)
13. Burns, T., Rogers, S., Ruck, D., Oxley, M.: Discrete, spatiotemporal, wavelet multiresolution analysis method for computing optical flow. Optical Engineering **33**(7), 2236–2247 (1994)
14. Starck, J.L., Candès, E.J., Donoho, D.L.: The Curvelet Transform for Image Denoising. IEEE Transactions on Image Processing **11**(6), 670–684 (2002)
15. Candes, E.J., Demanet, L., Donoho, D.L., Ying, L.: Fast Discrete Curvelet Transforms. Multiscale Modeling and Simulation **5**, 861–899 (2006)
16. Donoho, D.L., Duncan, M.R.: Digital curvelet transform: Strategy, implementation and experiments. Proc. SPIE **4056**, 12–29 (2000)
17. Abramovich, F., Sapatinas, T., Silverman, B.W.: Wavelet thresholding via a Bayesian approach. J. R. Statist. Soc. B, 725–749 (1998)
18. Zhang, W., Yu, F., Guo, H.-M.: Improved adaptive wavelet threshold for image denoising. In: Control and Decision Conference, Chinese, pp. 5958–5963 (2009)
19. Chui, M., Feng, Y., Wang, W., Li, Z., Xu, X.: Image Denoising Method with Adaptive Bayes threshold in Nonsubsampled Contourlet Domain, American Applied Science Research Institute (2012)

Efficient Pancreas Segmentation
in Computed Tomography Based on Region-Growing

Tran Duc Tam$^{(\boxtimes)}$ and Nguyen Thanh Binh

Faculty of Computer Science and Engineering,
Ho Chi Minh City University of Technology, Ho Chi Minh City, Vietnam
tamtd@hcmup.edu.vn, ntbinh@cse.hcmut.edu.vn

Abstract. Pancreas segmentation in computed tomography data is one of difficult problems in medical area. Segmentation of pancreas tissue in computed
tomography is difficult even for human, since the pancreas head is always
directly connected to the small bowel and can in most cases cannot be visually
distinguished. In this paper, an efficient method to extract the pancreas from
such computed tomography images is proposed. Histogram equalization is used
to enhance the contrast of computed tomography images. After that, region-
growing technique is applied to label pancreas region and return the result of
segmentation. The proposed method will be experimented and evaluated by
using Jaccard index between an extracted pancreas and a true one. For evaluating the proposed method, we have compared the results of our proposed method
with the other recent methods available in literature.

Keywords: Computed tomography · Pancreas · Segmentation · Medical image

1 Introduction

Nowadays, the computed tomography (CT) is most widely used to determine and
diagnose medical problems. With this technique, we can detect abnormal organs to
treat as soon as possible. For example, pancreatic cancer is the most difficult type of
cancers to treat, which has a high mortality. It is the first leading cause of cancer-
related mortality in many countries [1]. In order to detect pancreatic cancer, the entire
abdominal area will be scanned. However, segmentation of pancreas tissue in CT is
difficult even for a human, since the pancreas head is always directly connected to the
small bowel and can in most cases cannot be visually distinguished. Additionally,
pancreas is an organ that includes pancreatic juice as liquid. Therefore, the CT scan of
pancreas has a low contrast.

In recent years, some algorithms have been built to pancreas segmentation [2]. The
algorithm of Shimizu [3, 9] based on anatomical and radiological observations. He
proposed an automatic pancreas segmentation algorithm from contrast-enhanced mul-
tiphase CT and verify its effectiveness in segmentation. The algorithm is characterized by three unique ideas as: the two-stage segmentation strategy with a spatial
standardization of pancreas, a patient-specific probabilistic atlas-guided segmentation,
and fine segmentation incorporated with a classifier ensemble learned by a Boosting
algorithm tomography.

© Institute for Computer Sciences, Social Informatics and Telecommunications Engineering 2015
P.C. Vinh et al. (Eds.): ICTCC 2014, LNICST 144, pp. 332–340, 2015.
DOI: 10.1007/978-3-319-15392-6_31

In the other works, Marius [4] gets information about liver and spleen and uses them as starting points for detection of splenic and mesenteric veins where pancreas lies near. He detected clinically meaningful support structures and building a classifier that models local spatial relationships between the pancreas and the support structures. Furthermore, performance texture descriptors based on wavelets and cosine transform are proposed to model local appearance. Marius uses texture descriptors to build the final pancreas tissue feature vector $\vec{Z}(\vec{t}) = \{\vec{F}(\vec{t}), \vec{\Phi}(\vec{t}), \vec{W}_\eta^-(\vec{t}), \vec{W}_\eta^+(\vec{t}), \vec{H}(\vec{t})\}$ as details in [4]. All the methods discussed above have local advantages or disadvantages depending on the features they have used.

In this paper, we have proposed an efficient approach for pancreas segmentation, using region-growing technique with intensity value. In order to enhance the contrast of medical images, we also use histogram equalization method for increasing equality. We also base on the ideas of general method for segmentation which is mentioned in the above part to improve the proposed method. By using intensity value as a feature to distinguish pancreas with other surrounding organs, we can detect and segment the pancreas image in the area which localized in [4]. Therefore, the proposed method can get a good result. For performance measure, we computed the Jaccard index (J.I) between an extracted region and a true one, which was manually defined by an expert and compared with the method of Shimizu [3] and Marius [4].

The rest of the paper is organized as follows: in section 2, we described the background of histogram processing and region-based segmentation; in section 3, we shown details of the proposed method; the result and conclusion of the paper are orderly presented in section 4 and section 5.

2   Background

2.1   Histogram Processing

Histograms are the basis for numerous spatial domain processing techniques. Statistics obtained directly from an image histogram can be used for an image enhancement. The histogram of a digital image [5, 10] with intensity levels in the range $[0, L - 1]$ is a discrete function

$$h(r_k) = n_k \tag{1}$$

where r_k is the kth intensity value, n_k is the number of pixels in the range with intensity r_k and L is the number of possible intensity levels in the image.

Let r denote a discrete random variable representing intensity values in the range $[0, L - 1]$ and let $p(r_k)$ denote the normalized histogram component corresponding to value r_k, and it is viewed as an estimate of the probability that intensity r_k occurs in the image from which the histogram was obtained.

The probability $p(r_k)$ of intensity level r_k occurring in a given image is estimated as

$$p(r_k) = \frac{n_k}{MN} \qquad k = 0, 1, 2, \dots, L - 1 \tag{2}$$

where MN is the total number of pixels.

A transformation function of particular importance in image processing has the form

$$s = T(r) = (L-1) \int_0^r p_r(w)dw \qquad (3)$$

where w is a dummy variable of integration. The right side of this equation is recognized as the Cumulative Distribution Function (CDF) of random variable r. The discrete form of the above transformation is:

$$s_k = T(r_k) = (L-1) \sum_{j=0}^{k} p_r(r_j) \qquad k = 0, 1, 2, \ldots, L-1 \qquad (4)$$

Thus, a processed image is obtained by mapping each pixel in the input image with intensity r_k into a corresponding pixel with level s_k in the output image. The transformation $T(r_k)$ is called a histogram equalization transformation. Figure 1 shows the CT image of enhanced image using histogram equalization.

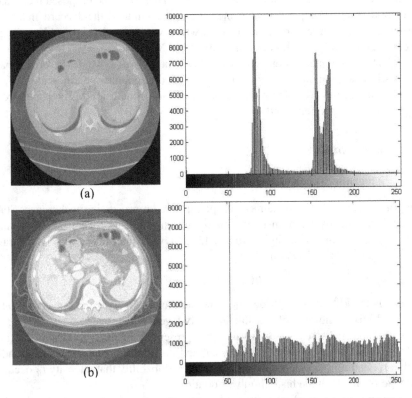

Fig. 1. The CT image of abnormal area and its histogram: (a) Original image, (b) Enhanced image using Histogram Equalization

2.2   Region-Based Segmentation

Region-based segmentation methods attempt to partition or group regions according to common image properties [5]. These image properties consist of:

(i) Intensity values from a given image or a processed image;

(ii) Textures or patterns that are unique to each type of region;

(iii) Spectral profiles that provide multidimentional image data;

In this paper, intensity value is used as a characteristic in region-growing algorithm. Using a seeding and region-growing technique, a segmented pixel set is created by initially selecting one or more pixels from the image (called the seed pixels). The seeds are often specified interactively by the user and start from these growing regions by appending to each seed those neighboring pixels that have predefined properties similar to the seed. The region-growing algorithm will then add to the segmented pixel set all the pixels that are r-connected to the initial seed pixels and fall within the threshold limits. To be r-connected to one another, two pixels must share at least r corner points. The algorithm recursively adds to the segmented pixel set all the pixels that are connected to the current members of the pixel set. Region growth should stop when no more pixels satisfy the criteria for inclusion in that region.

Let: $f(x,y)$ denote an input image array; $S(x,y)$ denote a seed array containing 1s at the locations of seed points and 0s else where; and Q denote a predicate to be applied at each location (x,y). Arrays f and S are assumed to be of the same size. A basic region-growing algorithm based on 8-connectivity may be stated as follows [5].

(i) Find all connected components in $S(x,y)$ and erode each connected component to one pixel; label all such pixels found as 1. All other pixels in S are labeled 0.

(ii) Form an image f_Q such that, at a pair of coordinates(x,y), let $f_Q(x,y) = 1$ if the input image satisfies the given predicate, Q, at those coordinates; otherwise, let $f_Q(x,y) = 0$.

(iii) Let g be an image formed by appending to each seed point in S all the 1-valued points in f_Q that are 8-connected to that seed point.

(iv) Label each connected component in g with a different region label. This is the segmented image obtained be region growing.

After that, we have to specify a predicate and append to each seed all the pixels which are k-connected to that seed as well as similar to it. Using intensity differences as a measure of similarity, our predicate applied at each location (x,y) is

$$Q = \begin{cases} TRUE & \text{if the absolute difference of the intensities between the seed and the pixel at (x,y) is} \leq T \\ \\ FALSE & \text{otherwise} \end{cases}$$

where T is a specified threshold.

3   The Proposed Method

In this section, we propose an efficient approach for pancreas segmentation that is based on region-growing technique combine to histogram equalization.

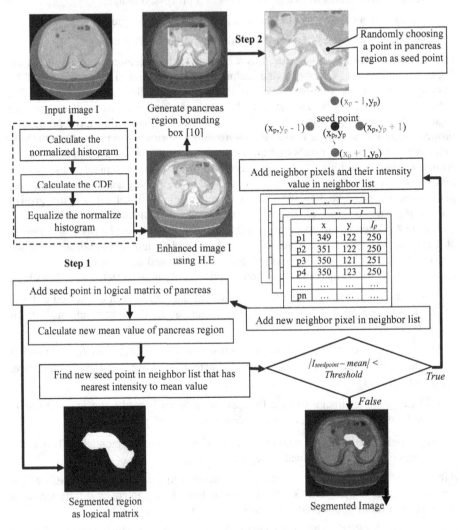

Fig. 2. Block diagram of the proposed method for pancreas segmentation

Because pancreas has unusual shape and dual location in the abdomen [1], the head of the pancreas always contact the superior mesenteric vein while body and tail follow the pathway of the splenic vein, thus the segmentation is so complex and time-consuming. Therefore, in order to reduce a number of processed data, we utilize the described anatomical information. Liver and spleen are automatically segmented by [6]. The axis-aligned bounding boxes $\vec{l}$ and $\vec{s}$ of the liver and spleen masks are computed and a pancreas region bounding box $\vec{p}$ is generated. All subsequent calculations are limited to the region described by $\vec{p}$.

$$\vec{p} = \left(\frac{l_{xmax} - l_{xmin}}{2}, \min\left(l_{ymin}, s_{ymin} \right), \frac{s_{xmax} - s_{xmin}}{2}, \max\left(l_{ymax}, s_{ymax} \right) \right) \qquad (5)$$

Figure 2 presents a flowchart of proposed algorithm. The input, which has low-contrast, will be enhanced by histogram equalization method as a pre-processing data. The second step performs a segmentation method based on region growing technique using difference of intensity between pancrease and other organs in abdomen.

Firstly, we enhance the input image by Histogram processing. In this stage, this stage can be described as follows:

1. Calculate the histogram of the input image according to Eqn. (1)

2. Calculate the CDF of the input image according to Eqn. (4)

3. Equalize the histogram of the input image.

$$I_p = T(I_p) \qquad (6)$$

where I_p is intensity value of pixel in the input image

Secondly, we choose a one point on the pancreas region to be a seed point (x, y). Pancreas region is segmented by region growing technique. This stage can be described as follows:

1. For each pixel (x, y) has four neighbors whose coordinates are given by

$$(x + 1, y), (x - 1, y), (x, y + 1), (x, y - 1)$$

Check if neighbor pixel is still inside the image and not already part of the neighbor list then add new neighbor pixel to neighbor list and mark them as checked pixels.

2. Add current seed point in segmented region.

3. Find pixel with intensity nearest to mean value of segmented region and use it as a new seed point in next iteration. The minimum distance is the difference between the chosen pixel and mean value of intensity:

$$min_{distance} = \min_{i=1..n} |I_i - m_{mean}| \qquad (7)$$

where I_i is an intensity of pixel p_i in neighbor list, m_{mean} is mean of the segmented region which is calculated by:

$$m_{mean} = (m_{mean} * |R| + I_p)/(|R| + 1) \qquad (8)$$

where $|R|$ is size of segmented region.

4. Calculate the new mean of the segmented region and remove the chosen pixel from the neighbor list.

5. Repeat the above processes until distance between region and possible new pixels become higher than a certain threshold.

Proposed algorithm will return the segmented region as a logical matrix that contains pancreas region which has the same characteristics to seed point.

4   Experiments and Evaluation

In this section, we implemented the proposed approach in section 3 and achieved good results in our segmentation experiments as demonstrated. We applied the proposed method for single-phase CT data that obtained from many cases, the number of slices per case ranged from 92 to 112. Inter-slice spacing was 2mm abdominal control standard protocol whereas spacing within an axial slice varied between 0.6 mm and 0.7 mm.

To evaluate the segmentation performance quantitatively, we computed the Jaccard index (J.I) between an extracted region and a true one [7], which was manually defined by a medical expert.

$$JI(A, B) = \frac{|A \cap B|}{|A \cup B|} \times 100 \tag{9}$$

where A is extracted region, B is true region. If A and B are both empty, we define $JI(A, B) = 100$. The index ranges from 0 to 100%, with higher values representing better performance. Resolution of tested images are 512 x 512 and threshold is used in experiments ranges from 0.06 to 0.1. We have experimented on many image. Here, we report the results in some cases as Figure 3.

Figure 3 shows results separately for the original images and compares the result of the proposed method with others (using value of Jaccard index). Generally, the below results have high accuracy giving the low contrast of pancreas regions.

As mentioned in section 3, we find pixel with intensity nearest to the mean of segmented region and use it as a new seed point in next iteration to add to segmented region. Although this predicate is based on intensity differences and uses a single threshold, we could specify more complex schemes in which a different threshold is applied to each pixel, and properties other than differences are used. In this paper, the preceding predicate is sufficient to solve the problem. Therefore, our proposed method is better than other methods.

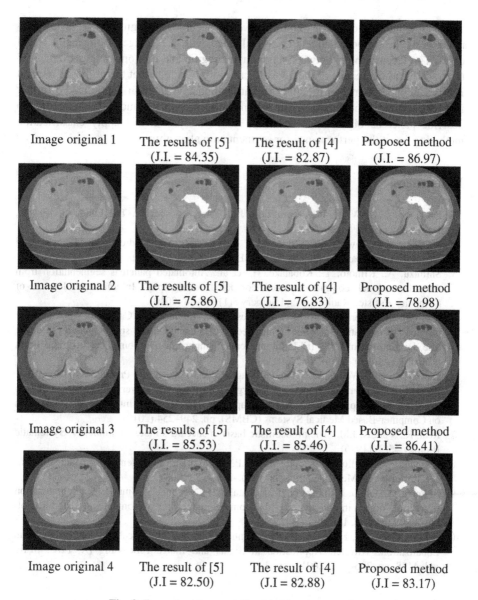

Image original 1   The results of [5]   The result of [4]   Proposed method
                    (J.I. = 84.35)   (J.I. = 82.87)   (J.I. = 86.97)

Image original 2   The results of [5]   The result of [4]   Proposed method
                    (J.I. = 75.86)   (J.I. = 76.83)   (J.I. = 78.98)

Image original 3   The results of [5]   The result of [4]   Proposed method
                    (J.I. = 85.53)   (J.I. = 85.46)   (J.I. = 86.41)

Image original 4   The result of [5]   The result of [4]   Proposed method
                    (J.I = 82.50)   (J.I = 82.88)   (J.I = 83.17)

Fig. 3. Exemplary segmentation results on unseen data

5   Conclusion and Future Work

This paper presented an efficient pancreas segmentation algorithm from CT images. Histogram equalization is used to enhance the contrast of computed tomography images. After that, region-growing technique is applied to label pancreas region and return the result of segmentation. Based on the prior work, the proposed method allows to enhance the contrast and improve the accuracy of segmentation. The effectiveness of the proposed method was validated with CT images from many tested cases. The Jaccard index between an extracted region and true one ranges from 73.37 to 86.97. From the results of the above section, we conclude that the proposed method is efficient and better than the other recent methods available in literature. To further improve accuracy and flexibility of the method, we will use more characteristics to describe pancreas objects more clearly. Additionally, we will apply classification method to boost the performance for segmentation algorithm.

References

1. Li, D., Xie, K., Wolff, R., Abbruzzese, J.L.: Pancreatic cancer. The Lancet **363**(9414), 1049–1057 (2004)
2. Shimizu, A., Nawano, S., Shinozaki, K., Tateno, Y.: Medical Image Processing Compettion in Japan. In: WC 2009. IFMBE Proceedings 25/IV, pp. 1814–1817 (2009)
3. Shimizu, A., Kimoto, T., Kobatake, H., et al.: Automated pancreas segmentation from three-dimensional contrast-enhanced computed tomography. International Journal of Computer Assisted Radiology and Surgery **5**(1), 85–98 (2010)
4. Erdt, M., Kirschner, M., Drechsler, K., Wesarg, S., Hammon, M., Cavallaro, A.: Automatic pancreas segmentation in contrast enhanced Ct data using learned spatial anatomy and texture descriptors. In: 2011 IEEE International Symposium on Biomedical Imaging: From Nano to Macro, pp. 2076–2082 (2011)
5. Gonzalez , R.C., Woods, R.E.: Digital Image Processing, 3rd edn. Prentice Hall (2002)
6. Erdt, M., Kirschner, M., Steger, S., Wesarg, S.: Fast automatic liver segmentation combining learned shape priors with observed shape deviation. In: IEEE International Symposium on Computer-Based Medical Systems (CBMS), pp. 249–254 (2010)
7. Real, R., Vargas, J.M.: The probabilistic basis of Jaccard's index of similarity. Systematic Biology **45**(3) (1996)
8. Ghaneh, P., Costello, E., Neoptolemos, J.P.: Biology and management of pancreatic cancer. Postgraduate Medical Journal **84**(995), 478–497 (2008)
9. Shimizu, A., Ohno, R., Ikegami, T., Kobatake, H., Nawano, S., Smutek, D.: Segmentation of multiple organs in non-contrast 3d abdominal images. Int. J. Computer Assisted Radiology and Surgery **2**, 135–142 (2007)
10. Jin, Y., Fayad, L., Laine, A.: Contrast Enhancement by Multi-scale Adaptive Histogram Equalization. Wavelet: Application in Signal and Image Processing IX, Proc. SPIE, vol. 4478, pp. 206–213 (2001)

Object Classification Based on Contourlet Transform in Outdoor Environment

Nguyen Thanh Binh[✉]

Faculty of Computer Science and Engineering,
Ho Chi Minh City University of Technology, Ho Chi Minh City, Vietnam
ntbinh@cse.hcmut.edu.vn

Abstract. Classification of objects is an important task in computer vision. In the case that the objects are occlusion or outdoor environment, classification of objects is a challenging problem. The primary goal of this paper is to classify the object into two classes: human and car in an outdoor environment. In order to detect object classification, most of existing methods separated detecting object region from pre-defined background model. Here, we propose a method to implement classification of human and car in outdoor environment using contourlet transform combined with support vector machine as a classifier for classification of objects. The proposed method tested on standard dataset like PEST2001 dataset. For demonstrating the superiority of the proposed method, we have compared the results with the other recent methods available in literature.

Keywords: Object classification · Contourlet transform · Support vector machine

1   Introduction

Classification of objects is an important task in computer vision, where we classify human and non-human objects in real scene [1]. There are two tasks for image understanding: object detection and classification in the past decades. The object classification aims to predict the existence of objects within images while the object detection is localizing the objects [2]. Any object classification algorithm is to develop a method having capability to interpret the objects into different groups. Object classification algorithm must work under real-time constraints and must be robust in variation in natural conditions, different sizes of human objects, etc [10]. Feature selection and machine learning are the key components in any classification algorithm. Most of object classification algorithms developed base on Machine learning methods [3].

In the past, many algorithms have been built to object classification. Lowe [4] used Scale Invariant Feature Transform as a feature descriptor for object recognition. Lu [5] proposed a visual feature for object classification based on binary pattern. Dalal [6] proposed Histogram of oriented Gradient (HoG) as a feature descriptor for object detection. Cao [7] proposed a method by extending the HoG to boosting HoG feature.

© Institute for Computer Sciences, Social Informatics and Telecommunications Engineering 2015
P.C. Vinh et al. (Eds.): ICTCC 2014, LNICST 144, pp. 341–349, 2015.
DOI: 10.1007/978-3-319-15392-6_32

All the methods discussed above have local advantages or disadvantages depending on the features they have used [10].

Yu [8] proposed wavelet method for visual classification. This method uses real valued discrete wavelet transform. Real valued wavelet transform has three major problems: lack of shift sensitivity, poor directionality and lack of strong edge detection [11]. This drawback affects the process of feature selection. To increase the ability to identify objects, we use contourlet transform to overcome these problems.

In this paper, we propose a method to implement classification human and car in an outdoor environment using contourlet transform combined with support vector machine as a classifier for classification of objects. The proposed method was tested on a standard dataset like PEST2001 dataset. For demonstrating the superiority of the proposed method, we have compared the results with the other recent methods by Lu [5] and Renno [9]. We use three different performance metrics: average classification accuracy, true positive rate (recall), and predicted positive rate (precision) for this comparison.

The rest of the paper is organized as follows: in section 2, we described the basic of feature selection, contourlet transform and details of the support vector machine classifier; the proposed method is presented in section 3; the results of proposed method are given in section 4 and conclusions in section 5.

2   Background

2.1   The Contourlet Transform

Real valued wavelet transform suffers from three major problems: lack of shift sensitivity, poor directionality and lack of strong edge detection. Do [12] proposed a solution to overcome these problems by contourlet transform (CT).

Contourlets constitute a new family of frames that are designed to represent smooth contours in different directions of an image. A contourlet is easily applied in image processing because its representation is a fixed transform [12, 16]. The contourlet not only inherits the main qualities of wavelet transform, such as multiscale and time-frequency information, but also captures direction characteristics. It holds the geometrical formation of images and implements a true sparse representation of images. The contourlet allows for a different number of directions at each scale and aspect ratios. This feature allows an efficient contourlet-based approximation of a smooth contour at multiple resolutions. The discrete contourlet transform is a multiscale and directional decomposition using a combination of Laplacian pyramid (LP) and directional filter bank (DFB) [12, 16].

The idea of the contourlet construction [12] is: let $a_0[n]$ be the input image, the output after the LP step is I bandpass images $b_i[n]$, $i = 1, 2,..., I$ and a lowpass image $a_I[n]$. Each bandpass image $b_i[n]$ is decomposed by an ℓ_i-level DFB into 2^{t_i} bandpass directional images $c_{i,k}^{(l_i)}[n]$, for $k = 0, 1,..., 2^{t_i}-1$.

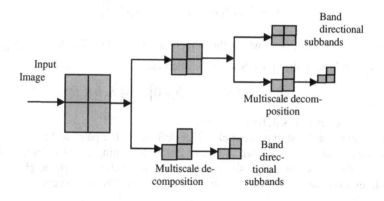

Fig. 1. Contourlet decomposition

In the discrete contourlet transform, the multiscale and directional decomposition steps are decoupled. Therefore, we have different numbers of directions at different scales. Contourlet decomposition proceeds through two main steps: first, LP multiscale decomposition is performed; then directional filter bank decomposition is used to link point discontinuity to linear structures. In more detail, an image is decomposed into a low pass image and bandpass images by the LP decomposition. Each bandpass output is further decomposed by the DFB step. The output of the DFB step consists of smooth contours and directional edges. In this paper, each directional subband at each level consists of 2^n element, where n is a positive integer. Figure 1 shows a contourlet decomposition [16]. Human and car object classification are a problem where the objects may present in translated as well as rotated form among different scenes. Contourlet transform has the time-frequency-localization and multiscale properties of wavelets. It offers a high degree of directionality and anisotropy. Therefore, the properties of contourlet transform will be useful for classification of human and car object.

2.2   Support Vector Machine Classifier

Support vector machines (SVM) include associated learning algorithms that analyze data and recognize patterns, used for classification and regression analysis in machine learning. SVM can efficiently perform a non-linear classification, implicitly mapping their inputs into high-dimensional feature spaces.

SVM is a popular classifier. The classifier objects are into two categories: object and non-object data [13]. In here, we detect two types: human and car object.

An n-dimensional object x has n-coordinates.

$$x = \left(x_1, x_2, x_3, \ldots \ldots, x_n \right),$$

where, each $x_i \in R$ for i=1, 2, 3,....,n.

Each object x_j belongs to a class $y_j \in \{-1, +1\}$. Consider a training set T of m patterns together with their classes,

$$T = \left\{ \left(x_1, y_1 \right), \left(x_2, y_2 \right), ..., \left(x_n, y_n \right) \right\}$$

and a dot product space S, in which the objects are embedded: $X_1, X_2, ..., X_m \in S$.

Any hyperplane in the space S can be written as:

$$\left\{ x \in S \mid w.x + b = 0 \right\}, w \in S, b \in R$$

The dot product w.x is defined by [10]:

If there exists at least one linear classifier defined by the pair (w, b) which correctly classifies all objects as shown in Figure 2 then a training set of objects is linearly separable [10]. The linear classifier is represented by the hyperplane H (w.x+b=0) and defines a region for class +1 and another region for class -1 objects.

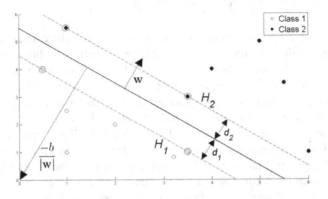

Fig. 2. Linear classifier [10] defined by the hyperplane H

After training, the classifier is ready to predict the class membership for new objects, different from those used in training. The class of object x_k is determined with the equation [10]:

$$class\left(x_k \right) = \begin{cases} +1 & if \quad w.x_k + b > 0 \\ -1 & if \quad w.x_k + b < 0 \end{cases}$$

2.3   Feature Selection

Feature selection is to select a subset of input variables with no predictive information by eliminating features. It can significantly improve the comprehensibility of the resulting classifier models. A feature is a function of one or more measurements computed so that it quantifies some significant characteristics of objects [15]. In any object classification algorithm, the selection of appropriate feature is very important. We see that the performance of classifier will increase if the correct feature is selected for classification algorithm. In our proposed work for human and car classification, we have used contourlet transform coefficients as a feature set. We have taken combination of two different features – contourlet transform and support vector machines. A brief description of these two features and why they are useful for human object classification are described in subsection 2.1 and 2.2 respectively.

3   The Proposed Method

In this section, we propose a method for object classification. The proposed method uses contourlet transform coefficient as a feature evaluation set and support vector machine as a classifier for classification of data into two categories: human object and car object. Steps of the proposed method are described as figure 3:

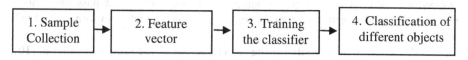

Fig. 3. The process of the proposed method

Fig. 4. Sample images with car and human objects of PEST2001 dataset

Firstly, we collect sample images for training and testing the classifier. In here, we have taken PETS2001 dataset [14] images for training and testing purpose. We have created our own dataset that consists of 500 images (300 images for training and 200 images for testing). We have shown some car and human objects of PEST2001 dataset [14] in figure 4.

The images in PEST2001 dataset are of different size. To reduce complexity, we should require normalization of these images. The collected images are scale normalized to 256 x 256 pixel dimensions. We also converted to the gray level images from the RGB color space.

Secondly, we compute feature vectors. In the proposed method, image frames are decomposed into complex wavelet coefficients using contourlet transform. After applying contourlet transform, we get coefficients in form of two filters: low-pass filter image and high-pass filter image as shown in figure 1. The value of high-pass filtered image is used as feature values of different images, because high-pass filtered image provides detailed coefficient of images, which is in form of complex values. We have skipped the value of the low-pass filtered image, because the low-pass filter image provides the approximation of coefficients of the image, which is in form of real values.

Thirdly, we train the classifier using feature values as the same algorithm in [10], which we have got in step 3. We have used SVM classifier, in which we have assign value '0' for car object data and value '1' for human object data by detecting car and human from image to image. By using feature value of images and assigning value of data, SVM classifier trained for classification. Detailed information of SVM classifier is given in section 2.

Finally, we are to classify the test data into one of the two categories: car and human object. For this process, we compute the feature vector of image using step 3 of the proposed method, then this computed feature value is supplied into SVM classifier, where SVM classifier analyzes this feature value by previously trained data and gives the result of two value '0' and '1', where '0' indicates car object data and '1' indicates human object data. The same process will be repeated for all test data.

4   Experimental and Evaluation

In this section, we apply the procedure described in section 3 and achieved a superior performance in our object classification experiments as demonstrated in this section. For performance evaluation, we compare the results of the proposed method based on combined contourlet transform (CT) with SVM with the methods: method proposed by Lu [5] and Renno [9].

The quality of car and human object is increasing by comparison with the value of average classification accuracy, True positive rate (TPR) (Recall), and Predicted positive rate (PPR) (Precision). The proposed method has been tested on PEST2001 person dataset [14]. We have evaluated the proposed method for multiple levels of contourlet transform coefficients (L = 1, 2, ..., 6).

The different performance metrics, such as Average classification accuracy (ACA), True positive rate (TPR) (Recall) and Predicted positive rate (PPR) (Precision), are depended on four values: True Positive (TP), TN (True Negative), FP (False Positive) and False Negative (FN), where [10]:

+ TP is the number of images, which are originally positive images and classified as positive images.

+ TN is the number of images, which are originally negative images and classified as negative images.

+ FP is the number of images, which are originally negative images and classified as positive images.

+ FN is the number of images, which are originally positive images and classified as negative images.

All above three performance metrics are defined in [10]. In here, we review parameters following:

+ ACA is defined as the proportion of the total number of prediction that was correct: $ACA = \dfrac{TP+TN}{TP+TN+FP+FN}$

+ TPR is defined as the proportion of positive cases that were correctly classified as positive: $TPR\,(Recall) = \dfrac{TP}{FP+FN}$

+ PPR is defined as the proportion of the predicted positive cases that were correct: $PPR(Precision) = \dfrac{TP}{FP+TP}$

Now, we have experimented on PEST2001 dataset. Here, we report the results as shown in figure 5.

Fig. 5. Car and human classification in PEST2001 dataset (image in RGB color space)

Table 1 shows the value of TPR, PPR and ACA of proposed method with other method.

From table 1, one can observe that the proposed method gives better than performance results at higher levels of contourlet transform in comparison to other methods [6, 9], as a feature, for human and car object classification.

5   Conclusions

In the present work, our aim is to classify objects into two types of classes: human and car. We develop a method for object classification in real scenes using contourlet transform as a feature set. Contourlet allows for a different number of directions at each scale and aspect ratios. This feature allows an efficient contourlet to have based approximation of a smooth contour at multiple resolutions. Human and car object classification is a problem where the objects may present in translated as well as rotated form among different scenes. Contourlet transform has the time-frequency-localization

Table 1. Performance Measure Values TPR, PPR and ACA

Methods Name	TPR (Recall) (%)	PPR (Precision) (%)	ACA (%)
The Proposed method with CT (Level-1) as a feature	88.00	88.00	88.00
The Proposed method with CT (Level-2) as a feature	91.00	89.87	89.01
The Proposed method with CT (Level-3) as a feature	93.00	92.17	92.50
The Proposed method with CT (Level-4) as a feature	94.00	94.89	95.05
The Proposed method with CT (Level-5) as a feature	94.00	94.89	95.05
The Proposed method with CT (Level-6) as a feature	95.00	96.02	96.50
Method used by Lu [5]	91.00	86.14	87.00
Method used by Renno [9]	90.00	85.34	86.07

and multiscale properties of wavelets. It offers a high degree of directionality and anisotropy. Therefore, the properties of contourlet transform will be useful for classification of human and car objects.

The proposed approach first trains SVM classifier by using contourlet coefficients of data as a feature set and then classifies testing data into one of the two categories: human and car objects. The proposed method is compared with other methods proposed by Lu [5] and Renno [9]. Experiments show that the proposed method gives better classification results at higher levels of contourlet transform and provide better results than other methods. The proposed method can detect human objects in a complex background.

References

1. Hu, W., Tan, T.: A Survey on Visual Surveillance of Object Motion and Behaviors. IEEE Transaction on System, Man, and Cybernetics **34**(3), 334–352 (2006)
2. Song, Z., Chen, Q., Huang, Z., Hua, Y., Yan, S : Contextualizing object detection and classification. In: IEEE Conference on Computer Vision and Pattern Recognition, pp. 1585–1592 (2011)
3. Wang, L., Hu, W., Tan, T.: Recent Developments in Human Motion Analysis. Pattern Recognition **36**(3), 585–601 (2003)
4. Lowe, D.: Object recognition from local scale invariant features. In: Proceeding of 7th IEEE International Conference on Computer Vision, pp. 1150–1157 (1999)
5. Lu, H., Zheng, Z.: Two novel real-time local visual features for omnidirectional vision. Pattern Recognition **43**(12), 3938–3949 (2010)
6. Dalal N., Triggs, B.: Histograms of oriented gradients for human detection. In: Proceeding of IEEE International Conference on Computer Vision and Pattern Recognition, pp. 886–893 (2005)
7. Cao, X., Wu, C., Yan, P., Li, X.: Linear SVM classification using boosting HoG features for vehicle detection in low-altitude airborne videos. In: Proceeding of IEEE International Conference on Image Processing, pp. 2421–2424 (2011)
8. Yu, G., Slotine, J.J.: Fast wavelet-Based visual classification. In: Proceeding of IEEE International Conference on Pattern Recognition (ICPR), pp. 1–5 (2008)

9. Renno, J.P., Makris, D., Jones, G.A.: Object classification in visual surveillance using Adaboost. In: Proceeding of IEEE International Conference on Computer Vision and Pattern Recognition, pp. 1–8 (2007)

10. Khare, M., Binh, N.T., Srivastava, R.K.: Dual tree complex wavelet transform based human object classification using support vector machine. Journal of Science and Technology, Vietnam Academy of Science and Technology **51**(4B), 134–142 (2013)

11. Binh, N.T., Khare, A.: Image Denoising, Deblurring and Object Tracking, A new Generation wavelet based approach. LAP LAMBERT Academic Publishing (2013)

12. Do, M.N., Vetterli, M.: The Contourlet Transform: An Efficient Directional Multiresolution Image Representation. IEEE Transactions on Image Processing **14**, 2091–2106 (2005)

13. Noble, W.S.: What is Support Vector Machine. Nature Biotechnology **24**(12), 1565–1567 (2006)

14. PEST2001 Dataset. http://www.cvg.rdg.ac.uk/PETS2001/pets2001-dataset.html (last Accessed November 11, 2014)

15. Castleman, K.R.: Digital Image Processing. Prentice Hall, Englewood Cliffs (1996)

16. Thanh Binh, N., Dien, T.A.: Object detection and tracking in contourlet domain. In: Hung, N.M., Suzuki, J., Tung, N.T., Vinh, P.C. (eds.) ICCASA 2012. LNICST, vol. 109, pp. 192–200. Springer, Heidelberg (2013)

Motion Detection Based on Image Intensity Ratio

Pham Bao Quoc[1]([⊠]) and Nguyen Thanh Binh[2]

[1] Faculty of Information of Technology,
Ho Chi Minh City University of Technology, HUTECH, Ho Chi Minh City, Vietnam
nationpham@hotmail.com
[2] Faculty of Computer Science and Engineering,
Ho Chi Minh City University of Technology, VNUHCM, Ho Chi Minh City, Vietnam
ntbinh@cse.hcmut.edu.vn

Abstract. Motion detection is the first important step in large applications of computer vision. Motion detection extracts moving objects from the background. There are many methods to do that. However, in most methods, if the input video has noise and light change, moving objects will not be extracted accurately. In this paper, we propose the method for motion detection which extracts moving objects from the background based on the image intensity ratio concept that is not affected by light change; therefore, the sensitivity with light change is overcome. The image intensity ratio is computed by the average intensity of current frame and the intensity of every pixel in that frame. The intensity ratio of a pixel is nearly unchanged between two frames. We apply the Lucas-Kanade optical flow method based on that image intensity ratio. Our proposed algorithm has good noise tolerance and is not affected by light change. For demonstrating the superiority of the proposed method, we have compared the results with the other recent methods available in literature.

Keywords: Motion detection · Intensity ratio image · Moving object

1 Introduction

Real-time object tracking is a popular application of computer vision. It faces up to complex problems. Although the algorithms have to do a lot of manipulation, they must be fast enough to finish processing a video frame in the extremely short time between two frames. The motion detection is a very important and complex step in the real-time object tracking system. In this step, moving objects will be extracted from the background. It is not easy to extract moving objects. In the input video, there is a lot of noise and light change because of the effect of the outdoor environment, which makes the moving object extraction inaccurate and some parts of the background become moving objects.

In the past, there are many methods to extract moving objects from the background. In image subtraction methods [1], the current frame will be subtracted with a reference frame. The reference frame may be the background frame (background subtraction) or the previous frame (frame difference). This method is very sensitive with noise and light change. Noise and light change makes the current frame different

© Institute for Computer Sciences, Social Informatics and Telecommunications Engineering 2015
P.C. Vinh et al. (Eds.): ICTCC 2014, LNICST 144, pp. 350–359, 2015.
DOI: 10.1007/978-3-319-15392-6_33

from the reference frame. These different pixels become the foreground and make the moving object extraction inaccurate. In Gaussian mixture model [2], Stauffer has proposed a probabilistic approach using a mixture of Gaussian for identifying the background and foreground. This method is not affected by noise and sudden light change. However, if the light changes continuously, some parts of the background will become foreground objects. In Lucas-Kanade optical flow method [4, 5, 6, 7, 8], two continuous frames are used to compute the velocity of moving objects by the spatial and temporal derivatives. This method has good noise tolerance. However, if the light changes suddenly and continuously, some parts of the background will become moving objects.

In this paper, we propose the method for motion detection extracts moving objects from the background based on the image intensity ratio concept that is not affected by light change; therefore, the sensitivity with light change is overcome. The intensity ratio image is computed by the average intensity of current frame and the intensity of every pixel in that frame. The intensity ratio of a pixel is nearly unchanged between two frames. Then, we apply the Lucas-Kanade optical flow method based on that image intensity ratio. Our proposed algorithm has good noise tolerance and is not affected by light change. It is suitable for the real-time object tracking system. For demonstrating the superiority of the proposed method, we have compared the results with the other recent methods available in literature.

The rest of the paper is organized as follows: in section 2, we described the basic of Lucas-kanade optical flow; details of the proposed method are given in section 3; the results of the proposed method are presented in section 4 and our conclusions in section 5.

2   Lucas-Kanade Optical Flow

The Lucas-Kanade optical flow method is proposed by Lucas and Takeo [4]. This optical flow method is used to compute the velocity of moving objects between two continuous frames by the spatial and temporal derivatives. It is fast and has a low computational cost, and good noise tolerance [5]. It tries to compute the motion between two continuous frames at time t and $t + \Delta t$. Assuming the intensity of a pixel does not change between two frames, we have equation:

$$I(x, y, t) = I(x + \Delta x, y + \Delta y, t + \Delta t) \qquad (2.1)$$

Assuming the movement between two frames is small, the equation (2.1) with Taylor series can be derived to give:

$$I(x + \Delta x, y + \Delta y, t + \Delta t) \approx I(x, y, t) + \frac{\delta I}{\delta x} \Delta x + \frac{\delta I}{\delta y} \Delta y + \frac{\delta I}{\delta t} \Delta t \quad (2.2)$$

From (2.1) and (2.2), we obtain the following:

$$\frac{\delta I}{\delta x} \Delta x + \frac{\delta I}{\delta y} \Delta y + \frac{\delta I}{\delta t} \Delta t = 0 \qquad (2.3)$$

or

$$\frac{\delta I}{\delta x}\frac{\Delta x}{\Delta t}+\frac{\delta I}{\delta y}\frac{\Delta y}{\Delta t}+\frac{\delta I}{\delta t}\frac{\Delta t}{\Delta t}=0 \qquad (2.4)$$

and the result is:

$$\frac{\delta I}{\delta x}V_x+\frac{\delta I}{\delta y}V_y+\frac{\delta I}{\delta t}=0 \qquad (2.5)$$

where V_x and V_y are the x and y components of the velocity and $\frac{\delta I}{\delta x}, \frac{\delta I}{\delta y}, \frac{\delta I}{\delta t}$ are the spatial and temporal derivatives at x, y, t. Set I_x, I_y, I_t as those derivatives, we have equation:

$$I_xV_x+I_yV_y=-I_t \qquad (2.6)$$

Assuming the neighboring pixels move at the same velocity with the pixel under consideration, we have the following:

$$\begin{cases} I_{x_1}V_x+I_{y_1}V_y=-I_{t_1} \\ \vdots \\ I_{x_m}V_x+I_{y_m}V_y=-I_{t_m} \end{cases} \qquad (2.7)$$

The (2.7) can be written as:

$$\begin{bmatrix} I_{x_1} & I_{y_1} \\ \vdots & \vdots \\ I_{x_m} & I_{y_m} \end{bmatrix}\begin{bmatrix} V_x \\ V_y \end{bmatrix}=\begin{bmatrix} -I_{t_1} \\ \vdots \\ -I_{t_m} \end{bmatrix} \qquad (2.8)$$

Set $A=\begin{bmatrix} I_{x_1} & I_{y_1} \\ \vdots & \vdots \\ I_{x_m} & I_{y_m} \end{bmatrix}$, $v=\begin{bmatrix} V_x \\ V_y \end{bmatrix}$, $b=\begin{bmatrix} -I_{t_1} \\ \vdots \\ -I_{t_m} \end{bmatrix}$, we have equation:

$$Av=b \qquad (2.9)$$

Use the least squares method to solve equation (2.9), we have the following:

$$v=(A^TA)^{-1}A^Tb \qquad (2.10)$$

And the result is:

$$\begin{bmatrix} V_x \\ V_y \end{bmatrix} = \begin{bmatrix} \sum_{i=1}^{m} I_{x_i}^2 & \sum_{i=1}^{m} I_{x_i} I_{y_i} \\ \sum_{i=1}^{m} I_{y_i} I_{x_i} & \sum_{i=1}^{m} I_{y_i}^2 \end{bmatrix}^{-1} \begin{bmatrix} -\sum_{i=1}^{m} I_{x_i} I_{t_i} \\ -\sum_{i=1}^{m} I_{y_i} I_{t_i} \end{bmatrix} \qquad (2.11)$$

We can use Gaussian function in computational derivative step and add a Tikhonov constant to (2.11) for the better result [8].

3   The Proposed Method

Real-time object tracking is a complex problem and a popular application of computer vision. In this section, we propose an approach for motion detection which extracts moving objects using an image intensity ratio based on Lucas-Kanade method (IRI-LK). We apply the Lucas-Kanade optical flow method based on the intensity ratio image. We propose the image intensity ratio concept because it is not affected by light change.

In input video, assuming the different pixels of actual interested moving objects between two frames is small. If the light does not change between two continuous frames, the average intensity of two continuous frames is different slightly. Else, the intensity of all pixels is changed and the average intensity is significant different between two continuous frames, which means the average intensity depends on the light change. Assumingly, the intensity of all pixels will change with a same coefficient λ when the light changes.

Set $I(x, y, t)$ and $I(x+\Delta x, y+\Delta y, t+\Delta t)$ as the intensity of pixel at time t and $t + \Delta t$, we have equation:

$$I(x, y, t) = \lambda I(x + \Delta x, y + \Delta y, t + \Delta t) \qquad (3.1)$$

Set $\bar{I}(t)$ and $\bar{I}(t + \Delta t)$ as the average intensity of the frame with the size m x n at the time t and $t+\Delta t$, we have the following:

$$\bar{I}(t) = \frac{\sum_{y=1}^{n} \sum_{x=1}^{m} I(x, y, t)}{m.n} \qquad (3.2)$$

and

$$\bar{I}(t + \Delta t) = \frac{\sum_{y=1}^{n} \sum_{x=1}^{m} I(x + \Delta x, y + \Delta y, t + \Delta t)}{m.n} \qquad (3.3)$$

From (3.1), (3.2) and (3.3), we have equation:

$$\overline{I}(t) = \lambda \overline{I}(t + \Delta t) \tag{3.4}$$

Set $R(x, y, t)$ and $R(x+\Delta x, y+\Delta y, t+\Delta t)$ as the intensity ratio of pixel at time t and $t+\Delta t$, we have the following:

$$R(x, y, t) = \frac{I(x, y, t)}{\overline{I}(t)} \tag{3.5}$$

and

$$R(x + \Delta x, y + \Delta y, t + \Delta t) = \frac{I(x + \Delta x, y + \Delta y, t + \Delta t)}{\overline{I}(t + \Delta t)} \tag{3.6}$$

From (3.1), (3.4), (3.5) and (3.6), we have equation:

$$R(x, y, t) = R(x + \Delta x, y + \Delta y, t + \Delta t) \tag{3.7}$$

The equation (3.7) means the intensity ratio of pixels do not change when the light changes. Therefore, the intensity ratio image is not affected by light change. If the Lucas-Kanade optical flow method is based on the intensity ratio image, the sensitivity with light change of it is overcome.

The proposed method IRI-LK algorithm which we propose is depicted in figure 1. This model includes four steps. The two main steps are intensity ratio image computation and optical flow computation.

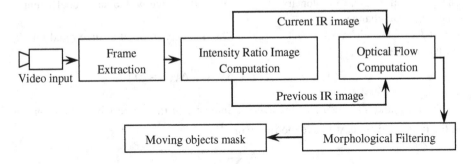

Fig. 1. Image Intensity ratio based on Lucas-Kanade model

Firstly, the frame extraction. Frame sequences are extracted from input video. Frame by frame are converted to intensity images. Then, the intensity image is standardized. The intensity value will be a real number between 0 and 1. In this step, we can use an image processing function to resize the frame in an appropriate size.

Secondly, the intensity ratio image computation. Each intensity image in turn is used to compute the image intensity ratio. We use the equation (3.2) to compute the average intensity of the current intensity image. Then, we use the equation (3.5) to compute the image intensity ratio. We can multiply the image intensity ratio with a coefficient α which depends on the highest intensity ratio. This makes the intensity ratio value always in a correct range.

Thirdly, optical flow computation. The Lucas-Kanade method is applied to compute the velocity of moving objects. The spatial and temporal derivatives are computed based on the current image intensity ratio and previous image intensity ratio using Gaussian function. We use the equation (2.11) to calculate the velocity vector $\begin{bmatrix} V_x \\ V_y \end{bmatrix}$ of moving objects. The velocity magnitude $V(x, y)$ is calculated by the following:

$$V(x, y) = \sqrt{V_x^{\,2} + V_y^{\,2}} \tag{3.8}$$

For returning binary foreground mask $B(x, y)$, the velocity magnitude $V(x, y)$ is taken threshold by the following:

$$B(x, y) = \begin{cases} 1 & (V(x, y) \geq Threshold) \\ 0 & (V(x, y) < Threshold) \end{cases} \tag{3.9}$$

Finally, we apply some morphological filtering to remove noise and small blobs such as morphological closing, image fill, and binary area open.

4   Experimental Results

In this section, we illustrate the results of IRI-LK algorithm. The implementation of developed algorithm has been tested under MATLAB platform. The input video is captured by a static camera with the resolution of 160 x120 pixels, at the frame rate of 15fps. We choose coefficient $\alpha = 6$ and Tikhonov constant $= 0.005$. We tested many video clips. In here, we present some frames. In the input video, there are many frames having light change. Video clips for testing are taken from standard datasets and some clips from cameras on the streets. For demonstrating the superiority of the proposed method, we have compared the results with the Lucas-Kanade (LK) method, and Gaussian Mixture Model (GMM) method.

In figure 2, we show three input frames that have light change. The light is darker from frame 39 to frame 41. For the Lucas-Kanade optical flow method, we receive a flash at frame 40 and frame 41. For the Gaussian mixture model method, we receive a flash at frame 41. For the proposed method, the segment result is very good.

Table 1 compares the motion segment error between LK method, GMM, and the proposed method (IRI-LK). Look at table 1, we have the percentage of the motion segment error is LK: 12.40%, GMM: 8.26%, IRI-LK: 0.00%. The LK gets the motion segment error when the light changes suddenly and continuously. The GMM gets the motion segment error when the light changes continuously. The IRI-LK is very good for this input video.

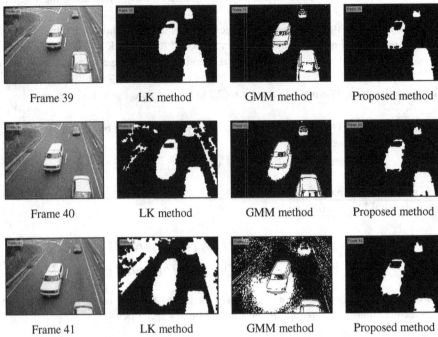

Fig. 2. The segment of Car video compared the proposed method with the other methods

Table 1. Comparing the motion segment error of LK, GMM, and IRI-LK

Frame	Average Intensity	LK method	GMM method	Proposed method
1	0.5220			
...				
21	0.5030			
22	0.5056			
23	0.4628	Error		
24	0.4717			
25	0.4854			
...				
38	0.5165			
39	0.5035			
40	0.4643	Error		
41	0.4166	Error	Error	
42	0.3714	Error	Error	

Frame	Average Intensity	LK method	GMM method	Proposed method
43	0.3922		Error	
44	0.3374	Error	Error	
45	0.3814	Error	Error	
46	0.4026	Error	Error	
47	0.4345	Error		
48	0.4829	Error		
49	0.4818			
50	0.4809			
...				
76	0.4764			
77	0.4975			
78	0.4472	Error	Error	
79	0.4056	Error	Error	
80	0.4237		Error	
81	0.4068		Error	
82	0.4551	Error		
83	0.4925	Error		
84	0.4890			
85	0.4892			
...				
98	0.4790			
99	0.4677			
100	0.4200	Error		
101	0.4282			
102	0.4330			
103	0.4267			
104	0.4704	Error		
105	0.4875			
106	0.4872			
...				
121	0.4891			

In another test, the input video is captured by a static camera with the resolution of 640x360 pixels, at the frame rate of 29fps. We choose coefficient $\alpha = 6$ and Tikhonov constant = 0.001. We add 10% brightness at frame 160 and 20% brightness at frame 161 for testing. Three input frames are shown in figure 3.

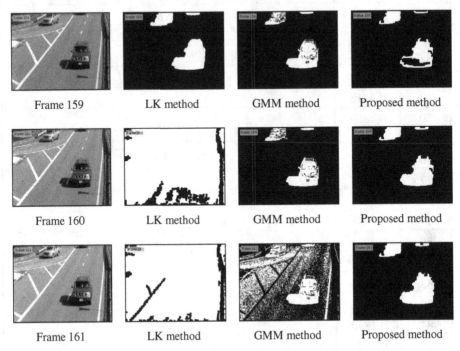

Frame 159	LK method	GMM method	Proposed method
Frame 160	LK method	GMM method	Proposed method
Frame 161	LK method	GMM method	Proposed method

Fig. 3. The segment of clip, which was captured by a static camera, compared the proposed method with the other methods

In figure 3, we also show three input frames that have light change. For the Lucas-Kanade optical flow method, we receive a flash at frame 160 and frame 161. For the Gaussian mixture model method, we receive a flash at frame 161. For the proposed method, the segment result is also very good.

5   Conclusion

In motion detection, the noise and light change makes moving object identification inaccurate because the Lucas-Kanade optical flow method works well with the assumption that the intensity of pixels does not change. We propose the image intensity ratio concept that is not affected by light change in accordance with the Lucas-Kanade optical flow method. The proposed method has good noise tolerance and is not affected by light change. It is good for the real-time object tracking system. In fact, the light does not change with the same coefficient λ at all pixels. The intensity ratio of a pixel has a small difference between two continuous frames. It makes the segment result not good in all cases. Despite that, our proposed method greatly improves the result of motion detection in the light change.

References

1. Moeslund, T.B.: Introduction to video and image processing: Building real systems and applications. Springer (2012)
2. Rout, R.K.: A survey on object detection and tracking algorithms. Diss (2013)
3. Stauffer, C., Grimson, W.E.L.: Adaptive background mixture models for real-time tracking. In: IEEE Computer Society Conference on Computer Vision and Pattern Recognition, vol. 2. IEEE (1999)
4. Lucas, B.D., Takeo, K.: An iterative image registration technique with an application to stereo vision. In: IJCAI, vol. 81 (1981)
5. Lu, N., et al.: Motion Detection Based on Accumulative Optical Flow and Double Background Filtering. World Congress on Engineering (2007)
6. Frantc, V.A., et al.: Video inpainting using scene model and object tracking. In: IS&T/SPIE Electronic Imaging. International Society for Optics and Photonics (2013)
7. Shirageri, M.S., Udupi, G.R., Bidkar, G.A.: Design and development of Optical flow based Moving Object Detection and Tracking (OMODT) System. vectors 2.4 (2013)
8. Karlsson, S.M., Josef, B.: Lip-motion events analysis and lip segmentation using optical flow. In: 2012 IEEE Computer Society Conference on Computer Vision and Pattern Recognition Workshops (CVPRW). IEEE (2012)

Vehicle Tracking in Outdoor Environment Based on Curvelet Domain

Nguyen Thanh Binh[✉]

Faculty of Computer Science and Engineering,
Ho Chi Minh City University of Technology, Ho Chi Minh City, Vietnam
ntbinh@cse.hcmut.edu.vn

Abstract. Vehicle tracking is a difficult part in intelligent traffic system. The images of vehicles on the streets, picked up from cameras, are usually in occlusion because of effecting outdoor environment such as lack light, weather, etc. Therefore, vehicle tracking is a challenging problem. This paper proposed a method for vehicle tracking in an outdoor environment. We use curvelet transform combined with object deformation of contour. The light of background may change from this frame to the other frame. The proposed algorithm has significantly improves the edge accuracy and reduces the wrong position of objects between the frames. For demonstrating the superiority of the proposed method, we have compared the results with the other methods.

Keywords: Curvelet transform · Vehicle tracking · Contour

1 Introduction

Vehicle tracking is a difficult part in intelligent traffic system, particularly for visual-based surveillance system. In the real world, an intelligent video surveillance system requires being fast and reliable. Tracking system designed consists of three function blocks: moving object detection, object classification and object tracking. The techniques of moving object detection used background subtraction, statistical models, temporal differencing, optical flow, etc [1]. The most popular methods to detect moving objects are based on background subtraction. This method is to create a background model that is quite similar to the real one. After that, they make differential operation with every frame of video and background image to set changing area as moving objects [2] such as: eigen backgrounds, median filter, mean filter, temporal median filter, Kalman filter and sequential kernel density approximation [3]. When the environment is crowded with scenes, the background is hard to model. The solution to this problem is to use optical flow method. In this method, the pixels compared in frame sequences for the pixel position are calculated based on the vector position [1]. However, its drawbacks are sensitive to noise and have high computational complexity.

For vehicle tracking, there are four main groups: feature-based tracking, model-based tracking, region-base tracking, contour-based tracking [5]. The commonly used

© Institute for Computer Sciences, Social Informatics and Telecommunications Engineering 2015
P.C. Vinh et al. (Eds.): ICTCC 2014, LNICST 144, pp. 360–369, 2015.
DOI: 10.1007/978-3-319-15392-6_34

methods are Kalman filter, Kanade-Lucas-Tomasi, mean-shift, particle filter, etc. However, most of these methods are complex, slow processing as the object is in occlusion. Vehicle tracking is to detect locating position of vehicles through consecutive frames [4] in the video. The video picked up from cameras, are usually in occlusion because of effecting outdoor environment such as lack light, weather, illumination variability, background noise, partial overlapping and occlusion, etc. In the last decades, although many different approaches have been proposed. Vehicle tracking is still a challenging problem.

In this paper, we propose a method to implement a vehicle tracking in outdoor environment using curvelet transform combined with object deformation of contour. For demonstrating the superiority of the proposed method, we have compared the results with the wavelet transform method and curvelet transform method. The rest of the paper is organized as follows: in section 2, we described the basic concepts on curvelet transform. Details of the proposed algorithm have been given in section 3. In section 4, the results of the proposed method for vehicle tracking have been shown and finally the conclusion in section 5.

2   Curvelet Transform

In this section we explain what curvelets are, how they are constructed, and what are their main properties are. Curvelets are basically 2D anisotropic extensions to wavelets that have a direction associated with them. Analogous to wavelets, curvelets can be translated and dilated. The dilation is given by a scale index j that controls the frequency content of the curvelet, while the translation is indexed by m_1 and m_2 in two dimensions.

The anisotropic scaling relation is a key difference between wavelets and curvelets. The parabolic scaling is also a key ingredient to prove that curvelets remain localized in phase-space (i.e., remain curvelet-like) under the action of the wave operator provided the medium is smoothed appropriately prior to propagation [6].

The idea of curvelets [7] is to represent a curve as a superposition of functions of various lengths and widths obeying the scaling law $width \approx length^2$. This can be done by first decomposing the image into subbands, i.e separating the object into a series of disjoint scales; then, each scale is analyzed by means of a local ridgelet transform.

Curvelets are based on multiscale ridgelets combined with a spatial bandpass filtering operation to isolate different scales. This spatial bandpass filter nearly kills all multiscale ridgelets which are not in the frequency range of the filter. In other words, a curvelet is a multiscale ridgelet which lives in a prescribed frequency band. The bandpass is set so that the curvelet length and width at fine scales are related by the scaling law $width \approx length^2$ and so the anisotropy increases with decreasing scale like a power law. There is a very special relationship between the depth of the multiscale pyramid and the index of the dyadic subbands. The side length of the localizing windows is doubled at every other dyadic subband, hence maintaining the fundamental property of the curvelet transform which says that elements of length about $2^{-j/2}$ serve for the analysis and synthesis of the jth subband $[2^j, 2^{j+1}]$.

Like ridgelets, curvelets occur at all scales, locations, and orientations as shown in Fig.1. However, while ridgelets have global length and variable widths, curvelets in addition to a variable width have a variable length and so a variable anisotropy does.

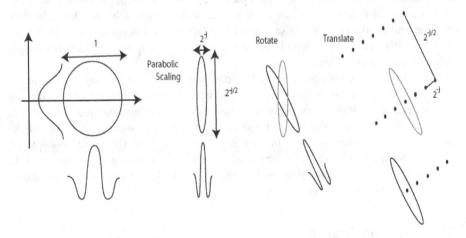

Fig. 1. Curvelets parameterized by scale, location, and orientation (source [8])

The length and width at fine scales are related by the scaling law *width ≈ length²* and so the anisotropy increases with decreasing scale like a power law. Recent work [7] shows that the thresholding of discrete curvelet coefficients provided near optimal N-term representations of otherwise smooth objects with discontinuities C^2 along curves.

The curvelet dictionary is a subset of the multiscale ridgelet dictionary, which allows reconstruction. The "à trous" subband filtering algorithm [9] is especially well-adapted to the needs of the digital curvelet transform. The algorithm decomposes an n by n image $f(x, y)$ as a superposition of the form

$$f(x, y) = c_J(x, y) + \sum_{j=1}^{J} w_j(x, y) \tag{1}$$

where c_J is a coarse or smooth of the original image $f(x, y)$ and w_j represents the details of *Im* at scale 2^{-j}.

The discrete curvelet transform of a continuum function $f(x_1, x_2)$ makes use of a dyadic sequence of scales, and a bank of filters $(P_0f, \Delta_1f, \Delta_2f, \ldots)$ with the property that the passband filter Δ_s is concentrated near the frequencies $[2^j, 2^{j+1}]$, e.g.,

$$\Delta_s = \Psi_{2s} * f$$
$$\widehat{\Psi_{2s}}(\xi) = \widehat{\Psi}(2^{-2s}\xi) \tag{2}$$

In wavelet theory, one uses a decomposition into dyadic subbands $[2^j, 2^{j+1}]$. In contrast, the subbands used in the discrete curvelet transform of continuum functions have the nonstandard form $[2^j, 2^{j+1}]$. This is nonstandard feature of the discrete curvelet transform well worth remembering.

The basic process of the digital realization for curvelet transform is given as follows:

(1) *Subband Decomposition.* We define a bank of filters P_0, $(\Delta_s, s \geq 0)$. The image f is filtered into subbands with à trous algorithm [9]

$$f \rightarrow (P_0 f, \Delta_1 f, \Delta_2 f, ...) \qquad (3)$$

The different subbands $\Delta_s f$ contain details about 2^{-2s} wide.

(2) *Smooth Partitioning.* Each subband is smoothly windowed into "squares" of an appropriate scale.

$$\Delta_s f \rightarrow (w_Q \Delta_s f)_{Q \in Q_s} \qquad (4)$$

where w_Q is a collection of smooth window localized around dyadic squares.

$$Q = [k_1 / 2^s, (k_1 + 1) / 2^s] x [k_2 / 2^s, (k_2 + 1) / 2^s] \qquad (5)$$

(3) *Renormalization.* Each resulting square is renormalized to unit scale

$$g_Q = (T_Q)^{-1} (w_Q \Delta_s f), \qquad Q \in Q_s \qquad (6)$$

where $(T_Q f)(x_1, x_2) = 2^s f(2^s x_1 - k_1, 2^s x_2 - k_2)$ is a renormalization operator.

(4) *Ridgelet Analysis.* Each square is analyzed in the orthonormal ridgelet system. This is a system of basis elements p_λ making an orthonormal basis for $L^2(R^2)$:

$$\alpha_\mu = \langle g_Q, p_\lambda \rangle \qquad (7)$$

We see that the performance of vehicle tracking will increase if the correct feature is selected for tracking algorithm. In our proposed work, we have used curvelet coefficients as a feature set.

3   The Vehicle Tracking Based on Curvelet Domain

In this section, we describe a method for moving vehicle tracking in outdoor environment using curvelet transform. The common approach for vehicles tracking consists of two periods: detecting vehicles and tracking vehicles as the following in figure 2. A video sequence contains a series of frames. Each frame can be considered as an image. The proposed method also consists of two periods. Firstly, curvelet coefficients are used for detection of vehicles. Secondly, we track vehicles in the sequence of frames. If an algorithm can track moving vehicles between two digital images, it should be able to track moving vehicles in a video sequence.

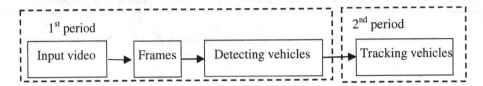

Fig. 2. The common approach for vehicles tracking system

The common approach for detection of vehicles consists of three steps: background modeling, foreground detection and data validation. We assume there are only two modes for each pixel in a single frame: background and foreground. The basic of background subtraction method is to compare the frame background with a threshold (T) which we are pre-defined. If the difference of a pixel is smaller than T, then it is background, otherwise, it is foreground. To detect objects, the curvelet coefficients and their statistical values were extracted as the features of object images. We define a discrete warped curvelet transform which goes across the region boundaries. We compute the image sample values in each region of the partition and also describe its implementation together with the inverse resampling. A warped wavelet transform with a sub-band filtering along the flow lines is implemented. At the boundaries, warped curvelet still have two vanishing moments. The curvelet coefficients of a discrete image are computed with a filter bank.

The step of pre-processing stage raws input video. Background modeling is the current background scene. We can know that the background is to acquire a background image which does not include any moving objects. Foreground detection checks if the input pixels are background or foreground. Foreground pixels are calculated by the Euclidean norm at the time t:

$$\left| PI_t(x, y) - BG_t(x, y) \right| > T \tag{8}$$

where, PI_t is the pixel intensity value, BG_t is the background intensity value at time t and T is the foreground threshold.

$$PI_t = \left[PI_{1,t} ... PI_{n,t} \right]^T$$
$$BG_t = \left[BG_{1,t} ... BG_{n,t} \right]^T$$

where, n in the number of image channels. The foreground threshold T is determined experimentally.

The goal of tracking is find position of vehicle between two adjacent frames. The tracking algorithm searches the position of the vehicles in the next frame according to the value of object boundary energy, which is computed from the three previous frames and direction of movement. Our algorithm is capable of tracking an object whose size changes within a range in the various frames. The processing of vehicles tracking system as the following in figure 3.

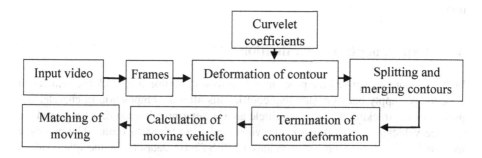

Fig. 3. The processing of vehicles tracking system

Firstly, the video input is divided into image sequence I(S), where S denotes a frame number, S =1, 2, 3, ….. Support $p_i(x_i(t), y_i(t))$ represent a contour model, where t is the number of iterations at each frame. If it is the first time, S is set to be 1. We set the number t = 0 at each frame. When S=1, we set an initial contour $p_i(x_i(0), y_i(0))$ for all moving objects [12].

Secondly, deformation of contour. In this step, we use the greedy algorithm [11] and move all contour points $p_i(x_i(t),y_i(t))$ (where i=1, 2,…,n) by minimizing a contour energy E_{snakes} and t = t + 1. The number moved points are stored in C_{move}. We detect object boundary by minimizing the following energy functional:

$$E_{snake} = E_{int}(p) + E_{image}(p) + E_{ext}(p)$$

where E_{int} is an internal energy associated with splines, E_{image} is an image energy such as edge potential and E_{ext} is an external energy associated with external forces.

Thirdly, splitting and merging contours. We divided a contour into multiple closed contours by detecting its self-crossings. The area E_{ext} of a contour model $p_i(x_i, y_i)$ (i=1, 2, 3,…,n) is defined as:

$$E_{ext} = \frac{1}{2}\sum_{i=1}^{n}\left[x_i(y_{i+1} - y_i) - (x_{i+1} - x_i)y_i\right] \qquad (12)$$

where $p_{n+1}(x_{n+1}, y_{n+1}) = p_1(x_1,y_1)$. After that, we will be merging multiple contours. The process of merging two contours into a single one. To create new contour points, a new contour point between two adjacent points p_i and p_{i+1} must satisfy the condition $|p_{i+1} - p_i| > Dis_{TH}$ where Dis_{TH} is a threshold which maximums the distance between adjacent discrete points [12].

Fourthly, termination of contour deformation. If $C_{move} \leq C_{TH}$ or $t_{max} \leq t$ then terminate the contour deformation at the image I(S) and proceed to step 5 else proceed to step 2. C_{TH} and t_{max} are predetermined thresholds.

Fifthly, calculation of moving vehicle. We calculate intensity histogram within the region surrounded by each contour model as the feature of moving objects.

Finally, matching of moving vehicle. In each frame, cumulative intensity histogram $H_m(k)$ is computed within a region extracted by a converged contour model as a moving object. Set S = S+1 and proceed to step 1. The test cases will present in section 4.

4   Experiments and Evaluation

In this section, we applied the procedure described in section 3 to track the vehicles in a video. We apply hard thresholding coefficients after decomposition in curvelet domain. For the tracking period, the vehicle area is determined in the first frame and we find the vehicles in each frame of the video and from frame to frame. The proposed method has been done on many videos in PEST2001 dataset and the other videos picked up from cameras on the streets. Here, we report the results on some video clips. Our experimental approach is as follows. For demonstrating the superiority of the proposed method, we have compared the results with the wavelet transform (WT) method, curvelet transform (CT) method.

Our experiments are on vehicle video clips with the frame size 254 by 254. Most of videos are fuzzy videos. The proposed method processes this video clip at 24 frames/second. We have experimented on the video up to 3000 frames. Here, we report the results up to 2000 frames. Some results achieved as shown in figure 4 and figure 5.

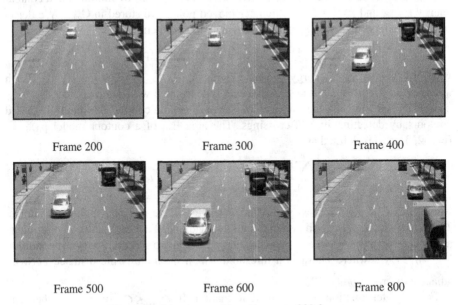

| Frame 200 | Frame 300 | Frame 400 |
| Frame 500 | Frame 600 | Frame 800 |

Fig. 4. Tracking in car video clips up to 800 frames

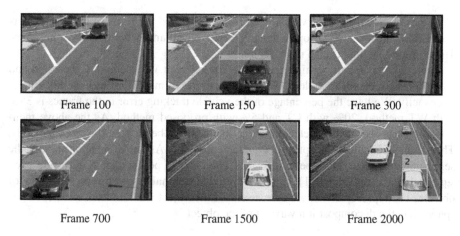

Frame 100   Frame 150   Frame 300

Frame 700   Frame 1500   Frame 2000

Fig. 5. Tracking in the other car video clips up to 2000 frames

Table 1. Comparing the vehicle tracking error of WT, CT and proposed method

Frame	WT method	CT method	Proposed method
50			
100			
150	false	false	
200			
250	false		
300			
350			
400			
450			
600			
650	false		
700			
750	false	false	
800		false	
850	false		
900			
950	false	false	false
1000	false		

In these figures, we observe that the proposed method performs well. Other experiments also show that the proposed method works well and better than the other ones. The proposed method is also more accurate.

Table 1 compares the vehicle tracking error between WT method, CT method and the proposed method. In table 1, we put false in the frames which vehicle tracking is not exactly. We have the percentage of the vehicle tracking error in the frames is 35% with WT method, 20% with CT and 5% with proposed method. As the above mention, the proposed method detecting object boundary is better than the other methods. Therefore, the results of the proposed method are good. As above mentioned, a dyadic segmentation of curvelet coefficients and choice of a polynomial flow inside each square define a curvelet B(T). Curvelets provide optimally sparse representations of objects. The representations are as sparse as if the object were turn out to be far more sparse than the decomposition wavelet of the object.

5   Conclusion and Future Work

Vehicle tracking is a difficult part in intelligent traffic system. The images of vehicles on the streets, picked up from cameras, are usually in occlusion because of effecting outdoor environment such as lack light, weather, etc. Vehicle tracking in these cases is not easy. In this paper, we have constructed a method for detecting and tracking of vehicles for outdoor environment. We use curvelet transform combined with object deformation of contour for tracking objects in outdoor environment. The proposed algorithm significantly improves the edge accuracy and reduces the wrong position of objects between the frames. However, if the quality of the frames in videos is very bad then the estimation ability is reduced. In the future work, we will compare the proposed method with the other methods and improve it in case of light change.

References

1. Shuigen, W., Zhen, C., Hua, D.: Motion Detection Based on Temporal Difference Method and Optical Flow Field. Second International Symposium on Electronic Commerce and Security **2**, 85–88 (2009)
2. Zhang, R., Ding, J.: Object Tracking and Detecting Based on Adaptive Background Subtraction. International Workshop on Information and Electronics Engineering **29**, 1351–1355 (2012)
3. Masafumi, S., Thi, T.Z., Takashi, T., Shigeyoshi, N.: Robust Rule-Based Method for Human Activity Recognition. International Journal of Computer Science and Network Security **11**(4), 37–43 (2011)
4. Ritika, G.S.S.: Moving Object Analysis Techniques in Videos - A Review. IOSR Journal of Computer Engineering **1**(2), 07–12 (2012). ISSN : 2278-0661
5. Zang, Q., Klette, R.: Object Classification and Tracking in Video Surveillance. In: Petkov, N., Westenberg, M.A. (eds.) CAIP 2003. LNCS, vol. 2756, pp. 198–205. Springer, Heidelberg (2003)
6. Smith, H.F.: A Parametrix Construction for Wave Equations with C1,1 Coefficients. Annales de l'institut Fourier, tome. **48**(3), 797–835 (1998)

7. Cand`Es, E., Donoho, D.: Curvelets: A Surprisingly Effective Nonadaptive Representation for Objects with Edges. In: Schumarker, L.L., et al. (eds) Curve and Surface Fitting: Saint-Malo 1999, pp. 105–120, Vanderbilt University Press, Nashville, TN (2000)
8. http://www.crm.umontreal.ca/imagerie06/pdf/montreallecture2.pdf. (last accessed: July 30, 2014)
9. Starck, J.L., Candès, E.J., Donoho, D.L.: The Curvelet Transform for Image Denoising. IEEE Transactions on Image Processing **11**(6), 670–684 (2002)
10. Araki, S., Yokoya, N., Iwasa, H., Takemura, H.: Real-time Tracking of Multiple Moving Objects using Split-and-Merge Contour Models Based on Crossing Detection. Systems and Computers in Japan **30**(9), 25–33 (1999)
11. Williams, D.J., Shah, M.: A Fast Algorithm for Active Contours. Proceedings of Third International Conference on Computer Vision, pp. 592–595 (1990)
12. Hoa, D.T.T., Binh, N.T.: Adaptive Object Tracking Technique based on Bandelet Domain in Outdoor Environment. In: Proceedings of International Conference on Advanced Computing and Applications, Vietnam (2014)

Author Index